The
Organic Gardeners
Handbook

The
Organic Gardeners
Handbook

By

Frank Tozer

Green Man Publishing
Santa Cruz

First published in the United States 2008

ISBN: 978 - 0 - 9773489 - 1 - 6

Library of Congress Control Number 2008900192

Green Man Publishing
Santa Cruz
P.O. Box 1546
Felton
CA 95018

Contact us online @ greenmanpublishing.com

Contents

Introduction

Up until the twentieth century people in rural areas commonly produced a significant proportion of their own food in their vegetable gardens. This was an age old practice that dated back beyond memory; it was what people had always done. In those more uncertain times the garden was the most secure and reliable source of food. At many points in history it actually became a matter of life or death; it provided the food that kept people alive in times of crisis. Even when it wasn't essential for survival, the garden provided a margin of comfort and security, supplying its inhabitants with a better and more varied diet and making their lives easier. Indeed often the only difference between a comfortable family and an impoverished one was whether they had access to land for growing food.

In the twentieth century, industrialization and greater affluence broke the old bonds with the land. People moved to the cities and suburbs and the self-sufficient home vegetable garden became a thing of the past. To most people food is now just another commercial product, like shampoo or detergent. It is available year round, ready packaged from the supermarket. It is no longer our most vital link to the earth and as a result our view of nature has become distorted. We now see ourselves as so separate from nature that the health of the economy seems more important than the health of the planet.

The way our food is produced has also changed radically. We are often told that modern agriculture is the most efficient the world has ever seen, but it is really only efficient in terms of the amount of food produced relative to the amount of human labor expended. This has been made possible because massive amounts of fossil fuel energy have replaced human energy (as much as 10 calories of fossil fuel energy are now expended to produce 1 calorie of food energy). Industrial agriculture has undeniably made food cheaper, but this has come at a very high price. It requires an enormous amount of oil, electricity and natural gas, not only to run machinery and transport the food, but also to produce fertilizers, pesticides and other chemicals and to obtain irrigation water. Industrial agriculture also uses vast quantities of water and in many places this is being pumped from underground sources much more rapidly than it is being replenished (basically it is being mined). It also burns up so much topsoil that it's been said that we are already past the point of peak soil (if not peak oil). In parts of the plains over 50% of the topsoil has disappeared in less than 100 years. Not only does the loss of soil threaten future food production, but it also has another, more immediately damaging effect. When this soil vanishes, its organic matter is converted into huge quantities of greenhouse gases. When a tonne of soil disappears it liberates about three tonnes of carbon dioxide, along with nitrous oxide (which is much more powerful greenhouse gas), together the equivalent of about 33 tonnes of carbon dioxide. Many farms are losing several tonnes of soil per acre annually, so it's no surprise to learn that our system of industrial agriculture creates 40% of all greenhouse gases.

Cheap food has also cheapened the most essential human activity of all and made growing food into a menial task. The people who do the work of actually growing food are near the bottom of the heap in terms of status and wages. This is why they are often emigrants; doing work Americans consider to be beneath them. We live in a strange world when the activity that is most essential to human life is though to be beneath our dignity.

The industrial methods we have been using to produce food won't work for much longer. There is no alternative to eating, so how will our food be grown in the future? Do we increase out reliance on a brave new world of technology, machines, chemicals, genetically engineered organisms and multi-national corporations (whose primary responsibility is to their shareholders), or do we look to more sustainable and self reliant ways of producing food?

Part of the answer to this question is as close as your backyard. If you look at food production per acre (or in relation to the amount of energy, water and other inputs), home gardens are the most productive way of growing food that humans have ever devised. It is possible to produce a significant proportion of your own fruits and vegetables in the average backyard. If every house had its own productive vegetable garden, it could revolutionize the way food is grown in this country and how household wastes are disposed of. If we are ever to succeed in building a truly sustainable "Green economy", the organic home vegetable garden must become an essential component of every household. To quote Christopher Alexander "In a healthy town every family can grow vegetables for itself. The time is past to think of this as a hobby for enthusiasts; it is a fundamental part of human life".

Not only do we need a dramatic increase in the number of home vegetable gardens, we also need a new kind of urban and suburban farmer, growing food intensively on small plots of land, in and around our cities. Some imaginative pioneers have already done this successfully in various cities, as did our ancestors around all major cities, before cheap transportation became available. The Maraichers who worked the land around Paris during the nineteenth century are the best known of these.

The United States in a unique position to be at the forefront of a new green revolution, because it has a benevolent climate and plenty of space for anyone who wants to have a garden. In recent decades suburban sprawl has swallowed up vast tracts of prime farmland, so the land is often right where people live. Some estimates say there are 30 million acres of irrigated suburban lawn in this country, as well as enough small tractors to supply the third world. If some of this land were devoted to home food production, the changes could be awesome.

The benefits of a vegetable garden

Fine food

I love great food and have found that the best way to get it is to grow it myself. One of the greatest pleasures of growing a vegetable garden is in eating the best food that can be obtained anywhere. With a little effort you can grow foods that are of exceptional flavor and quality and often simply aren't available commercially. All serious home gardeners are familiar with the superior flavor of homegrown food; it can be so much better it doesn't even taste like the same thing. This superiority may be due to homegrown food being fresher, the use of superior tasting varieties, because the plant receives better nutrition or maybe occasionally just because you have grown it yourself.

Health

Organic food, fresh from your own garden, is the most nutritious you can get and it can improve your health significantly. It's been noticed that domestic animals will usually eat organic food in preference to that grown with chemicals. Obviously they know something that we don't. Organic foods commonly have more protein, vitamins and minerals to begin with, largely because they aren't bloated with water to make them bigger (the much vaunted high yields of chemically dependent agriculture are often simply extra water). When you are harvesting from your garden the food can be eaten at the peak of freshness, before their vitamins and other nutrients have started to break down.

Of course organic foods don't contain any pesticide residues, which is significant because we really don't know the long-term effects of pesticides in the body. This is particularly important for children, as they consume larger quantities of pesticides in relation to their body weight. Many conventional farmers have an organic garden for their own consumption.

Health is more than just good food of course and gardening helps here too. It is both a pleasant way to relax and one of the best forms of exercise, with benefits far greater than the simple burning of calories would suggest. Working out in the fresh air, creating a beautiful garden, working at your own pace, doing a meaningful activity you enjoy, growing the food that sustains you. All of these contribute to psychological health. It's even been suggested that a persons stress level is directly related to how close they are to plants; that plants are actually a biological need for humans.

Environmental

A home vegetable garden can significantly lessen your impact on the earth, by reducing your consumption of resources. Indirectly you will use less fossil fuel, because you will be eating food produced with only a fraction of the energy used by commercial agriculture and there are no transportation costs. It also has a significant impact on the amount of stuff you throw away. You can eliminate a lot of the packaging that comes from purchased foods and you can recycle a lot of the stuff you do acquire, by composting food waste, paper packaging, and most natural materials. Using rainwater catchment and waste gray water from the house could help to reduce the amount of water needed to grow food. An even bigger step would be to recycle human wastes though the garden. A system to safely do this would be a momentous step forward in reducing water use and pollution, and in recycling nutrients back to where they can be a valuable resource.

The vegetable garden can also teach you a significant lesson in how you don't always have to spend money to enjoy yourself. When you get down to the fundamentals, life can actually become richer and more satisfying when you consume less.

Financial
A vegetable garden can save you money. If you have a well paying job this may not seem like much, but if you are trying to raise a family on a limited income it can be significant. Many poor people, in this country and around the world, depend upon their home vegetable gardens to keep them well fed and they would be considerably poorer without them. Just because you are poor doesn't mean you have to eat badly. If you want to eat organic food and don't have much money, this is probably the only way to make it happen.

I have never thought of saving money as a big reason to have a vegetable garden, because food has always been relatively cheap in this country. However at the time I am finishing this book, food prices have risen more rapidly than at any time I can remember. Maybe in the future saving money will become an important reason.

Security
The ability to produce your own food also gives you a measure of psychological security. The number of Americans who remember the last serious economic upheaval is diminishing rapidly, but many will testify that their vegetable garden was an invaluable buffer against economic crisis. If food ever becomes scarce or very expensive you can always grow your own. Americans have rarely lived with the threat of not having anything to eat, but in other parts of the world it is an all too frequent reality. I recently read an account of how many city dwelling Russians survived the demise of communism and the resulting economic collapse. Many depended upon their gardening relatives in the country to supply them with food and without this lifeline they would have been in dire circumstances.

Spiritual
Working with the earth to fulfill the basic need for food is a fundamentally benevolent activity, that can help you to re-connect with nature. It can bring you back to the reality that we are totally and absolutely dependent on the earth for our well being, and that we should look after it a little more carefully.

For me gardening is about using human energy to make a place more productive, more diverse, and biologically richer than it would be otherwise. It's been said that "Gardening is the natural activity of man" and that pretty much sums it up. It is one of the most gratifying and fulfilling activities a person can engage in. I love to be out in the garden, nurturing the land and bringing crops to fruition. If you garden long enough you will begin to understand what is meant by the expression "the garden cultivates the gardener".

About this book

After spending nearly 30 years reading and criticizing other peoples gardening books, I decided it was time to see if I could do any better. The Organic Gardeners Handbook, and its companion The Vegetable Growers Handbook, are the result; the gardening books I always wanted. I prefer substance over appearance, so these books aren't as pretty as many others, but I believe they will be more useful. My aim has been to give the beginning gardener a thorough understanding of the most significant aspects of intensive gardening, in an easily accessible and usable format. The techniques I describe are simple, but used together they allow you to grow the maximum amount of food, in a relatively small area, with the minimum use of resources (soil, nutrients, water, labor). Gardening is a pretty straightforward activity that is mostly learned by doing. Generally all you need are a few clear pointers, what to do, what not to do, when to do it and you can work the rest out for yourself. I have also given you a little of the theory behind the practice, so you know why you are doing these things.

I love working in my garden, but I'm not a workaholic. I don't make work for myself and am always looking for ways to get the maximum results for the effort I expend. This is why I have come to depend upon the methods I describe here. Together they allow you to grow the most food, with the least work, land and expense.

As someone who has lived a life of mostly voluntary (and occasionally involuntary) simplicity, I know what it is like to live with little money and I have tried to bring that experience into these books. Organic vegetable gardening should be an activity that saves you money. It should not be another excuse to buy more stuff. The house and garden can provide most of the fertilizer you need (the rest can be obtained for free, as they are usually someone else's unwanted waste). Seed doesn't have to be bought every year, as it is easy to save seed from most crops. Tools can be obtained from yard sales. You can even make money from your garden by selling surplus food, seedlings or even seed.

These books are a reflection of my experiences in the garden and I hope you find them useful. If you have any comments, suggestions or corrections I would like to hear from you. I am always interested in other viewpoints.

1 Getting started

Gardening is a pretty simple activity, anyone with a few square feet of sunny soil and some seeds can be successful. However you will have more success if you approach the job with some degree of organization. It helps to have some idea of what you want to accomplish and what you need to do to get there. Here are a few suggestions on how to get started.

Small is beautiful

Creating a productive vegetable garden takes time. You don't need to do everything at once, so be patient. Start small and close to the house, no matter how grand your eventual plans. The commonest beginners mistake is to be too ambitious initially. Most gardens are started in spring, a time of year when energy and enthusiasm are abundant. Don't let this tempt you to bite off more than you can chew, start modestly. As you gain more experience you will be in a better position to judge how to expand. It is often suggested that one 100 square foot bed will be plenty for your first year. This is probably good advice, but it always seemed a little too modest to me. Of course you are a better judge of what you can handle. The condition of the soil, climate, personal preferences, ability, strength and enthusiasm, all have a part to play in how quickly you want to expand. I wouldn't start with more than 200 square feet though.

Soil improvement

All gardening begins with the soil (except hydroponics of course), so you need to put a lot of effort into soil improvement. This is particularly important in the first few years, as you work to build up your soil.

One of your first priorities is to improve the soil. Begin by doing everything necessary to stimulate soil life: add nutrients, adjust the pH, add and cultivate to loosen the soil (if necessary) and add organic matter.

Initially you should concentrate on the growing beds you are going to plant immediately, but you don't have to stop there. If you know where you are going to be putting beds in the future, you can start improving their soil right now.

If there are any persistent perennial weeds you must work on getting rid of them. In extreme cases this may even involve covering the entire area in black plastic for several months. If you don't have any such problems, you could cover the area of planned beds with a long-term green manure (Sweet Clover or Alfalfa are both very good).

The more organic matter in the soil, the more water it can hold, and the more nutrients it will have. One of your main tasks will be finding a source of organic matter and then getting it into the soil. The more you can get, the better your garden will be. Use a mulch to protect the soil from harsh sun and conserve moisture.

You may also want to have a soil test, so you know what you are working with, and (most important) if there are any serious deficiencies that need remedying.

If you are to have as much compost as you could use, you will have to devote some time to making it regularly.

Timing

Probably no factor is more critical to success in vegetable gardening than starting your plants at the right time. Many crops simply won't produce a useful crop if planted at the wrong time. Conversely if planted at exactly the right time they may produce for months, with no further attention.

In the intensive garden we don't just plant in spring, we keep planting and replanting as long as there is any plant growth. This makes the garden far more productive than it would otherwise be (but places greater demands on soil fertility).

Raising plants

Growing plants, either by direct sowing or by raising transplants, is one of the most technical aspect of gardening and takes a fair amount of care and attention. It is also one of the most rewarding, as you see your garden filled with beautiful plants you grew from tiny seeds.

Crop selection

Some crops are much harder to grow than others. I strongly advise that you start with the easiest ones, as you are more likely to have success with them and will be encouraged by the experience. Of course these should also be crops you will use, don't fill your garden with Radishes and Jerusalem Artichokes. The easiest crops are not necessarily the commonest ones though. A crop like Spinach can be quite tricky if not planted at exactly the right time, whereas Amaranth (an equally good potherb) grows itself.

Maintenance

It is essential to look after what you have planted. This is why it is usually recommended that you concentrate on a small area initially, until your skills improve. Plants really want to grow and need relatively little help from you. However when they do need help, they need it at very specific times and if they don't get it they won't be very fruitful. Some gardeners love starting plants and getting them established, but don't spend enough time actually maintaining them. Needless to say their gardens are not usually very productive.

Watering is probably the most critical maintenance operation in dry climates. When plants need water, they need it immediately, otherwise growth will be impaired. In humid climates weeding may be more important than watering. You won't get much of a harvest if your plants are crowded by weeds. Mulch and drip irrigation (with a timer) can significantly reduce the amount of time you have to spend on these tasks.

Controlling pests is another significant task. Your crop plants are attractive to a variety of creatures and you will often have to intervene to protect them.

Observation

A walk around the garden should be part of your daily maintenance routine. Most gardeners do this because they enjoy it, but it is also an important part of successful gardening. You need to see what is going on with your plants, so you can give them the attention they deserve.

Garden journal

I strongly advise new gardeners to keep a journal. This is not so you can sit back and reminisce in years to come, it has a very practical purpose. The journal will help you to work out the best times to plant crops in your particular climate. It can help you become a more efficient and effective gardener.

Make your journal an everyday record of all that happens in the garden, planting, harvesting, fertilization, the weather and more. You should also write down which species of flowers bloom when you plant various crops and when pests first appear. This will give you a better idea when to plant in the future and when to anticipate pest problems.

There are lots of pretty garden notebooks available, but they are not usually big enough, so it is much better to make your own. Print out some master pages, make as many copies as you need and keep them in a ring binder. Keep it conveniently at hand in the tool shed (with a pen). If you are so inclined you might choose to have a page for each crop and divide the pages into sections for each bed. This makes it easier to note actual planting dates, varietal notes, experiments and crop information. If you can't get it together to make a journal, then get a large calendar and make notes on that.

It's easier to recommend good record keeping than to practice it. In reality it's often the first thing to be neglected when you are tired. I often find myself trying to remember what happened a week ago, having neglected to write it down at the time. Even this is much better than nothing.

Your journal will become an invaluable aid to planning and day-to-day activities. All you have to do is look at the current page to determine what needs to be done. When everything is written down, it's much easier to keep to schedule and you are less likely to get behind (it's like having your own supervisor).

2 Site selection

Most gardeners decide where to put their gardens by default, it goes where there is enough sunny space. If you are lucky enough to have a choice of locations, there are several factors to consider. A garden site is usually a compromise, you choose the place with the most advantages and the fewest disadvantages. If you can't find a single site that is large enough for your requirements, you could put the garden in several smaller areas.

Sunlight

Plants live on sunlight, so this is the most significant factor when siting the garden. If plants don't get at least 6 to 8 hours of direct sunlight a day, they won't grow well and won't produce very much. It is the one thing you can't afford to compromise on.

In small gardens getting sufficient sunlight can be a problem because of shade from neighboring buildings and trees. In such situations you have to put the garden where it will get the most light. Some crops will tolerate light shade (leaf crops, carrot, pea, onion, radish, cauliflower and cucumber), but none really like it.

Sunlight also affects how quickly the soil warms up, how hot it gets and how frequently you need to water.

Distance from your living space

This may seem like a trivial matter but it is a basic fact. The further the vegetable garden is from your house, the less you will take care of it and use it. Ideally it should be located right outside the kitchen door. You might think this doesn't really apply to you, because you are so enthusiastic. One hundred feet really isn't that far, but it will make a difference as to how often you enter your garden. Someone once estimated that the harvest declined by 30% if the garden was over 100 feet away. At the very least plant a small salad and herb garden near the house.

Soil

It is nice to start with rich soil, but this is actually one of the least important considerations when choosing a garden site. You can completely transform the soil by good gardening methods, but you can't create more sunlight.

Slopes

Gardeners tend to avoid them, but slopes often have better microclimates for gardening than level land and some of the best garden sites can be found in the middle of gentle slopes. The orientation of a slope has a considerable effect on its' microclimate, because the maximum solar gain is received when the sun strikes the soil at right angles.

Slopes also drain faster than flat land, which can be a significant advantage in rainy climates.

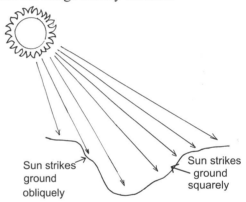

Sun strikes ground obliquely

Sun strikes ground squarely

Eastern slopes: These warm up fast in the morning sun, which is useful in spring and autumn. Such slopes are commonly sheltered from prevailing winds, which makes them somewhat warmer.

Southeastern slopes: These are probably the ideal garden sites. They warm up rapidly like eastern slopes, but get warmer. They aren't as hot and dry as south facing slopes.

Southern slopes: These have the warmest growing climate, because the sun hits them more directly. If flat land gets 100 units of sun, then a south-facing slope may get 106. This is effectively like moving the land further south. These slopes warm up faster in spring and get hotter in summer. They also dry out more quickly.

Western slopes: These are exposed to the afternoon sun, so get very hot and dry out rapidly. Prevailing westerly winds can exacerbate this drying effect. These winds may also cool the soil in spring and fall and

13

can cause physical damage. On frosty mornings these slopes thaw out more slowly, which can mean less frost damage.

Northern slopes: These get less solar gain than flat land. They may only receive 86 units of sunshine, as compared to 100 units for flat land. This means they have a cooler and somewhat shorter growing climate, just as if the land was further north. In addition they are often exposed to cold northerly winds, which further lowers the temperature. Like western slopes they thaw out slowly in winter, which can reduce frost damage. In temperate climates such slopes don't make very good garden sites, but in very hot climates they may be preferred for some crops.

Frost pockets

At night cold air flows downhill (rather like molasses) and collects in valleys. This makes low flat areas more vulnerable to frosts than somewhat higher elevations (contrary to what you might expect, as it is supposed to get colder at higher elevations). Low lying areas, where cold air sits, are known as frost pockets and can suffer from severe frosts, even when higher areas nearby are relatively frost free. Don't put your garden in a frost pocket

If a barrier (wall, hillock, tree or hedge) blocks the flow of cold air down a slope, the cold air may build up behind it and form a frost dam. By careful landscaping with solid barriers on the uphill side of the garden, you can re-direct the downhill flow of cold air so that it keeps on moving and misses your garden area. You should also ensure that fences on the downhill side of the garden have gaps to allow cold air to pass through them, rather than damming up to form a frost pocket.

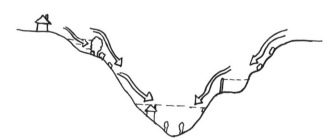

Frost pockets can be dissipated by wind, but of course too much cold wind can chill plants also. Frost pockets aren't always bad, they are sometimes used in mild winter areas to ensure that fruit trees get sufficient chilling.

Wind

Plants don't like strong wind. It can increase transpiration to the point where plants have to shut down (and stop growing) to conserve moisture. This can cut total crop yields in half. Wind also wastes water by increasing evaporation from the soil.

Wind also has other negative effects. It lowers air temperature (exposed areas may be 5° F cooler than sheltered ones), inflicts physical damage to the plants, causes erosion of dry topsoil and blows heat out of cloches and cold frames.

If your area is particularly windy, you might be able to site the garden where the topography of the land will protect it. If this isn't possible you will have to create a windbreak, which can be expensive and time consuming

Windbreaks: A good windbreak should be fairly permeable (only about 50% solid), so it slows the wind, rather than merely deflecting it over the top and causing increased turbulence on the other side. It is said that a windbreak will block the wind for a distance of about four times its height.

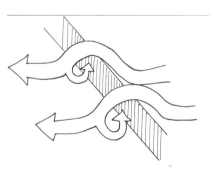

Hedgerows and trees make good windbreaks (and also provide habitat for predators), but take a while to get established. They also compete for nutrients and water and can reduce rainfall immediately around them by as much as 75%.

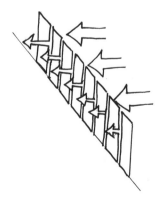

14

Wooden fences are an instant solution (even a 3' tall one will help), but are expensive and can cast unwanted shade.

Some crops make good windbreaks (Fava Beans, Sunflowers), but you will probably have to reinforce them with stakes to help them withstand strong wind. Blackberries trained on a trellis make a great windbreak.

In very windy areas it may help to orient your beds to act as windbreaks and plant vulnerable crops downwind. (See **Bed Orientation** below)

Pollution
Contamination of the soil from human made chemical pollutants is an increasing problem for gardeners and one you should be aware of. Though the possibility of serious problems is fairly remote in most places, once a toxic substances gets into the soil it may be impossible to remove.

Make sure the garden is a minimum of 100 feet away from well traveled roads, as they are a source of many dangerous pollutants. The soil around old buildings may contain high levels of lead, leached from old paint. Heavy metals such as lead and cadmium have been found in composted sewage sludge. Wood that has been pressure treated with chromated copper arsenate (or other preservatives) may leach toxins into the soil (it may also have been burned). Old farms might still contain persistent pesticides such as DDT or lead arsenate. Anywhere people have worked on machinery can contain waste oil. Ground water pollutants in irrigation water are another possible hazard.

Garden size
Gardeners sometimes say that a large garden is a liability, not an asset. By this they mean that you can easily become a slave to a garden that is too big. The smaller the garden the more efficiently you can use the space and the less empty space there is to grow weeds, or waste fertilizer and water on. The smaller the garden, the better you can take care of it and the higher the yield per acre.

The size of your garden will depend upon how much food you want to grow and how good a gardener you are. You don't need a very large space for an intensive garden, because the greater efficiency enables you to easily double the yield per square foot of conventional gardens. For a beginning gardener 200 square feet of bed

space is plenty, unless you want to grow a lot of space demanding crops such as Corn or Melons. Even a very large vegetable garden for 4 people doesn't have to be much more than 5000 square feet (an area roughly 70 feet square).

Apparently the average American vegetable garden is 500 to 600 square feet.

There is one good reason to make the garden larger and that is so you can devote some space annually to growing soil improving crops. If you make it a third larger than you need for crops, you can take a third out of production annually and plant it to green manures. This is an easy way to make a big contribution to soil fertility.

Fencing
In many areas a fence is necessary to keep out dogs, children, deer, raccoons, rabbits and other predators. The type of fence you select will depend on the job it's required to do and your budget. Fencing large areas to keep out deer or raccoons can be quite expensive, so you might want to enclose only a minimum area for vulnerable crops. The fence must be up to the job, or it's worthless (see **Pests**). If you must fence the garden make sure you put up a nice functional gate so it's easy to get into the garden (so many garden gates seem to be held together with string).

A fence can be more than merely a barrier; it can also give privacy, provide support for crops and act as a windbreak. In cold climates fruit trees were once trained against south facing stone walls, as these hold the suns heat and provide a warm microclimate.

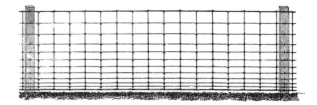

Trees
Trees are not very compatible with intensive vegetable gardens. Trees to the south side of the garden block out direct sunlight. The roots of all trees will compete for water and nutrients. In this situation you can either cut them all down (not very satisfactory), or get creative.

Wide beds

Vegetable gardens in this country traditionally consisted of long rows of crops separated by areas of bare soil. These imitated the fields of commercial growers, who needed the wide areas between rows for machine cultivation. In recent years wide raised beds have gained broad acceptance as a more efficient and productive way to use garden space. In these intensively cultivated beds all of the effort and fertilizer goes into the soil where the plants grow and none is wasted on paths. Equally important the soil isn't compacted by walking on it. See **Bed Preparation** for more on the advantages of these beds.

Bed orientation

Gardeners have long argued about it, but it probably doesn't make much difference whether your beds are aligned north/south or east/west. You do have to ensure that small plants aren't shaded excessively by taller ones. This is most easily accomplished by aligning the plants north/south, as then you don't have to worry about tall crops shading those to the north of them.

In very cold areas you may want to designate a couple of beds for early and late crops. These should ideally be located on a south facing slope to maximize solar gain. Failing this you can orient the beds on an east/west axis and tilt them slightly to the south. Also make sure they are not in a frost pocket.

In very windy areas it's usually best to situate the beds at right angles to the wind, so each bed protects the ones downwind. For maximum wind protection you might also stagger the paths (to prevent the wind travelling down the paths unhindered).

Bed size

The width of the beds is usually decided by how far you can comfortably reach to the center. This usually works out to a bed somewhere between 3 to 5 feet wide. Narrow beds are easier to dig from each side and step over, so there is less chance you will stand on them (you can also straddle them with a wide garden cart). It is convenient to standardize the width of a bed, as it facilitates planning and record keeping and you can use standard size cold frames and row covers. French market gardeners made their beds to conform to the standard size cold frames they had available.

Bed length is less critical than the width and is often dictated by site conditions. Don't make the beds too long, or it becomes a nuisance to walk all the way around them. You can of course simply cut long beds in half with a path. One way to decide on a length for the bed, is to make the length multiplied by the width into a nice round number (e.g. 4 ft x 25 ft = 100 sq. ft, or 5 ft x 40 ft = 200 sq. ft).

To maximize growing area the paths between beds are kept fairly narrow (in small gardens they can be as narrow as 12″ to 14″). If you make the paths narrow don't make the beds too long, as you can't easily get a wheelbarrow down very narrow paths. You don't want to have to carry spadefuls of compost half way down a 100 foot bed. Generally it's best to bisect your garden with a nice wide path, so the furthest distance you would have to carry that spade would be 25 feet.

If you have lots of space you can make your paths much wider (18″ to 24″), to facilitate getting a wheelbarrow between them. The disadvantage of wide paths is that you have more unproductive area to weed and take care of.

Enclosed Beds

Some gardeners enclose their beds with railroad ties (beware of toxic chemicals), concrete blocks, bricks, stone or wooden 2 x 10's or 2 x 12's. These look neat, make mulching paths easier and they reduce stooping (good for elderly gardeners). They are most useful for very poor soils (such as highly alkaline or rocky ones), as you can simply import soil to fill the frames. They are the best way for creating Gopher free beds, simply staple the wire to the bottom of the frame (make a good tight fit). Wooden frames also make it easy to create a modular system for attaching drip irrigation, trellis or cloche hoops. See **Bed preparation** for more on them.

There are drawbacks to enclosed beds. The materials for the sides cost money and aren't very ecologically sound (they use wood and it usually doesn't last very long unless treated with toxic chemicals). The beds are labor intensive to create and their edges can provide hiding places for pests (soil sometimes shrinks away from the boards slightly, leaving a perfect hiding place).

Bed Shape

The shape of the beds greatly affects the appearance of the garden, so is worth a little thought. If you just want to grow as much food as you can then straight beds may be preferable. They are easier to enclose with wood (see below) and protect with Gopher wire and bird netting. They may also be easier to set up for irrigation and to calculate the square footage of your crops. If you want the garden to have a more informal and attractive appearance then curved beds may be your choice, or even circular ones. They are certainly much more interesting visually.

Circular keyhole beds are favored by permaculture gardeners. They say there is more growing area and less path and they are easily irrigated with a single sprinkler. I also like the way they make the garden look.

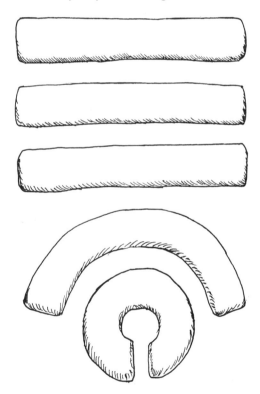

Laying out the beds

Use string and pegs to lay out straight lines in the garden. Use hose pipes and ground limestone to mark out curved lines. Draw arcs and circles with string and pegs to get nice clean accurate curves. Marking out lines on the ground gives you a good idea of your layout, so you can correct any problems easily. Find a high vantage point (hill, roof, tree) to get a good view.

Some extra facilities you may want

When planning the layout of your garden you might think about whether you will need the following and where you might put them.

Garden shed

It is really convenient to have a shed for storing tools, seeds, soil amendments, stakes, hoses, irrigation components and all of the other equipment the garden requires.

The shed should be located close to the vegetable garden for ease of getting tools and putting then away (then hopefully they won't get left out in the weather). If it is on the north side of the garden it won't cast shade on growing beds.

My ideal tool shed would have a covered area (with a transparent roof) adjacent to it, where you can work in rain. This area acts like an extended open greenhouse and gives you an extra place to store tender plants in winter. You can even grow some tender plants under it permanently. Run rainwater from the gutters to storage barrels (or directly to plants) underneath.

If you don't have a full shed, at least have some kind of covered rack to store tools. This could be right in the middle of the garden for maximum convenience.

Greenhouse

The greenhouse is an essential outbuilding for the serious gardener. Until you have had one you have no idea how useful it can be. Not only does it greatly expand your plant raising capabilities, but it also adds a lot to the pleasure of gardening. See **Greenhouses** for more on this.

Garden Plumbing

It is nice to have water faucets conveniently spaced around the garden. You can waste a lot of time going to turn distant faucets on and off (and it often means plants don't get all the water they need).

Water pipes should be buried at least 18″ deep, otherwise they may freeze in winter, or you may hit them while digging.

If you live in a dry climate you should think seriously about installing a drip irrigation system. It will quickly repay the labor and expense of installation.

If your climate is suitable (you get some rain all summer) I would also strongly advise a rainwater collection system, to collect rainwater from the roof. This particularly makes sense if you use expensive city water. See **Watering** for more on this.

Compost Area

In a small garden this might simply be a plastic bin, to take care of kitchen waste. In large gardens it might be a large shaded area for windrow type composting. It is very important that the area doesn't become a feeding station for rats and flies and other undesirable creatures (I once had a bear on my pile). In the city an unenclosed bin will inevitably attract rats. If this is the case a worm bin might be a better alternative

The compost area should be close to the vegetable garden, so you aren't transporting materials and finished compost for long distances. If you import a lot of bulk materials it should also have easy access to the road. The area needs a source of water and protection from extreme weather (in hot areas it needs shade, while in cold areas it needs sun and protection from wind and rain. The compost area might also be used to store leaf mold, manure, wood chips and soil.

Propagation/nursery Area

The propagation and nursery area (ideally with a greenhouse) should be a high priority, as it can play a crucial role in filling the garden with plants.

The nursery area supplies plants for expanding the garden as well as for replacing those harvested, or lost to other causes. It should have a protected area for starting seedlings outdoors, maybe also cold frames and areas for growing on cuttings and seedling trees.

It is nice to have an area for growing on seedlings, protected with bird netting and maybe even shade cloth. This area might even have its own automated watering system. The logical place for these features is near the greenhouse and growing beds area.

Potting bench

This will usually be near the shed and propagation area. It provides you with a solid surface to perform a variety of gardening tasks, not just potting up plants.

Garden sink

Not a very exciting feature, but one that helps to make the garden work better. It makes cleaning vegetables and other things easy and helps to keep the house sink clean. Newly harvested crops can be washed and stripped of waste parts before they go inside (the waste stuff going straight on the compost pile, the water going back into the garden (it even helps to conserve water). A sink doesn't need to be connected to anything permanent, attach a hose for water and have a bucket underneath to drain into.

The sink should be located near the greenhouse, propagation area and potting bench, so it can serve all of these areas.

3   Soil

Soil is not dirt. It is the source of human life, it is where our bodies come from and where they eventually return to. It is no coincidence that the words' humus and human have the same root. Our agricultural ancestors treated the soil with reverence, as their well being so obviously depended directly upon it. We are just as dependent upon the soil as they were, though many of us live so far removed from it that we forget. There is a direct relationship between the health of the soil and the health of the people who depend upon it. When you build up the soil you not only improve your plants health, but you can also improve your own.

Soil is the part of the earth's crust that supports plant life. A reactive spongy matrix in which plants anchor themselves, it accumulates and holds plant nutrients and water and keeps them available to plants. In some ways the soil resembles a living organism. It's powered by sunlight, it breathes (inhaling and exhaling) and it digests particles of organic matter, freeing up their nutrients for plants use (it's been likened to a stomach for plants).

Properties of the soil

As gardeners our main interest in the soil is how it supports plant life and how we can enhance this ability. I will now go into some detail about the soil, what makes it fertile and how it affects plant growth. I find it useful to have a basic idea of basic processes we are dealing with here. If you are of a more practical inclination, you might want to jump to the next section.

Soil texture

When we talk about soil texture, we are referring to the size of the individual mineral particles of which it is composed. Texture is a major factor in soil fertility, because it affects the ability of the soil to hold nutrients, as well as aeration, moisture holding capacity, drainage, temperature, structure and vulnerability to erosion.

Soil is composed of mineral particles of various sizes. The larger particles: boulders (above 24″), stones (10 to 24″), cobbles (3 to 10″) and gravel (2 mm to 3″), don't affect soil texture, though they do have physical effects.

Up to 10% of larger particles can be beneficial in heavy soils, as they absorb heat, increase water infiltration, improve drainage and provide habitat for soil organisms. They don't usually have much effect on plant growth, because roots simply grow around them (though some tap-rooted crops may be adversely affected). Of course such obstacles can interfere with cultivation, making the soil harder to work.

Particles smaller than 2 mm (sand, silt and clay) affect soil properties in many ways. They are collectively known as fine earth and the proportion of each defines the texture of a soil.

Sand: These are the largest fine earth particles and are approximately the size of sugar granules. A coarse sand consists of particles from 2 to 0.2 mm, with a combined surface area of about 23 sq cm per gram. A fine sand has particles from 0.2 to 0.02 mm, with a combined surface area of about 91 sq cm per gram. This is a very small surface area, so they have a low cation exchange capacity (see below for an explanation of this) and the pore spaces between them are so large they don't hold much water. These particles are too big to move around in the soil very much.

Silt: These particles are formed like sand, by mechanical grinding action, but they are much smaller. They are so small they are hard to see and have a silky feel, rather like white flour. Individual particles range in size from 0.02 mm down to 0.002 mm and have a combined surface area of about 450 sq cm per gram on average. This is still pretty low and so they also have a low cation exchange capacity. Silt doesn't usually make up a very high proportion of any soil, except in situations where it is deposited by water (there are few pure silt soils).

Silt particles don't cluster into aggregates very easily and when they do they aren't very stable. In some situations they tend to break apart into individual particles very easily. This can cause capping of the soil surface, or particles may move down and clog the soil pores (the particles are quite mobile in the soil).

Clay: The smallest soil particles are the flat plate-like particles of clay. They are formed chemically, rather than mechanically, by the weathering of parent rock by water and weak acids and are 1000 times smaller than sand. These minute particles measure less than 0.002 mm and have a total surface area of as much as 800 square meters per gram of soil. An ounce of clay particles might have a total surface area of 6 acres. (My apologies for mixing up the units of measure).

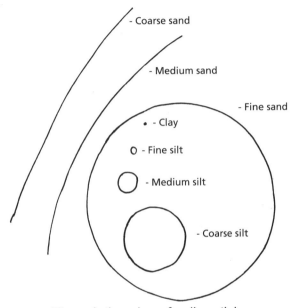

The relative size of soil particles

You probably know what clay feels like, it is plastic and amorphous like putty. The individual particles are so small they have a negative electric charge, which makes them very chemically active. They are continuously exchanging ions with the soil water solution and plant roots. Clay is the only size particle to have a significant cation exchange capacity (in poor soils it's the main source of C.E.C's), so it has been called the engine of chemical activity in the soil.

Though individual clay particles are small, their electric charge enables them to attract each other and clump together into larger aggregates.

Clay is by far the most important textural element; a soil need have only 40% clay to be a 'clay soil', whereas it must be 90% sand to be a 'sandy soil'. Most fertile soils contain at least 20% clay.

Assessing soil texture

It is helpful to know the texture of your soil because this affects fertility in many ways. You can get a rough idea of the dominant type of particle in the soil by the way it feels and how you can manipulate it.

Take a handful of soil, moisten thoroughly (traditionally with spit), knead it to break down its structure and rub it between your fingers. Roll the moistened soil into a ball and then squeeze it into a ribbon between thumb and forefingers. The longer the ribbon the more clay it contains.

Sand: The large individual grains are visible. It has a gritty feel and makes a grating sound when squeezed between the fingers. Sandy soils don't readily hold together in a ball and don't stick to the fingers.

Sandy loam: This resembles a sandy soil in that it feels gritty and the particles are visible. However it is more cohesive and can be shaped into a cube, or rolled into a ball. If you try and roll the ball into a cylinder it will break apart. It doesn't stick to the fingers.

Silt: These particles have a smooth, silky, feel and you can't distinguish the individual particles. Silt soils roll into a cylinder quite easily and stick to the fingers. Dry silt crushes to dust.

Silt clay: These soils have a silky feel, but are also somewhat sticky. They can be rolled into a thin thread and then shaped into a rather delicate ring. They stick to the fingers and make them dirty.

Clay: Wet clay is sticky and almost as malleable as putty when moist. Dry clay is very hard and doesn't crumble. A thread of clay soil can be shaped into a fairly strong ring. It doesn't stick to the fingers.

Loam: Most soils don't consist of a single particle size (a soil is rarely more than 50% clay), but of varying proportions of the three types. When no one size particle predominates, the soil is known as a loam. The ideal loam consists of 40% sand, 40% silt and 20% clay and has the positive characteristics of each. When one kind of particle is slightly more abundant then the others then you have a clay loam, silt loam or sandy loam, with more of their associated characteristics.

See **Soil Improvement** for more on soil texture and how it affects fertility.

Soil Structure and porosity

The way the individual particles are arranged in the soil determines its structure. A well-structured soil has large crumbs (from 0.5 to 5 mm in size) and a system of continuous pores, reaching from the surface to the subsoil (like well-risen bread). The large spaces between the aggregates are known as macropores (larger than 0.1 mm). They are filled with air most of the time and act as air ducts. They are home to bacteria, algae, protozoa, mites, springtails and countless other organisms. The much smaller spaces between the particles are known as micropores (smaller than 0.1 mm) and usually remain full of water. Root hairs penetrate them in search of water and they provide a home for water loving micro-organisms.

In a healthy soil there is a good balance of large macropores (which hold air and encourage vigorous root growth) and small micropores (which hold water). Such a soil is very stable and doesn't break down under adverse conditions.

You could say that an important component of the soil is empty space, though it's not really empty. Generally half of this pore space is filled with water and the rest is filled with air, though these proportions vary proportionally, as one increases the other declines. The amount of space between the individual soil particles (and their aggregates) determines soil porosity, which dictates how easily air and water can move through the soil. Porosity affects drainage, water retention, aeration and the amount of life in the soil.

You might imagine that a soil composed of large particles, would have more pore space than one composed of smaller particles, but the opposite is usually true. This is because the smaller particles clump together into much larger aggregates (or crumbs), whereas the larger ones don't. The amount of pore space varies considerably, from 60% of soil volume in an open, well-structured soil, down to 30% of volume in a sandy soil. Down in the subsoil it may be only 25% of soil volume, or even less.

Soils with a large proportion of macropores contain a lot of air, but don't hold moisture very well. Soils with a large proportion of micropores don't hold much air, but often hold so much water they are poorly drained.

Roots like to grow into spaces that are at least as big as themselves (0.3 mm up) and don't readily go into spaces smaller than this. This is why most plants dislike dense, heavy soils (roots may penetrate 4 times further in a light sandy soils than in a heavy clay).

Factors affecting soil structure

The most important factor in determining soil structure is the readiness with which individual particles cluster together to form aggregates. As I already mentioned, this is largely determined by the soil texture.

Organic matter and humus also significantly affect soil structure. Humus particles are electrically charged like clay and so cluster together with other tiny particles to form aggregates. The larger organic matter particles also loosen up the soil, reducing its' density.

Biological activity also has an effect on structure. When soil organisms break down organic matter, they release gums that help to glue soil particles together and encourage crumb formation. These gums can even glue the larger silt and sand particles together into stable aggregates. Fungal hyphae (threads) also bind soil particles together. Pressure from plant roots is also significant in improving and maintaining good soil structure. Earthworms are justly famous for their beneficial effect on soil structure.

Expansion and contraction from freezing, thawing and cycles of wetting and drying also affect soil structure. They compress soil particles into solid masses and break them apart again. This can cause a homogenous mass of particles to break up into various smaller aggregates.

Calcium has the ability to bind clay particles into aggregates (see **Soil management**).

Soil components

Soil is composed of four very different parts.

Mineral (45%)
Soil is formed when the parent rock is broken down by the process known as weathering. This is not only caused by actual weather (freezing, rain, wind), but also by the physical abrasion of glaciers, streams and waves. Some living organisms (bacteria and lichens) secrete acids that can dissolve rock. Weathering also occurs in the soil, when the acid soil solution dissolves minerals.

The type of parent material generally isn't very significant with regards to potential fertility, though it may affect the pH.

Four elements; silica, iron, oxygen and aluminum, make up 90% of the mineral component of the soil.

Water (25%)
A good soil at field capacity contains roughly equal amounts of air and water. The proportion of each of these varies inversely, when one increases (with precipitation, watering, evaporation and transpiration) the other decreases proportionally. For most of the time the soil is holding an enormous quantity of water.

When rainfall hits the ground it either runs off into streams or soaks down into the soil. The speed with which it enters the soil is known as the rate of infiltration, the speed with which it moves down through the soil is known as the rate of percolation. Both of these depend on soil structure and porosity.

When water enters the soil, it combines with carbon dioxide in the soil air to form a weak solution of carbonic acid. This dissolves out mineral ions from the parent material, which then go into the soil solution. Once in this solution the nutrient ions become much more mobile, as they can move through the soil with the water and be picked up by plant roots. Soil water keeps moving (taking nutrients with it), either from the effect of gravity, or by capillary action as water moves from wetter to drier areas. In this way soil water acts as a nutrient transport system, transferring nutrient ions from soil particles and cation exchange sites to plant roots. As roots absorb these nutrient ions they are replaced in the soil solution from cation exchange sites or mineral particles. See **Watering** for more about water and soil.

Cation exchange capacity

Cation (pronounced cat-ion) exchange capacity (C.E.C.) is a measure of the number of cation exchange sites in a soil, which indicates the soils ability to hold on to nutrients. This makes it a useful measure of the potential fertility of a soil. Cation exchange sites are negatively charged colloids (minute particles) of clay and organic matter, which attract and hold the positively charged nutrient particles (ammonium, calcium, iron, magnesium, manganese, potassium) called cations (a process known as adsorption). These sites hold on to nutrient cations that might otherwise be leached out by rain or irrigation water. Soils with a low C.E.C. need to be fertilized frequently, whereas those with a high C.E.C. are able to store nutrients until needed. A high C.E.C. also buffers the effect of toxic minerals such as aluminum and iron.

The cation exchange capacity of a soil is determined by the amount of organic matter and clay it contains. It is measured in milliequivalents per 100 grams of soil.

Sandy soils: 2 - 4 meq
Loam soil: 10 - 20 meq
Clay soils: 25 - 50 meq
Pure humus: 30 - 300 meq

Air (25%)
Air is the least obvious component of the soil, yet a good soil at field capacity contains as much air as water (about 25% or more). A well-aerated soil has all of the air required by plant roots and soil organisms and has good air circulation to vent out toxic gases.

Oxygen in the soil air is used by plant roots for the essential task of respiration, whereby the products of photosynthesis are converted into energy for plant growth. If plants don't get enough oxygen they can't respire and grow properly, so the amount of air in the soil directly affects their growth. Oxygen is also essential for aerobic soil microorganisms that mineralize organic matter and make nutrients available.

Soil air contains less oxygen than atmospheric air (from 20% near the surface, down to as little as 5% in the subsoil). The importance of air in the soil is apparent when you examine the subsoil. Topsoil and subsoil are made up of the same parent material, yet subsoil is much less able to support life, because of its much reduced aeration.

Soil air also contains a lot more carbon dioxide than atmospheric air (sometimes several hundred times more). Some of this seeps out of the soil and is used for photosynthesis and some enters into the soil water solution to form carbonic acid. This weak acid dissolves nutrients from minerals and makes them available to plants.

The other main component of air is nitrogen, but this is unavailable to plants, except through the intermediation of nitrogen-fixing organisms (see **Nitrogen**).

The ability to maintain a good balance between air and water is a very important aspect of soil fertility. Aeration is best in porous well structured soils, with large aggregates and continuously connected macropores that reach from the surface right down into the subsoil. Well-aerated soils can hold some air even when very wet and drain quickly. Poorly structured soils, or those subject to compaction have fewer macropores, so tend to be wet and poorly aerated.

Effects of poor aeration

If roots don't get enough oxygen they stop growing. If the wet conditions persist for very long the roots will eventually die. Root tips and hairs are especially sensitive to lack of oxygen and won't grow into poorly aerated soil (such as subsoil). Minor root damage from poor aeration may not be immediately obvious, but there may be an increased incidence of disease, or deficiency symptoms. Some crops are much more tolerant of waterlogging than others, but all suffer if this condition persists.

The commonest cause of poor aeration is too much water. Plants fail to grow in waterlogged soil, not because there is too much water, but because there is too little oxygen for root respiration. When soil remains waterlogged for more than a few days, the aerobic (air breathing) organisms normally involved in soil activity are suppressed, (some die, others go dormant) and anaerobic organisms (which don't need air) become active. These organisms give off toxic gases such as

hydrogen sulfide, methane and ethylene, which inhibit plant growth. Denitrifying bacteria also become more active in anaerobic conditions, so nitrogen may be lost from the soil. Some anaerobic organisms obtain oxygen from oxides of iron and manganese and in the process may make these nutrients available in toxic amounts. Carbon dioxide may also accumulate in the soil in toxic amounts.

Effects of excessive aeration

Though air is essential for a healthy soil, it's possible to have too much of a good thing. Too much air in the soil (such as from too much cultivation) can reduce organic matter by oxidizing humus and by encouraging an explosion of aerobic organisms that actually consume organic matter.

Soil breathing

Air in the soil is exchanged with atmospheric air in two ways. When barometric pressure is high, air is forced down into the soil and when it's low it is sucked back out. Rain also helps the soil to breathe, by driving out old air and replacing it with water. When this water drains away, fresh air is drawn back into the soil.

Organic matter and humus (5%)

The fourth component of the soil makes up only a small proportion of its volume, but it is vitally important in terms of soil fertility. The most beneficial thing you can do for your soil is to add more organic matter (some of which will eventually become humus).

Organic Matter

Organic matter is any dead plant or animal material and is mainly composed of carbohydrates, proteins, cellulose, lignins and waxes. It may be identifiable as to its origins, or simply indistinguishable organic debris. Either way it is still identifiable as being of plant or animal origin. Organic matter is good for the soil for a number of reasons.

Organic matter is the source of food for soil organisms, so drives most of the life processes in the soil. These in turn perform many functions that are beneficial to plants and to the soil.

Plant nutrients are recycled through organic matter (95% of the nitrogen, 60% of the phosphorus, 90% of the sulfur). The nutrients in organic matter were quite recently taken up by plants and when it decays these elements are released in a form that plants can readily use. Hence it is the main source of fertilizer for plants

Organic matter acts like a slow release fertilizer, holding nutrients in a stable state so they can't leach away, yet in a form that can become available fairly quickly.

The coarse structure of organic matter opens up the soil and improves structure, aeration and drainage.

Acids in organic matter react with inert mineral particles and make their nutrients more available to plants.

Organic matter can hold up to 4 times its own weight in water, which is very important for water retention. A soil with only 1% organic matter may retain about 1" of water, whereas a soil with 5% organic matter might hold 6" of water (six times as much). This is extremely important in light soils, in arid areas, or when irrigation water is scarce or expensive.

Humus

Humus is the end result of the decay of organic matter and is sometimes called stabilized organic matter. It is a dark amorphous jelly-like mix of minute sticky particles, which are insoluble in water. It has a large surface area and a soapy texture, rather like silt, but isn't usually present in sufficient quantity to affect any texture appraisal. Humus consists of long chains of carbon molecules that are very resistant to further decay (some humus in the soil may be several hundred years old). However it can be destroyed by oxidation, which converts it into water, carbon dioxide and heat.

- Humus doesn't contain many nutrients itself, but it has a very high cation exchange capacity (it may hold 10 times as many nutrients as an equal amount of clay) and so increases the soils capacity to retain nutrients. You can double the C.E.C. of a light sandy soil by increasing its organic matter content from 1% to 5%.

- The high C.E.C. of humus also means it can help stabilize the pH of the soil, by absorbing excess hydrogen, calcium and sodium ions.

- Humus darkens the soil, enabling it to absorb heat more efficiently, so it gets warmer (up to 5° F). The dark color of rich soils is usually caused by humus.

- Humus coats the larger soil particles and glues them together into larger aggregates and so improves soil structure. It actually repels minute clay particles, so helps prevent their compaction.

How much is enough?

Every soil has a stable natural level of organic matter and humus, dictated by vegetation, temperature and rainfall. This ranges from almost 100% in some peat soils, to almost 0% in some desert soils. Most soils contain less than 5% and this is mostly concentrated in the top 3″ to 12″ (organic matter content drops quickly with depth). A good garden soil may contain 5% organic matter. With a lot of work you could increase the organic matter content up to as much as 10%, but it's not necessarily desirable to go higher than that. Very high levels of organic matter can lead to unforeseen problems. For example decomposing organisms, such as Earwigs and Sow bugs, may become so numerous that they become pests.

If you regularly cultivate and remove crops without fertilizing, you deplete the reservoir of organic matter and the soil deteriorates. This manifests itself by reduced yields, crusting, compaction, poor drainage, rapid drying and fewer earthworms. See **Soil Improvement** for more on this.

Soil pH

See **Soil pH Adjustment** for information on this

Soil life

The carbon in plant material provides food for almost all soil organisms (directly or indirectly) and so is the energy source that keeps the soil alive and running. All soil organisms are full of plant nutrients, so the more life there is in the soil the more nutrients there are available.

The soil is a hospitable place for living creatures, with water, air, plenty of food, relatively stable temperatures, lots of hiding places and no lethal ultraviolet light. Consequently it provides a home for countless organisms. Some creatures burrow, others live in the soil pores, crumbs or cracks, or in the soil water. Anaerobic organisms live in the center of the larger crumbs, where they are protected from oxygen. Some creatures live on decaying plant material and some on living plants. Of course many soil organisms eat other soil creatures.

You can see the effects living organisms have on the soil by looking at a rotting fence post; it rots only in the top few inches of soil where life is most active. You can also see the difference between subsoil and topsoil, both come from the same parent material, yet topsoil is alive with activity and much more able to support plant growth.

Soil life and fertility

Soil organisms improve the soil in many ways.

- Their secretions glue particles together into aggregates. For example a single crumb of soil may contain 5 meters of fungal hyphae (threads).

- Tunneling organisms aerate and drain the soil.

- Soil organisms store nutrients in their bodies, preventing it being lost. These become available after the creatures die.

- Some soil organisms fix nitrogen and make it available to plants.

- Many essential nutrients in the soil are locked up in organic matter and only become available to plants when soil organisms break it down and release them. The decomposition of organic matter begins with a whole chain of creatures, slugs, woodlice, springtails, earthworms and many more. The products of decomposition are further broken down by fungi, bacteria and other organisms (as are the bodies of the decomposers themselves). The decay resistant material left at the end is humus (see above).

Encouraging Soil Life

One of the most basic principles of organic gardening is that you encourage the life in the soil. It's a mistake to think of soil organisms as of no consequence, or as pests and diseases to be "fought". They are all important and the more diverse and abundant the soil life, the less problems you will have. A diverse micro-flora means that there are so many different species that no single one gets out of hand. Logic says that when you upset all of these organisms you are asking for problems. It is why chemical fertilizers, herbicides and pesticides are such a disaster for the soil.

Most organisms are either beneficial or neutral, relatively few ever become a problem and then usually only when something isn't quite right (see **Pests** and **Diseases** for more on this).

It is easy to increase the population of active organisms in the soil. All you have to do is ensure it contains sufficient air and moisture (not too much or too little), has adequate organic matter (which supplies food (especially nitrogen) and a fairly neutral pH. A mulch also helps, by moderating soil temperatures and conserving moisture.

Types of Organisms

Protozoa (100 to 200 lb/acre) These organisms eat fungi and bacteria and so help control their population.

Actinomycetes (800 to 1500 lb/acre) These creatures come somewhere between bacteria and fungi and have a characteristic earthy smell. They break down rot resistant cellulose and lignins and produce important antibiotics (to help them compete for food against bacteria). They don't like acid soils.

Algae (200 to 500 lb/acre) Green algae photosynthesize their own food. Blue green algae fix nitrogen to make amino acids. They don't like acid soils either.

Bacteria (100 to 2000 lb/acre) There may be a billion bacteria (of 20,000 species) in a gram of soil. These may be aerobic (need air), anaerobic (don't need air) or facultative (can go either way). The most important role of bacteria is in breaking down organic matter in the form of plant and animal parts and waste products. They also glue soil particles together, make mineral nutrients more available and some can even break down toxic chemicals such as pesticides. Some produce antibiotics and other chemicals. A very few bacteria cause plant diseases (perhaps 1 in 30,000).

Some bacteria have the ability to fix nitrogen from the air, either in association with plants such as legumes (see **Green manure**), or as free-living organisms (*Clostridium*, *Azotobacter*). These are extremely important for the fertility of the soil.

Bacteria prefer a soil pH of 5.5 to 7.5 and soil temperatures of 40 to 90° F. In common with most soil organisms, they don't like synthetic fertilizers or pesticides.

Fungi (1500 to 2000 lb/acre) Molds, yeasts and mildews are all fungi. A few types of fungi are parasites and cause diseases of crops, but most are saprophytes and live by breaking down dead organic matter. They are particularly important for their ability to break down the tough lignins found in woody material. Their hyphae help to bind soil particles together into aggregates. Some fungi kill nematodes, others produce antibiotics.

Many plants establish a symbiotic association with mycorrhizal fungi, which supply nitrogen (and sometimes phosphorus) to their hosts, in exchange for carbohydrates or other nutrients. Some plants can only survive in certain soils if they have the appropriate mycorrhizal association to supply them with essential nutrients.

Earthworms (Up to 900 lb / acre) The best known beneficial soil organisms are the earthworms. They are so important that they are considered to be a good indicator of soil health. Most gardeners know that earthworms are good for the soil, but may not realize just how valuable they can be.

Earthworms are sometimes called "natures plow" because they may turn over 15 tons of soil per acre annually. They are also known as the "intestines of the soil" because of their ability to digest organic matter. They pull it from the surface down into the soil and break it down into smaller parts, which are then digested by smaller soil organisms. The bodies of these organisms (and their waste products) contain nutrients that eventually become available to plants. By breaking down organic matter they can also increase the C.E.C. of the soil.

Earthworm castings are not only rich in plant nutrients; they are also coated in a water-resistant gel, which improves soil structure and makes the aggregates more stable. Their constant burrowing creates channels in the soil, which aerates the soil and improves drainage.

Other organisms: Mites, Springtails, Woodlice, Millipedes, Nematodes, Pseudo-scorpions, Bristletails, Symphyla, arthropods and many and more. These organisms break down organic matter and aerate the soil with their tunneling. Some help to keep pests and diseases under control. A few may become pests.

The rhizosphere

The rhizosphere is the area of soil immediately adjacent to plant roots (it extends out about 2 mm) and is the most biologically active part of the soil. Plants can actually attract and control the kind of organisms that live there, by means of exudates from their roots. These organisms include bacteria, protozoa and fungi.

This is a very hospitable region for soil organisms because it is rich in carbonaceous material sloughed off by growing roots (this may amount to 5% of all the carbon fixed by the plant). The plants give some nutrients (carbohydrates, proteins) to these organisms and get others in return. They also get their nutrient rich waste products and when they die they get the nutrients in their bodies.

4 Soil pH adjustment

Most crop plants prefer to grow in a neutral, or slightly acid (pH 6.0 to 7.0) soil, because this is the range where most nutrients are most available. As the soil gets more acid, or alkaline, various nutrients become unavailable and some toxic elements may become more available.

You may be familiar with the concept of pH from high school chemistry. The letters pH stand for potential Hydrogen and measure the balance of positive hydrogen (H) ions to negative hydroxyl (Oh) ions. These are formed when water molecules break up (dissociate) and enter the soil water solution. There they combine with other particles to form new compounds, or attach themselves to particles of clay and humus (this is known as potential acidity).

The pH scale goes from 1 to 14, though soil is rarely below 4.0 or above 8.0 (extremes cases range from 3 to 11). It's a logarithmic scale, which means that a soil with a pH of 5.0 is ten times as acid as one with a pH of 6.0 and a hundred times more acid than one with a pH of 7.0. A soil below 7.0 is acid and contains a greater proportion of hydrogen ions. A soil above 7.0 is alkaline and contains a greater proportion of hydroxyl ions.

You can determine the pH with a simple soil test kit. If done carefully it will be accurate enough for most purposes (most errors come from an inability to compare the colors accurately). If it indicates that your soil is very acidic, or alkaline, you will have to correct it.

Acid soils

Acid soils are common in humid climates (especially in cultivated soils), because alkaline ions (calcium, magnesium, potassium, sodium) are readily leached out by water and are replaced by acid hydrogen ions. Phosphorus is unavailable in acid soils.

Organic matter tends to lower the pH, as organic acids are released when vegetation decays. In some areas, acid rain or irrigation water (which is sometimes as low as pH 3.0) also makes the soil more acid.

Low pH is a problem because it decreases the availability of many nutrients, including phosphorus, potassium, nitrogen, magnesium and molybdenum. It also increases the availability of some potentially toxic elements, such as aluminum and manganese, which are most available in acid soils. For example 75 times more aluminum is available at a pH of 4.5 than at a pH of 5.5. Most beneficial soil organisms don't like very acid soils and are much less active in them. Earthworms are often absent almost entirely.

Alkaline soils

These soils are common in arid areas, where there is insufficient rainfall to leach away the soluble alkaline ions (especially sodium). This problem is exacerbated if alkaline irrigation water is used, as when this evaporates it leaves yet more alkaline ions in the soil. Gardeners in such areas often have a struggle to maintain their soil at a reasonably low pH. Soils with a pH above 8.5 can become so difficult to alter that it may be easier to just replace the soil.

Alkaline soils are sometimes found in humid areas, if the soil is derived from limestone or similar rock.

pH adjustment

If the soil is very acid (much below 6.0) or too alkaline (much above 7.0) you will need to adjust it if you are to grow most crops successfully. This simple step can have a greater impact on soil fertility than just about anything else you can do.

Raising pH (Liming)

Soil pH is raised by adding a liming agent such as ground limestone (calcium carbonate). When you add lime to the soil, the calcium ions replace the hydrogen cations in the soil solution and on soil particles. The free hydrogen ions then combine with the carbonate to make water and carbon dioxide. When all of the hydrogen ions have been replaced the soil becomes neutral.

27

The pH scale

Few H+ ions

14 - Lye (drain cleaner)

13 - Bleach

12 - Soapy water

11 - Ammonia

10 - Great Salt Lake

9 - Baking soda - Higher limit of plant growth

8 - Sea water

7 - Neutral pure water - Preferred pH range for
most plants

6 - Urine

5 - Black coffee

4 - Acid rain - Lower limit of Plant growth

3 - Orange juice

2 - Lemon juice

1- Stomach acid

Lots of H+ ions

The benefits of liming

The application of liming materials has several beneficial effects. It increases the availability of many nutrients while decreasing the availability of some potentially toxic elements (aluminum and manganese). It increases the activity of beneficial soil organisms and decreases the incidence of diseases such as Clubroot. It can improve the texture of clay soil and of course it adds the nutrient calcium (if you use dolomitic lime it also adds magnesium).

Liming materials

Ground limestone: This is mainly calcium carbonate ($CaCO_3$) and is one of the commonest organic liming agents. It's safe, cheap and continues to work for several years. Its main drawback is that it is fairly slow to take effect.

Dolomitic limestone: Also known as Dolomite or magnesian limestone, this is calcium magnesium carbonate (it contains 60% $CaCO_3$ and 40% $MgCO_3$). This is slightly less soluble than calcitic limestone (it is only 85% as effective) so is even slower to start working. However it also adds magnesium to the soil as well as calcium, so is preferred for soils where magnesium is less than abundant.

Basic slag, marble, chalk, oyster shell: These are merely other forms of calcium carbonate and may be used like ground limestone. They are usually more expensive though.

Wood ash: This is more soluble than limestone and so acts more quickly, but is only about half as effective. It is actually a fertilizer as it supplies potassium and other nutrients as well as calcium. (See **Fertilizers** for more on this).

Quicklime: Also known as calcium oxide (CaO), it is made by heating calcium carbonate. Quicklime raises pH quickly, but the effect doesn't last for very long. It is also caustic, harmful to soil organisms, unpleasant to use (it's harmful to humans too) and energy intensive to produce. Organic gardeners rarely use it.

Slaked lime: Also known as hydrated Lime, this is sometimes confused with ground limestone (presumably because of its similar use) but it is quite different. It's made by adding water to quicklime to make calcium hydroxide (Ca $(OH)_2$). Inorganic farmers commonly use it because it is very soluble and works quickly even on heavy soils (which need a lot of lime to alter them appreciably). It isn't much used by organic growers because it is caustic, very energy intensive to produce and harmful to soil organisms. The pH raising effect of slaked lime doesn't last very long in the soil, it is quick in and quick out.

Applying liming materials

Liming materials are more effective when finely ground, as this increases their surface area and hence the speed with which they react and take effect. Calcium carbonate is insoluble in water, but is dissolved by the acids in the soil solution. Compost is said to increase the efficiency with which limestone neutralizes acidity.

When: You can add lime at any time of year. The important thing is to get it into the soil as soon as possible (it takes 6 to 12 months to take effect). You shouldn't apply lime at the same time as you add high nitrogen fertilizers, because the calcium can cause nitrogen to be converted to ammonia and lost. Hold off the nitrogen for at least 2 months after liming. This fits in well with autumn liming, as it's best to add nitrogen in spring, when it can be used fairly quickly. Nitrogen added in autumn may be leached out by rainfall.

How: Scatter the powder evenly over the surface of the growing beds and then fork it into the top 6". Be thorough, as calcium doesn't move in the soil very much.

How much: Of course how much lime you need to apply depends upon how much you need to alter the pH. It isn't practical to try and change the pH too drastically, in one treatment. The pH scale is logarithmic, so if it takes 10 lb of lime to raise it 1 point, it would take 100 lb to raise it 2 points. I would advise trying to change it by 1 point and then leaving it for a year. Test again and see what effect it had.

The type of soil affects the amount of lime you need to apply. Those with a high C.E.C (from lots of organic matter or clay) will need more lime to raise the pH than soils with a low C.E.C. A muck soil may need 10 times as much lime as a sandy one. As a rough guide, to raise the soil pH 1 point apply:

Sand: 3 lb ground limestone /100 sq ft
Loam: 5 lb ground limestone / 100 sq ft
Clay : 8 lb ground limestone /100 sq ft

If you only add enough lime to neutralize the hydrogen ions in the soil solution, they will soon be replaced from the cation exchange sites and the pH will drop again. You must add enough lime to neutralize this potential acidity, as well as that in the soil solution (this explains why liming takes time to work). The effects of lime usually last about three years, after which the pH may start to drop again.

Over-liming

In theory if you add too much lime you could raise the pH of the soil too much and then you could have a deficiency of boron, copper, iron and manganese. This is most likely to occurs in light sandy soils, but shouldn't happen if the soil has a reasonable amount of organic matter. To ensure it doesn't happen, add lime incrementally, rather than in one massive dose.

Lowering pH

Excessively high pH is rare in humid areas, but is a common problem for gardeners in arid areas. It can cause a deficiency of boron, copper, manganese or other trace elements. Occasionally you may want to increase the acidity of a neutral soil, for growing acid loving plants such as Blueberries or Cranberries, or to reduce the incidence of some diseases. The best way to lower the pH is with organic matter, such as Peat Moss, perhaps with a little sulfur to make it more effective (though this is more expensive than organic matter).

Acidifying materials

Cottonseed meal, Pine needles, Leaf mold, Peat moss

These materials reduce the pH of the soil by releasing various acids. Though slow to take effect, they continue to work for up to a year and are quite long lasting. They also add organic matter, which is always a good thing. Scatter a three-inch deep layer on the soil surface and fork it thoroughly into the top 3″ to 6″ of soil. There is a possibility that large quantities of these materials may cause a temporary nitrogen shortage as they decompose, so you may want to add extra nitrogen to compensate.

Iron sulfate Use 4 oz per square yard. It is quick to take effect (about 2 weeks), but it doesn't last for very long.

Sulfur powder

Incorporate 1 pound of sulfur for every 100 square feet for sandy soils (2 pounds for clay soil). It isn't very mobile in the soil, so must be thoroughly mixed into the top 6" of soil. It is slower to act than iron sulfate, but the effect lasts for longer.

5   Soil appraisal

It is helpful to understand the soil in your garden and to know its strengths and weaknesses. You will then be able to begin your program of soil building with the things it needs most.

Soil surveys

You might begin appraising your soil by consulting the U.S.D.A. Soil Conservation Service soil surveys, available from Department of Agriculture Extension offices, or your local library. They can tell you a lot about your soil, local climate and vegetation.

Depth

The usual way to determine the depth of soil is by digging (you can also use a soil auger, but this isn't as good). Vegetable crops generally prefer deep soils, so ideally the topsoil will be at least 6″ deep and preferably much more. If it's less than this you will have to work to make it deeper (new houses often have no appreciable topsoil, as it was removed during the construction process and never replaced). Building raised beds is the easiest way to increase the depth of soil.

Porosity

A fertile soil is loose and uncompacted. You should be able to push a fork at least 6″ deep. In a really good soil you might push a ½″ steel rod down a full 2 feet (if the soil is moist). Look out for subsurface compacted layers (hardpan).

Life

A rich fertile soil has plenty of earthworms and other soil life. Look for the large crumbs that are characteristic of earthworm activity.

Texture

I already discussed this in **Soil**.

Drainage

The moisture content of the soil (and hence drainage) varies considerably according to the time of year. A soil that doesn't drain at all in spring may be quite dry in summer when there is less moisture about. Ideally you should check drainage during the wettest time of the year (though this may not be the growing season).

A poorly drained soil can often be identified by the presence of specially adapted plants (Sedges, Rushes, Wiregrasses) that only grow where there is abundant moisture. Poorly drained subsoils are often gray or bluish in color and may have a faint smell of hydrogen sulfide from anaerobic bacteria.

A simple way to test soil drainage is with a large (46 ounce) juice can. Remove both ends and bury one end 4″ deep in the soil. Fill this with water and leave if for an hour. If less than 2″ of water has drained out then drainage is poor. If more than 5″ has drained out then water retention is poor.

Soil pH

You can test the pH of the soil with litmus paper, a home test kit, an electric pH meter, or as part of a commercial soil test (see **Nutrient Testing** below). Naturally occurring vegetation can also give you an idea of soil pH (see **Weed Indicators** below).

Chemical soil testing

The usual way to determine the nutrient content of the soil is with a chemical soil test. However these are rather imperfect because they only measure the concentration of nutrients in the soil solution and don't necessarily give a very accurate picture of the soils ability to supply plants. The availability of nutrients depends on several factors, the concentration of nutrients in the soil solution, the ability of the soil to maintain that concentration from the cation exchange complex and the rate at which nutrients are transferred to the soil solution.

When you first start a garden it may be worth having a comprehensive soil test done by a reputable testing lab. This will alert you to any major deficiency or excess in your soil and gives you a reference point to work from

Commercial soil testing laboratories are much more comprehensive than home test kits. They can test for macro and micronutrients, C.E.C and even for heavy metals and other pollutants (which might be a good idea if you have any grounds for concern). You can also get an agricultural water test to help you determine how good your water is for irrigation.

Large commercial growers now often use plant tissue analysis, which measures the concentration of nutrients in the plant sap to determine the available nutrients in your soil. This is too expensive for home gardeners though.

You can buy home test kits for measuring nitrogen, phosphorus and potassium. They can be quite accurate if used carefully and are certainly convenient. The biggest problem is that many people find it hard to match the colors in the charts accurately. The pH test is the most accurate.

There is a school of thought that argues that chemical tests aren't really necessary. That they are only really relevant to commercial growers. You would probably do much the same things to improve your soil even without one. I lean towards this view and don't often bother with them.

Testing procedure.
It doesn't really matter what time of year you test the soil, but for accurate comparison you should test at the same time annually, because the soil changes seasonally (more nutrients are available in summer for example). Fall is probably the best time to test (just before you put the garden to bed), as any fertilizers you need to add will have all winter to work. Spring is also good however, so decide on a time and mark it down in your garden journal.

To obtain a soil sample you normally take at least ten sub-samples (each about a tablespoon), five at a depth

of 1″ and five at a depth of 6″. Make sure you get a representative set of samples and avoid any unusual, or conspicuously different spots. To get the final sample you mix the sub-samples in a clean glass container for a minute or so and then take one sample from this. It's important not to mix samples from radically different soils and not to touch the soil with hands, fertilizers, or anything else that may affect the test.

Organic matter
The most obvious and useful indicators of high organic matter are a loose and friable soil with good structure and an abundance of earthworms. A high C.E.C, as indicated by a soil test is another good indicator.

It is possible to determine the organic matter content of the soil by drying a sample in an oven, weighing it and then burning off the organic matter. The % of weight lost is organic matter. Whether there would be any point to this is debatable, as you should already be adding as much organic matter as you can get hold of.

Soil color

The color of the soil can be informative. Generally soils in humid areas are darker than those in dry areas. Darker soils are better in cool climates because they warm up faster than light ones. Color can also give you more specific information:

Black or tan: Indicates high organic matter.

Brown or yellow: Indicates good aeration.

Blue: Indicates a lot of iron, but very little oxygen (wet).

Red: Indicates a lot of iron and oxygen, which means a dry soil.

Grey or blue subsoil: Indicates poor drainage. Such soils often smell of rotten eggs from anaerobic bacteria. Mottling indicates seasonal waterlogging.

White: Indicates a lot of salts and very little organic matter or iron (which would color the soil). White surface deposits indicate a high pH (8.0 or higher).

Weeds as indicators of soil type

The ultimate test of the fertility of a soil is whether it can support good plant growth. When looking at a potential garden site you should take note of the plant communities (not single species) that grow there. Many wild plants have quite specific requirements and are only found where their preferred conditions exist.

You should also note the condition of these plants. Are they deep rooted, healthy and vigorous, or shallow rooted, stunted and quick to bolt? Deep roots usually indicate deep soil, shallow roots indicate shallow soil. If a soil has a rank growth of vigorous healthy weeds it will probably grow good crops too.

Chickweed is a good indicator of a good garden soil, fertile, moist, well aerated and high in humus, nitrogen and other nutrients. Unfortunately it disappears in very hot weather.

Acid soil

Bracken, Buttercup, Corn Spurrey, Dock, Horsetail, Plantain, Sorrel.

Rich soil (high nitrogen)

Look for good growth of Amaranths, Chickweed, Chicory, Cleavers, Ground Elder, Groundsel, Lambs Quarters, Sow Thistle, Speedwell, Stinging Nettles, Yarrow.

Wet soil

Cattails, Green Algae, Horsetail (especially poor soil), Loosestrife, Mints, Mosses, Sedges, Wiregrass.

Dry soil

Broad Leaf Dock, Dandelion, Groundsel, Fireweed, Shepherds Purse.

Poor soil

Mullein, Wild Carrot, Wild Radish, Fireweed.

Compacted soil

Pineapple Weed, Great Plantain, Silverweed.

Alkaline soil

Poppy, Ox-Eye Daisy, Salad Burnet, Tansy, Yarrow.

6   Plant nutrients

Essential plant nutrients

It isn't necessary to know all the details about every single nutrient, but you may need to find out about specific nutrient at some point.

Only 17 of the elements in the soil are thought to be essential for plant growth. Those needed in the greatest quantities are referred to as major or macronutrients. Those needed in very small quantities are known as minor or micronutrients.

The terms major and minor nutrients is somewhat deceptive as they might lead one to believe that some are more important than others, but this isn't really the case. Plants need them all for healthy growth; they merely need more of some than others. Botanists commonly use an analogy of a barrel with staves of different lengths (representing nutrients available in varying amounts). The barrel (plant) can only hold as much water (grow) as the shortest stave (nutrient in least supply) allows.

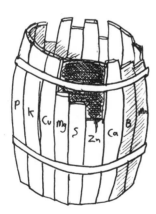

The following is a list of the 17 essential elements. This list isn't quite as finite as one might imagine, as some other elements appear to be essential in some plants but not in others and it's possible that other elements will eventually be found to be essential. In parentheses is the approximate proportion of the nutrient found in plants:

C - carbon (45%)
H - hydrogen (6%)
O - oxygen (45%)

These nutrients are used in the largest amounts (to make carbohydrates) and make up about 95% of all plant material. However they can safely be ignored by growers, because they are readily available from air and water and never present any problem of deficiency.

N - nitrogen (1.5%)
P - phosphorus (.15%)
K - potassium (1.5%)
These are sometimes called the primary nutrients, because they are absorbed from the soil in the largest amounts. They are needed in such large quantities that they are the most common causes of nutrient deficiency. Chemical fertilizers containing all three of these nutrients are known as "complete fertilizers", though of course they are far from that.

Ca - calcium (0.5%)
Mg - magnesium (0.2%)
S - sulfur (0.1%)
These three elements are known as secondary nutrients, though they are also absorbed from the soil in considerable quantities (plants often use more magnesium and calcium than they do phosphorus).

The six primary and secondary nutrients mentioned above are known as macronutrients.

B - boron (.002%)
Cu - copper (.0006%)
Fe - iron (.01%)
Mn - manganese (.005%)
Mo - molybdenum (.00001%)
Zn - zinc (.002%)
Cl - chlorine
These seven nutrients are known as micronutrients or trace elements. They are only needed in minute amounts for healthy plant growth (chiefly for producing enzymes) and actually become toxic if too abundant.

Co - Cobalt
This isn't used by most plants, but is essential for nitrogen fixation in legumes.

33

Macronutrients
Nitrogen

This is a unique nutrient because it isn't found in any parent rock, all of the nitrogen in the soil originally came from the air. Our atmosphere is 4/5 nitrogen, so there is 150,000 tons of nitrogen over every acre of soil - more than enough for even the most intensive garden. Unfortunately atmospheric nitrogen is useless to plants, as they can only absorb nitrogen in the form of nitrate (NO_3) or ammonium (NH_4). Fortunately it can become available to plants in several ways.

A small amount of nitrogen (about 5 lb/acre) is fixed by lightening in the form of oxides, or comes down to earth in rainfall. However most of the nitrogen used by plants is made available through the intermediation of nitrogen-fixing microorganisms. These include the Blue Green Algae, the symbiotic Actinorhizae and mycorrhizal fungi and various free living bacteria (notably Azotobacter and Clostridium species).

The best known nitrogen-fixing organisms are the mycorrhizal Rhizobium bacteria, that live symbiotically in nodules on the roots of members of the *Fabaceae* (Bean family). They convert nitrogen into amino acids for their own use and that of their host plant. When these organisms die the nitrogen is released into the soil. Organic growers commonly utilize these organisms by growing nitrogen-fixing plants as green manures. See **Green manures** for more on nitrogen-fixing crops.

Mineral soil contains very little nitrogen, but as the soil ages and improves it slowly accumulates in the form of organic matter and soil organisms. Once nitrogen has been captured and absorbed into plant tissue it may be recycled through plants and animals and if conserved by good cultural practices, soil fertility will slowly increase.

Nitrification: The nitrogen stored in the organic matter in the soil is not directly available to plants, but becomes available through the action of micro-organisms. The process whereby it is made available is known as nitrification and is carried out in two stages, by two distinct groups of microorganisms. Both groups must have sufficient moisture and temperatures of at least 50° F.

The nitrification process begins when bacteria digest organic matter to get the energy rich carbohydrates. In the process the proteins and amino acids are broken down into ammonia (NH_3) and then into ammonium (NH_4). The bacteria that do this don't need oxygen, so it can occur in wet soils. The ammonium thus released may then be used by plants, held at cation exchange sites, or other bacteria may break it down further into nitrite (NO_2) and then into nitrate (NO_3). The bacteria that do this need oxygen, so it occurs more readily in summer when the soil is dry (and when the soil is alkaline).

Loss of nitrogen

- Plants can utilize nitrate more easily than ammonium, but it isn't held at cation exchange sites (it is negatively charged), so it leaches from the soil quite readily. This is why it isn't desirable to have too much available at one time. In wet areas most of the available nitrate in the soil is leached away over the winter and is only replaced (from organic matter) when microorganisms become active in spring.

- Nitrogen can also be lost from the soil by the process of de-nitrification, which (as the name suggests) is the reverse of nitrification. This process most often occurs in warm, poorly aerated or waterlogged soils (and in wet compost piles). Anaerobic bacteria convert the nitrate into nitrite (they do this to obtain oxygen for their respiration) and then into ammonia, which is released into the atmosphere.

- De-nitrifying bacteria have long been maligned for wasting valuable nitrogen, but they play an important role in breaking down the nitrate fertilizers polluting groundwater and watercourses.

- Nitrogen is also lost from the soil by intensive cropping (more than any other nutrient) and this must be replaced if you are to maintain fertility.

Use: Nitrogen has a greater effect on crop growth than any other nutrient and is needed in the largest amounts (2% of dry weight of the average plant is nitrogen). It is a component of chlorophyll, so is essential for leaf growth and hence all plant growth. It's also needed for the synthesis of nucleic acids and amino acids (and hence proteins), for respiration and for the regulation of potassium and phosphorus use.

Deficiency: Nitrogen is the most commonly deficient nutrient in commercial agriculture, because it is needed in the greatest quantities, but is easily lost. Fortunately a deficiency is quite distinctive and if dealt with promptly it doesn't seriously affect a crop. Nitrogen deficiency affects the entire plant and is characterized by poor growth. There is severe chlorosis, the older leaves may turn uniformly yellow (their veins also) and die back from the tip. Younger leaves aren't as green as they should be, and if the shortage persists they may turn yellow. Older leaves and stems sometimes develop a reddish, purplish or orange tint (especially in Brassicas).

Nitrogen is quite mobile in the plant and when in short supply it is transferred from older leaves to newly developing ones. This degrades the performance of the older leaves, resulting in less functioning leaf area, less photosynthesis and slow, often stunted growth.

Cauliflower and Cabbage are good indicators of nitrogen deficiency.

Excess: An excess of nitrate nitrogen isn't uncommon in heavily manured or chemically fertilized soil. It causes an abundance of succulent dark green (sometimes bluish) foliage and tall weak stems that often fall over from their own weight. Such plants have thin cell walls and are more vulnerable to attack by pests and disease organisms and more susceptible to frost damage. Flowering and fruiting may be delayed in favor of leaf production and the fruit don't store well.

Nitrogen is rarely abundant in nature, so when plants find more than they need (such as when growing in heavily fertilized soil) they often store it (as nitrates) in their leaves for later use. These can become mildly toxic to humans, especially babies.

Reasons for deficiency

Lack of nitrogen: There may be insufficient available nitrogen in the soil, as a result of natural infertility, over-intensive cropping, denitrification, leaching or the incorporation of a large volume of highly carbonaceous organic matter (see **Soil improving Crops**).

Poor nitrification: In spring the nitrogen in the soil may be unavailable because it is too cold (below 40° F) for the nitrifying bacteria that make nitrogen available.

Excessively wet conditions may also inhibit these bacteria and hence nitrogen availability.

High pH: Nitrogen is most available at a pH of 5.5 and up. High acidity also inhibits nitrifying bacteria.

Nutrient imbalance: For plants to utilize nitrogen properly they need adequate amounts of calcium, magnesium and phosphorus.

Nitrogen sources:

If your plants are deficient in nitrogen, don't take any action until you have determined whether the soil is actually deficient, or whether it is simply unavailable for one of the reasons mentioned above. If it's merely unavailable then applying more nitrogen won't necessarily achieve anything. In fact the plants might eventually get too much, resulting in other problems.

Nitrogen is stored in the soil in organic matter (up to 95% of all the nitrogen in the soil), the bodies of living organisms (plant and animal) and as ammonium on cation exchange sites. The amount of nitrogen immediately available for use by plants (and soil animals) varies greatly according to conditions. When you add nitrogen fertilizer only about half of the nitrogen it contains will become available in that year.

The best source of nitrogen is organic matter in the form of compost. This is slow acting and remains in the soil until needed. Only about a third of the nitrogen in organic matter is released in the first year.

Manure is another valuable source of nitrogen, especially if it contains lots of bedding and urine. Be careful however, some types contain too much nitrogen and can burn plants (see **Fertilizers** for more on this).

Human urine is a good source of nitrogen, in the form of ammonium.

Green plants contain a lot of nitrogen and can be incorporated into the soil, composted, or made into tea.

Blood meal is a very concentrated and rapidly available source of nitrogen, but its use can present problems (see **Fertilizers**).

Liquid feeds such as manure or Comfrey tea can be used to give plants a quick shot of soluble nitrogen.

Phosphorus

Though phosphorus is common in many soils (especially cultivated ones), it is the second most commonly deficient nutrient (after nitrogen) because it readily combines with iron and aluminum to form insoluble phosphates. Even when a highly soluble chemical fertilizer is applied to the soil, only about 15 to 20% is actually taken up by plants, the rest is quickly rendered unavailable. It's been estimated that 90% of the phosphorus in the soil is completely unavailable, 9% is slightly available and only about 1% is readily available.

Phosphorus is one of the most difficult nutrients to deal with because of this lack of availability. Usually the problem is to get the soil to release the phosphorus it already contains, rather than supplying more. Chemically fertilized fields often contain huge reservoirs of phosphorus, while the plants growing in them may be phosphorus deficient. Phosphorus only becomes available when weathering releases ions from the slightly soluble phosphates. Once phosphorus has been absorbed by plants it is recycled through soil organisms and organic matter. Almost half of the available phosphorus in the soil is in organic matter.

Phosphorus isn't found in the soil solution in high concentrations (only 1 to 2 ppm of available phosphorus) and plant roots quickly absorb this. When roots have taken all of the phosphorus ions in range they have to wait for more to move closer, or they must grow more roots to reach out for it. Plants vary greatly in their ability to forage for phosphorus, so you must do everything you can to ensure your plants get all the phosphorus they need, especially when young. In the wild many plants get around the phosphorus problem by forming a symbiotic association with mycorrhizal fungi, which send out hyphae to forage for available phosphorus ions. These are then exchanged for other nutrients. This is a more efficient arrangement than for the plant to produce extra roots merely to get phosphorus.

It's important to replace the phosphorus removed when harvesting crops, especially if you are growing and harvesting large numbers of young plants (such as salad greens). Conserve this important nutrient by returning all healthy crop residues to the soil.

Use: Phosphorus is a component of the high energy compounds adenosine diphosphate (ADP) and adenosine triphosphate (ATP) which are essential for photosynthesis. It also helps to produce strong roots, increases resistance to disease and is needed for respiration.

Plants also use phosphorus for cell division, so need a lot of it when young. They use half of all the phosphorus they will ever need in the first fifth part of their life. In later life it's transferred from the roots to maturing seed and fruit.

Deficiency: Phosphorus deficiency isn't very distinctive. Growth is slow and stunted, while the undersides of older leaves develop a purplish / bluish coloration. Phosphorus is quite mobile in the plant so is transferred from older to newer growth when necessary. There may also be poor fruit set, or fruit drop (sometimes with good leaf growth). Problems are most obvious with small seedlings, as plants need phosphorus most acutely when young. A deficiency of phosphorus is hard to correct quickly

Kale, Tomato and Turnip are good indicators of phosphorus deficiency. Corn leaves may develop a purplish coloration by the time they are 2 feet high.

Excess: Phosphorus is so readily fixed and made unavailable in the soil that an excess simply isn't a concern.

Reasons for deficiency:
Lack in soil: Phosphorus is naturally deficient in many soils.

Poor availability: Phosphorus is only available in a fairly narrow pH range (5.5 to 6.5), so it is often unavailable to plants. In alkaline soils (above 7.0) it binds with calcium or magnesium and in acid soils (below 6.0) it binds with iron or aluminum. For maximum availability you should keep the soil close to neutral.

Nutrient imbalance: Too much zinc can prevent the uptake of phosphorus.

Sources: Deep cultivation can help increase phosphorus uptake by encouraging vigorous root growth (roots grow to search it out). Conversely anything that impedes root growth may inhibit its uptake.

The commonest source of phosphorus for gardeners is rock phosphate (20 to 30% phosphorus). This isn't in a very available form so you should add plenty (you can't add too much). It should be ground as finely as possible to increase its availability (the most finely ground rock is known as colloidal phosphate).

Phosphorus isn't very mobile in the soil so should be thoroughly mixed into the top few inches of soil, where it will be most available for good seedling growth. For large plants it's common practice to put some phosphate in the planting hole. Soil organisms and organic acids will slowly make it available to plants over the next ten years or so. Many gardeners add rock phosphate to the compost pile because the acids released by decomposition can help to make the phosphorus more available (see **Composting**).

Bats, seed eating birds and ocean dwelling birds accumulate phosphorus in their droppings. This is commonly known as guano and was once an important commercial source of this nutrient. A tea made from these materials is probably the best fast acting source of phosphorus. The droppings of humans are also a good source, though they need treatment before they are safe to use in the vegetable garden. Worm castings are also rich in available phosphorus

Other sources of phosphorus include bonemeal, fish emulsion, dried blood, tankage and basic slag. Some detergents contain a lot of phosphorus, so it may be found in gray water. Human urine is also a good soursce of available phosphorus.

In the mature garden phosphorus is most often supplied in the form of organic matter, especially as compost. Phosphorus accumulating plants include the Legumes (especially deep-rooted ones such as Alfalfa and Sweet Clover), Buckwheat, Mustard and Hemp. These can be used to make the phosphorus already in the soil more available (they can be composted, or turned in as green manure).

Potassium

Potassium occurs naturally in most soils (some soils contain as much as 1% potassium) and slowly becomes available through chemical weathering and biological activity. However only 0.5 to 1% of the potassium in the soil is actually available for plant use at any time.

Use: Potassium is essential for photosynthesis, protein synthesis, enzyme activity and the opening and closing of stomata. It is probably best known as the nutrient that promotes good root growth, so is especially recommended for root crops. It also helps form strong stems (it helps prevent lodging), improves storage life, aids in the assimilation of nitrogen and phosphorus and increases resistance to disease, drought and cold. Seedlings need a lot of potassium.

Deficiency: Only nitrogen is used in greater quantities than Potassium and it is the third most commonly deficient plant nutrient. Deficiency symptoms tend to be quite distinctive and appear most reliably on older leaves. There are interveinal chlorotic streaks, necrotic lesions and yellowing or scorching of the leaf tips and edges (which eventually roll inward as the leaf dies). Potassium is mobile in the plant so is transferred from older leaves to new growth. There is also slow growth, reduced vigor, poor root growth (even rotting) and weak stems that may lodge (fall over).

Cauliflower, Fava Bean and Potato are good indicators of potassium deficiency. Beet roots may be tapered instead of round.

Excess: An excess of potassium is similar to one of nitrogen; growth is sappy and prone to disease and insect attack. Another problem is that it can make other nutrients (notably phosphorus and magnesium) less available.

Reasons for deficiency
Leaching: Potassium occurs naturally in most soils and is steadily made available by chemical weathering and biological activity. Unfortunately available potassium is quite soluble and if not held at cation exchange sites it is easily leached out by rainfall. This is why potassium is most often deficient on light soils (especially those that are low in organic matter).

Low pH: Potassium is most available at a pH of 6.0 and up and may be unavailable in acid soils.

Nutrient imbalance: An excess of magnesium and calcium (usually the result of over-liming) can interfere with the absorption of potassium.

Sources: The commonest sources of potassium for gardeners are the rock powders, greensand (6 to 7% potassium) and granite dust (3 to 8% potassium). These forms of potassium only become available slowly by the action of the acids from micro-organisms, earthworms and organic matter. They are often composted to increase their availability (see **Composting**).

Wood ash is an excellent source of available potassium (6 to 10%) and many trace elements. It is so soluble that it can sometimes cause a temporary excess of potassium in the soil, and can raise soil pH excessively. However it also leaches from the soil very easily.

Compost is an important source of potassium. Make it from a variety of materials and fortify with rock powders if necessary.

Other sources of potassium include dry leaves (0.4 to 0.7%), urine (3%) and Comfrey leaves (6%). A tea made from urine or Comfrey (or urine and Comfrey), is a good way of getting potassium into plants quickly.

Magnesium

Some clay soils contain as much as 0.5% magnesium. This is slowly made available to plants by the action of carbonic and other acids, but is readily leached from the soil if not held at cation exchange sites.

Use: Magnesium is the central component of chlorophyll. It is also used for phosphorus metabolism and enzyme activity.

Deficiency: Magnesium is the most commonly deficient secondary nutrient. In many cases deficient plants show no obvious symptoms, except reduced yields. The most common visual symptom is the yellowing of older leaves, especially in the areas between the veins (leaf margins and veins stay green), giving the leaves a mottled effect. These yellow patches

may eventually turn into necrotic lesions. The leaves (or their margins) often take on a reddish hue and their tips may curl upward. Affected leaves commonly drop and it can eventually defoliate most of the plant. Magnesium is quite mobile in the plant, so symptoms first appear in older leaves.

Cauliflower and Potato are good indicators of magnesium deficiency.

Reasons for deficiency:

Leaching: Magnesium cations are easily leached, so a deficiency sometimes occurs in light sandy soil in humid areas.

Low pH: Magnesium is most available at a pH of 6.0 to 8.5, so may be unavailable in acid soils. Simply raising the pH may solve a deficiency problem.

Nutrient imbalance: An excess of potassium or calcium can cause a deficiency of magnesium.

Sources: Organic matter in the form of compost or manure is the best source of magnesium for a mature organic garden.

The commonest source of magnesium for the garden is dolomitic lime (calcium magnesium carbonate). If your soil is deficient in magnesium always lime with this in preference to calcitic limestone. Basic slag is another liming agent that contains magnesium.

In alkaline soils you can't use dolomitic lime, because it will raise the pH even further and can lead to other problems. In such a situation you can dissolve 10 ounces of Epsom salts (magnesium sulfate) in 10 gallons of water for every 100 square feet of soil.

If a magnesium deficiency shows up in the early stages of growth, you can use Epsom salts as a foliar feed (3 ounces in a gallon of water). You may also try a liquid seaweed fertilizer.

Sulfur

As a native of Britain, I am more accustomed to the spelling sulphur, rather than sulfur, but my spelling checker doesn't like it. Could anyone explain why it likes phosphorus but not fosforus?

Use: Some plants use large quantities of sulfur. It is needed for the manufacture of chlorophyll, vitamins, enzymes, hormones and amino acids (and hence proteins). It is also used for protein synthesis and root growth.

Deficiency: A sulfur deficiency resembles nitrogen deficiency in that there is a general chlorosis of the leaves (no necrotic lesions) and growth is stunted and spindly, but it is much less common. It differs from nitrogen deficiency in that the young leaves are the first to exhibit symptoms (sulfur isn't mobile in the plant) and they don't usually die. A deficiency may delay maturation of fruit and seeds.

Cabbage, Onions and Asparagus are good indicators of sulfur deficiency.

Reasons for deficiency:
Lack in soil: Sulfur is rarely deficient because it is found in most soils and isn't much affected by pH (it's readily available above 5.5). However it is easily leached by rainfall, so is sometimes deficient on light soils.

Sources: Organic matter contains 80 to 90% of all the sulfur in the soil, so compost is the best source (indeed other sources are rarely used). Sulfur dioxide and other pollutants (especially in rainfall) supply sulfur in industrial areas.

Sulfur powder is sometimes used to lower the pH of the soil (see **Soil pH Adjustment**), in which case it also adds sulfur of course. Epsom salts (magnesium sulfate) given to supply magnesium, will also supply sulfur.

Calcium

Use: Calcium is extremely important for good plant growth, though this isn't often evident because it is rarely deficient. It is needed for nitrogen absorption, protein synthesis, meristematic growth, enzyme activity, to neutralize toxic by-products and to make other nutrients (phosphorus, potassium) available. In the form of calcium pectate it is a component of cell walls and helps maintain their permeability. It also improves the storage life of crops.

Deficiency: Symptoms of calcium deficiency commonly show up in meristematic tissue, the leaves of terminal buds tend to have characteristic hooks and often die back, which may cause the entire bud to abort. Leaves may show tip burn and growth is generally slow. Calcium is needed for new growth and isn't very mobile in the plant, so symptoms first show up in young parts.

Roots are more prone to calcium deficiency than the tops and may be stunted and short (though this may not be apparent of course).

The Brassicas are good indicators of calcium deficiency. Lettuce may show tip burn, Tomatoes may get Blossom End Rot.

Reasons for deficiency:
Some plants use large amounts of calcium, but deficiency is rare in most areas because calcium is routinely added to the soil to raise pH and improve structure. Alkaline soils already have calcium, in fact pH is a good indicator of calcium level. If it's reasonably high there is probably enough calcium for good growth. Calcium is most available at a pH of 6.0 to 8.5.

Leaching: Carbonic acid in the soil converts calcium carbonate into soluble calcium bicarbonate. This is easily leached from the soil, if not held at cation exchange sites.

Nutrient imbalance: Calcium, magnesium and potassium must be balanced for good growth.

Sources: Calcium is most often added to the soil to raise its pH, rather than as a nutrient. (See Liming materials in **Soil pH Adjustment** for sources of calcium.)

If you need to add calcium, but don't want to raise the pH you can use gypsum.

Milk or eggshell tea can be used as a quickly available source of calcium.

Micronutrients

Micronutrients are vital for healthy plant growth, fortunately if your soil is rich in organic matter then it will contain plenty of micronutrients. If it isn't rich in organic matter then the best thing you can do is add plenty of compost or aged manure. You should also make sure the pH is close to neutral, so the individual nutrients are most available. It is very risky to add individual micronutrients to the soil, as they are needed in such small quantities there is a significant danger of adding too much.

Boron

Use: Boron is used for enzyme activity, nutrient transport, protein synthesis, water uptake, cell division, pollen production and fruiting. It affects calcium absorption.

Deficiency: Boron deficiency doesn't usually show up in the leaves, so a deficiency may be hard to identify at first glance. It is pretty distinctive though, the commonest symptom is internal cracking or rotting of the roots or heart. Less common symptoms include death of the growing point (similar to calcium), slow growth, short stems and distorted terminal leaves. The best way to determine if boron is lacking is with a soil test.

Cauliflower, Radish, Rutabaga, Turnip, Beet, Celery and Fava Bean are good indicators of boron deficiency. The interior of roots may rot, while the stems of Brassicas may become hollow.

Excess: High concentrations of boron occur naturally in some arid area soils. If the soil is very acid, and low in organic matter, it may be available in excess, as it's most available at a pH of 5.0 to 7.0. Fortunately arid area soils tend to be more alkaline. This isn't usually a problem in humid areas because boron is quite soluble and leaches easily.

An excess of boron is so toxic to plants that borax has been used as a weed killer. It causes slow growth, lack of vigor, pale coloration (cereals may be almost white), vulnerability to disease and insect pests and low yields. Organic matter reduces these problems.

Reason for deficiency:

Excess alkalinity: Boron becomes unavailable above pH 7.0. Boron deficiency is a common result of over-liming,

Nutrient imbalance: Excess calcium can affect boron uptake.

Lack in soil: Some crops have an affinity for boron and if grown frequently may exhaust the soils reserves, so subsequent crops become deficient. This is most often a problem on light sandy soils where it has been leached away.

Sources: Boron is needed in such small quantities it is usually adequately supplied by organic matter. The best way to treat boron deficiency is to add plenty of good compost.

Granite dust contains some boron.

Traditionally a boron deficiency was remedied with household borax. It is important to realize that boron is only essential in very small amounts and it's easy to add too much. The difference between deficiency and toxicity is smaller for boron than any other nutrient. Try an ounce of borax per 1000 square feet (mix it with water or sand) and see how that works. It is easy to add more, but harder to remove.

If you use gray water regularly be careful which detergent you use. Some detergents contain potentially toxic amounts of boron.

Manganese

Use: Manganese is used in the synthesis of chlorophyll, enzymes and nucleic acid and for nitrogen metabolism and fixation.

Deficiency: Manganese deficiency isn't uncommon, though it may not be obvious because the symptoms aren't very distinctive and vary with species. It can resemble an iron, nitrogen or sulfur deficiency.

Manganese is quite mobile in the plant, so a deficiency may not affect younger parts at all. The commonest sign is a mottling of older leaves caused by interveinal chlorosis, which may eventually turn into necrotic lesions (this doesn't happen with iron). The whole leaf may eventually turn yellow, or even the whole plant. Growth is slow and plants don't mature well. Young plants normally have enough manganese in the seed to get them going.

Beet, Brassicas, Pea and Potato are good indicators of manganese deficiency.

Excess: Manganese is most available in acid soils and may be absorbed in toxic amounts if the pH is below 5.5 (moderate liming will prevent this). High heat can release manganese, so an excess sometimes occurs in soils that have been heat sterilized.

Reason for deficiency:

High pH: Manganese is most available at a pH of 4.0 to 5.5 and may become deficient as the pH increases (a possible result of excessive liming).

Lack in soil: Manganese is found in most soils, though some peat or sandy soils are deficient.

Nutrient imbalance: Excess copper, iron, potassium and zinc can reduce the uptake of manganese.

Sources: Often simply adjusting the pH will correct a deficiency. Seaweed is a good source of manganese.

Iron

Iron is needed in larger amounts than any other micronutrient. Fortunately it is abundant in most soils (sometimes as much as 4%), so deficiencies are rare.

Use: Iron is used for producing enzymes, proteins and chlorophyll (though it's not a component),

Deficiency: Because iron is needed to make chlorophyll a deficiency resembles that of magnesium (also used in producing chlorophyll). It initially manifests itself as interveinal chlorosis in the younger leaves and in extreme cases they may turn almost completely white (they don't usually drop off and there are no necrotic lesions). Older leaves remain green, because iron isn't very mobile in the plant. The stems may be spindly and short and new shoots may die back.

Cauliflower and Cabbage are good indicators of iron deficiency.

Reasons for deficiency:

High alkalinity: Deficiency sometimes occurs on alkaline soils, as iron is most available at a pH of 4.0 to 5.5. This is a possible effect of over-liming.

Sources:

Sources of iron include compost, manure and blood meal. Acids from organic matter help make iron available to plants.

Copper

Use: Copper is used for enzyme activation, chlorophyll synthesis, metabolism, respiration and possibly nitrogen fixation.

Deficiency: The most distinctive symptom of copper deficiency is when the young leaves become twisted and misshapen (they may also be chlorotic, wilted, or have necrotic spots). The terminal bud usually isn't affected. Growth may also be slow. A soil test is often the best way to identify copper deficiency.

Beet, Cabbage, Spinach and Tomato are good indicators of copper deficiency.

Excess: Copper is only needed in very small amounts and is extremely toxic in excess. Symptoms of copper toxicity include stunted growth and yellowing of leaves.

Reasons for deficiency:

Copper is rarely deficient in plants, as it is common in most soils and is needed in very small amounts (1 Ppm is adequate).

High pH: Copper is most available at a pH range of 4.0 to 5.5 and a deficiency may occur as a result of over-liming.

Lack in soil: Some sandy soils are deficient in copper.

Unavailable: Copper can get tied up in organic matter, so is sometimes unavailable in peaty soils.

Sources: The best way to prevent a copper deficiency is to maintain a well-balanced pH and add plenty of organic matter (especially manures). Once a crop shows deficiency symptoms it's hard to save it, so think ahead.

Traditionally copper deficiency is remedied by applying a very small quantity of copper sulfate (1 lb per acre every 5 years. If you try this be aware that copper can be toxic and be very conservative in the quantity you add.

Copper sulfate is sometimes added to the soil inadvertently, in the form of the fungicide known as Bordeaux mixture. It is also found in some types of manure.

Zinc

Use: Zinc is used in the production of chlorophyll, proteins and enzymes and for cell division.

Deficiency: Zinc deficiency shows itself by poor growth and a mottling of older leaves from interveinal chlorosis (which may then spread to the veins). There may also be necrotic lesions, distorted leaf margins and small leaves with short internodes. Fruit trees are frequently deficient in zinc (which shows itself by early leaf fall). Beans are a good indicator of zinc deficiency.

Excess: Zinc is sometimes imported in toxic amounts in sewage sludge.

Reasons for deficiency:

High pH: Zinc deficiency is most common on alkaline soils, as it is most available at a pH of 4.0 to 5.5. A deficiency may be the result of over-liming.

Sources: Zinc is usually supplied in the form of compost, manure or in rock phosphate. Fruit trees sometimes have zinc glaziers points pushed into the sapwood.

Molybdenum

Use: Molybdenum is used by symbiotic bacteria for nitrogen fixation and by plants for protein synthesis and nitrogen uptake.

Deficiency: Molybdenum deficiency isn't very common and can be hard to identify. The young leaves become chlorotic, rolled and distorted and their leaf edges die and turn brown. Translucent patches may appear close to the midribs and holes develop. New leaves may fail to develop properly, the leaf blade being very narrow and the leaf consisting mostly of stem (known as Whiptail in Broccoli and Cauliflower). There may also be mottled interveinal chlorosis of older leaves. A soil test is the best way to identify this deficiency. A lack of molybdenum may result in a nitrogen deficiency.

Cauliflower, Lettuce and Legumes are good indicators of molybdenum deficiency.

Reasons for deficiency:

Molybdenum is present in most soils and is needed in smaller quantities than any other element (less than 1 ppm), so a deficiency is fairly uncommon. Once a deficiency appears it's too late to treat the present crop.

Low pH: The commonest reason for molybdenum deficiency is excessive acidity. Raise the pH to 6.0, or more, to increase its availability.

Sources:

If raising the pH doesn't solve a deficiency, then try seaweed.

Chlorine

Use: Plants accumulate chlorine in greater amounts than any other micronutrient. It's involved with water absorption.

Deficiency: Chlorine is so widely available that deficiency doesn't usually occur.

Source: Chlorine mainly comes from rainwater or salt.

Cobalt

Use: Plants don't use Cobalt directly, but the bacteria responsible for nitrogen fixation do (as do many other soil organisms). Hence it is necessary for plants that associate with nitrogen-fixing bacteria.

Deficiency: A deficiency only affects nitrogen-fixing plants and results in poor nodulation of roots. It only usually occurs on alkaline soils.

Sources: Compost, manure, basalt rock.

Common deficiencies for various soil types

Light soil: Boron, copper, magnesium, manganese, molybdenum, potassium, zinc.

High organic matter soil, peat: Copper, manganese and zinc.

Acid soil: Calcium, magnesium, molybdenum, phosphorus, potassium.

Alkaline soil: Boron, copper, iron, manganese, nitrogen, phosphorus, zinc.

Clay soil: Phosphorus

Plant nutrient deficiencies

Identifying nutrient deficiencies isn't always easy because plants don't necessarily show the classic deficiency symptoms. When diagnosing a problem you have to think like a detective (or doctor) and take all of the possible variables into account.

- Minor deficiencies may not show up visibly, but may manifest themselves in other ways, such as low yield, or an increased incidence of disease or pests.

- A deficiency may occur because root damage (from disease, pests, waterlogging) prevents the plant from absorbing nutrients properly. This can happen even if the soil is bursting with available nutrients.

- Often the same symptom may be caused by disease, frost, toxicity (excess of a nutrient), drought, waterlogging or other cause.

- Consider the crop (some are more susceptible than others), time of year, soil pH, climate (wet or dry), the relative abundance (or rarity) of the element generally, even an excess of other elements.

- You must also take into account the nature of the suspected nutrient. Is it easily leached? Does it become unavailable at extreme pH? Is it usually abundant or scarce? These nutrients don't work in isolation, but interact with one another. A deficiency or excess of one may cause a deficiency of another.

- Be aware of what nutrients are most likely to be deficient or unavailable in your growing conditions.

If you have reason to suspect that your soil is deficient in some nutrients, you can save yourself a lot of time and aggravation by having a comprehensive soil test done. Alternatively if you have the time you could simply monitor the most susceptible crops for the characteristic symptoms.

43

Nutrient deficiency key

A: Color of lower/older leaves affected.........................**B**

AA. Color of upper / younger leaves affected.............**F**

B. Leaves chlorotic...**C**

BB. Leaves brownish or purplish..................................**E**

C. Leaves at base turn yellow and often die (sometimes have a reddish tint) growth is slow, spindly and stunted...**Nitrogen**

CC. Yellowing interveinal..**D**

CCC. Leaves chlorotic, especially around leaf edges, which then brown and die. Leaves may develop yellow chlorotic streaks. Poor root growth and weak stems may cause lodging...**Potassium**

D. Leaf mottled from interveinal chlorosis, areas often have reddish color. Leaves eventually die and fall. Leaf margins and tips may die, leaving only newest leaves......
....**Magnesium**

DD. Interveinal chlorosis on older leaves (which may then occur on younger ones too). Leaves pale, rolled, distorted or narrow. Growing point dies.........................
....**Molybdenum**

E. Leaves dark green, but may be purplish underneath. Older leaves may turn yellow and die. Stems may be slender and growth slow. There may also be poor fruit set or premature fruit drop (sometimes with good leaf growth)...**Phosphorus**

EE. Leaf tips wilt, brown and die.....................................
....Excess **Chlorine**

F. Pale white or yellow areas on leaves.........................**G**

FF. Pale patches, death of growing points....................**K**

G. Whole plant uniformly chlorotic, growth poor........
....**Sulfur**

GG. Not like G..**H**

H. Young leaves are wilted, misshapen, tip burned, but not usually chlorotic. Terminal bud may wilt. Growth is slow…..…...**Copper**

HH. Not as in H...**I**

I. Interveinal chlorosis, spreads to veins. If severe also affects older leaves so whole plant may be almost white, alkaline soils…....................................………**Iron**

II. Veins not chlorotic..**J**

J. Young leaves mottled yellow from interveinal chlorosis and necrotic lesions, spreads to older leaves. Plants grow slowly and don't mature well.......................
....**Manganese**

JJ. Leaves develop interveinal chlorotic spots and necrosis (eventually spreading to veins), also distorted leaf margins. Newer growth may show a reduction in leaf size and internodes...**Zinc**
.

K. Terminal leaves pale and distorted and buds finally die. Stems short and sometimes splits, leaves brittle and distorted..**Boron**

KK. Growth is slow and stunted, leaves curl, tip burn, margins die, terminal buds abort. Similar to calcium deficiency…..................................………....**Calcium**

7 Soil management

It has been said that the primary aim of organic gardening is to grow soil and that growing plants is secondary. As organic gardeners we strive to make the soil as biologically active and diverse as possible, in the knowledge that this will increase its ability to sustain healthy plant growth. Diseases and pests are considered to be symptoms of a deficiency or imbalance in the soil, rather than simply random attacks by malevolent organisms. If the soil is good then plants will grow steadily and vigorously without interruption and will be more productive, healthier and more resistant to pests and diseases (it will all be so easy).

One of the keys to creating a healthy soil is to get soil organisms to work, by giving them all of the organic matter and nutrients they can use. These creatures will then multiply rapidly and can transform even the most impoverished soil into a vegetable paradise. Obviously the better the soil you start with the sooner you will get good crops, but almost any soil can produce abundantly if treated well. You've probably heard the stories of gardens established on soil little better than a parking lot, well it can be done if you know what to do and put a lot of effort into doing it. One benefit of starting with such a poor soil is that you will have more to brag about in a few years time. Imagine the effect when you say "of course this was all blacktop and parking meters three years ago. The hardest part was composting all those cars" Save a sample of old soil (or oil stained blacktop) to show astonished visitors.

Steps for soil improvement

Understanding your soil
You have already read about the factors that make up a fertile soil and how to determine the strengths and weaknesses of your soil. You must now decide how to correct its deficiencies.

Soil pH
One of the most important steps to improving the soil is to correct any excessive acidity or alkalinity. See **Soil pH Adjustment** for more on this.

Fertilization

A chemical soil test may be helpful in indicating any serious deficiencies or excesses, though I don't usually use one. Of course the correction of nutrient deficiencies is a critical aspect of soil improvement. See **Using Fertilizers** for more on this.

Organic matter

I already discussed the importance of organic matter in the section on **Soil**. Organic matter really is a complete fertilizer and contains all the nutrients your plants need (hardly surprising when you consider that it actually is mostly decomposed plant material). In the intensively cropped garden it is constantly being used up and must be replenished frequently, otherwise fertility will decline. Not only must you replace that used by plants, you should also try to increase the amount in the soil. For all practical purposes you can't add too much organic matter.

One of the biggest criticisms of chemically dependent farming is its disregard for organic matter. This essential element of fertility is consumed to produce crops.

Every soil has its own natural level of organic matter and it takes a lot of work and material to raise it. Only about 5 to 10% of the weight of compost actually remains in the soil as organic matter, so you must be quite diligent if you are to raise the soils organic matter level significantly. It also takes quite a long time, even with generous quantities of compost or manure it may take 5 years to increase it by 50%.

If you are growing a lot of crops, you must add organic matter regularly to maintain a high level in the soil. If you neglect to replace the organic matter consumed by soil organisms and growing plants, then the proportion in the soil will start to decline. In hot climates organic matter breaks down very quickly, so you must be even more diligent.

Managing organic matter

- Always replace the organic matter you remove as crops and more.

- The most significant source of organic matter for the garden is compost. You can't add too much compost to the soil, the more the better. The main problem I have had with compost has been not having enough of it. See **Compost** for more on this, the gardener's panacea. If you don't have enough compost, then aged manure is the next best thing.

- Mulching is another good way to add organic matter. It's easier than composting and has the added benefit of keeping down weeds, conserving moisture and protecting the soil surface. See **Mulching** for more on this.

- Green manures (especially grasses) add organic matter to the soil if done in the right way. This takes time, but doesn't involve the importation of large quantities of material. Green manures also protect the soil surface and help to conserve the organic matter already in the soil. See **Soil improving Crops** for more on these.

- Wherever possible you should leave the roots of crops in the ground to decay (and form channels for air and water penetration). Roots make up 50% of the weight of some crops and can add an appreciable amount of organic matter to the soil. Of course you should also return as much of the above ground portion as possible, incorporated directly or as compost or mulch.

- Keep cultivation to a minimum, as excessive aeration oxidizes organic matter.

- Put your organic matter in the top 2″ to 3″ of soil and it will eventually move down deeper.

- Dig narrow trenches down into the subsoil and fill them with organic matter (this is known as vertical mulching). I sometimes dispose of excess kitchen waste in this way.

Soil structure

This is a major factor in soil fertility and you want to do all you can to maintain and improve it. There are a number of things you should (or shouldn't) do to improve and maintain a healthy soil structure:

- Add organic matter (you should have guessed). I have mentioned this so many times I'm getting tired of writing it, but organic matter cures almost every soil problem, it truly is the soil panacea.

- Never work the soil when it is too wet. This can seriously damage its' structure.

- Avoid excessive cultivation (especially rototillers), burning, flooding, vehicles, walking and chemical fertilizers.

- Encourage soil life.

- Keep the soil surface covered with plants or mulch. Don't leave it bare for any length of time.

- Don't take out more organic matter than you are putting in. Be sure to fertilize sufficiently to compensate for the level of cropping (and more).

Soil Compaction

Compaction can reduce the amount of pore space in the soil to the point where it can inhibit root growth by as much as 90%. By reducing the amount of oxygen in the soil it also reduces the activity of soil organisms.

It takes time and effort to improve a poorly structured soil to the point where it is porous, well aerated and fertile, so don't do anything that might cause compaction.

Avoiding soil compaction

- Keep all traffic off the soil, including trucks, tractors, tillers, wheelbarrows, carts, children, dogs, bare feet and hands. A footstep may create only 6 psi which doesn't seem like much, but as little as 4 psi may be enough to cause damage. This means strictly separating growing areas from traffic areas and is easy if your garden is set out in raised beds. You really have no excuse for walking on the soil.

- Avoid excessive cultivation; the soil doesn't like being dug. You should particularly avoid rototillers. So many gardeners amend and rototill the soil to make it nice and fluffy and then walk on it. This is one of the worst things you can do to the soil structure. The vigorous cultivation breaks apart the soils fragile crumb structure, while walking mashes the fragments into dense clods. Rotary cultivation also tends to cause a plow pan in heavy soils, as the tines smear and compact the soil at their maximum depth (this effect is exacerbated in wet soil).

- If you must use a tiller on your beds try to use a machine that allows you to walk to the side of it on the paths, rather than behind. At least then you can avoid walking on the newly tilled soil.

Subsurface Pan

This is a layer of compacted soil beneath the surface and is common in some soils. It may be formed naturally by the leaching down of clay particles, or we can create it by repeated plowing at the same depth. (they are sometimes called plow pans). If the soil has a serious hardpan you must break it up, by deep plowing, double digging, or with a steel bar and a sledgehammer. A minor pan can sometimes be broken down by plantinga strongly taprooted plant such as Chicory or Daikon Radish. You could also create raised beds, to get a greater depth of soil above the pan.

Cultivation

Advantages: Many soils are too dense for optimal root growth in their natural state and in such cases cultivation (loosening the soil mechanically) can have a major effect on crop growth. It allows plant roots, air and water to penetrate the soil more easily and improves drainage.

Cultivation is also used to incorporate fertilizers and amendments, to create a good tilth for seed beds and to break up highly compacted soil and subsurface pans. It can also be used to remove (or bury) weeds and other surface vegetation and to incorporate soil improving crops.

Disadvantages: Though there are definite benefits to some cultivation, you can have too much of a good thing. Don't think that by repeatedly hoeing, forking and digging you are somehow improving the soil. All that lovely crumbly soil may be aesthetically satisfying, but exposing it to the sun and air is detrimental to its health. Nature rarely does much digging.

Excessive cultivation damages soil structure, oxidizes nutrients and even decrease its organic matter content (the extra oxygen stimulates the soil organisms that consume it). It also brings fresh weed seeds to the surface (where they can germinate) and disturbs or kills soil organisms. The excessive loosening can also damage soil structure

If your soil is in very good condition you might think seriously about ceasing to disturb the soil altogether (see **No-Dig gardening** in **Mulch**). If digging is a lot of work and isn't really necessary (or even harmful) then why do it?

Rules for cultivation

- Perform only the minimum amount of cultivation necessary to grow your crops and no more

- Digging must be done when soil conditions are exactly right. Working soil which is too wet or dry can seriously damage its structure (obviously in inclement weather this can cause delays).

- Do not invert the soil when digging. When topsoil is buried under the subsoil many of the microorganisms die from lack of oxygen. Plant feeder roots are mostly found in the top few inches of soil. If this is disturbed subsoil (which doesn't contain as much soil life or available nutrients) the plants will have to work harder to get what they needs. Subsoil is also poorly structured in many cases and sometimes contains toxic levels of some elements. The fork (or broadfork) is the best tool for aerating the soil without inverting it.

Soil life

In an ideal world you could simply add beneficial organisms such as earthworms to the soil and they would improve it. Unfortunately this doesn't work. If such creatures aren't already there it's because the soil can't support them for some reason. If you simply put some in your soil they would either leave or die.

The way to get more life into the soil is by fertilizing, amending, aerating and otherwise making it into a more hospitable habitat. If you do all of the things mentioned above you will soon notice increased activity in the soil.

Earthworms like a relatively neutral (pH 6.5) soil, light, porous, moist, well drained, with lots of organic matter and mulch (which provides food and moderates the soil temperature). They don't like constant cultivation and disturbance, especially in spring and autumn when they are most active. I've seen beautifully rich French Intensive beds with very few earthworms in them.

Soil Air

Soil aeration is largely a factor of its structure. A well-structured loose soil consisting of large aggregates will usually have good aeration. Aeration is improved by adding organic matter, careful cultivation (especially double digging), the activity of soil organisms, improving drainage, careful cultivation and by growing soil improving crops.

Soil Water

The soil must contain enough moisture, not only for plant growth, but also for the soil life that is so vital for soil fertility. Both extremes of moisture cause problems:

Too Dry: A dry soil doesn't hold much moisture, so can't support plants for very long without irrigation. Such soils also tend to be low in soil life (earthworms don't like dry soil). You can increase the moisture holding capacity of the soil by double digging and adding organic matter (preferably compost) at every level. Adding 10 pounds of compost per square yard, annually, for six years can increase the water holding capacity of the soil by 25%.

Too wet: Water is removed from the soil by plant transpiration, evaporation and gravity. If this isn't enough to remove excess water then the soil becomes waterlogged and there will be a deficiency of air. This inhibits new root growth and causes existing roots to rot, so plants won't grow well. Wet soil also inhibits the activity of soil organisms, including nitrogen-fixing ones.

Wet soils tend to be cold and only warm up slowly in spring, because evaporating water has a cooling effect. Simply draining off excess water has been known to raise soil temperature by as much as 6° F. If your soil is waterlogged you must remove the excess water before you can do anything else.

Reasons for waterlogged soil

There may be several reasons why the soil is holding too much water.

- Soil is most often waterlogged at the start of the growing season, when there is a lot of water about and temperatures (and hence evaporation) are low.

- The soil may have a sub-surface layer that prevents water from draining away. This may be caused by mechanical compaction, or it may be a chemical hardpan.

- A heavy clay soil may naturally have poor drainage. This can be corrected by improving its texture. Add organic matter to open it up and stimulate soil life.

- The water table may be so shallow that it rises to the surface in wet weather. Raised beds can be a big help in such situations. Underground water can be removed with drains, which lower the water table immediately above them (so long as there is somewhere for them to drain to).

- Low lying land may be waterlogged because the surrounding area drains on to it. If this is the case you must put in ditches or drains up slope, to intercept the incoming water and channel it away from the garden (if you are ambitious this water might be used to create a small pond or wetland).

Drainage

Ditches: These work best in light soils where water moves quickly, though they must be quite deep if they are to be effective. Open ditches provide interesting ecological niches for growing Watercress, Mint or other moisture loving plants. They can also be mosquito breeding grounds you can fall into (it depends upon your perspective). If you don't want open ditches they can be filled with brush or rubble. Obviously this is safer, but they won't last as long, or be as interesting.

Pipe drains: These are labor intensive and expensive, but more permanent than ditches. They are the best way to drain heavy slow draining soils. As a rule of thumb a pipe or ditch will drain as many feet of soil above it as it is inches deep in the ground (though this also depends on soil texture). This means a pipe buried 9″ deep will drain an area 9 feet wide. Drains must have a slight fall (slope) so water moves out of the pipe (one foot in 100 feet is sufficient). There must also be an outlet to take the water away (hopefully not to your house or neighbors garden).

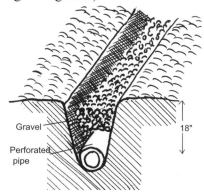

Gravel

Perforated pipe

18″

Once you have drained seriously waterlogged land you should probably double dig (to aerate) and incorporate organic matter. Soil organisms will then be able to get to work improving it.

Soil texture and type

The texture of the soil greatly influences its potential fertility and the methods needed to bring it to maximum productivity. Soil texture is determined by the type of parent material and it isn't very practical to try and alter it. To make a significant difference to a clay soil you would need to add a ton of sand for every 100 square feet of bed. Each type of soil has its own problems that you must work to overcome. If all else fails you can always build wooden sided beds and fill them with an imported mix of soil, compost and other amendments.

Sandy soil

Sandy soils are light and so drain well. They also warm up quickly in spring, so are good for early and overwintering crops. Their low C.E.C. means that nutrients tend to leach out easily, so they are often low in nutrients. Their low buffering capacity makes them prone to large fluctuations in pH, they can turn acid quickly and are easily over-limed. Such soils tend to be well aerated and can lose organic matter through oxidation.

Structure: Soils with a high proportion of fine sand don't make very stable aggregates, so structure is often poor and they are prone to capping.

Cultivation: Sandy soils are easily worked and can be cultivated even when at field capacity (unlike clays or silts). This means they can be dug at almost any time of year. They are so loose they don't compact easily and are the best soils for root crops.

Sandy soils don't need cultivation for aeration, but they may need it for the incorporation of organic matter. It may be worthwhile to cultivate deeply when first starting your garden, to get lots of organic matter down deep into the soil. Green manures and mulches are very beneficial.

Moisture: Sandy soils don't hold much water, so are not good for sustaining crops in hot dry weather (they should be watered little and often). Raised beds in sandy soil should have a low profile, otherwise they will dry out quickly.

Fertilization: Organic matter is beneficial for these soils because it increases their moisture holding capacity and C.E.C. It also encourages the large particles to cluster together to form aggregates, which they don't do naturally. These light soils need fertilizing regularly to replace nutrients that have leached out.

Sandy soils should always be cover cropped over the winter to prevent the loss of nutrients (especially nitrogen) and mulched in summer to reduce water loss by evaporation.

Silt soil

Soils are rarely very high in silt, but the particle does have a significant effect on the soils properties. These medium textured soils have characteristics somewhere between sand and clay and can be very good for growing most crops. They are better aerated than most clay soils and are easier to cultivate. Like sandy soils they have a fairly low cation exchange capacity, so nutrients tend to leach out easily.

Structure: As with sand, the individual silt particles are too large to cluster into aggregates readily and their structure is quite unstable. In heavy rains the aggregates tend to break down into individual particles, clogging soil pores and causing capping and erosion (keeping the soil surface covered will largely prevent this happening).

Cultivation: Silt soils compact easily if compressed or worked when wet. They were traditionally dug in autumn and left over the winter for frost to break down the clumps. This is not a good idea though, it's much better to not create the clumps in the first place.

Moisture: Silt soils retain more water than sandy ones, but still usually drain well (unlike many clays).

Fertilization: Silt soils are improved by adding organic matter to increase their C. E. C. and improve their structure. They need regular fertilization to replace nutrients leached away.

Clay soil

Clay soils can be heavy and difficult, but if you persevere they can be very fertile and productive. Ideally your soil will contain at least 20% clay, but no more than 35% (or you can have problems).

Clay particles are so small they have a significant C.E.C, which helps them to hold on to nutrients. Under the right conditions their tiny particles readily cluster together to form aggregates, in which case aeration can be good. Clay soils often contain a lot of nutrients, though you may have to adjust the pH to make them available.

Structure: Roots have a hard time penetrating poorly structured clay soils because the pores are so small and the particles so densely packed they aren't pushed aside easily. It is hard to get a good tilth for seedbeds in high clay soils. Given plenty of organic matter and soil life the minute particles will cluster together to form larger aggregates.

Cultivation: Clay soils are easily damaged by careless cultivation and can only be safely dug in a fairly narrow moisture range. A dry clay soil is so hard it is almost impossible to dig, let alone work to a suitable tilth. The soil cracks into large chunks which crumble to dust. When this dust gets wet it sets rock hard, almost like plaster. Cultivation of wet clay is even worse, as the aggregates break down into their individual particles, damaging the soil structure. These sticky soils also compact very easily when wet, even walking will do it.

Traditionally clay soils were roughly dug in autumn when relatively dry and left over the winter for frost to break down the large clumps to a fine tilth. Under the right conditions this can actually improve the soils structure. If the soil is fairly well drained and freezes slowly the repeated freezing and thawing compresses the soil into aggregates. If the soil is very wet and cold it will simply freeze solid and the thawing will break any soil crumbs into individual particles.

Clay soils benefit greatly from double digging to incorporate organic matter and calcium. Use raised beds to improve aeration and prevent future compaction.

Moisture: Clay soils hold a lot of water (up to eight times as much as a sandy one) and are slow to dry out. This is an advantage in times of drought, but in wet climates it means they get waterlogged easily. If clay aggregates are soaked for a long period they may dissolve and disperse uniformly, ruining the soil structure.

Wet clay soils tend to be cold and slow to warm up in spring. For this reason many plants don't over-winter well on clay soils. Slight slopes make good garden sites on clay soils, because they drain more quickly. Raised beds should be quite high to help them drain and warm up. Clay soils crack when they dry out. These cracks increase evaporation and make the soil hard to re-wet because water simply drains away down the cracks. Obviously you should never allow the soil to get so dry that it gets into this state. If it does you must cultivate the soil surface.

Fertilization: Add well decomposed organic matter to improve drainage and aeration. At one time it was recommended that you add sand to improve the texture of clay soil, but organic matter is easier, works just as well and has other benefits as well. If you really want to add some sand then add it to the compost pile.

Green manures improve structure, add organic matter and remove excess water. Liming is very beneficial on clay soils. Not only does it reduce acidity, it may also help to improve their structure (see **Soil Management**).

Flocculation: Calcium has the ability to cause clay particles to cluster together to form aggregates the size of silt particles, (a process known as flocculation). It does this because it has two positive charges, so can link up with two clay particles to form a larger particle (which may in turn be connected to other particles of calcium and clay). This only works if the soil is low in calcium. These aggregates aren't very stable or long lasting by themselves, but may be useful to improve soil structure temporarily, until you can get sufficient organic matter and soil life into the soil.

In acid soils you can use any liming agent with a high proportion of calcium. In alkaline soils gypsum is usually used, as you don't want to raise the pH any further. A common mix is 80% gypsum and 20% dolomitic lime, using an ounce of this mix per square foot of soil in spring and again in fall. This may be repeated for a second year, while adding as much organic matter as possible.

Alkaline soils

Alkaline soils are most commonly found in arid areas, where there is insufficient rainfall to leach away soluble alkaline ions. They also occur in humid areas, on soils derived from limestone or other high calcium parent material. They present their own particular problems and aren't the best soils for growing vegetables, but can be made very productive if you work at it.

Fertility: Alkaline soils tend to be light and easily leached, so are not usually very fertile. In addition some nutrients are unavailable due to their high pH, while others may be available in excess.

Moisture: These soils are usually porous and well drained and need organic matter to increase their water holding capacity.

Fertilization: The first thing you have to do with alkaline soils is to bring down the pH to make nutrients more available (see **Soil pH**). The next thing is to add organic matter and keep adding it (it burns up quickly in warm soil). This adds humus and nutrients, increases the depth of soil, lowers pH, improves water retention and raises the C.E.C. Green manures are also a good idea to improve structure, prevent nutrient leaching and supply organic matter. The texture of alkaline clays can by improved with gypsum.

8 Fertilizers

Obtaining fertilizers

One of the reasons I garden is to reduce my impact on the earth. Therefore I try to avoid purchased inputs wherever possible, by recycling everything that comes from the garden back into the garden and more. If you are creative you can find many sources of free fertilizers, which would otherwise be discarded as waste. Many of the most useful soil amendments and fertilizers are someone elses garbage (notably manures, kitchen waste, dry leaves, grass clippings and wood chips) and they are usually only too happy to get rid of them.

If you need specific nutrients, such as are supplied by rock phosphates, greensand or seaweed, and can't find an alternative, you will have to buy them. I try to get these in bulk from farm supply stores or wholesale nurseries, as these are usually cheaper than garden centers. When buying these materials don't simply look at the price however, you must also consider the quality and availability of the nutrients, to see which gives you the most value for money.

Problems with imported fertilizers

If you are importing materials to build up the soil, you should be aware that there are problems with some organic fertilizers and amendments. Many of the organic materials offered for sale to gardeners are not particularly environmentally benign. Some come from non-renewable resources (I would include some types of peat in this category) and in some areas mining them has had a severe environmental impact that is in no way sustainable in the long term. Even products that are renewable often have hidden environmental costs. For example they may use lots of fuel for processing and transportation (most amendments are heavy). Even renewable is a relative term, peat may be renewable in the long term, but many English peat bogs have disappeared into gardens. I personally have an ethical problem with supporting the intensive industrialized livestock industry (which gives us blood and bone meal and packaged manure).

When choosing fertilizers and amendments you should take these things into account and use the more environmentally sound and sustainable types where possible.

Contamination

When importing amendments be aware that you may be introducing problems into the garden as well as nutrients. The commonest imported problems are the weed seeds, pests and diseases that come in with bulky sources of organic matter such as manure. It's difficult to be absolutely sure such materials are clean and you may not have any alternatives to using them. In which case the safest option is to compost all of the stuff you import. A less obvious problem concerns more dangerous chemical pollutants such as various metals. The most serious of these are the heavy metals, as once they get into the soil there's no way to remove them. In some places sewage sludge is used as a soil amendment. This seems like a great idea, taking a waste product and recycling it into a useful commodity. Unfortunately it is commonly contaminated with cadmium and other heavy metals from industrial sources (it got there when industrial waste mixed with human waste in the sewers). It should be avoided at all costs.

There are other sources of contamination also. Hog manure often has high levels of copper, cow manure often contains a lot of salt and sometimes hormones and antibiotics. Tree leaves from heavily used streets may contain a variety of pollutants. Cottonseed hulls, straw and other agricultural wastes may contain herbicides. Fortunately a lot of these are broken down during the composting process and don't present a long-term problem.

Common fertilizing materials

Almost anything which was once alive can be used as a fertilizer, as well as many things that weren't (but will be).

Animal manures

It's a sign of the diversity of organic gardening that some growers think animal manures are the best fertilizers of all, while others believe they are detrimental to the soil and should never be used. Of course both schools of thought work.

Nutrient content of manure: Animals eat plants, so their manure is an excellent plant food. In fact manure could be looked upon as a form of quick compost, produced by anaerobic fermentation in only a few days. It is most valuable as a source of organic matter, nitrogen and trace elements, but also contains a moderate amount of phosphorus. Farmyard manure (manure mixed with urine soaked bedding) is even more useful, because urine contains nitrogen and potassium, while the bedding contains organic matter. The manure of young animals is less useful than that of older animals, because they need more minerals for growth, so digest their food more completely.

Finding manure: There is a lot of manure about if you look for it (it's been estimated that American cows alone produce two billion tons of manure each year!) and it's often available free for the hauling. You can use as much manure as you can get when first starting a garden, so it pays to establish a regular source of supply. This isn't difficult in most places, as manure often presents a disposal problem, so you are doing them a favor by taking it (they will often load it for you if you have a truck). Look in the Yellow Pages for riding stables or other farms. Some stables do a great job of composting their manure and have huge piles that heat up enough to kill any pathogens or weed seeds. If you are lucky you will find one of these.

If you can't find a source of free manure or don't have a means of transporting it then I suggest having a few truckloads delivered. Failing that you can fill garbage bags or cans, though it's hard to get enough in this way The French market gardeners would use over 1000 tons of horse manure per acre annually for the first three years of a new garden. They used to fill their carts with horse manure when returning from delivering vegetables to market.

In suburban areas horse manure is the most commonly available, but cow, hog and poultry manure can also be found. The type of litter affects the value of the manure, as it absorbs a lot of the urine and supplies humus building carbon. The best litter is straw, but hay, sawdust and wood shavings are all good. In time you may become a connoisseur of manure and will handle it affectionately and without hesitation. Is it aged or fresh? Does it smell strongly of ammonia? Does it look and feel nice?

Problems with manure

- The commonest problem with some manures is that they contain viable grass and weed seeds, either from the bedding or from feed. This will often pass through the animal undigested (only chickens kill all of the seeds they eat). By using such manure directly you may be planting weeds. Aged manure left in a pile may have heated up sufficiently to kill weed seeds in the center of the pile, but not at the edges, while dispersed manure may not have heated up at all.

- Fresh manure may contain so much nitrogen it burns plants.

- Some manures contain a lot of salt and this can build up in the soil if you use a lot. Salt is not only harmful to plants, but can damage the structure of clay soils.

- Manure from factory farmed pigs may contain large amounts of copper, which can be toxic.

- Manure may also contain disease or insect pests. Unless you are very familiar with the manure it's hard to know whether it will bring problems.

Storing manure: Ideally manure should be stored in a steep sided pile, with compacted sides to reduce the loss of nitrogen. It's important to keep the moisture content of a pile constant, otherwise it won't mature properly. In wet climates you should keep the pile covered with plastic sheet to prevent waterlogging and leaching. If it gets too wet it must be uncovered (and possibly turned) to allow it to dry out. If the pile dries out too much it won't break down. In which case it should be moistened, either by leaving it uncovered in the rain, or with a sprinkler.

You might want to leave a pile of manure somewhere to age. Simply left out in the rain it will lose a lot of nutrients, but it will still be an excellent source of organic matter.

Ways to use manure: Fresh manure may contain so much nitrogen it acts like a chemical fertilizer. It may burn the leaves and stems of any plants it comes into contact with. It may also cause sappy growth, lodging and delayed maturation of fruit. You can avoid this problem by applying fresh manure to the bed in autumn to age over the winter and incorporate it in spring. You can also spread it in late winter to leach for a month or so before planting. Fresh manure can also be used to make liquid fertilizer (see **Using Fertilizers**) and for making hotbeds for growing crops in cool weather. See **Season Extension** for more on this.

Aged manure is much gentler than the fresh stuff and can be used in the same ways as compost.

Generally the best way to use manure is to get it fresh and compost it yourself. You then know that it hasn't lost nutrients through leaching and has been heated enough to kill weed seeds and break down potentially toxic chemicals.

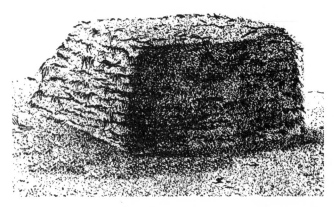

Types of manure

Chicken: Bird droppings combine feces and urine, so are very high in nitrogen. In fact they can be so high that they can present some of the same problems as chemical fertilizer. Chicken manure is too strong for direct application to the soil, so is best used as liquid fertilizer, or to supply nitrogen to the compost pile. It is especially useful for composting high carbon materials.

Cow: This is the favorite of biodynamic gardeners, who say it's the most balanced of all manures. Cows stomachs contain organisms that digest cellulose, which is why it is so different from horse manure. Cow manure tends to be fairly moist and not too hot (it's relatively low in NPK).

Horse: This is generally the most readily available manure, as there are riding stables almost everywhere. It is very well balanced, containing large quantities of nutrients (it is fairly hot) and a lot of organic matter (horses don't digest their food very well). The best manure includes bedding of straw, which catches a lot of the nitrogen rich urine. Wood shavings or sawdust are often used as bedding, but are inferior because they break down more slowly (they are a good source of organic matter though). Horse manure is excellent for compost piles. One potential drawback is that the uncomposted manure often contains lots of viable seeds.

Pig: This is another excellent fertilizer, though that from pig factories may contain a lot of copper so should be avoided (I wouldn't want to deal with such a barbaric system anyway).

Sheep: This would be one of the best manures for garden use, but isn't usually available in quantity. This is because sheep are usually kept in fields, rather than penned together, so their manure doesn't accumulate.

Cat and dog: The manure of carnivorous animals is rich in nutrients, but isn't safe for direct garden use, because it contains some rather nasty pathogens that can infect humans.

Human manure

This is the manure that most garden writers prefer to avoid (in more ways than one). Some people deny it, but humans produce useful manure. At one time human manure was considered to be the very best, which isn't really surprising considering the varied diet of its producers. My dad once asked a prize winning Onion grower in England what was his secret to growing such fantastic Onions. His answer was: human manure!

Using human manure for fertilizer is a logical way to recycle the valuable nutrients taken from the garden as crops. It is also a good way to solve the waste disposal problem. Unfortunately there are some significant problems associated with its use. The most obvious problem in western countries is the serious social stigma. There are not many things you can do that are as socially unacceptable as using your own feces. A more valid objection is that human waste contains pathogens that make it unsafe to use without treatment (apparently vegetarian waste is less toxic than that of meat eaters).

In parts of the third world human waste is far too valuable as fertilizer to be used to pollute rivers. In China untreated human waste has been used to fertilize fields for centuries, but there is a danger of spreading disease in this way (this is why food is always cooked in China). More recently the waste has been piped into methane digesters and processed to provide methane for fuel and then used for fertilizer.

In this country disguised human waste is sometimes available in the form of commercially processed sewage sludge. There are two kinds of sludge, digested sludge, which has been fermented anaerobically and activated sludge, which has been aerated to encourage aerobic decomposition (this type contains a lot more nitrogen). Unfortunately neither of these treatments has any effect on the heavy metals that commonly enter sewage from industry. These are very serious pollutants and you do not want them anywhere near your garden.

Probably the easiest way to process your own waste for garden use is by treating it in a good composting toilet (put this out in the garden) and then using it to fertilize fruit trees, compost crops, or other non-food crops. Of course these are not inexpensive.

The Humanure Handbook (by Phillip Jenkins) suggests collecting the manure in 5 gallon buckets, using sawdust to cover it and render it inoffensive. When you have enough full buckets you then compost it in the middle of a hot compost pile. This simple and inexpensive method is much less polluting than the traditional earthen pit outhouse and produces valuable fertilizer too.

Vent pipe

Composting toilet

Finding new ways of using human waste, locally and safely, should be a priority of agricultural researchers. This could provide large quantities of valuable fertilizer, while at the same time reducing household consumption of water enormously. In addition it would reduce the pollution of our waterways, oceans and groundwater. You know it makes sense.

Other organic matter sources

Compost

Compost has become one of the foundations of modern organic gardening, because it has far more value to the soil than its rather meager NPK analysis would indicate. Quite simply it is the best thing you can add to the soil. Unfortunately you can't just get compost, you have to make it, or pay someone to make it for you (which alters the economics of gardening somewhat). See **Composting** for more on this.

Spent mushroom compost

The specially made manure and straw compost used for growing mushrooms is a useful source of organic matter. Exhausted mushroom compost is often sold or given away to anyone who wants it and is easily available in some areas. It usually contains pesticide residues however.

Peat Moss

Peat moss is commonly used by gardeners as a source of organic matter. However it contains few nutrients and so isn't really of much use as a fertilizer. It is also quite expensive, very acidic (the pH may be as low as 3.5) and is hard to re-wet if it dries out. It has only been widely used in horticulture in the last 50 years or so, as an industry has grown up to exploit and promote its use. Gardeners once got along fine with the much superior leaf mold, turf loam and compost.

In England the mining of peat for gardens has become an important environmental issue, as some of the last remaining English lowland peat bogs have being destroyed to supply gardeners. Many English gardeners have stopped using peat altogether and are using alternatives such as Coconut fiber (coir), leaf mold or composted bark, wood shavings or sawdust. In North America the situation isn't nearly as extreme, as there are much greater areas of peat bog available. However the use of peat still means the unnecessary destruction of peat bogs and we should be aware of this. I should also point out that in some countries peat is actually burned in power stations to generate electricity. Putting it in the soil certainly seems preferable to that.

In my opinion the only valid use of Peat is as an ingredient for seed starting mixes and then only if better alternatives aren't available (see **Sowing Mixes**).

Tree leaves

In wooded areas tree leaves can be one of your most important fertilizers. They are one of the best sources of organic matter available anywhere and you should feel lucky to have them. Bagging them up and sending them to the dump or burning them is just plain silly.

Contrary to popular belief most tree leaves don't lower the pH of the soil significantly and it's easy to add lime if there is any problem. The presence of decaying organic matter may slightly inhibit the growth of some crops (they give off toxins), but the addition of organic matter and nutrients far outweighs any temporary detrimental effect.

The best leaves are those from Oak and Beech, though any deciduous tree leaves may be used.

Evergreens aren't nearly as useful, because they tend to contain toxic resins that can inhibit plant growth.

Gathering leaves: If there are many trees around your garden one of your autumn jobs should be to stockpile as many leaves as possible (mark it in your journal). If you don't have trees of your own (or even if you do) then beg, gather, buy or steal as many leaves as you can from elsewhere. Some people even go so far as to get street cleaners to dump truckloads of leaves in their gardens. If you do this you should be aware that street leaves may have high levels of various pollutants in them.

If you have a power lawn mower you can run it over the leaves to shred them. If you have a weed wacker you can use it to shred leaves in a garbage can. This isn't really necessary, but the resulting chopped leaves are easier to handle, much less bulky, less prone to compaction and they decompose a lot faster.

Using leaves: Leaves can have a dramatic effect on soil fertility. Just put them on the surface as a mulch and they will break down in one season (especially if chopped). They can also be incorporated into the soil when double digging and rot quickly when buried (conveniently the best time to do this is in autumn, as they then have all winter to decompose). If you have a large quantity of leaves this is a good way to prepare a large area for future planting. Tree leaves can also be used to make hot beds, simply replace half of the manure with leaves (See **Season Extension**).

Leaf mold: Leaves can also be used to make leaf mold. This valuable soil amendment holds 5 to 10 times its own weight in water and is richer in nutrients than peat (Peat moss has been called an expensive and inferior substitute for leaf mold).

Leaf mold can be dug from any woodland, but you shouldn't take large amounts from any one area. Woodland leaf mold is inferior to that you can make, because it tends to be very acidic and may contain substances that inhibit seed growth. Much better and more ecologically sound, is to make your own, as described in **Composting**). You can never have enough leaf mold for the greenhouse and garden, so make as much as possible.

Plants
All green plants are rich in nutrients and are an excellent fertilizer.

- Weeds, lawn mowings, prunings, harvest trimmings, aquatic weeds, bed skimmings, cover crops and any other green material can be used.

- Don't just think of the materials in your own garden, be creative and go out foraging. Lawn clippings can be obtained from many apartment buildings (often ready bagged), as professional gardeners are usually only too happy to have someone haul them away.

- Landscapers will leave you their tree trimmings, lawn mowings, hedge clippings and other organic waste. In fact they are often looking for places to dump the stuff.

- Aquatic weeds often become a problem in streams, canals and lakes and can sometimes be obtained in quantity (use as green manure or compost material).

- Some invasive plants (Japanese Knotweed, Kudzu, Ivy) can also be obtained in quantity.

- Make sure that any vegetable material you receive from outside the garden isn't contaminated with weed seeds, diseases, pests, insecticides or herbicides.

- You may want to grow some plants specifically to supply greens for making compost, or for fertilizer. Good plants for this include Comfrey, Horsetails, Stinging Nettles, Sweet Clover and Sunflowers. See **Soil improving Crops** for more on these.

Other organic fertilizers

Animal processing by-products
Slaughterhouse by-products such as blood meal, bone meal, feathers, tankage, as well as fish and crab meal and eggshells, are very rich in soluble plant nutrients and make excellent fertilizers. Personally I don't want to support the intensive livestock industry in any way (I don't like packaged composted cow manure for similar reasons). These materials are usually quite expensive anyway.

Food and agricultural processing wastes
Cotton gin trash, cottonseed meal (cotton wastes tend to be full of pesticides), buckwheat hulls, rice hulls, oil-seed waste, spent hops, wool shoddy, cocoa bean hulls, grape and apple pomace and more. These are all valuable soil amendments, or compost materials, and if you search around, or are in the right place at the right time you can get them for free.

You can often get garbage cans full of food waste from supermarkets, restaurants and markets. These can be a useful source of nutrients, though you have to compost them promptly or they will attract pests. Actually it's probably more ecologically sound for these food materials to be fed to livestock rather than composted, though of course composting is preferable to dumping.

Kitchen and household garbage
The best way to dispose of household waste is to re-use or recycle it. If this is not possible any organic material can be composted. Kitchen scraps are the most obvious compostable household waste, but paper, wool, cardboard, cotton, hair, cellophane, leather, can also be used. If you don't want to go to the trouble of making a compost pile, you could get a worm bin, or bury the stuff in trenches in the garden (see **Composting**). You might think that you don't produce enough of this to bother with, but in a year a household throws away a lot of valuable nutrients (a half-ton or more per person).

Seaweed
Seaweeds are rich in potassium and all of the trace elements needed by plants (most micronutrient deficiencies can be resolved by applying seaweed). They also contain growth-stimulating hormones, that encourage plants to grow vigorously and increase

their resistance to disease and pests. They are also rich in alginates, which improve soil structure, increase bacterial activity and may help prevent nutrients leaching from the soil. Seaweeds are useful for rejuvenating worn out soils and as an activator for compost piles. They

aren't usually necessary in the mature garden.

There are a number of commercial seaweed preparations, in powders or liquid form, but they are quite expensive. If you are lucky enough to live in coastal areas, you may be able to gather seaweed that has been cast onto beaches after autumn and winter storms (leave it in the rain for a while to wash off the salt). Fresh washed seaweed can be used like manure, applied at a rate of one barrow per 100 square feet. It rots quickly when dug into the soil.

Too much seaweed can stunt growth and add a lot of sodium to the soil, so use it carefully.

Urine

Human urine probably ranks as one of the most overlooked of all plant fertilizers. Like human manure it's one that is either a resource or a pollutant. Urine is much easier to deal with than solid waste because it is usually sterile and safe for direct use in the garden (a notable exception is that hepatitis can be transmitted through urine).

The average quantity of urine produced by one person in a day contains about 12 g nitrogen, (mostly as ammonium) 1.0 g phosphorus, 2.5 g potassium, 1.0 g sulfur and 5.0 g sodium (too much urine might cause salt buildup). Depending upon the diet of its producer, it also contains a variety of useful micronutrients.

Probably the most popular way to use urine is as a source of nitrogen for the compost pile. It can also be diluted with four parts of water for use as a liquid fertilizer (it may burn plants if used undiluted). Some people use it regularly as a foliar fertilizer. Urine is also an effective fungicide.

Wood wastes

Sawdust, bark and wood chips are all good sources of humus for building long term soil fertility, but there are problems with their use. These materials have a very high carbon to nitrogen ratio (see **Composting**) and if dug directly into the soil they may cause a temporary shortage of nitrogen. This happens because the organisms that break it down need nitrogen to work and must take it from the soil. They give it back eventually, but can cause problems in the meantime.

The best way to use wood wastes (especially sawdust) is to compost them with a highly nitrogenous material such as fresh manure or urine. See **Composting** for ways to deal with such materials. You can also dig these materials directly into the soil, if you also add a high nitrogen source, such as fresh manure, to ensure there is enough nitrogen for rapid decomposition. Don't try and bury too much at one time however, or it will take a long time to break down.

Shredded bark and wood chips can also be used as a long lasting, weed suppressing mulch.

Miscellaneous wastes

Creative and determined gardeners accumulate many other kinds of waste organic material for the garden. Wool wastes, hair from hairdressers, paper processing waste, wool or cotton from old mattresses, shredded documents and much more.

Straw and Hay

These materials are valuable and readily available sources of organic matter. Hay is made from whole dried grasses and weeds and contains most of the nutrients found in green plants. It is quite a good fertilizer and breaks down quickly in the soil. The problem with hay is that it is usually full of weed seeds. The best way to use it is to add it to the compost pile, as this will kill any weed seeds.

Straw is made from the stems of grain crops and isn't as rich in nutrients as hay. It is also slower to break down, but is usually free of weed seeds. It is a great mulch material, and can also be added to the compost pile

An old bale of straw makes a good garden urinal. It will trap the nitrogen and the nitrogen will help it decompose more rapidly.

Vermicompost

The nutrient rich castings of earthworms are a valuable fertilizer, but aren't usually available in sufficient quantity for general use. They are most often used in seed starting mixes, or for amending individual planting holes. See **Composting** for more on this.

Simple fertilizers

Rock powders

The nutrients in rock powders are fairly insoluble in water and only become available slowly, by the action of organic acids and soil organisms. Only small quantities of nutrients will be available initially (only 2% of colloidal phosphate becomes available in the first year and only 18% ever). The rest will remain in the ground for a long time.

Basalt rock: A source of calcium, iron, magnesium, phosphorus, potassium, cobalt and boron. 10 lb / 100 sq. ft.

Granite dust: 5% potassium and trace elements. 10 lb / 100 sq. ft

Greensand: 5% potassium and trace elements. 15 lb / 100 sq. ft.

Gypsum: Gypsum is calcium sulfate and so supplies both calcium and sulfur. It is the only common source of calcium that doesn't raise the pH.

Gypsum can also be used to improve the structure of saline soils, by displacing sodium ions.

Rock or colloidal phosphate: 25 to 30% phosphorus. 10 lb / 100 sq. ft.

Wood ashes

Wood ashes contain most of the elements that went into making wood, so are obviously a good plant fertilizer (and one which might otherwise be wasted). Their nutrient content varies according to the kind of wood burned, but generally they are an excellent source of calcium and potassium and a good source of magnesium and phosphorus. They also contain sulfur, iron, copper, manganese, boron and zinc. With a pH as high as 10.0 they make the soil more alkaline, so are often considered a liming agent.

When using wood ashes it's very important to know what has been burned to make them. Residues of plastics, paints, oil, glossy colored paper, painted wood and other materials contain some fairly unpleasant substances that shouldn't be in the garden. I like to put wood ashes through a ¼″ screen to remove any pieces of charcoal, as these don't decompose very well and will remain in the soil for a long time (I suppose you could crush them). Store wood ashes in a watertight container until needed.

Wood ashes are very soluble and leach from the soil easily. They should be dug into the top 3 to 6″ a couple of months before planting, or added later as a top dressing.

If the soil is already alkaline you have to be careful about using wood ashes, as they are a liming agent (from 20 to 90% as effective as calcium carbonate). Make sure they don't make the soil too alkaline.

Making your own fertilizer

Some gardeners like the convenience of a ready mixed powder they can apply at any time and which contains a full range of plant nutrients in the appropriate proportions. You can buy many ready made organic mixes, or you can formulate them yourself. Just make sure they contain a full range of nutrients rather than just NPK. Try this for a start.

2 parts cottonseed meal
2 parts colloidal phosphate
3 parts wood ash, greensand or granite dust
1 part Kelp meal.

NPK content of common fertilizers

	% Nitrogen	% Phosphorus	% Potassium
Animal products			
Blood meal	9 - 13	0.8 - 3.0	0.7
Bone meal	0.3 - 4.0	15 - 34	0.1
Eggshell	1.0	0.5	0.1
Feather meal	15		
Fish emulsion	4.0	4.0	1.0
Fish scraps	7.8	7 - 13	4.0
Hair	12 - 16		
Hoof and horn meal	6 - 13	1.6	2.0
Leather dust	5 - 12		
Tankage	5 - 13	2 - 20	
Wool shoddy	5 - 14	2.0	1.0
Manures			
Bat	12	8.0	3.0
Chicken	1.0	1.5	0.5
Dog	2.0	10	0.3
Horse	0.5	0.3	0.4
Pig	0.6	0.4	0.3
Pigeon	4.2	2.5	1.4
Rabbit	2	1.4	0.6
Sheep	0.4	0.3	0.8
Sewage, raw	2.3	2.0	0.5
Sewage, Activated	5 - 6	2.5 - 6.0	0.5
Urine, Human	1.5	0.5	1.0
Worm Casts	2.0	4.0	1.0
Food and farm by-products			
Apple pomace	0.2	0.02	0.15
Brewers grain	0.9	0.5	0.05
Castor pomace	5.5	1.5	1.25
Cocoa hulls	1 - 2.5	1.5	2.7
Coffee grounds	2.0	0.4	0.25

	% Nitrogen	% Phosphorus	% Potassium
Corn stalks	0.8	0.4	1.0
Cottonseed meal	3 - 7	2 - 3	1 - 2
Hops, spent	0.6	0.2	
Milk	0.5	0.3	0.18
Tea leaves	4.1	0.2	0.3
Alfalfa hay	2.4	0.5	2.1
Clover hay	2.0	0.1	2.1
Grass hay	0.5 - 1.5	0.5 - 2.0	2.0
Salt hay	1.1	0.25	0.75
Vetch hay	2.8	1.8	2.3
Barley Straw	0.1 - 0.5	1.0	
Oat Straw	1.1	0.1	1.5
Wheat Straw	0.5	0.1	0.8
Plant products			
Bracken Fern	2.0		3.0
Cattails	2.0	0.8	2 - 3
Comfrey, wilted	0.7	0.25	1.1
Compost, good 0.4	0.5 - 1.0	0.25	1.0
Grass clippings	1.2	0.3	2
Mud, Freshwater	1.3	0.2	0.2
Mushroom compost	0.7	0.3	0.3
Seaweed, dry	1.3 - 2.8	0.22 - 0.75	2.0
Oak Tree Leaves	0.8	0.5	
Sedge Peat	0.8	0.35	0.15
Water Lily	2.0	0.8	3.4
Wood ashes	0.1	0. 1- 1.0	0.1 - 13.0
Rock Powders			
Basic Slag		2.0 - 17	
Greensand		0.5 - 2.0	5 - 7
Limestone, Dolomitic		18 - 30	
Phosphate, Rock		30 - 50	

9 Using fertilizers

The aim of chemically dependent horticulture is to feed plants nutrients in the most available and soluble form, to grow the biggest plants in the shortest time. The aim of organic horticulture is to feed the soil, in the knowledge that fertile soil will grow healthy plants.

The line between chemical and organic fertilizers isn't really as cut and dried as you might think. It's commonly said that organic fertilizers are slow acting and so feed the soil rather than the plant, but this isn't always the case. Some fertilizers approved for use by organic certification organizations are actually more soluble (and hence more rapidly available) than some chemical ones. Some organic fertilizers (e.g. steamed bone meal and blood meal) are also energy intensive to produce. The extraction or mining of some organics also causes considerable environmental damage (see below).

There are "organic growers" who think and act like chemically dependent ones. They feed their monocultures with highly soluble fertilizers and spray their crops with toxic pesticides. The difference is that their fertilizers and pesticides are "organic", their techniques are the same.

Nutrient Availability

Weathering
Plant roots take up nutrients by exchanging negative or positive ions (electrically charged particles) with the soil solution. They don't absorb inert atoms, so the large stores of nutrients in the soil aren't directly available to them (such nutrients are said to be labile, which means stored or inert). Weathering is the process whereby mineral nutrients become available. We think of weathering as a mechanical process, whereby rocks are broken down by wind, ice, heat (in a word weather), but it is also a chemical process.

Chemical weathering occurs because of the disequilibrium between the soil solution and soil particles. The soil particles have a much greater concentration of nutrient ions than the soil water, so ions move into the water to correct this imbalance.

Once these ions are released into the soil solution they become quite mobile and move through the soil water by diffusion. As these ions are removed from the soil solution by plants or by leaching, the concentration of ions gets less, so others move in to take their place. Ions are also transferred from the soil solution to cation exchange sites (they are then said to be exchangeable) and may remain there until needed.

If ions in the soil solution aren't absorbed by plants, or held on cation exchange sites, they may eventually leach out of the soil and be lost. This occurs most dramatically in light acid soils in high rainfall areas. In extreme cases (such as tropical rain forests) soils are so leached they contain very few nutrients. They have either leached away, or are stored in soil organic matter and living plants and animals.

Generally the most readily available nutrients are those that have recently been incorporated into plants or animals in the form of organic matter. Though these must be made available by the process of mineralization before their constituent parts can be utilized.

The least available nutrients are those in their pure mineral form, such as rock powders. These can be made somewhat more available by grinding them as finely as possible (hence the greater value of colloidal phosphate over rock phosphate). This makes them slightly more chemically reactive, but they still they need chemical or biological action to convert them to the available ionic forms. The most effective way to make this happen is to increase the biological activity of the soil (composting them may also help). For maximum availability of organic fertilizers, soil organisms must be active, which means the soil should be warm, have the right pH and be rich in organic matter.

We commonly think of plants as passive organisms, that just sit in the ground (rooted to one spot) and take what comes along, but this is far from accurate. Plants can be very active in searching out nutrients, sending out feeder roots and root hairs wherever they find rich sources. Some plants are much better at this than others, which partly explains the difference in nutrient requirements·

Causes of nutrient deficiency

Once you have determined a plant is suffering from a deficiency you have to determine the cause. See **Nutrients** for more on this important topic. The most obvious reason is a lack of nutrients in the soil, but there are many other possible causes. Keep these possibilities in mind:

Root restriction / damage: Nutrient uptake will be reduced if roots can't absorb them properly. The roots might be restricted by compacted soil or poor drainage, or they may have been damaged by poor transplanting practices, disease, insect pests or waterlogging. Examine the soil and plant roots carefully for signs of problems.

Competition: Competition from weeds, or too closely spaced neighboring crop plants, can prevent a plant from getting all of the nutrients it requires. You can see this effect quite clearly when plants are left crowded in containers for too long; they soon start to show deficiency symptoms. Make sure your plants don't suffer in this way by planting at the proper spacing and by thinning and weeding promptly.

Disease and insects: Sucking insects such as aphids can remove so much sap from plants that they can cause a nutrient deficiency. Root eating or boring insects may damage roots or stems to such an extent that plants can't get all of the nutrients they need. Some diseases can affect a plants ability to absorb nutrients.

Soil pH: Extremes of pH affect the availability of nutrients and can cause a deficiency, (especially if a nutrient isn't particularly abundant to begin with). It's impossible to have the perfect pH for all nutrients because some are more available in acid soils (manganese, cobalt, iron, etc) and others in alkaline soils (nitrogen, sulfur, calcium, magnesium, molybdenum). Low pH may also exacerbate problems by causing toxicity from liberated aluminum and manganese ions. The best compromise is a pH of 6.0 to 7.0, as this is where the most nutrients are most available. See **Soil pH Adjustment** for more on this.

Soil temperature: Low soil temperature affects nutrient availability. The speed of any chemical reaction (including life processes) doubles with every 18° F rise in temperature and below 40° F there is little biological activity in the soil. This is significant because soil microorganisms are needed to make nutrients available. The nutrients most commonly deficient in cold soils are nitrogen and phosphorus. There are two ways to correct the problem of low soil temperature. You can either give your plants nutrients in a highly soluble form such as manure tea, or you can raise the soil temperature with cloches or plastic mulch.

Nutrient imbalances: Some nutrients have an antagonistic effect on others, so that an excess of one nutrient can reduce the uptake of another. If one kind of nutrient ion is more abundant and available than any other it will tend to be absorbed more frequently on to cation exchange sites, or into roots. This may result in other cations being leached away and lost. This is known as antagonism and is a common problem when chemical fertilizers are used.

This problem could get quite confusing if you tried to deal with each nutrient individually and tried to calculate the exact quantities of nitrogen, potassium, molybdenum you need. Fortunately when you are supplying your nutrients in complex organic forms, you can afford to be casual. You don't have to worry too much about toxicity, as nutrients locked up in organic materials are only made available slowly. A comprehensive soil test can tell you if you have a serious excess of any particular nutrient and you can then watch out for potential problems.

Variation in crops: Some crops are much less efficient at absorbing certain nutrients than others and some crops have higher demand for certain nutrients. Both types of plant are more likely to show deficiency symptoms, so you should watch these crops carefully when trying to determine the cause of a nutrient deficiency.

Nutrient excesses

These can present problems in several ways. An excess of nitrogen or potassium may delay maturation and cause plants to become susceptible to disease and pests (nitrate nitrogen can actually make green leaves mildly toxic). All of the micronutrients are needed in very small amounts and can be toxic if too much is available (especially copper and boron). If you have to add micronutrients then do it very sparingly, it's easy to cause problems by adding too much.

Fortunately nutrient excesses are rarely a problem for organic gardeners, because most organic fertilizers aren't highly concentrated and only become available slowly. You do have to be careful with the highly soluble ones such as wood ashes and blood meal though.

Fertilization

When we fertilize a growing crop, only a small proportion of the nutrients actually find their way into the growing crop. Most go to replace the more readily available nutrients the plants have removed from the soil and those leached out by rainfall or excessive irrigation.

When to fertilize: You will generally be fertilizing the soil, not the plants, so it doesn't really make too much difference when you apply fertilizers. A good rule is to apply organic materials when you have them. Don't hoard them in piles, get them into the soil where they can do some good.

For maximum growth, plants must have all of the nutrients they need readily available. If you feel it necessary to feed the plants directly then the stage of growth is the main determining factor. Plants have the greatest need for nutrients when they are young. A young plant may only make 10% of its growth in its first 10 weeks, but may use almost half of its total nitrogen uptake and a fifth of its potassium and phosphorus. By the time a plant is half way through its life, it has used almost all of the nitrogen and potassium it will need.

Fertilizer solubility: You want plants to be able to absorb nutrients as they become available, otherwise they may simply leach away (especially on light soils with low organic matter).

Highly soluble fertilizers such as wood ashes and blood meal, should be applied just before planting, so they are available when needed.

Fresh manures are usually applied in autumn, as they can burn plants if applied during the growing season. Some nutrients (notably nitrogen and potassium) will probably be leached out by rainfall, but the valuable organic matter will remain. The loss of nutrients through leaching can be reduced by planting a cover crop immediately after fertilizing. Aged manures can be applied at any time.

Insoluble fertilizers, such as rock powders, only become available through weathering or biological action. This takes a while, so mix them thoroughly into the soil as soon as possible. Such materials are commonly applied in the fall, so the nutrients have all winter to break down into usable forms before they are needed.

Trace elements: We don't usually worry too much about individual micronutrients, but rather make sure that the soil gets a good mix of nutrients in the form of plenty of organic matter. The addition of individual trace elements is a difficult business, because they are needed in such small quantities (sometimes as little as one ounce per acre is enough) and there is a danger of adding too much. If you are looking for a more concentrated source of micronutrients then try seaweed.

How much to apply: Fertilization isn't simply a matter of adding as many nutrients as you can to the soil. That would be wasteful in terms of resources, money and labor and may even be counter-productive, as you can fertilize too much.

If you are going to rely on your garden for a large part of your food, or as a source of income you may want to have the soil tested professionally. Such a test will tell you whether you have any serious deficiencies or excesses that must be dealt with immediately. This could quickly save you the expense of having the soil tested.

For the average home garden a chemical soil test is by no means essential. You can simply fertilize with the assumption that the soil needs all of the plant nutrients and fertilize according to a pre-set formula (see below). Most nutrients will be applied in the form of organic matter anyway and you can't go wrong with this.

Observe how well the plants grow and examine them regularly for signs of deficiency symptoms. Pay particular attention to those crops that are most likely to show deficiencies of certain nutrients.

How well a plant responds to a fertilizer depends on whether the plant is deficient in the nutrient supplied. It won't respond markedly to fertilization if it already has all of the nutrients it needs. However if the soil is deficient in a single element then adding that nutrient can greatly improve plant growth. I already mentioned the analogy of the barrel with one stave shorter than all the others (the nutrient in shortest supply). The barrel can only hold as much water as the shortest stave, in the same way as a plant can only grow well until supplies of the least available nutrient are exhausted.

Conventional wisdom recommends giving nitrogen to leaf crops, potassium to root crops and phosphorus to seed or fruit crops. There is some basis to this, young vigorously growing leaf crops do need a lot of nitrogen, but it's not really so simple. Root crops also have a high demand for phosphorus, fruit and seed crops need potassium and all young plants need phosphorus for healthy root development. This is another reason why it's better to rely on feeding the soil rather trying to feed each crop individually.

A fertilization program

I don't worry about exact quantities or single nutrients, but aim for a general increase in the bank of nutrients in the soil. The simplest way to do this is to apply a standard formula to each 100 square feet of bed.

For the first two years apply a 3″ layer of compost or aged manure to supply organic matter (this is always the highest priority, as it adds all of the other nutrients at the same time). You should also add 10 lb of cottonseed meal for nitrogen, 10 lb of colloidal phosphate for phosphorus, 10 lb of greensand (or 2 lb of wood ashes) for potassium and 1 lb of kelp for trace elements.

In following years you should add 2″ of compost annually in spring. You will also fertilize the soil with specific nutrients before planting any heavy feeding crop and any time you feel it might help.

Fertilizer application

Spread the fertilizers evenly over the surface of the bed and incorporate into the top 4" to 8" of soil. Though plant roots often go down quite deep (4 feet isn't unusual), most feeder roots stay in the top 12" of soil. Nutrients slowly leach down into the soil with water and gravity.

If you decide to double dig the garden it's a good idea to put some organic matter and less soluble nutrients, down deep in the soil (as much as 24"). This encourages deep rooting.

Bulky organic materials such as compost can be incorporated into the soil in several ways. You can add it when double digging. You can simply fork it into the top few inches of soil. You can also simply leave it on the surface as a mulch and let soil organisms incorporate it.

Manure should be incorporated into the soil as soon as it is spread, otherwise it will lose nitrogen as it dries out (up to 25% in the first 24 hours.) Don't leave manure in small piles as nitrogen may leach down into the soil (causing problems of excess in those spots).

If you only have a very limited amount of fertilizer, or if a crop is hungry for a specific nutrient, you might want to put the fertilizer in the planting trench or hole.

Don't apply high nitrogen fertilizer at the same time as lime, because the calcium in the lime can cause nitrogen to be converted to ammonia gas and lost. It is better to add lime in the fall (which gives it time to work) and add nitrogen in spring (when there is less time for leaching).

Highly soluble fertilizers such as wood ashes and blood meal are easily leached from the soil, so are usually applied as top dressings. In this way they leach down into the root zone, rather than away from it.

Post planting fertilization

Though most fertilization is done before planting a crop (it's easier for one thing), there are situations when growing crops need a quick boost of a specific nutrient. In such cases you can use some form of post planting fertilizer. Reasons for fertilizing after planting include:

- It can help you get reasonable yields when you are first establishing a garden and the soil isn't very fertile. Fast growing crops such as Radish and Spinach may be fed weekly and will greatly benefit from the steady and continuous supply of nutrients.

- It can help over-wintered crops get off to a fast start, by giving them a shot of nutrients (especially nitrogen) when the soil is cold and nutrients are least available.

- It can be used to give an easily absorbed boost to rapidly growing plants, or those that have been stressed by transplanting, harvesting or pests.

- It can be used to help maximize yields by giving plants the nutrients they need at critical times in their development (such as when food storage organs are enlarging).

- It can help long season crops get all the nutrients they need, even after they have exhausted the locally available nutrients.

- It can be used to save a nutrient deficient crop, by supplying the necessary nutrient in an easily absorbed form.

Brewing manure tea

Foliar fertilizers

Foliar fertilization consists of spraying a dilute solution of liquid fertilizer onto the leaves of a plant. It works because plants are able to take up small quantities of nutrients directly through their leaves (apparently this is 8 times as efficient as absorbing them through the roots). Some organic purists frown upon the use of foliar fertilizers as "unnatural", because it concentrates on feeding the plant rather than the soil. It is sometimes used as a way of growing plants without building up the soil and this certainly isn't good practice. However it can be useful in some circumstances. It is most often used when raising transplants, to supply the seedlings with all the nutrients they need for good growth.

The simplest way to foliar feed is with commercially prepared liquid fertilizer such as fish emulsion or seaweed. These are convenient and have minimal smell, but are quite expensive. A cheaper alternative is to make your own, from compost, manure, Comfrey or whatever you have readily available.

Old fashioned compost/manure Tea

I like this for its simplicity. It is easily prepared from locally available materials (a renewable resource), doesn't cost anything and supplies all of the most soluble nutrients found in those materials. The problem with this kind of tea is that it has a horrible sewage-like smell and may contain large quantities of pathogenic bacteria. The anaerobic decomposition is smelly enough to discourage many people from making it more than once. You wouldn't want to use it in your house and in towns you could well get complaints from neighbors.

Prepare the tea by filling a plastic bucket one third full of manure, or half full of compost and topping it up with water (larger quantities can be made with woven plastic sacks and 50 gallon oil drums). Cover with a tight fitting lid and leave to steep for 7 to 10 days (depending on how warm the weather). The tea is then strained into a bucket and diluted one part tea to 2 parts water (if you have two more buckets of equal size simply pour a third into each of the other buckets and then fill all three buckets with water). Some people add a ½ teaspoon of soap per gallon as a wetting agent, to help it stick to leaf surfaces (some leaf surfaces are hard to wet). You can also use molasses for this.

Modern compost/manure tea

In recent years the making of compost tea has undergone a radical transformation. Those who were repulsed by the old stinky anaerobic compost tea now have an alternative in the form of actively aerated compost tea or AACT. This is made in a similar way to the old compost tea, with one big difference. Air is bubbled through the liquid for the whole time it is being made. This results in an aerobic tea with only a mild earthy smell.

Making actively aerated compost tea

To make this kind of tea you need to be able to bubble air through the liquid for the entire time it is brewing. You can buy commercially made aerating systems, but it is much cheaper to make your own. All you need is an aquarium aerator, a three gang valve, some plastic hose and a 5 gallon bucket. If you buy the right parts it probably doesn't take you any longer to make your own than it does to assemble a commercial system.

The compost (or vermicompost or aged manure) is put in a bag (a pair of old panty hose works great) to make a kind of teabag. This prevents the manure from clogging the hose. This is then left in the bucket for 24 to 48 hours, with air bubbling through it. It should be kept at a temperature of 70 to 80° F and it should be in the dark. The end product should not be offensive in any way. If it is then it didn't brew properly and you have made old fashioned manure tea.

The finished product is diluted and used like traditional manure tea.

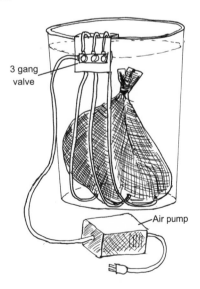

3 gang valve

Air pump

Plant teas

Comfrey: This is best known as a source of potassium, but is also rich in nitrogen, phosphorus, calcium and magnesium. It is especially valued for feeding young plants.

Stinging Nettle: A quick source of nitrogen, phosphorus and iron.

Alfalfa: A source of phosphorus.

Horsetail: Biodynamic gardeners believe Horsetail tea increases plants resistance to disease.

Oak bark: Rich in calcium.

Seaweeds: Rich in nitrogen, potassium and many trace elements (wash thoroughly before use to remove salt)

Yarrow: A source of potassium and silica. It is believed to increase disease resistance.

Grass: Lawn clippings are an easily available source of nitrogen.

Plant teas: Green plants can also be made into foliar fertilizer. If a specific nutrient is in short supply you might want to use a plant that accumulates that nutrient. You can also mix different plants of course, or add liquid seaweed.

The usual method of preparation is pretty much the same as for old fashioned compost tea. You fill the plastic bucket with as much foliage as it will hold (best for Comfrey, Seaweeds, Nettles), top it up with water, then cover and leave for 2 to 5 days. Unfortunately these smell just as bad as manure tea.

You may also want to experiment with making aerated teas as described above. These are much less offensive and so much nicer to work with.

Applying foliar fertilizers

Plants only absorb nutrients through their leaves as they need them, so it's more effective to use frequent applications of very dilute fertilizers. If they are applied in too high a concentration they may burn the plants and you will waste nutrients. Don't apply foliar fertilizers to water stressed plants, as it may do them more harm than good. In such cases remedy the water stress first and then feed.

The best way to apply foliar fertilizers is with a sprayer, as this enables you to wet both sides of the leaves for maximum nutrient absorption. To cover larger areas you can get an injector system that attaches to a hose and watering wand. You could also use a hand sprayer or backpack unit normally used for spraying pesticides. If you have nothing else you can use a watering can with a fine rose (though it's harder to cover the undersides of the leaves).

The best time for applying a foliar feed is in early evening, because the nutrients are most easily absorbed at night when leaf stomata are open (it is up to 10 times more effective at this time). It also helps if the air is still and humidity is high. Early morning is also good. Ideally the plants shouldn't get wet again until they have had 24 hours to absorb the nutrients through their leaves (wetting will wash off the nutrients). Generally it is better to give several light applications, rather than one heavy one.

In less than ideal soils it may be necessary to fertilize several times during the growing season. Perhaps begin with a feed as soon as the plants have recovered from transplanting, to get them up and going. Feed them again just before they start developing the food producing part and once again as this part is sizing up. Of course, rather than keeping track of every crop and stage of growth, you could just feed everything in the garden every couple of weeks

Don't harvest and eat green leaf crops within 2 weeks of fertilization, as nitrogen rich feeds can temporarily increase the level of toxic nitrates in the plant. Of course you wouldn't want to eat salad greens that have just be sprayed with diluted manure anyway.

Liquid fertilizers

The difference between liquid fertilizers and foliar ones is in the manner in which they are absorbed. The same materials are used and for the same purposes. Rather than being absorbed through the leaves, liquid fertilizers are absorbed through the roots in the usual way.

Liquid fertilizers are easily applied with a watering can. You merely pour water on to the soil around the plants individually, as if you were watering them in after transplanting. After applying the fertilizer you then irrigate the whole bed to soak the nutrients down to the root zone.

Top dressing

Top dressing is another method of applying fertilizers to growing plants. It usually means sprinkling small quantities of soluble fertilizers onto the soil around the plants to give them a quick boost. They will be washed down to the root zone by rain or irrigation water.

10 Bed preparation

Growing beds

The past 30 years have seen a big change in vegetable gardening, with wide beds (often raised) largely replacing row cropping. These beds have become popular because they have a number of advantages over the traditional rows.

Advantages

- The beds are never walked on so compaction is kept to a minimum. Plant roots can then spread widely in the loose well-aerated soil.

- Water and fertilizers are used more efficiently because they are only applied to the soil in the growing beds, none is wasted on the paths (and weeds). The high level of fertilization on these beds means plants can be spaced closer together, giving higher yields per square foot of ground.

- When the beds are raised above the surface of the ground, the soil warms up faster in spring than traditional flat row gardens. This can be a significant advantage in heavy soils and in cool climates. Raised beds also drain faster, and in very heavy rains the beds may stand out like little islands.

- The closely spaced plants quickly form a dense canopy of foliage across the bed. This discourages weeds, keeps the soil cool and conserves moisture.

- Using raised beds reduces the amount of work you have to do, by minimizing the area to be cultivated, fertilized, weeded, watered and tended.

- The clearly defined permanent beds make crop rotation easier.

Disadvantages

- Raised beds can dry out quickly in hot, dry climates. In such situations it makes more sense to make the growing bed flat (you still get all the other benefits).

- In some soils a raised bed may be hard to re-wet when it gets dry, the water simply runs off rather than soaking in. In such cases you can give the bed a concave top (see **Bed Shapes** below).

Preparation of growing beds

I will begin with a basic procedure for preparing a "standard" raised bed and will then mention some of the many variations. The initial establishment of a raised bed garden is quite a lot of work, especially if you intend to double dig it all. Unless you are very strong and fit don't try and double dig the entire plot in one year. Fortunately much of the heavy work of establishment need only to be done once. In later years digging becomes easier because the soil is so much better.

When to prepare beds: The right time to prepare the beds depends on the soil type and moisture content. Clay and silt soils are commonly dug in autumn, as the soil tends to be drier at this time (such soils drain slowly in spring and are easily damaged if worked when wet). They were traditionally left rough over the winter to allow the frost to break them down to a fine tilth, but using a cover crop is a much better idea. Clay and silt soils can be prepared in spring if they are dry enough. Light sandy soils can be worked while quite wet, so may be dug in spring or fall. I prefer to do most of the preparation in fall (including double digging) and then plant a cover crop to protect the soil over the winter.

Moisture: Before you do any kind of cultivation the moisture content of the soil must be right. If the soil is too wet, or too dry, not only will it be much more difficult to work, but also you may damage its structure. Start monitoring the moisture level a few days before you want to start digging.

Too wet: One of the quickest ways to damage the soil is to cultivate it while it's too wet. This mashes the softened soil particles together, closing pore spaces, driving out air and destroying the crumb structure. It is also physically harder to dig wet soils, as it sticks to your spade and boots rather than sliding off.

Soil texture largely dictates how wet a soil can be worked. Clay soil must be quite dry, whereas sandy soils can be worked when fairly wet (even at field capacity).

To test if the soil is suitable for digging take a handful of soil and lightly squeeze it into a ball. Drop this from waist height, if it doesn't break up it's too wet to work with (obviously sandy soils don't stay together as readily as clay ones). If you poke your finger into the ball it should fall apart. If you walked upon the wet soil (which of course you won't) your footprints would initially be shiny as they squeezed water from the soil.

If the soil is too wet you must postpone working until it has dried out. I have hastened drying in wet weather by covering beds with plastic sheeting or cloches (these are also useful to help the soil warm up). Of course raised beds drain a lot faster than flat areas. Cover crops can help the soil to dry out faster in spring.

Too dry: Dry soil often becomes a problem in hot weather. Clay soils are the most problematic, as they can bake very hard when dry (they may be almost impossible to penetrate) and tend to crumble to powder when cultivated. When the powdered soil gets wet again it sets solid almost like concrete and becomes impossible to dig. The soil is too dry if it won't hold in a ball when squeezed in your hand.

The remedy for dry soil is simple, just water with an overhead sprinkler overnight. It's important to apply enough water initially, as a dry soil can absorb a lot of water (sometimes several inches of water!). Don't apply too much of course, you don't want to have to wait for it to drain before you can start work.

Water has a miraculous effect on dry clay soils, when it is dry you need a pick to make a mark, but once it is moist you can push a fork into it.

Clearing vegetation

Before you can prepare new beds you have to deal with the existing vegetation. The easiest way to do this is to cover the soil with black plastic for several weeks, which kills most plants by heating and depriving them of light. This is a good way to deal with tough sod with a dense network of roots.

The commonest way to deal with the vegetation is to incorporate it as you dig the beds, but this is a lot of work (see **Soil improving Crops** for more on this). You can also remove the vegetation from the soil surface and compost it separately.

Loosely rooted old crops, weeds and soil improving crops can often be pulled by hand, but well established crops may require thorough skimming. If there is a lot of vegetation, you could scythe off the tops for composting and incorporate the roots into the soil.

Removing tough grass sod is particularly hard work. You may have to cut through a section on all sides, slide the spade underneath to cut the roots and then lever it from the ground. The end result should be a totally clean area of soil with no plant material on it at all. Don't bury perennial weeds or grass clumps, as they may start to grow. It is amazing what will survive and grow if you give it a chance, I've seen Alder twigs root themselves.

Clearing established beds: Skimming well-established plants isn't an easy task, but it can be made easier if you use the proper technique. A flat spade is the right tool for this (I can't imagine using anything else). Make sure it is sharp (see **Tools**), as you want to be able to slice through the vegetation cleanly, rather than simply tearing it out in chunks.

Hold the spade low when skimming, with the blade almost parallel to the ground and the tip just below the soil surface. You don't want to move around any more topsoil than necessary. Swing the spade vigorously so that it cuts using the momentum of the spade to do the work rather than your arms. Be on the lookout for perennial weeds as you work, as you need to remove them completely, roots and all, don't just cut the tops off. If they are pernicious (see **Weeds**) don't allow them to get mixed in with the harmless stuff or you won't be able to compost any of it.

For maximum efficiency you should work in a specific pattern. Begin by clearing a small area at one end of the bed (or where you intend the bed to eventually be), then skim sideways, slowly moving down the bed. The motion of your spade deposits the plant material onto the already cleared area, so you then only have to move the material once. If you skim randomly you will deposit vegetation on top of unskimmed areas and will then have to move it to get at the stuff underneath. Work your way along the bed, depositing material onto the area you have just cleared, until you get to the end of the bed. Then go to the other side and skim straight across, depositing the skimmings onto the recently cleared area. You then work back down to where you first started. Once the bed is cleared you can remove the accumulated skimmings from the surface of the bed all at once.

The vegetation you remove can be composted, or it can be buried while double digging. Grass sod can be composted in a special pile to make valuable turf loam (see (**Compost and composting**).

Marking out

The next step is to mark the layout of the beds. Most gardeners use rectangular linear beds because they are more efficient (easier to water, set up drip irrigation, lay Gopher wire), though curved ones are more visually appealing (see **Site Planning** for more on curved beds). I once rejected linear beds completely, but have returned to them because it is easier to protect them from gophers.

Linear beds: Once you have decided on the size and location of the beds set out string lines to define the edges. Keep these almost at ground level initially, so they are out of the way while digging. You don't have to bother with lines if you don't care about the beds being straight and uniform, but it's almost impossible to keep the edges straight without them.

Non linear beds: To lay out curved beds use a hose pipe to define the required curves and then mark out the shape with ground limestone or wood ashes (fill a coffee can with ground limestone and punch a ¼″ hole into the plastic lid). To inscribe a perfect arc or circle, make a compass from a length of string and two stakes. Perfect circles look a lot better than misshapen ones.

Making the beds

There are several different ways to create the growing beds. How you do it depends partly on the fertility of the soil and partly on your strength and enthusiasm (and endurance).

Double digging

This is the best known, most thorough and effective way to prepare beds. By loosening the soil down to a depth of 24″ or more, it has a number of beneficial effects:

- It aerates the soil deeply and so increases the activity of soil life and the subsequent release of nutrients.

- It allows you to enrich the soil to a much greater depth than normal (effectively making the topsoil deeper). This means you can grow plants closer together, thus obtaining higher yields from a given area. This is one of the keys to intensive cultivation.

- It improves drainage and hastens the warming of the soil.

- It is the most effective way to deal with compacted soil layers.

There is some debate as to whether double digging is really worth the effort. Some people point out that in a rich soil most of a plants feeder roots will be in the top 6″ to 12″ of soil. They say it isn't necessary to dig any deeper than that. However it isn't just about fertility. Research has shown a definite increase in yields after double digging, an effect that lasted for several years. This is mainly because roots were able to penetrate more deeply in search of water in times of drought (double digging is of great value in dry areas).

Drawbacks to double digging

Double digging is hard on the soil in that the disturbance damages soil structure, destroying the tunnels created by worms and often inverting soil.. Earthworms don't like it, as it can physically injure them. It is also hard on your body and if you are not careful it can result in some chiropractors bills.

To double dig or not?

So do you double dig or not? That really depends upon your soil. Double digging can dramatically improve heavy or compacted soils (those that are hardest to dig). These will definitely benefit from an initial double digging, to open them up and get organic matter down deep. Light soils might benefit from double digging to incorporate organic matter deeply, but doing it routinely would be a waste of time. I didn't double dig my present garden because the topsoil is loose, very deep and fertile (the gardeners dream soil)

You don't have to double dig straight away, you could wait and see how the garden performs and then decide if it would be worthwhile.

The tools for the job

Double digging is hard enough without trying to do it without the right tools, so get a good garden fork and spade. Make sure your spade is sharp and clean and that its handle is long enough. In heavy soils you might use a fork for double digging in preference to a spade (ideally a flat tined spading fork). See **Tools** for more on these).

How to double dig

1) Start by digging a trench 10″ to 12″ deep by 18″ to 24″, wide and the breadth of your bed. If you are only digging one bed put the soil from this trench into a wheelbarrow and take it to the other end of the bed (you will use it to fill in the last trench). If you are digging more than one bed simply put it to one side and use it to fill in the last trench on the next bed (start that one from the opposite end). Remove any roots, large rocks and perennial weeds as you go (be thorough).

Some people double dig from the side to avoid compacting the soil, or they stand on a digging board (a piece of ¾″ plywood 2″ x 4″). I usually just stand on the bed, as it's going to be dug anyway.

2) Put a layer of organic matter (fresh or aged strawy manure, compost, inverted sod or surface skimmings) in the bottom of the trench. This is a good place to use immature compost, or manure with lots of weed seeds, as it will be buried too deeply to present a problem. Put some rock powders in there too.

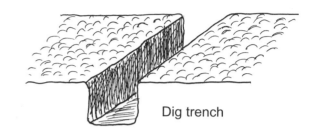

Dig trench

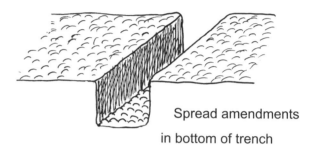

Spread amendments

in bottom of trench

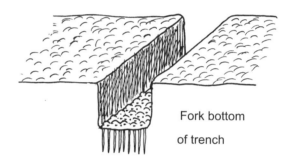

Fork bottom

of trench

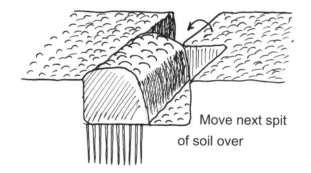

Move next spit

of soil over

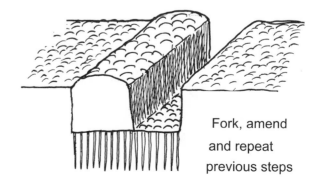

Fork, amend

and repeat

previous steps

71

3) Next use your fork to loosen the soil in the bottom of the trench. Make deep cracks 10″ to 12″ deep every 3″ to 4″ all the way across the trench. Don't pulverize the soil to a fine tilth, or it may compact again more quickly.

4) Start the next trench alongside the first, by sliding spadesfull of earth across to fill in the first trench. Try to keep these fairly intact, you don't want them to fall apart. Also take care not to invert them, as subsoil is much inferior to topsoil for plant growth. This can be a little tricky initially, but you will soon learn how to slide, lever and flip the soil from one section to the next. In sandy soils the spadesfull of soil tend to break apart, unless they are quite moist. In heavy clay soils you may have to break up the large clods with the side of the spade, otherwise they may dry out into hard lumps. The addition of lots of organic matter will eventually alleviate both of these problems.

If you invert the soil, putting topsoil underneath and subsoil on top, you are "Bastard Trenching", presumably done to make the topsoil deeper?

5) Repeat these operations on down the bed. When you get to the end of the bed, fill it in with the soil from the wheelbarrow (or from first trench of the adjacent bed).

Keep the edges of the bed straight, otherwise plants at the edge of the bed may end up growing into compacted soil. Compensate for any unevenness in the bed as you dig, by moving extra soil around as necessary, filling in low spots or cutting down high ones. If you do this well the bed should be quite level when you finish, and should have a fairly fine tilth that needs little further work. If the bed is very uneven you should rake soil from high spots to fill in the low ones (use a wheelbarrow if there's a lot to move).

When you finish digging, skim loose topsoil from the paths (leave the subsoil) and throw it onto the beds. If the beds are already high enough then don't bother with this.

Making digging easier

In difficult soils, double digging a large area can become a monumental task. Expect to take four hours to dig a bed 4 feet x 25 feet, though you could do it in half that time (or less) if you are strong and experienced. Fortunately there are ways to reduce the work (and the stress on your body) to manageable proportions.

- Don't exert yourself any more than you would in your everyday life, or try to do too much at once. This is especially important in spring when your muscles have weakened from winter inactivity (this is the commonest time of year for injury). If you have any medical problems I suggest you avoid double digging altogether, as it is strenuous.

- Double digging is hard work, but it can be enjoyable if you work slowly and carefully. Dig only a small section at a time (perhaps 30 minutes a day), resting as necessary. I am fairly fit and strong and I find the repetitive hard labor of double digging quite therapeutic in small doses. More like a combined exercise and meditation than an unpleasant chore. Break yourself in slowly and you will soon be able to double dig from dawn to dusk (or even dusk to dawn).

- Don't strain yourself by picking up more soil on your spade than you can comfortably lift. Two small loads are a lot less tiring than one big one. You should also understand how your body works, even the strongest people can injure themselves through poor body mechanics. Bend your knees when lifting, rather than bending from the waist (I admit this is one I have never quite got the hang of). Use your strongest hand to hold the bottom of the spade (where the weight is) and use your weakest arm to counterbalance and maneuver it around.

- Dig efficiently. Jump on to the spade and use the weight of your body to push it into the ground (not your arms and back). Use your heel or the middle of your foot to press down on the spade. Learn to lever and slide the spades full of soil into position rather than lifting them (they break up less and it greatly reduces back strain). Push your spade (or fork in heavy soil) into the ground vertically for deepest penetration.

- You don't HAVE to dig down the full 24″ the first time. If it's a lot easier to only go down 15″ to 20″ that's fine. You can go deeper next time, when the soil is looser and the digging is easier.

- If you have enough time you could plant deep rooted cover crops for a season to loosen the soil before digging (see below). This is a good argument for establishing the garden incrementally, over several years.

Alternatives to double digging

Forked beds

This is a quick and easy way to prepare beds. Begin by scattering the appropriate amendments on to the bed, and then thoroughly fork them into the soil to a depth of 8″ to 10″. The flat tined spading fork is the best tool for this, as it's more effective at opening up the soil. Throw the topsoil from the paths onto the beds and shape raised beds with a rake. These beds work very well on light soils that are already in good condition (such as ones that are already gardens). Shallow, poor or compacted soils usually need more intensive treatment.

Single digging

This is then next step up from forked beds as it allows you to more thoroughly incorporate fertilizers and amendments. The process is simply the first part of double digging, dig the first spit, then throw a layer of organic matter into the trench in the usual way and throw the soil from the next trench on top (I often give it a token forking).

Tilled beds

Commercial market gardeners (and large-scale home gardeners) often make raised beds with tractors or rototillers. The resulting beds aren't as good as double dug beds, as they aren't cultivated very deeply and are usually remade each year so the soil often gets compacted. However they require a lot less labor and they are better than conventional row cropping.

There are several drawbacks to the use of mechanical tillers. They are noisy, smelly, expensive, hard to handle and kill earthworms and other soil organisms. Worst of all they pulverize and compact the soil, which has a horrible effect on its structure. They also tend to cause a plow pan on heavy soils where the tines smear and compact the soil at their maximum depth

If the soil has a lot of pernicious weeds you can't use a tiller, as you will simply propagate the weeds when you chop them up.

Begin by marking out the entire area to be covered in beds, and spread out all of the amendments in a layer. Then till to loosen the soil to the maximum depth possible (this may take several passes). If it's a large area you can save a lot of time and effort by hiring a tractor.

Once the area is thoroughly tilled, set out stakes to mark the outline of the beds (always keep to the paths) and string lines between the stakes. Then transfer surplus soil from the paths to the beds (there is actually a tiller attachment which does this for you). You then fork in any other amendments, shape the beds and plant.

Triple digging (Trenching)

This is sometimes used in very poor clay soils. Suitable for the serious penitent only, this is "Extreme Gardening", a form of self-flagellation that is even more work than double digging. Basically it's similar to double digging, but quite a bit more work. You dig and move 2 spits deep and then fork the third spit. Incorporate organic matter at the bottom of both spits.

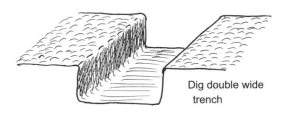

Dig double wide trench

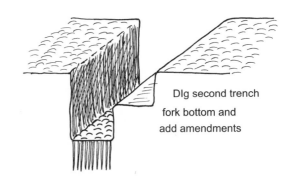

Dig second trench fork bottom and add amendments

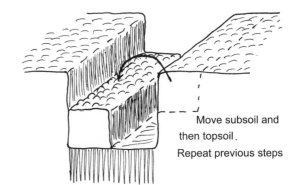

Move subsoil and then topsoil. Repeat previous steps

Lazy beds

Lazy beds work best if you first plant a vigorous crop like potatoes, that doesn't mind a rough seedbed.

This is a simple way to prepare new beds on grassland. Start by covering the bed area with a barrow load of manure for every 50 sq. ft, then skim the turf from the paths and throw it upside down on to the beds. Finish by removing any topsoil from the paths and scattering it on the bed. In cool weather the decay of the bed can be hastened by covering it with black plastic.

A more elaborate method is to skim off the turf, lay down a layer of woody brush and then replace the turf upside down (include the turf from the paths). You then add layers of manure, compost or other organic matter and finally a layer of soil skimmed from the paths.

Enclosed Beds

These beds are created by filling the (usually) wooden frames with a mix of soil, organic matter and other amendments. I really don't like enclosed beds, but have adopted them because they work very well with gopher wire).

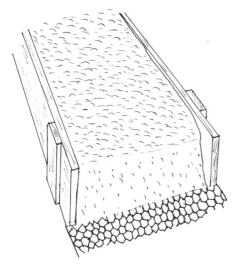

Gophers

If you live in Gopher country, you will want to line the bottom of some beds with wire mesh (ideally plastic coated for longer life), to prevent their getting into the beds (see **Pests** for more on this). This is usually preferable to killing them, but is time consuming and expensive. It is why many people in Gopher areas use wooden sided beds.

Amendments

Once you have the beds thoroughly dug, the next step is to add the appropriate fertilizers and amendments to the top 6″ of soil (if you didn't mix them in already). See **Fertilizing** for more on this.

Tilthing

The prepared bed is tilthed to break up any remaining soil clods and leave a fine loose tilth. The larger lumps of soil are broken up with glancing sideways blows with the fork (sideways to minimize the compaction that might result from downward blows). This should be done immediately after digging, otherwise the soil may dry out leaving hard clumps that are almost impossible to break apart. If you did your cultivation well then only a minimum of tilthing should be necessary.

Shaping the bed

The best tool for shaping beds is the back side of a rake (the front side doesn't work very well because the tines have a tendency to dig in and move too much soil). Begin shaping by removing any leftover debris, hard clumps of soil, rocks and weeds (rake them into the path and remove - clods of soil can be walked upon to break them up). To get the required shape pull soil from high spots to low spots, then rake diagonally both ways, as well as straight across. It's easier to work from the opposite side of the bed, pulling soil up towards you, rather than pushing. I raise the string about 9″ off the ground while shaping, so it doesn't get tangled in the rake.

The intended crop dictates how thorough your preparation must be. A crop like Carrot needs much more thorough soil preparation than a fruit or leaf crop. For a seed bed the surface particles should be small, roughly the same size as the seed which will go into them, for transplants the bed may be a lot rougher. See **Direct Sowing** for information on preparing seed beds.

Beds shouldn't be too tall (10″ at most), I've seen raised beds that were 18″ above the paths and looked more like graves or fortifications than a garden. Beds in clay soils can be higher than sandy ones, because they hold water better and benefit from increased aeration. If they get too high, you must either raise the path, or remove some soil (this can be added to the poorest beds, or used for propagation or composting).

Shapes

The shape of the bed depends on the soil, climate and the crop to go in it. There are a number of variations.

- Gently rounded beds are preferred for numerous small plants such as Lettuce or Spinach. These go right to the edge of the bed (especially if they are to be broadcast) and this shape gives you the greatest growing surface.

- Beds with flat tops and steeply sloping sides (no more than 45° or they will erode) are used with root crops such as carrots (they ensure a more even depth of soil). They may also be used when only a few plants will go in the bed (e.g. Tomatoes, Cucumbers), or where plants will be in rows (such as Peas or Beans). If the soil isn't very good you may want to create a lip at the edges to help it hold water. In some cases the center of the bed may even be slightly sunken to facilitate the penetration of water.

- In northern areas beds are sometimes tilted slightly (5 to 10°) to the south, to help them absorb the suns heat, so they warm up faster. These beds might also be surrounded by a windbreak to conserve warmth. They are sometimes even bermed.

- Beds don't even have to be raised at all. In hot dry climates the beds should be flat, or only raised a few inches, so they don't dry out so quickly.

- In very arid areas the beds may actually be sunken by a few inches, to maximize the use of water. Such beds may also be useful in humid areas, for growing semi-aquatic plants such as Water Spinach or Watercress. To prepare such beds you basically dig a trench the size of the bed, fork the bottom and re-fill it with soil, organic matter and other necessary amendments. Remember to keep the topsoil to one side for re-filling the bed and remove the subsoil only.

The back of this type of rake is the best tool for shaping beds

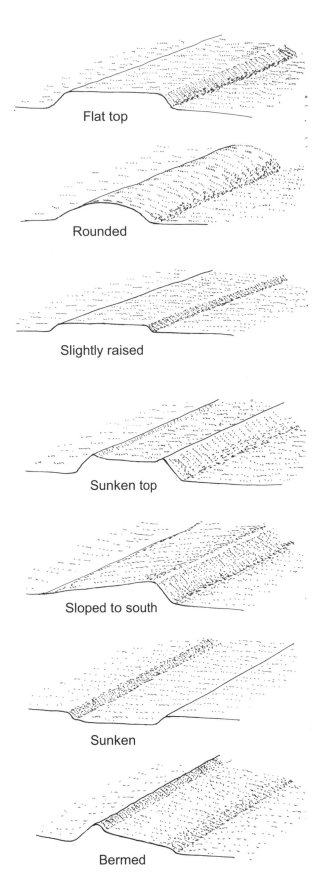

Flat top

Rounded

Slightly raised

Sunken top

Sloped to south

Sunken

Bermed

75

Watering

Once the bed is prepared it must be watered like a seedbed to keep it moist, even if it isn't going to be planted immediately (ideally you should plant into the bed as soon as it is prepared). This is also the time to install drip irrigation.

Paths

When the beds are finished you should clean up the paths and rake off any debris. Make sure their width is even their entire length and that each path is of equal width (they should be if you used string to mark the ends). Attractive paths do a lot to make the garden look good.

In dry areas you can leave the paths bare, they will bake hard to create a good walking surface. In wet areas bare soil can get muddy, so you may want a covering of sawdust or wood chips. This will rot down in a couple of years and can then be incorporated into the soil (this is actually a good way to add highly carbonaceous material to your soil).

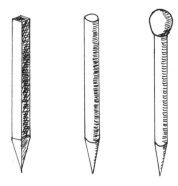

Corner stakes

When you remove your string and temporary stakes it's a good idea to replace them with attractive, permanent, rot resistant stakes, such as 2 x 2's. These stick up about a foot or so above ground and permanently define the edges of the beds. They prevent encroachment at the corners and prevent hoses dragging across the beds. These can be quite decorative if nicely made

One disadvantage of permanent corner stakes is that they are easy to trip over. You might want to round the tops to minimize scraping your shins on them.

Finished

Don't walk on the finished beds again. If you absolutely must stand on a bed for any reason, lay down a board and stand on that.

Preparation of established beds

Once the beds are established and the soil is fertile the amount of bed preparation work is reduced considerably. There is no need to cultivate deeply every year, in fact I usually simply dump manure or compost on the bed, along with any other amendments, rake it out evenly and then fork it into the soil. All that is left is to rake them to the desired shape.

If you really want to cultivate more deeply, the easiest way to do it is with a broadfork, which is specifically designed for this task.

To maintain the highest possible yields on heavy soils it might be worthwhile to double dig every 4 or 5 years (perhaps double dig a quarter or a fifth of the garden beds annually). This will be easier the second time around, as the bed is more defined, the soil is looser and you can dig deeper with less effort. You can tell when you get to the edge of the bed because the soil will be more compacted in the path and so a lot harder to dig. Of course putting string lines back on the corner stakes will help to define the edges of the bed.

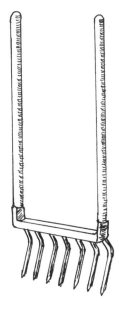

A broadfork

Supports

These aren't directly connected with making beds, but this seems like a good place to discuss them. A number of crops require support, vines such as Beans and Peas need something to climb upon, while weak stemmed top heavy crops such as Tomatoes need help to prevent their falling over. By training low growing, sprawling crops (Cucumbers, Winter Squashes, Melons) on supports you can greatly reduce the amount of bed space they need. Properly supported plants usually produce more usable food, as there is less pest damage and disease. Also the fruits are cleaner and of higher quality.

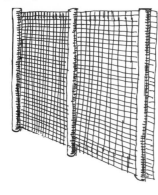

The simplest method of support is to train plants up existing fences. This works very well and makes the fences look more attractive. It doesn't work if the fence is intended to exclude deer, as they will eat whatever plant parts hang on the outside.

The next simplest supports are 6 to 8 foot poles of bamboo, scrap wood, or even metal pipe, stuck into the ground. These are very versatile and can be used singly, lashed together into various configurations, or combined with string.

Bamboo can be grown in the garden to supply poles for garden use.

Permanent supports might be installed at strategic places around the garden. These can be 4″ x 4″ fence posts, eight feet long and sunk 18″ to 36″ into the ground. Put metal eyes

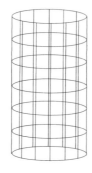

in them and you can put string (or galvanized wires) between them as needed.

Tomato cages are very versatile and can be used for a variety of crops. You can buy them, but commercial ones tend to be too small (I find them more useful for flowers). It's much better to make your own from 4″ concrete reinforcing wire, as you can make them almost any size (mine are six feet tall). Tall cages should be tied to stakes to stop them falling over.

You can also open up these wire cylinders and spread them across the bed like semi-cylindrical wire cloche frames. The plants will grow up through the mesh and sprawl on the top. This can be covered with plastic to protect the plants early in the season and taken off as the weather warms up.

Many structures (walls, arbors, buildings, etc) can be used as support by running strings up them. You can use climbing plants to hide ugly features in your garden, or act as screens.

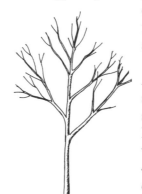

A traditional English plant support is the Pea stick, a slender but sturdy branch of Hazel (many other woods would be just as good) about 4' tall. The twigs are trimmed of branches on two sides to leave a flat branches support (see illustration). They are flat so they can be inserted into the soil in close rows. I like these because you can make them for free and they will eventually recycle themselves.

Fall clean up

It's common for gardeners to get a little burned out by autumn, but putting the garden to bed properly is very worthwhile. It helps you get an early start in spring, reduces pest problems and is an important part of a soil building program.

Begin the fall clean up by removing crop debris to prevent pests over-wintering. Ideally you will be able to empty entire beds at once, or at least large sections of them. Remove all weeds at this time and compost all of the plant material. This is a good time to add rock powders such as rock phosphate and to lime the soil. Plant cover crops into the clean beds and tend as necessary.

In mild winter areas the fall cleanup is complicated by the fact that growth never really stops. Many crops will continue to produce well into winter, or even right through it. You can often sow a cover crop underneath an existing crop. Just watch out for birds eating it (they will think you were very kind to put it out for them).

11 Compost

Introduction to composting

Composting is a process whereby complex organic plant and animal matter is broken down into simpler forms that plants can use. The artificially warm and humid environment of the heap gives you a way to accelerate and control the process of decay that goes on in nature all the time. There is alchemy in composting, do it poorly and nothing happens, do it right and you get magic.

The benefits of composting

- Compost is the best source of organic matter and humus for the garden. It is so valuable that the pile has been called the heart of the organic garden.

- Compost is the main source of nutrients in a mature organic garden. These are securely held in the form of microorganisms and organic matter, and are slowly made available to plants as these materials break down.

- Compost encourages a healthy population of soil organisms. A teaspoonful of compost may contain 1 billion bacteria, 2500 protozoa, 300 feet of fungal hyphae and 150 nematodes.

- Composting is a great way to dispose of organic household and garden waste and turn it into useful fertilizer.

- Compost suppresses a variety of soil pathogens, including Damping Off (Compost tea works also).

- The composting process breaks down toxins such as pesticides and can bind heavy metals to make them unavailable to plants.

Composting provides all of these benefits without costing anything. You really don't have to spend any money to make compost. There is no need for bins, inoculants, nitrogen sources, or anything else. All you have to do is use the right materials, in the right proportions and put them together in the right way.

Problems with compost

- One problem with compost is that it takes work and foresight, so most gardeners rarely have enough.

- A more serious problem with poorly made compost is that it may not have heated up enough to kill weed seeds. In such a situation spreading compost can plant thousands of weed seeds.

- Poorly made piles may attract scavengers such as flies, raccoons and rats. They may also smell bad.

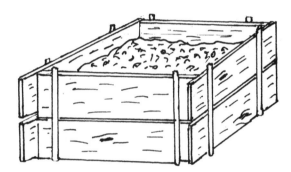

Composting as a means of recycling

In recent years we have begun to realize the importance of recycling wastes, rather than discarding them and composting is particularly useful in this regard. It allows you to take materials that would otherwise end up in the landfill and convert them into a valuable product. The most commonly composted household material is kitchen waste, but almost anything that once lived can be composted (so long as it hasn't been treated with toxic chemicals).

Non-gardeners often think that compost making must be a smelly affair. They assume that decaying vegetation, food scraps and manure must smell and attract flies and vermin. Actually there is a big difference between a well-made compost pile and a heap of garbage. The compost pile doesn't attract pests or smell very much. Indeed composting is one of the best ways to dispose of this kind of material without such problems.

How composting works

The workings of the compost pile have been studied closely and are now fairly well understood. The process starts when micro-organisms in the newly completed pile start to break down the most easily digested materials, the simple sugars and starches (these can be broken down by many organisms). The abundant food source causes a population explosion and the respiration of billions of organisms causes the pile to heat up rapidly. At the same time other organisms get to work on the more resistant materials. Cellulose can only be broken down by a few organisms (snails, termites and bacteria) that secrete the enzyme cellulase. This breaks cellulose down into simple sugars, organic acids and carbon dioxide. Proteins are broken down into amino acids, then into ammonium, then nitrates and (sometimes) then into ammonia gas (this is why some piles smell strongly of ammonia). Lignin, waxes and resins are very decay resistant and require a sequence of organisms to break them down.

When the readily available food has been consumed many of these organisms die and the ensuing reduction in respiration causes the temperature in the pile to drop. As organisms die they in turn are broken down and release nutrients. The stuff remaining at the end of the composting process contains a large proportion of humus, a stable form of organic matter that is very resistant to decay.

During the fermentation process a lot of material in the heap is lost to volatilization. As much as three quarters of the carbon in the pile may be released as carbon dioxide, causing the C : N ratio of the pile to drop from around 30 : 1 to around 8 or 12 : 1. Some nitrogen is also lost as ammonia, especially if the C : N ratio starts out lower than 30 : 1 (the final C : N ratio will still be around 8 : 1).

Composting organisms: Compost piles are alive with almost countless organisms. The bacteria are the most important decomposing organisms and are active from the beginning of the process until the end (some even fix atmospheric nitrogen in the pile). Fungi go to work on a pile within a week or so, but can only work in the cooler and well-aerated outer layers. Actinomycetes also work on the well-aerated outer layers and give the pile a grayish white color and a distinctive earthy smell. They appear during the final stage of decomposition and

their arrival indicates the pile is almost finished. Other organisms are active during various stages, including earthworms (not the same as those which inhabit soil), beetles, protozoa and woodlice.

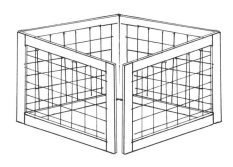

Compost temperature: While the compost pile is cool (up to 10° C) it is said to be in the cryophilic stage and decomposition happens no faster than in the soil. As biological activity increases, heat is generated faster than it can dissipate from the well insulated mass of the pile. When the interior of the pile heats up to 112° F (40° C), the composting process enters the mesophyllic stage. Mesophyllic organisms are most efficient at these higher temperatures, so decomposition proceeds rapidly as it gets warmer. As the heat builds in the center of the pile it gets hotter and hotter, until these organisms either die off, or migrate to cooler areas. The thermophyllic stage is then reached and specially adapted heat loving organisms take over (these can survive up to 180° F (80° C). Temperatures above 140° F (60° C) are needed to kill pathogens, weed seeds and pernicious roots, but decomposition slows somewhat at such high temperatures.

When most of the available nutrients are consumed the pile begins to cool down and mesophyllic organisms take over again (some of these survived out at the cooler edges of the pile). These keep on working as the pile cools, until the temperature gets low enough for cryophilic organisms such as earthworms and Actinomycetes to come in and finish the job.

You might think that the hotter the pile gets, the better, but this isn't the case. You don't want it to go much above 150° F. Very hot piles waste nutrients through volatilization, so that (60% or more of the volume of the pile may disappear. You can cool a pile down by turning, adding soil, or even by adding more carbonaceous material.

Temperatures to kill pathogens
30 minutes at:

176° F (80° C): Weed seeds
158° F (70° C): Insects, bacteria, viruses
140° F (60° C): Slugs, Fusarium, Botrytis
122° F (50° C): Fungi, nematodes

The compost pile doesn't heat up uniformly all the way through. The well insulated center gets the hottest and it gets progressively cooler towards the exterior, where it is easier for heat to escape. This is significant because it allows many organisms to avoid being killed by the intense heat of the center, by moving out to a zone more to their liking. As the pile cools they migrate back to the center. To ensure that all parts of the pile heat up sufficiently for good decomposition (and to kill weed seeds and pests), you must turn it at some point (see below).

Composting tools: The most important composting tools are the fork (ideally a manure fork) and a wheelbarrow for moving all the materials around. It's also helpful to have secateurs, a spade, a machete and perhaps a large wooden block to facilitate smashing woody materials.

Composting containers: These aren't necessary when making compost on a large scale, but they can be useful in some cases.

Home garden piles are generally too small for optimal heating, they simply don't have sufficient mass. Compost bins help to insulate the pile, so that it can heat up sufficiently for good decomposition. Bins are particularly useful for fast piles.

Small open piles lose or gain moisture quickly when exposed to heavy rain or hot sun. Enclosing them in a bin reduces this tendency. This is especially important in winter (a cover is also necessary) as rain not only leaches out nutrients, but also drains away heat.

Flies love compost

In small city gardens compost piles can attract the attention of one of the most difficult of all garden pests, complaining neighbors. A neat compost bin can help to minimize complaints by hiding the pile completely. Remember compost piles are illegal in some places.

The most useful bins have separate compartments, with removable partitions, so the compost is easily turned from one to another. Three compartment systems are the best because the pile can be started in the first bin, transferred to the second one and eventually to the third. By the time it's finished in the third bin the compost is ready to use.

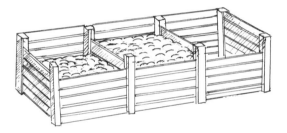

Bins may be made from new or salvaged materials, bricks, old pallets, wire, salvaged wood, concrete blocks or corrugated iron. The cheapest and fastest bin is a length of wire fencing made into a large (at least 3 to 4 foot) diameter cylinder. This can be lined with cardboard to hold in moisture or heat, or black plastic to absorb the suns heat. In cold weather you can make a bin out of spoiled hay bales, covered with corrugated cardboard (these materials are eventually composted too). Winter piles are sometimes made in pits to keep them warm, but in rainy climates there can be a problem with waterlogging.

When to compost
You need to make a real effort to keep up with compost making if you want to have enough for your needs. It can take 6 months or more for a pile to mature so it's important to plan ahead. Some people merely build piles whenever they have a sufficient accumulation of materials on hand, others go out actively searching for materials. It's a good idea to schedule your compost making activities (acquiring materials, building piles,

turning piles) in your garden journal, otherwise they are often among the first things to get neglected when you get busy.

There is no best time to build a compost pile. You can make one any time the air temperature is high enough for the composting process to get started. Many people concentrate on pile building in spring and fall as materials are most readily available at those times. In spring you have skimmings from the beds, weeds and cover crops, while in fall you have large quantities of fallen leaves, skimmings from beds and crop residues.

The demand for compost is greatest in spring, when you are preparing a lot of beds in a short time. Keep that in mind when planning.

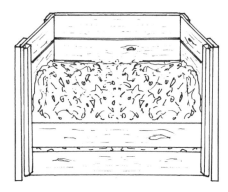

Siting the pile

The most important requirement is that the pile be located near to the garden, to reduce the work of hauling materials back and forth. Ideally there should also be access for a truck for unloading manure, leaves and other organic materials. In urban areas or small gardens it may be necessary to keep the pile hidden from the sight of neighbors. In hot climates the pile should be in light shade to reduce water loss from evaporation. In cold climates it should be in a warm sunny place that is sheltered from cold winds.

You might designate a permanent composting area, or you might move the piles around the garden, to spread out the benefit of the soluble nutrients that leach from the pile. If you put the autumn pile on the bed it will work over the winter and can be removed in spring to leave a warm, clean, fertilized bed ready for planting. Another idea is to put the piles on areas of poor soil you want to improve for eventual inclusion in the garden.

The factors involved in composting

When I first started gardening I piled plant debris in a wire cage, added some compost activator tablets and waited for it to become a compost pile. Needless to say it never happened, because I didn't give the composting organisms what they needed. It helps to think of your compost pile as a big pile of tiny animals. Your goal is to keep these animals happy, so they will multiply and make compost for you. When you build a pile you are not making compost, you are creating suitable habitat for these creatures, providing them with food and shelter. They do the work of making compost.

Gathering materials

You need a lot of material for a compost pile, so you may need a place to store it until you have enough. It's not nearly as effective to build a pile in stages. Good organic gardeners are often good foragers, getting materials from a variety of sources.

Particle size and texture

The size of a particle largely determines how quickly it can break down. Theoretically the smaller the particle the greater its surface area (in relation to volume) and the faster it will break down (this is most important for quick piles). However if the particles are too small they are easily compacted, which excludes air and so slows decomposition. The ideal particle size is about 1″ to 2″.

You could chop larger materials (such as Brassica stems) with a machete or a sharp spade, or you could lay them on your driveway to be run over by cars. Small woody material can simply be used as a base layer under the pile. When it comes to turning the pile it will be half decayed and can be chopped more easily

Shredding

You can hasten decomposition and produce finer compost by chipping stems, prunings and other bulky garden refuse in a shredder. However it is not really necessary. I bought an almost new shredder at a yard sale, but (like the first owner) I have never really used it.

Shredders can be useful for making very fine compost quickly, but this hardly justifies their cost. They fulfill an urge for neatness by reducing everything to a satisfying homogenous mass, but at some cost in noise, fuel, frustration and money (you could probably buy all of your hand tools for the price of a shredder).

Mixing

Ideally the materials would be completely homogenous throughout the pile, but in practice we usually make the pile in thin layers of various materials, alternating nitrogenous materials (green matter, manure) with carbonaceous materials (straw, leaves and other dried plants) and the occasional thin layer of soil (for bacteria and minerals). We never have large masses of a single material, as this would slow decomposition. A shredder can be used to mix the materials in the pile, by simply alternating the materials you put through the shredder.

Carbon to nitrogen ratio

One of the most important factors in successful composting is keeping the materials in the pile in the right proportions. These are divided into two types, those with a high proportion of carbon (sawdust, hay, dry leaves) and those with a high proportion of nitrogen (green leaves, waste food, manure). For a pile to work well there should be a balance of approximately 25 to 30 parts carbon for every 1 part nitrogen. If there is a higher proportion of nitrogen the excess will simply be given off in the form of ammonia and wasted (you will be able to smell it). If there is too much carbon the pile won't heat up quickly, or get very hot. See the chart of carbon to nitrogen (C : N) ratios at the end of this section.

Some gardeners prefer to make piles with a slightly higher carbon to nitrogen ratio (35 : 1 or more) so they won't heat up as rapidly, or get as hot (only up to about 90° F). They believe cooler piles are better as they don't lose so many nutrients through volatilization. The drawback is that they may not get hot enough to kill all weed seeds, pernicious weed roots, or diseased plant material. Of course the simple solution to this problem is to not put such stuff in the pile.

Pile size

Big is beautiful in the case of compost piles, because the larger the pile the smaller the surface area in relation to its volume and the better it's able to retain heat (a critical factor in rapid decomposition). The only limit on how large a pile can be is in its height. If a pile is higher than 6 feet the weight of the pile compresses the interior and it becomes difficult for air to reach the center (unless specially ventilated). If it can't get enough air then anaerobic organisms may take over. A very tall pile may also be so well insulated that it gets too hot in the center (they have actually been known to catch fire). Of course you aren't likely to want to make a pile anywhere near 6 feet tall, because it becomes difficult to get the heavy materials up that high. In reality the size is more limited by your ability to obtain sufficient materials and construct it.

Garden compost piles tend to be fairly small because of the limited amount of material available to compost and because most people aren't physically capable (or willing) to handle large quantities. The minimum size for a freestanding pile is about 3 feet by 3 feet by 3 feet. Smaller piles should be enclosed to help them retain heat and moisture.

Pile shape

The only restriction on the shape of a pile is that it should have as small a surface areas as possible for its volume. This usually means the pile is fairly close to a cube in shape. In wet climates the pile should have a peak to help it shed rain.

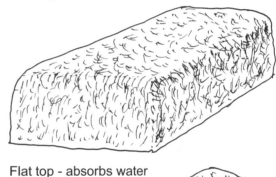

Flat top - absorbs water
used in dry climates

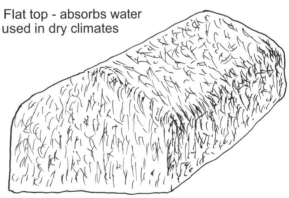

Sloped top - sheds water
used in wet climates

Moisture content

Too dry: Another important factor is moisture. In dry California I've seen so many compost piles that weren't working because they had dried out too much. Moisture is probably even more important than the carbon to nitrogen ratio as a limiting factor in composting. A pile must contain 50 to 60 % water if it is to work well. If there is less than 45% water the pile may not heat up at all. As you add materials to the pile make sure they contain as much moisture as they can hold. This is especially important for dry materials such as dry leaves or straw. In very dry climates you may want to enclose the pile, to stop it losing too much moisture (though this may reduce the amount of air it gets also).

Too wet: In cool wet weather you must make sure the compost pile doesn't get saturated with water. Too much water means too little air and can result in smelly anaerobic decomposition. Excess moisture can also result in leaching of nutrients. Well made compost has the texture of a wrung out sponge, it's wet, but you can't squeeze water out of it.

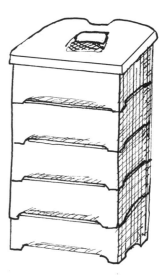

pH
For most rapid decomposition the accumulated materials in a pile must be close to neutral (pH 6.0 to 7.0), just like a healthy soil. If the pH is too high or too low soil organisms won't get to work in sufficient numbers and the pile won't heat up properly. Bacteria prefer the pH of a pile to be around 6.0 to 7.5, whereas fungi are slightly more tolerant of acidity (pH 5.5 to 7.5). In practice the lower end of the pH range is preferable, as a higher pH increases the production of ammonia and hence loss of nitrogen. Never add lime to a pile to alter the pH, as it can cause nitrogen to be lost.

Air
The compost pile must have a good supply of air for rapid breakdown. Make sure you don't get the pile too wet, make it too tall, or compact it by walking, sleeping, or performing fertility rites on it. Always be aware of the potential for compaction, especially when using a large proportion of succulent greens or other wet material. You could easily end up with rotten silage rather than compost. If this happens you must turn and aerate the pile (see below for more on this).

Air must be able to get to the center of the pile for it to work. It's common practice to put a layer of brush on the ground underneath a pile to improve aeration. You could also use old Bamboo, or the thick hollow stems of Tithonia, Sunflower or other large plants. The huge piles of municipal composting operations are aerated with perforated pipe.

Time
The time it takes for a pile to decay is governed by all of the factors mentioned above and is limited by that factor which is present in the least amount (the old barrel with a short stave again). If all of these are taken care of optimally your compost could be ready in 3 months or less. If they aren't then it might take a year or more. Quick compost (see below) can be ready for use in as little as 2 or 3 weeks, simply because it gives the microorganisms ideal conditions for their growth.

If you aren't in a hurry you could ignore most of the advice I've given here and just throw stuff into piles. Almost anything will decompose if given sufficient time (and kept moist).

Compost starter
There are commercial 'inoculants' that are advertised as speeding up decomposition by supplying the right organisms, but they aren't necessary. The right organisms can be found everywhere and if given the right conditions they will multiply rapidly. If the right conditions aren't present then inoculants won't help.

Rats love compost too

84

Building the compost pile

There is no great mystery to making compost, basically all you have to do is moisten all of the materials and combine them in the right proportions. The chart of C: N ratios is a useful guide, but you would need a weighing scale and a computer to calculate the exact C : N ratios and proportions of materials for the average pile. Fortunately you don't have to be that precise. A pile with too much nitrogen will simply vent off the excess nitrogen. A pile with too much carbon will just take longer to work (urine can be added to a finished pile to supply extra nitrogen).

A variation of the Indore method

Before you start the pile you may want to fork the ground to better connect the pile to the ground. Begin by laying down a 6″ base layer of somewhat woody material (small brush, Brassica or Sunflower stems). This defines the bottom of the pile and improves drainage and aeration. In dry climates you can forget about this base as you want to conserve moisture. Cover this with a 4″ deep layer of weeds, green manure and bed skimmings, followed by a 2″ to 3″ layer of manure (horse or cow is good). Follow this with a sprinkling of rock powders (not liming agents), then a 3″ layer of wetted straw or dry plants and finally a thin 1″ layer of soil. If any of these layers are dry you should moisten them thoroughly as you lay them down. You could even soak them beforehand to get them thoroughly wet (you can't make them too wet, as excess water will soon drain off).

Repeat these four layers (greens, manure, straw, soil) alternately until the pile is of the desired height (4 to 5 feet is good). Concentrate on building the sides of the pile, keeping them as nearly vertical as possible and the inside will take care of itself. If the sides start to slope inwards then pull them back out to near vertical with a fork. When you get near the top start to slope the sides inwards to give a slight pitched roof effect (a steeper pitch is good in wet climates). Some gardeners finish off the pile with a thick layer of straw, while others prefer to cap it with a layer of soil.

Piles don't have to be built exactly in this way, there is a lot of room for improvisation. No material is indispensable, you can use whatever is available, so long as you keep it in roughly the right proportions of carbon to nitrogen.

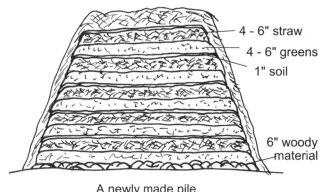

4 - 6" straw
4 - 6" greens
1" soil
6" woody material

A newly made pile

A finished pile

Examples of various piles

80% manure, 20% straw
50% green, 50% straw
20% manure, 40% green, 40% straw
33% green, 33% straw, 33% soil

Heating

You can tell when a pile is heating up without even going near it, because it shrinks rapidly (often overnight) as the material consolidates. Before the pile shrinks visibly you can check whether it is heating up by putting your hand into it. At a depth of 6″ it should be warm, at 12″ it should be almost too hot to comfortably hold your hand there. In cool weather a pile may be slow to heat up, or may not heat at all. There's nothing necessarily wrong, it just takes longer for the bacteria to reach a critical mass when it's cold. If you could get it going somehow it would eventually generate enough heat to sustain itself. Old carpet, bins, straw bales, or black plastic can help insulate the pile, but it's always best to get the pile going before it gets so cold that these measures are needed. In many areas winter is too cold for good decomposition (piles need to be enormous to hold enough heat at this time).

A compost thermometer is helpful for accurately recording the progress of your piles and gives you a way to compare different mixes of material.

Monitoring moisture content

Don't just build the pile and forget about it. It is a living thing and needs to be cared for as if it were another growing bed. Check its moisture content regularly and adjust as necessary.

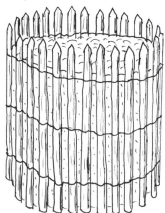

Dry: A pile can lose a lot of moisture from surface evaporation in hot dry weather. If you suspect this is a happening then cover with old cornstalks, a mulch of straw, or a plastic sheet (this can reduce air circulation though). Remove this cover when it rains. Regular light watering will replace the small quantity of water lost through evaporation, though you have to be careful not to get the pile too wet. Don't let the pile dry out too much, or it will be necessary to break it apart to re-wet it properly. It's hard to get the pile evenly moist simply by watering from above, some areas get wet, while others stay dry.

Wet: In cool humid conditions the pile might have to be covered during heavy rain to prevent waterlogging. If the pile gets too wet it may mat down into a gluey anaerobic mess. If this happens it will have to be turned to dry it out and get air into it. It takes a lot of effort to turn the heavy wet mush, but it's the only way to dry it out effectively.

Turning the pile

It isn't really necessary to turn a well-made and maintained pile, but it speeds up the composting process and ensures that the whole pile heats up uniformly. If you don't turn a pile, the outer 10″ layer of the pile won't heat up sufficiently to decompose properly, or kill pathogens and weed seeds. When an unturned pile is complete this outer part can be stripped off separately and composted again.

A newly turned pile will heat up a second time as more air is supplied and the goodies in the outer layers are consumed. It won't get as hot as it did the first time though. Some gardeners turn their piles a third time to speed up decomposition (and sometimes again - see **Quick Composting**).

If you want to add lime to the pile do it the last time you turn it, after it has cooled down. Don't add it when first building a pile, because it can cause nitrogen to be lost as ammonia gas.

Pests

If your pile heats up promptly you should have few problems with foraging pests. Meat, bones and other animal products are the cause of most problems, so they are often kept out of the pile, though any recognizable food waste is a potential lure. A cap of soil or straw will keep flies out of a pile until it starts to heat up (then it will soon get too hot for them).

Skunks, rats, raccoons, dogs and other animals (I've had a bear) can become a problem in poorly made compost piles, or those made in stages (as there is always edible food in them).

When is it ready?

It takes about 6 months to produce fully mature compost. The end result has a rich brown color, no easily identifiable parts (85% of it will go through a half inch screen) and a sweet earthy smell (the smell tells you when it's ready). The presence of earthworms indicates it has cooled down sufficiently to be ready for use.

If you really need the compost urgently you can use it after it cools down the first time. It will break down fully in the soil. Immature compost is sometimes added to clay soil to improve its structure, or put in the lower spit when double digging.

To get really fine compost for sowing mixes turn the pile twice and then leave it for a year to decompose fully.

Mature compost contains about 20% organic matter, 5% humus, 1% nitrogen, .7% phosphorus, .5% potassium and a lot of beneficial fungi, bacteria and other organisms.

Using compost

This is pretty much covered in other parts of the book. There is really no best time to apply compost. It is most often applied in spring, because that's when most bed preparation goes on, though it's also applied throughout the summer when preparing the beds for planting.

Don't leave mature compost standing around for very long, get it into the soil where it can do some good. If you must keep it for any reason (such as for spring seed starting) keep it covered to prevent leaching, drying out or oxidation.

Troubleshooting

Composting is a quite predictable process and if something goes wrong it's fairly easy to diagnose. These are the commonest problems:

Pile doesn't heat up

Too dry: Turn and moisten.

Too cold: Wait until the weather warms up, insulate, or build a bigger pile

Insufficient nitrogen: Add more nitrogen (urine is good - if you can get it).

Too small: There is insufficient volume to the pile, make it bigger

Pile smells:

Too much nitrogen: The pile is giving off nitrogen in the form of ammonia. You could turn the pile and add more carbon material, or you could do nothing.

Too wet: Turn and aerate

Quick composting

Also known as rapid or fast rate composting, this is a way to make compost in weeks rather than the 3 to 6 months needed by most piles. This isn't a replacement for conventional composting (it's hard to make in sufficient quantities), but is useful under some circumstances. The advantage of this kind of pile is the speed with which it is ready. It is also hot enough to kill pathogens and weed seeds (and even destroy many toxins). The disadvantage is that it is more labor intensive.

Quick composting isn't very mysterious, it works in exactly the same way as conventional composting. The difference is that you give the decay causing microorganisms optimal conditions for their growth at all times. This means shredding or chopping the materials to increase their surface area and turning the pile frequently to give them plenty of oxygen. Turning is the most important step, it will go quickly even without shredding.

Building: Quick piles are usually made in bins because they are relatively small and the bin helps to hold in heat. The 3 section wooden bin is ideal as you simply transfer the compost from one section to the next. The commercial rotating barrel composters also work, though they don't hold much compost at one time.

Begin the quick pile by laying down a base layer of chopped leaves or sawdust to absorb leachate. Then build the pile as described above, but with thinner layers and no additional soil. Keep out woody materials and chop the semi-woody stuff to increase its surface area. Some people use shredders to chop the materials, but I already explained why I don't like them. Remove as much soil from the roots of plants as possible, as it can slow down the decay process. Water the layers regularly to moisten.

Turning: The key to quick composting is frequent turning. The pile should start to warm up within 24 hours and should be ready for turning after two or three days. Be sure to turn the pile inside out, putting the outer parts into the center and the center part outside. Repeat this process every two or three days, the more often you turn it the quicker it will be ready. When it ceases to heat after turning it is ready for use. Quick compost isn't as thoroughly broken down as conventional compost, but the component parts are no longer identifiable and it still smells good.

Worm Composting

Also known as vermicomposting, this is a method of using earthworms to convert kitchen waste into very high quality compost. It can be used for treating continuous small quantities of kitchen waste and is so clean and odor free that it is used by many city apartment dwellers. It's main drawback is that it involves keeping live animals, that need special habitat and some care.

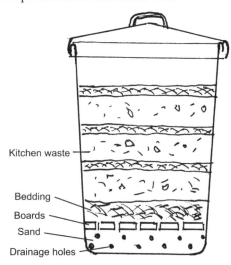

Kitchen waste

Bedding

Boards

Sand

Drainage holes

Making a worm bin

The worms need a suitable habitat in the form of a worm bin. The simplest type of bin is an old discarded plastic garbage can, with a series of holes punched into the bottom 4″ of the sides for drainage. The bottom is then filled with 6″ of sand or gravel to provide good drainage and water is added to provide humidity. A series of boards are set on top of the gravel (to keep it separate from the compost) and 3″ of bedding goes on top of this. The bedding is where the worms live initially and could be mature compost, peat moss, aged manure or leaf mold, mixed with an equal amount of torn newspaper. This should be quite moist, like a wrung out sponge. Finally a layer of newspaper (or straw) covers the whole thing to hold in moisture and the lid is replaced. I like these plastic bins, because they don't deteriorate and its easy to a get more (at the town dump). I started out with one bin, but am now up to four.

Keep the bin within the temperature range of 55 to 75° F. In winter you may have to move it to a warmer location (a shed, basement or greenhouse is good), while in summer you may have to put it in the shade to keep it cool. A full bin gets very heavy, so moving it isn't as easy as it sounds (move it after emptying it).

The worms

Common earthworms are not used in worm bins, you need special compost worms (*Eisenia foetida*) (or *Lumbricus rubellus*) and these aren't found in large numbers in the soil. You can get such worms from an old compost or manure pile, from another worm bin, through the mail, or from a fishing tackle shop. They feed on decaying vegetable matter of almost any kind, except very acid materials such as Citrus peel) or those that heat up very quickly (such as grass clippings).

I got my worms out of an old, badly made, compost pile, that had a lot of kitchen scraps. I have now had them longer than I have had my youngest daughter (at least 7 years)

Using the bin

The kitchen scraps are added to one side of the bedding at a time and covered with newspaper. The amount of waste that can be disposed of depends upon the number of worms and the temperature. The smaller the particles the faster they will decompose. It is best to give them too little food rather than too much (it's always easier to add more). Large quantities of food may heat up, or start to go anaerobic and smell. You may need to add water to keep it moist and add lime if the pH is too low. If you go away for a while and the worms run out of food they may die, but they will lay eggs that will hatch later. Obviously you should try to avoid this happening.

Other composting methods

Anaerobic composting

Conventional compost piles are driven by oxygen breathing aerobic organisms, however it is also possible to compost with anaerobic organisms. This process more closely resembles animal digestion than aerobic composting and has several advantages. It is fast, very little nitrogen is lost in the process and it takes place in sealed containers, so if done properly is completely odorless (it can even be done indoors). The disadvantage is that it doesn't heat up sufficiently to kill weed seeds or pathogens. It is a good way to dispose of pernicious weeds, but not their seeds.

The materials should be in the same 30 : 1 ratio of carbon to nitrogen as in conventional piles. They should be moistened thoroughly and then put in a heavy duty plastic garbage bag. This is squeezed to remove excess air, sealed tightly with a wire tie and put in a warm place. In cool weather use black plastic bags and leave in the sun for maximum solar heat gain. In 1 to 4 weeks (depending on the temperature) you will have some excellent manure-like fertilizer.

If you keep herbivorous animals then their stomachs can take care of your anaerobic composting. The compost is in the form of manure of course.

Leaf composting

Leaves for composting should be gathered as soon as they fall, because they lose water and nitrogen if they lay on the ground for any length of time. This makes them less valuable as fertilizer and more resistant to decay.

If you have the space and time the simplest way to compost tree leaves is to pile them up in a heap and leave them for 2 to 3 years to break down into leaf mold. They take so long because they contain a lot of rot resistant lignin.

If you are in a hurry you can compost leaves to make leaf mold within 6 to 12 months. The leaf pile should be as large as possible to help it hold moisture and heat. A container is very useful to keep the leaves together and stop them blowing around. Any composting bin can be used, but a simple wire cage is as good as any. The leaves can be shredded to increase their surface area, improve aeration and reduce their tendency to mat down. This greatly hastens their decomposition and can often be done while gathering, by running over them with a lawn mower. They should also be moistened thoroughly, as they won't break down if they are dry. You might also add a little soil to the pile to add decomposing organisms, and supply a little additional nitrogen. Urine, diluted 4 : 1 is ideal, if you can get it. As with other forms of composting turning the pile speeds decomposition.

You can compost leaves even more quickly by anaerobically composting them in plastic bags, as described above.

Trench composting

Trench composting isn't really composting, but is a simple and quick way to dispose of kitchen garbage and recycle its nutrients back into the soil. Begin by digging a trench the width of the bed as if double digging (you can actually double dig slowly). Throw you kitchen scraps into this trench and cover them with soil dug from another trench alongside it. Then fill this trench with garbage and cover with soil from the next one and continue this on down the bed. This is a good way to enrich the soil where you plan to build new beds, or plant fruit trees.

A simple way to get rid of excess kitchen waste is to bury it in small holes near fruit trees (so they can benefit from the nutrients).

Wood waste composting

Woody materials such as bark, shavings, sawdust and chips are very resistant to decay, because of their high carbon to nitrogen ratio (up to 500 : 1). However they are readily available in quantity and can be a valuable soil conditioner. They break down to give a high proportion of humus, so are worth using.

The best way to compost large quantities of wood wastes is in their own special pile, with a rich source of nitrogen such as fresh chicken manure. Simply cover the finished pile and leave for 6 to 12 months.

Brush composting

Woody brush and prunings are perhaps the most difficult garden wastes to dispose of because they are bulky and resistant to decay. These materials are slow to break down because their open structure allows them to dry out quickly and they have a high carbon to nitrogen ratio (they are mostly cellulose).

The commonest way to get rid of them is by burning, but this wastes a valuable source of nutrients and organic matter (only the ashes remain as fertilizer).

A more sensible alternative is to shred the brush in a chipper, as this reduces them to a much more compact mass (this is easily kept moist and will decompose more rapidly). However renting a suitable machine is always a hassle and quite expensive (and it uses fossil fuel). You can save up your woody stuff until you have enough to be worthwhile, or share the rental with neighboring gardeners. The chips can then be composted or used as mulch.

If you don't want to use a shredder you can make a slow (several years) compost pile by stacking the brush in an out of the way corner. Break them up as much as possible (after a year or so they get brittle and break up easier) and add a nitrogenous source of manure to hasten decay.

One of the best ways to use woody material is to make berms. These are low mounds that protect the garden from wind, create sun traps and intercept rainwater (allowing it to soak in to the ground). Make a pile of brush, then cover with a layer of manure and a covering of soil. As the woody material decomposes, the pile will shrink to about a third of its original height.

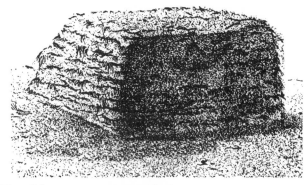

Turf loam composting

Before peat moss became widely available, turf loam was commonly used for starting seeds (it was even available commercially). It is superior to peat moss in that it contains a lot more nutrients.

Turf loam is made in late spring, by stacking strips of sod (ideally of a medium loam) upside down and leaving them to decompose. A richer mix can be made by adding a 2″ layer of strawy manure in between alternate layers of turf (if the pH is below 6.0 add a sprinkle of ground dolomitic lime between the other layers). The pile is then moistened thoroughly and covered to keep out rain. It takes 6 to 12 months for the turf to fully decompose.

If the turf is very weedy it should be covered with black plastic to exclude light and kill them. If it contains wireworms the pile should be sealed completely in plastic to prevent them from escaping.

C: N ratio of common materials

Activated sludge	6 : 1
Alfalfa hay	12 to 20 : 1
Apple pomace	12 : 1
Blood meal	3 : 1
Bonemeal	4 : 1
Bracken Fern	48 : 1
Cardboard	150 : 1
Comfrey	10 : 1
Corn stalks	60 : 1
Cottonseed meal	5 to 20 : 1
Dry leaves	50 : 1
Grass hay	80 : 1
Green plants	15 to 25 : 1
Humus	12 : 1
Kitchen garbage	15 to 25 : 1
Leaf litter	60 to 100 : 1
Leaves, Alder	25 : 1
Oak	50 : 1
Pine	60 to 100 : 1
Legume hay	12 to 25 : 1
Manure, Chicken	7 : 1
Cow	18 : 1
Horse	25 : 1
Human	10 : 1
Oat straw	50 : 1
Paper	150 : 1
Seaweed	19 : 1
Slaughterhouse waste	2 : 1
Sawdust	150 to 500 : 1
Sewage	20 : 1
Soil organisms	7 : 1
Straw	75 to 150 : 1
Topsoil	11 : 1
Urine	0.3 : 1
Vegetable waste	12 to 25 : 1
Weeds	30 : 1

Compost materials

Almost anything that has lived can be added to the compost pile, so long as you keep them in the appropriate proportions of carbon to nitrogen (see above). You need a bulk source of high carbon materials and a source of nitrogen. Usually the biggest factors in what goes into the pile is availability, simply what can you get in sufficient quantity. Small gardens don't produce enough material to make an adequate supply of compost, so good organic gardeners also tend to be good scroungers.

Manure: This is almost synonymous with compost for many people, yet some people believe manure is detrimental and never use it. Manure provides the nitrogen component of the pile and is full of microorganisms. Composting manure makes it safer to use in the garden, as the heating destroys pests, pathogens and weed seeds. Some people compost human manure in hot compost piles and claim the end product is perfectly safe.

Urine: Sometimes known as H.L.A. (Household liquid activator) to disguise its true origins, urine can be the main source of nitrogen for the compost pile. If you aren't overly fastidious and are prepared to collect it, urine is actually a very convenient material and one that has to be disposed of one way or another. Dilute it (4 parts water to 1 part urine) before putting it on the pile. It is especially useful for getting a reluctant pile to heat up.

Soil: This provides the right decay causing micro-organisms and may help prevent the loss of nitrogen. However it isn't needed in large amounts (that clinging to the roots of old plants is generally sufficient) and too much soil may slow the pile down. Gardeners sometimes add soil to the compost pile to prevent it heating up too much.

Green vegetation: This is one of the main sources of nitrogen for the compost pile. The commonest materials are those you take straight from the garden, cover crops, weeds and finished crops, but you can also go looking for any abundant fast growing (non-pernicious) vegetation, such as Vinca, Japanese Knotweed, Kudzu, Ivy, aquatic weeds, algae and Cat-tails. Never add the roots of pernicious perennial weeds such as Bindweed, Bermuda Grass or Couchgrass to the pile, or any weeds that have set seed. They may come back to haunt you. See below for more on what not to use in the pile.

You can also plant fast growing plants specifically for composting (see **Soil improving Crops** for more on Compost crops).

Grass clippings: Grass clippings are a rich source of nitrogen and other nutrients. They are usually mixed with coarser materials, as they tend to mat down and go anaerobic if used alone. Occasionally grass clippings contain viable seeds. If this is a problem then compost them in a hot pile.

The best place to get grass clippings is from neighbors or professional gardeners (they will often unload their clippings on your property). You may also be able to pick them up from apartment complexes and sports fields. When gathering from such places you should be aware of the potential accumulation of toxins from nearby roads. Pesticides aren't as much of a problem as they are broken down in the composting process. The place not to get grass clippings from is your own lawn, they should remain there to feed the living grass (let's not get into a discussion about whether you should even have a lawn).

Seaweeds: These add valuable trace minerals to the pile and stimulate microbial activity, but don't add much humus. Fresh seaweed should be leached thoroughly to eliminate excess salt. Powdered seaweed is best added directly to the soil. There is no advantage in composting it.

Straw, hay and dried plants: These are an important component of the pile because they are high in carbon. Spoiled hay is often available for the hauling, though it's very heavy when wet. It often contains weed seeds, so must be composted at a sufficiently high temperature to kill them. Straw stems are hollow and so help to improve aeration. Tree leaves are excellent, but tend to mat down unless chopped or mixed with other materials.

These materials should be wet when added to the pile, as they don't break down easily when dry (straw was once widely used for thatched roofs).

Sawdust: This is ultimately a good source of humus, but the decay process is slow because sawdust contains so much carbon. It should only be used in small quantities on the compost pile and should be mixed with a rich source of nitrogen. If you have a large quantity of sawdust it can be composted in its own special pile (see **Wood Waste Composting** above).

Kitchen scraps: Vegetable kitchen scraps are high in nitrogen and other nutrients, so are an excellent addition to the pile. Meat, bone and other animal scraps can be used if you are careful, but are best handled by quick composting, to minimize the time they are attractive to scavengers.

The problem with kitchen waste is that it's produced in small quantities steadily, whereas for composting you need large quantities at one time. You can't simply add kitchen scraps to the pile as they are produced, as your pile will simply become a feeding station for flies, rats, skunks, raccoons, dogs or even bears, which isn't good for you or the animals.

Because it isn't very satisfactory to compost this kind of material incrementally, you have to find a way to store the stuff until you have accumulated enough for a pile. If you live in the country you could simply make a holding area, but the stuff smells and attracts flies, rodents and other pests. One solution is to empty your kitchen scraps into 5 gallon buckets, cover with a thin layer of shredded leaves or sawdust (to stop it smelling) and seal it with an airtight lid. As each bucket fills up store it in a cool place until you have enough to build a pile. This same system is sometimes used with human manure.

Some gardeners pick up large quantities of kitchen scraps from restaurants and grocery stores. This works well if you have the capacity and motivation to deal with that much stuff, but it can easily turn into a big mess. I once visited a house where the owner composted fish waste he picked up from the nearby wharf. His Kiwi vines were awesome, but the flies were horrendous. For ever after we knew him as "The lord of the flies".

Garbage: All organic based garbage; newspapers, cardboard, clothing (natural fabrics) and more, can be composted if there is no way to reuse or recycle them (which is a better way to go)
.

Highly carbonaceous material like paper and cardboard should be torn into shreds and mixed with succulent greens (don't merely throw folded up newspapers on the pile).

Semi-woody materials: You can compost small amounts of semi-woody materials such as Brassica stems, summer fruit tree prunings, semi ripe wood and vines. They take a while to break down, but add a high proportion of valuable humus to the pile. You can hasten decomposition by chopping or shredding. Hand chopping is easily done when turning the pile, as they will already be partially broken down.

Rock powders: Some gardeners add rock powders such as greensand and rock phosphate to the pile. The organic acids produced during decomposition may help to make their nutrients more available.

Ground limestone (calcium carbonate): Limestone may be added to compost to raise its pH and to makes the lime more effective at raising soil pH. It should be added when turning the pile for the last time, or just before application. Never add lime when building a pile, as this will increase the loss of nitrogen.

Gypsum (calcium sulfate): Is sometimes added to the pile to supply sulfur. It also contains calcium so should only be added after the pile has cooled down.

Non-compostable materials

Materials which should not be composted include:

Animal products: Many garden books caution against adding meat, fat, bones and other animal parts to the pile, as they attract unwanted insects and animals. I haven't had much experience with this, though I have composted a number of whole animals with no problems.

Dog and Cat manure: This is high in nitrogen, but may contain unpleasant parasites. It could be composted in the middle of a hot pile, but why bother? Its easier to just bury it near non food plants.

Pernicious perennial weed roots, weeds with seeds: If these survive the composting process they may cause trouble, as they would go straight back into the garden in a pile of rich compost. You can easily tell where seed filled compost had been applied, by the number of weeds.

It is possible to compost these materials, if you are careful to put them in the center of the pile, where it gets hot enough to kill them. If you aren't sure about this it is better to keep them out of the pile. It isn't worth the risk for the amount of material involved. Be conscientious about not mixing such materials with good compostable stuff (and always try to cut weeds before they set seed).

You can kill perennial weeds by drying them out in the sun before composting, but make absolutely sure they are dead. Perhaps leave them in a heap of their own for a year or so and then compost them. Perhaps the best way to compost pernicious weeds is anaerobically in a plastic bag.

Woody and thorny branches: These materials won't break down in a normal compost pile, they need special treatment (see **Brush Composting**. Keep thorny plants out of the pile because the thorns can easily end up in your hands.

Glossy and colored paper: Though these are now commonly made from non- toxic inks, some may still contain heavy metals and you can't be sure which are safe. I avoid it.

Pressure treated wood: This is very toxic and doesn't break very easily. No one in their right mind would try and compost this, in fact I don't even know why I'm mentioning it. Also avoid plywood sawdust.

12 Soil improving crops

Types of soil improving crops

Soil improving crops give you a way to maintain and build the fertility of the garden without importing nutrients and should be an integral component of the garden. They may be divided into several categories according to how they are used, though the same crop will often fulfill more than one purpose. For example most are eventually incorporated as green manure or compost, no matter what their original purpose.

Cover Crops

These hardy plants are planted in the fall to protect the soil over the winter. They prevent soil erosion and absorb soluble nutrients so they don't leach away over the winter. In mild winter areas they continue to grow right through the winter, giving an abundance of organic matter and a leaf canopy that protects the soil from driving rain. In colder areas cover crops usually die back to the ground when it gets very cold, but their dense root network binds the soil and protects it from erosion. In spring these crops grow rapidly and can produce a lot of biomass before they are incorporated. Cover crops can have a dramatic effect on the structure of the soil.

Green manures

As the name suggests, green manures are used to fertilize the soil and can be planted any time you have space available. They may be grown to improve the soil texture, mine the subsoil for nutrients, break up compacted subsoil, or to fix atmospheric nitrogen. Depending on the plant and when it's incorporated, they can be tailored to supply carbonaceous material, to increase the amount of humus in the soil, or to supply readily available nutrients for crop growth. Green manures are most useful in warm weather, where they grow quickly and create a lot of biomass in a short time.

Smother crops

Some particularly vigorous and fast growing plants can overwhelm and smother almost all competition. They can be planted very densely to suppress perennial weeds that are out of control.

Living mulches

These are low growing plants (usually nitrogen fixers) sown underneath a main crop to help keep down weeds, protect the soil surface and add organic matter and nitrogen.

Many people have experimented with living mulches without a lot of success, they usually run into trouble with the timing. It's important that the crop plant has a head start, otherwise it will have to compete with the living mulch and may be inhibited. However you can't wait too long or the crop will get too far advanced and can shade out the living mulch seedlings. Normally you give a direct sown crop 4 to 5 weeks to get going (it should be perhaps 6″ tall) before planting a living mulch, or (better) you use transplants.

Compost material crops

Most soil improving crops may be composted rather than incorporated, but some are grown specifically to supply material for the compost pile. These plants are selected for their fast growth, high productivity, ease of propagation, ability to regenerate after cutting and in some cases for their ability to fix nitrogen. Most of the crops mentioned below can be used, though Sunflowers, Comfrey, Corn, Sweet Clover, African Marigold, Mustards and various grasses are particularly useful. These can be fertilized with high nitrogen fertilizers such as Chicken manure or urine.

Dynamic accumulators are sometimes grown as compost crops to supply specific nutrients. These are plants that have a special affinity for a specific nutrient and accumulate it in greater quantities than most plants. They can be grown to make such nutrients more available.

Common accumulators include Yarrow (calcium, potassium, phosphorus, iron), Nettle (iron, nitrogen), Dandelion (iron, potassium, phosphorus), Comfrey (nitrogen, potassium), Hemp (phosphorus) Datura (phosphorus), Horsetail (silica).

Comfrey

The benefits of soil improving crops

Nutrient source
Succulent green manures provide the crop that follows them with a rich supply of easily available nutrients. This happens even with non-leguminous plants, though of course their nitrogen comes from the soil (the crop having merely accumulated it in a readily available form). They do this so well they have been known to increase crop yields more than synthetic nitrogen fertilizer.

Deep-rooted crops can obtain nutrients from down in the subsoil and convert them into plant material. When these roots decompose they leave channels full of organic matter, which improves soil structure. Of course they also release their nutrients for other plants to use.

Nitrogen fixation
Some of the most valuable soil improving crops are the nitrogen-fixing members of the *Fabaceae* family (formerly known as the *Leguminosae*). These have a symbiotic relationship with *Rhizobium* bacteria that live in nodules on their roots and fix nitrogen from the air. This nitrogen is shared with the host plant in exchange for nutrients and is released to the soil when the bacteria and plant dies. A good stand of a Leguminous green manure can add up to several hundred pounds of nitrogen to the soil per acre annually.

Properly managed nitrogen-fixing crops can supply all of the nitrogen your soil needs. They don't automatically supply nitrogen however, if the soil is already rich in nitrogen, the plants won't form nodules and there won't be any appreciable fixation. Also if the bacteria isn't present in the soil there won't be any nitrogen fixation. You can tell if the bacteria are present because they will form nodules on the roots. You can tell if these are producing nitrogen if the interior of the nodule is reddish. If it is pale white they probably aren't fixing much nitrogen. In such a situation the seed must be inoculated with the appropriate bacteria before planting. See **Direct Sowing** for details on inoculating seeds.

Other factors may affect the level of nitrogen fixation, such as soil pH (above 5.7), moisture level, soil aeration and availability of trace elements such as molybdenum, cobalt and boron.

Preventing nutrient leaching
One of the main virtues of winter cover crops is that they absorb soluble nutrients from the soil, thus preventing them from being leached away by winter rains. An uncovered soil may lose as much as 60 kg / ha of nitrogen and 45 kg / ha potassium annually.

Soil cover
Soil improving crops cover the surface of the soil, preventing damage and erosion by sun, rain and wind.

Soil structure improvement
Plant roots stimulate soil organisms in the area immediately around their roots (the rhizosphere) and the secretions from these organisms helps to glue soil particles into aggregates. You have no doubt noticed how the crumbs of soil stick to plant roots when you uproot them. Roots bind the soil into crumbly aggregates, make millions of tiny channels and add organic matter. The pressure from roots also helps particles form aggregates. By the time winter cover crops are incorporated in spring, the soil is in much better condition than it was the previous autumn.

95

Grasses are especially useful for improving soil structure. Cereals such as Rye and Barley develop an amazing root network and can have a dramatic effect on the tilth of the soil. It's said that a single Rye plant may have roots totaling 300 miles in length and that a cubic inch of soil may contain 1300 feet of root hairs.

Tap rooted crops (Chicory, Radish) can help break up compacted subsoil.

In spring soil improving crops can help dry out wet soil and make it ready for cultivation.

One of the easiest ways to bring compacted land into cultivation is to plant a vigorous deep-rooted cover crop. The roots can penetrate and loosen the soil to a considerable depth and improve drainage and structure. In one season such plants can loosen the soil to the point where double digging is relatively easy (or at least possible).

Beneficial effect on soil organisms

A green manure crop also produces food for soil organisms, especially down in the fibrous root network. When the crop is incorporated into the soil, the sudden abundance of food causes the microbial population to undergo an explosion in numbers. These organisms help improve the structure of the soil, make nutrients available and may even eliminate some soil pathogens.

Organic matter

Soil improving crops can enable you to grow most of your own organic matter, the single most important component of a fertile soil. This can be important if you are trying to make your garden as self sufficient as possible, or if other sources of organic matter aren't easily available.

To significantly improve fertility you need to have at least one third of the garden (up to half in northern areas) in soil improving crops of some kind (especially those that fix nitrogen). One of the best ways to increase the soils organic matter content is to leave it in grass for 2 to 3 years.

You have to be quite diligent if you are to add appreciable amounts of organic matter

by means of green manures. You have to be careful which plants you use and when you incorporate them. The best sources of organic matter are the cereals, though any highly carbonaceous crop is good. You can't increase the organic matter content of the soil with succulent green plants. In fact you may actually reduce it.

Pest suppression

Some soil improving crops have the ability to suppress specific pests. The best known of these is the African Marigold (*Tagetes minuta*) which has been used to eliminate nematodes from the soil.

Many soil improving crops (especially Clovers, Mustards and Buckwheat) help suppress pests indirectly by providing food for predatory insects and other beneficial insecs (See **Pests** for more on this). You just have to let them bloom long enough for it to be worthwhile.

Some species can be used as smother crops to suppress weeds (see **Weeds** for more on this).

Disadvantages of soil improving crops

- Often the biggest problem with soil improving crops is incorporating them. If you dig them directly in to the soil you must allow 1 to 4 weeks to decompose before you can plant in the soil (less time in warm soil, more time in cold soil). Incorporation is also a lot of work.

- These crops take up space which might otherwise be used for growing crops, so there is sometimes a conflict.

- Some of these crops extract a lot of water from the soil. In areas where water is scarce this may mean there isn't enough water left in the soil to grow the following crop.

Planning for soil improving crops

Selecting the right crop

There are soil improving crops for almost every conceivable growing conditions: cold, wet, acid, hot, dry, shady, or any combination thereof. It important that you select the right species (and variety) for the conditions, as it can mean the difference between success and failure.

Gardeners often grow several soil improving crops together, as different crops provide different benefits. For example you might choose a nitrogen fixer, a deep (or fibrous) rooted crop and a producer of abundant organic matter, (perhaps Bell Beans, Barley and Kale). Just make sure the crops like the same growing conditions and won't compete with each other too much.

Weeds as soil improvers

If you don't have the seeds of any suitable crop you can use weeds as a soil improving crop. Simply allow them to grow until they begin to flower and then incorporate them (never let them set seed or course). You could also go out and collect the seeds of wild green manure plants such as Sweet Clover or Sunflowers.

When to plant

Plant winter cover crops as early as possible, to give them time to get established before cold weather arrives. This is important because if a crop hasn't reached a minimum size it may not be hardy enough to survive the cold. Ideally the crop will be advanced enough to provide a solid canopy of foliage and a dense root network to protect the soil. This is especially important for legumes, as they won't begin to fix nitrogen until well established. If you plant them early enough in mild climates they may fix nitrogen right through the winter, if you wait too long they won't start fixing until spring.

There are ways you can get a jump on planting a cover crop. The best way is to sow it underneath a standing crop (just be careful when harvesting). This can give your cover crop several valuable extra weeks of growing weather. You can also pre-germinate the seeds to get them going faster. You could even start slow growing crops indoors (use multi-planting) and set them out as transplants.

Plant a summer green manure crop whenever you have a bed free for a few weeks. A fast growing crop like Mustard, Radish or Buckwheat can produce a lot of material in a warm summer month (this may not be worthwhile in spring or fall). When you want to plant into the bed, simply skim off the above ground parts for compost and prepare the bed as usual.

If you are very well organized you could plan your soil improving crop schedule while making up your garden calendar.

Where to plant

If you have enough space, it is a good idea to plant a proportion of the garden beds in soil improving crops each year. Take this into account while designing your garden and include a few more beds than you actually need for productivity. You can then grow some soil improving crops through the warmer months. This enables you to draw upon a wider variety of soil improving plants, including the long-term nitrogen fixers such as Alfalfa or Sweet Clover. This can make a significant difference to the fertility of your soil.

If your garden is small you will probably want to devote all of the space during the growing season to producing food crops. In such a situation you will only be able to use soil improving crops to a limited extent, perhaps occasionally as a living mulch, or (more often) only during the coldest part of the year. Of course this limits your choice of crops to the hardiest varieties, those that grow in cold weather and are hardy enough to survive the winter.

Planting

You don't need to be as meticulous when preparing and sowing these plants as you would be for other crops. Generally the smaller seeded species are broadcast onto a roughly prepared seedbed and incorporated 1″ deep with a rake. If seed is in short supply you can sow in drills. Larger seeded species such as Fava beans or Peas are usually sown in rows 6″ to 8″ apart.

Proper spacing is important for optimal coverage and growth. Sow too densely and seed is wasted (a very common mistake), sow too thinly and you won't get a good stand. Sowing rates vary greatly according to crop, so see the table for details on planting specific crops. See **Direct sowing** for more on planting seeds.

Some of the slower growing crops need careful nurturing to help them get established, so water and weed carefully. Smother crops may need help in competing against weeds until they get established.

Inoculating: Nitrogen-fixing plants should be inoculated with their required Rhizobium bacteria (each species needs a different inoculant). If you don't do this they may not fix much nitrogen. See **Seeds** for more on inoculants.

Incorporating

You can incorporate a soil improving crop any time it's convenient, but for maximum benefit allow it to grow for as long as possible. Generally the best time to incorporate a green manure crop is from when it first starts to flower up until 100% bloom. At this time there is the maximum amount of biomass and a good proportion of carbon to nitrogen for rapid decomposition (earlier you get more nitrogen, later you get more carbon). Don't leave a crop so long that it sets seed (unless you want seed of course).

Buried plants break down faster when the soil is warm, so late spring or early fall are good times to incorporate them. If you must clear a bed and plant while the soil is cold, it may be better to skim off most of the plants and compost them.

To get the maximum amount of carbonaceous material wait until a crop has flowered before incorporating it. This may temporarily cause a nitrogen deficiency, as the decomposing organisms soak up all available nitrogen, but this is only a temporary effect and eventually the soil will be enriched with humus (as much as 5% of the weight of a crop may eventually become organic matter). The nitrogen robbing effect can be put to good use in that the temporary nitrogen deficiency can inhibit weed growth for some time after incorporation.

If a nitrogen-fixing crop such as White Clover obtains more nitrogen than it needs for growth, it stores the excess in its biomass. When it needs this nitrogen for making protein rich seed it is readily available. This means that if the crop is incorporated while still young it will add a lot of nitrogen to the soil. If the crop is incorporated after it has matured seed it may not add any nitrogen to the soil at all (it may even take some out).

If you can't turn a crop under at exactly the right time, you can delay flowering by cutting the tops. This has an additional benefit of causing the roots to slough off material, which adds extra organic matter to the soil. This technique can be used to increase the productivity of a stand without removing and replanting. By cutting off the tops you get material for composting and you encourage root sloughing and faster regrowth. This is also a good way to treat long-term cover crops.

How to incorporate: The actual incorporation of the plants is the hard part of the whole process physically. There are two ways you can deal with the large amounts of above ground vegetation (the roots always stay in the soil), digging in, or removing and composting.

Digging in: Incorporating the tops directly into the soil conserves most of the nutrients in the plants and stimulates soil organisms. However the material must be given time to decompose before the bed can be planted. The time this takes depends on the crop and on soil moisture and temperature. A succulent Buckwheat crop may decompose in a matter of days if the soil is warm and moist, whereas a fibrous grass such as Winter Rye may take a month in cold spring soil. Unfortunately spring is when most crops need incorporating (it's said that the decomposing crop can help warm the soil).

A good time to incorporate these crops is when single or double digging. In fact this is one argument in favor of spring bed preparation (it's called killing two birds with one stone). Skim (or pull by hand) the material from the second spit and deposit it into the first trench, then bury it by moving the topsoil over. Long plant material is more awkward to incorporate. You could scythe it, or chop it up first (chopping also helps the material to break down faster, but is hard work and slows the job). I prefer to simply fold it up and bury it.

Ideally the material should be incorporated in the well-aerated top layers of soil, 6″ deep in heavy soils, 8″ deep in light soils. If it's buried deeper than this decomposition will be slower. In double dug beds it can be slightly deeper because aeration is so good.

An easy way to incorporate these crops into the soil is with a rototiller, but this presents its own problems (see **Soil Improvement**).

Caution: Highly carbonaceous crops take a long time to break down (which may delay planting) and temporarily rob the soil of nitrogen. If you are in a hurry you can speed decomposition by adding a supplemental source of nitrogen. A few crops (Brassicas, Tomatoes) can be planted directly into rotting vegetable matter, but not many.

It's important not to add more green material to the soil  than it can comfortably handle at one time. The decomposition of large amounts of green material may consume much of the oxygen in the soil, causing anaerobic bacteria to flourish. These may then produce acetic and other, acids that can inhibit seed germination and plant growth.

There are ways to increase the amount of green material the soil can handle. You can cut the foliage and leave it to wilt and dry for a week or so before incorporation (this wastes nitrogen though). You can also scythe off part of the tops and compost them and then incorporate the rest into the soil (this also reduces the work of incorporating).

Composting
The alternative way to deal with these crops is to remove the above ground parts from the bed and compost them (see **Bed Preparation** for more on skimming beds). This is slightly less work than digging in and the beds can be worked and planted almost immediately. This is a good system for early spring when the soil is cold, or for when you have to deal with large amounts of vegetation. The trade off is that some nutrients are lost and the soil doesn't get an immediate boost.

Mulching
If you are using a no dig system and don't want to incorporate the crops, or make compost, you can simply cut/skim the material and lay it on the soil as a mulch. Of course this is much easier, though it may waste some nutrients (covering with a layer of dry material, such as tree leaves may help to prevent this).

The best soil improving plants

The soil improving crops all share the same characteristics. They germinate and grow quickly, produce a lot of biomass in a short time, grow well in poor soils and have long lived seeds. Some of the best ones also fix nitrogen. The most commonly used plants include:

Nitrogen-fixing plants

Alfalfa *(Medicago sativa)*
This hardy perennial can be grown for a single season, but is so slow to get established it is more often used as a long-term crop for fallowing beds for a year or more. It is a very efficient nitrogen fixer and has deep roots  that enable it to search out and accumulate many minerals. It dislikes wet or acid soils, but is quite tolerant of drought. One drawback is that it's a perennial and once established it may take some work to eliminate.

Alfalfa is easily grown from seed, but it is quite slow to get established. When it gets going it can be cut several times during the course of a summer (usually when 10% of the flowers are blooming). The foliage can be used as a compost activator, green manure, compost material or foliar feed.

A close relative of Alfalfa is Medick (*M. lupulina*), a hardy low growing annual that prefers light neutral soils. It's tolerant of drought, shade and light frost and can be walked upon. It is sometimes used as a living mulch.

Austrian Field Pea
This legume doesn't produce large quantities of biomass, but is valued for its ability to fix nitrogen in cool weather. It is usually combined with grasses or other high organic matter crops.

Bell (Fava) Beans *(Vicia faber)*

This nitrogen-fixing annual is one of the most highly prized winter cover crops for heavy soils. It is hardy enough to grow right through the winter in milder areas. Fava Beans may grow to 5 feet in height and produces a lot of biomass. It can also produce edible beans.

This is a very versatile crop. The Egyptian variety Foul Muddammas is quite heat tolerant and can be grown as a summer green manure. The most popular winter variety; Banner, survives temperatures as low as 10° F.

If you cut the plants down carefully they can regenerate from the root.

Clover Alsike *(T. hybridum)*

This hardy perennial nitrogen fixer can be used as a short or long-term crop. It is the best Clover for poor growing conditions, because it tolerates wetter, dryer, cooler, or more acid soils than most other species (it can also be walked upon). It is not easy to get established though.

Clover Crimson *(T. incarnatum)*

This fast growing annual Clover has beautiful and distinctive crimson flowers. It grows best on light soils. It isn't very hardy.

Clover Red *(T. pratense)*

This deep-rooted hardy perennial prefers good soils.

All Clovers are attractive to bees and other beneficial insects. Quite a few species are persistent and can easily become weeds

Fenugreek

This fast growing half-hardy annual is used as a short duration, deep-rooted green manure for well drained soils.

Peas
Kudzu
Hyacinth Bean
Soybeans

These members of the *Fabaceae* are all good nitrogen fixers.

Lupin *(Lupinus angustifolius)*

This small, half-hardy, annual nitrogen fixer has very deep roots. It prefers light somewhat acid soils. It is quite tender and easily killed by frost.

Sweet Clovers, White or Yellow *(Melilotus)*

These biennials have been called the aristocrats of weeds. They produce a large amount of biomass and have deep taproots which can penetrate compacted subsoil. They also smother weeds and fix nitrogen. Their only drawback is that they take a long time to get established. They are commonly grown as a long-term cover crop for an entire season. They are sometimes planted with a nurse crop such as Oats.

Winter Vetch *(Vicia sativa)*

This hardy annual relative of Bell Beans grows fast in mild weather and produces lots of biomass. It likes heavy soil, either neutral or alkaline.

Plants that don't fix nitrogen

Buckwheat (*Fagopyrum esculentum*)

This tender annual is one of the best short-term soil improving crops for summer. It thrives on poor soils  and is so fast growing it can be grown in a few weeks in between two crops. Buckwheat may reach up to three feet in height in only a few weeks and grows so densely it can be an effective smother crop (it actually has an allelopathic effect on Quack Grass). A good way to establish a new garden is to plant and incorporate two consecutive crops of Buckwheat. The flowers are very attractive to Hoverflies that prey on aphids. It can't stand frost.

Chicory (*Cicorium intybus*)

This vigorous perennial produces a lot of biomass and has a deep taproot that breaks up compacted subsoil. It is usually planted with other crops.

Comfrey (*Symphytum officinale*)

Comfrey is one of the most important soil improving crops. It differs from most of the plants mentioned here, in that it is a perennial and is commonly planted in its own permanent bed. It is propagated from root cuttings and needs a year to get established, so only cut it once the first year (in midsummer) to prevent flowering.

An established bed may be cut every 6 weeks or so and will produce an abundance of organic matter. To keep it productive it can be fertilized with almost anything, fresh poultry manure, kitchen waste, human manure, urine.

Comfrey is particularly rich in potassium and nitrogen so is often used as a compost crop, or even as a fertilizer. The resulting biomass can be added to compost piles, used to make liquid or foliar fertilizers, or buried in the soil like green manure. Lawrence Hills wrote a whole book about using Comfrey as a fertilizer.

Hemp (*Cannabis sativa*)

Is a very good producer of biomass and also accumulates phosphorus. It is quite an attractive plant and makes a good deciduous screen. Try telling that to the police however, because of course it is also illegal to grow it in most countries.

Barley
Oats
Wheat
Rye (*Secale cereale*)

In mild climates these hardy species are commonly planted as over-wintering green manures, alone or with other crops. They produce a large fibrous root mass over the winter and can have a dramatic effect on soil structure and tilth.

In cold climates they may be sown in late summer to produce organic matter in the fall. They may not survive the winter, but their roots will still protect the soil.

Marigold, African (*Tagetes minuta*)

The specific name minuta refers to the flowers not the plants, as this plant may grow to 12 feet in height. It is best known for its nematocidal properties (see **Pests**), but is also a good compost or smother crop, as it produces a lot of biomass.

Mustards (*Sinapis alba*)
Rape
Kale
Tyfon

These crops are so fast growing they can be used as smother crops. They are members of the Brassicaceae and so unfortunately are prone to the many pests and diseases of the Cabbage family crops (notably Clubroot). On good soils they produce a lot of biomass in a short time. You can even harvest some edible greens from them.

California Bluebell (*Phacelia tanacetifolia*)

This half-hardy annual quickly produces an abundance of succulent foliage and is popular in Britain as a green manure or smother crop. It is not commonly used in this country however. This is a shame, as it is easily established, accumulates phosphorus, tolerates mild frost, is attractive to bees and other insects and isn't related to any important crop so can be used in rotation. Unfortunately the seed isn't widely available, so you may have to save your own. It has started to self-sow in my garden.

Radish, Fodder (*Raphanus sativus*)

This plant produces a lot of biomass (either green or carbonaceous), but is mostly valued for its deep taproot. This breaks up compacted subsoil and mines it for nutrients. It thrives in both warm and cool conditions. They are also members of the Brassicaceae and so can't be used in rotation with any members of the Cabbage family crops.

Sudan Grass (*Sorghum bicolor*)

This hot weather grass produces a lot of biomass in a short time.

Sunflowers (*Helianthus*)

These provide a lot of organic matter in a short time and are one of the best compost and smother crops. Easily grown from seed in any good garden soil, they can be harvested when 3 to 5 feet high, just before they start to get woody.

Weeds

Weeds are actually the plants that are best adapted for growing in your beds and can be very useful as green manures. All you have to do is prepare the seedbed and soon you will have a self-sown cover crop of weeds. These can be composted or used as green manure. Watch them closely so they don't set seed of course. In mild climates weeds will grow right through the winter.

Plant	Soil type	Seed/ 100 sq ft	Sowing depth	Time to sow	Weeks to mature	Benefits	Comments
Alfalfa	Dry	1½ oz	½"	May - Aug	12 - 20	N fixer, deep rooted	A long term crop, perennial
Barley	Not acid	4 oz	¾"	Mar - Oct	10 - 18	Carbon biomass	Good winter cover crop
Buckwheat	Any	2 ½ oz	¾"	May - Sept	4 - 10	Green biomass	One of best green manure crops
Chicory		1 ½ oz	¾"	Apr - Jul	14 - 18	Deep taproot	Breaks up compacted subsoil
Clover, Crimson		1 ½	½"	May - Aug	26	N fixer	A fast growing annual
Clover, White		1 ½	½"	May - Aug	26	N fixer	
Clover, Sweet		¾ oz	½"	May - Aug	26	N fixer	Breaks up compacted subsoil
Corn		4 oz	1"	May - Aug	10 - 14	Carbon biomass	
Fava Bean	Heavy soil	6 oz	1 ½"	Sept - Oct	14 - 26	N fixer	Nitrogen fixing cover crop
Guar		2 ½	1"	May - Jul	10 - 12	N fixer	
Hemp	Any	3 oz	¾"	May - Jul	10 - 14	Green biomass	Illegal, accumulates phosphorus
Kale	Any	½ oz	½"	May - Oct	10 - 12	Green biomass	Edible greens
Lespedeza	Acid soil	1 ½ oz	½"	Apr - Jun	12 - 16	N fixer	
Lupin	Acid soil	4 oz	1"	Apr - Jul	12 - 16	N fixer	
Marigold, African		1 oz	½"	May - Aug	10 - 14	Green biomass	Nematocidal, smother crop
Millet		1 ½ oz	½"	May - Aug	14 - 16	Carbon biomass	Fast growing
Mustard		½ oz	½"	Apr - Sept	6 - 10	Green biomass	Edible greens
Oat	Any	4 oz	1"	Apr - Oct	14 - 20	Carbon biomass	Winter cover crop
Pea		4 oz	1 ½"	Mar - Oct	8 - 10	N fixer	
Phacelia		¾ oz	½"	May - Aug	10 - 12	Green biomass	Fast growing
Radish, Winter		½	½"	Mar - Sept	10 - 12	Deep taproot	Breaks up compacted subsoil
Rape		½ oz	½"	Apr - Sept	10 - 12	Green biomass	Edible greens
Rye	Any	3 oz	¾"	Sept - Oct	16 - 20	Carbon biomass	Good winter cover crop
Soybean		4 oz	1 ½"	May - Jul	10 - 14	N fixer	
Sudan Grass	Any	1 ½ oz	¾"	May - Jul	10 - 12	Carbon biomass	Fast growing tropical grass
Sunflower	Any	1 ½ oz	¾"	May - Aug	10 - 14	Carbon biomass	Good compost crop
Vetch, Common	Any	2 ½ oz	¾"	May - Sept	18 - 20	N fixer	
Wheat		4 oz	¾"	Oct - Nov	16 - 20	Carbon biomass	

13 Mulch

Mulching is natures way of gardening and is so effective that some gardeners give up on cultivation altogether and become no-dig gardeners.

The benefits of mulch
A mulch is a layer of organic material that covers the surface of the soil. It provides a number of significant benefits in the garden.

Weed suppression
Most annual weeds are adapted to growing on newly disturbed soil, so if the soil is never left bare they won't be able to get established (this is an example of going along with natural laws rather than trying to fight them).

If the mulch material is free of weed seeds, it will eventually break down to form a weed free organic layer on top of the soil. Any weed seeds in the soil will slowly get buried deeper and deeper and won't get the chance to germinate. If you don't allow any more weeds to set seed and don't disturb the soil, you can eventually almost eliminate annual weeds entirely.

Mulching can also work with perennial weeds if it is thick enough and you give it enough time (maybe two years or more).

Soil protection
Sunlight damages bare soil by burning up humus, liberating nitrogen and killing soil organisms. A layer of mulch protects the soil surface from direct sunlight and prevents these things from happening. It can also prevent erosion and reduces surface crusting and capping.

Soil building
Mulching is the easiest and most natural way to add nutrients to the soil (it could be considered a form of composting) and improve it's structure. Most organic materials break down quickly once they are in contact with the soil (look at old fence posts), as the humid interface of soil and air is an ideal place for decomposing organisms. A two-inch layer of shredded leaves will have all but disappeared into the soil by the end of one season.

Water conservation
Mulch significantly reduces evaporation of water from the soil. Not only does it shade the surface from the sun, it also increases the humidity of the air under the mulch (that in direct contact with the soil). In dry climates this alone is enough reason to use mulch.

Soil temperature stabilization
On a sunny day the surface of bare soil may reach 90° F, while on a cold day it may freeze. Organic mulch insulates the soil and slows down temperature change. It keeps the soil warmer in winter (by reducing heat loss) and cooler in summer (by reducing heat gain, it can reduce the temperature by up to 10° F) It's common practice to cover root crops with mulch in winter to prevent the ground freezing.

Organic mulch is so effective at insulating the soil from the suns rays that it can prevent the soil from warming up in spring. For this reason it should be removed from beds at least 2 weeks before you wish to plant, to allow them to warm up. Light colored mulches keep the soil cooler than dark colored ones.

Plastic mulches can also be used to warm or cool the soil (see below).

Soil life
Mulch benefits soil organisms by providing food, blocking out the sun, stabilizing the soil temperature, giving refuge from predators and providing suitable habitat. It is one of the best ways to increase the number of earthworms in the soil.

Cleanliness
Organic mulches can make the garden look more attractive and well cared for. They also make it less muddy in wet weather, which reduces the amount of soil splashing onto leaves (and hence the spread of disease).

Winter protection
A thick mulch (up to 12″ deep) of straw, tree leaves or other bulky material, may be applied after the

temperature drops in late fall. It can protect late crops and tender plants and help them to survive in otherwise inhospitable situations. It keeps the soil warmer, reduces leaching and helps keep soil organisms (especially earthworms) active. It also keeps the ground from freezing, so you can harvest over-wintering root crops. This mulch should be removed in early spring to allow the soil to warm up.

Problems with mulch

* The biggest problem with mulch may be getting enough to use it effectively. It takes a lot to work properly

* In cool humid climates where snails and slugs are a problem, mulching may cause more problems than it solves, because mulch is a perfect habitat for these pests. In some situations mulch has been known to create conditions whereby normally harmless creatures such as Earwigs and Sowbugs become so numerous they become pests.

* It is well known that organic mulches can keep the soil cold in spring. Less well known is that a heavy mulch may actually increase frost damage to plants in cold weather. This occurs because the well-insulated soil releases less heat than bare soil. If given advance warning you can sometimes protect vulnerable plants by heaping mulch right over the top of them.

* Some mulches contain toxins that inhibit growth (sawdust, tree leaves, seaweeds). Others may contain lots of weed seeds (hay, manure), though this won't necessarily matter very much if your soil is permanently mulched.

The application of mulch

Before applying any kind of mulch you should remove any perennial weeds (otherwise they will simply grow up through it). If the mulch material is very high in carbon you might want to put down a high nitrogen layer before applying the mulch. A layer of compost might also be a good idea, as it provides extra decomposing organisms to get to work on the mulch.

A weed suppressing mulch must be continuous and impenetrable to be effective. The depth depends upon the material used, it might be a 6″ layer of straw, 3″ of chopped leaves, two layers of cardboard, or 6 to 8 layers of newspaper. Whenever you use a mulch to suppress weeds you must pay particular attention to the edges, as weeds will try to creep around the edges. This is especially true with plastic, so bury the edges to prevent it happening.

Types of mulch materials

A good mulch material should:

* Be relatively long lived.

* Be free or inexpensive.

* Be available in abundance.

* Add nutrients and organic matter to the soil when it decays.

* Be heavy enough that it doesn't blow away.

* Be free of weeds, weed seeds, pests, disease and chemical pollutants.

* Ideally it will also be attractive.

Organic mulches

See **Fertilizers** for more about these materials.

Tree leaves: (2″ to 3″) Deciduous tree leaves are one of the best mulch materials, as they add humus and nutrients, encourage fungi in the soil and are usually free of weed seeds, pests and disease. They can be used whole, but tend to blow away or mat down (mix with straw to prevent matting). They work better and break down faster if shredded (use a shredder or a lawn mower).

Broadleaf evergreens can also be used, but are best shredded to encourage decomposition.

The needles of coniferous evergreens can also be used, but aren't as good as deciduous leaves because they contain toxic resins and can lower the pH of the soil. They work best on acid loving plants such as Blueberries and evergreens, but can also be used with other plants if you add lime.

Straw: (4″ to 6″) This bulky material is clean, attractive and a rich source of humus. It can be used to enrich the soil, suppress weeds, protect plants from frost and to insulate the soil. It may contain pesticide residues, but this isn't normally a problem.

Hay: This is similar to straw in many ways, but contains more nutrients. However it also contains a lot of weed seeds, so isn't a good mulch material for intensive beds.

Manure: (1″ to 3″) This can be a good mulch material, if you can get enough of it. It is rich in nutrients and organic matter

Fresh manure may contain so much nitrogen that it can actually burn plants. It is often applied to the soil in autumn so some of the nitrogen leaches out over the winter.

Aged manure is safer because it has less nitrogen and can be used in much the same way as compost.

Composted manure is even better, as you know it has heated up enough to kill weed seeds (fresh manures often contain a lot of these).

Compost: (1″ to 3″) Compost is a good mulch material because it contains a lot of nutrients and can suppress some pathogens. However in warm weather some nutrients will be lost to oxidation, unless it is covered with a coarser mulch, such as straw or tree leaves. Most gardeners don't make enough compost to be able to use it as mulch.

Seaweed: (2″ to 3″) A rich source of trace elements, seaweed breaks down very quickly into the soil, but doesn't add much humus. It was once widely used in coastal areas.

Grass clippings: (2″ to 3″) These are rich in nutrients and humus, but decompose rapidly so need replacing regularly if they are to keep weeds down. They are best put down in thin layers as they become available. Thick layers tend to mat down.

Sawdust: (1″ to 3″) Sawdust is highly resistant to decay because it is very high in carbon, so is long lasting when used as mulch. If incorporated into the soil it may cause a nitrogen deficiency, but this doesn't happen very much if it simply remains on the surface. Fresh sawdust may also contain toxic terpenes and tannins, which can inhibit plant growth. When it does finally break down it is an excellent source of humus. If you really want to use a highly carbonaceous mulch such as this, you might want to put down a layer of high nitrogen material first.

Wood wastes:
Shredded bark
Shredded yard waste
Wood shavings
Wood chips: (2″ to 3″)
These woody materials are very durable and effective mulch materials, though they don't break down and add nutrients for a long time. When fresh they may contain toxins that actually inhibit plant growth. They are best suited for mulching paths and around permanent

perennial plantings such as trees. They don't rob the soil of nitrogen if they are left on the surface, as they would if they were incorporated.

Bracken fern: (3″) If you can get it in quantity it can be used enrich the soil, suppress weeds and protect plants from frost.

Newspaper: (6 to 12 overlapping sheets) It makes more sense to recycle newspaper where possible, but it can be used as a weed suppressing mulch. Newspaper adds few nutrients to the soil, but is readily available in quantity and is an effective weed suppressant. Avoid colored inks that may contain heavy metals. It is often used as a second layer underneath other mulches, to make them more effective.

If newspaper is too ugly for your garden (or you only have a small amount of mulch material), you can lay down a layer of newspaper and cover it with a layer of leaves, hay or other organic mulch. It is so light it may blow away if not weighted or pinned down.

Cardboard: (1 layer of corrugated) Another effective weed suppressing mulch that doesn't add many nutrients to the soil. It isn't quite as ugly as newspaper, but is still usually covered with a layer of more attractive material. Like newspaper it is often used as a second layer underneath other mulches, to make them more effective.

Carpet: May be organic or inorganic, depending on the fibers (I would avoid synthetics, otherwise you may end up with a layer of matted synthetic fibers in your garden) This is good for suppressing weeds and keeping the garden clean and is great for paths. Lay it down upside down for most natural effect, unless you really want to bring the indoors outside.

Miscellaneous materials: Cottonseed meal, Cocoa hulls, Spent Hops, tea leaves, coffee grinds, all make fine mulch, but are rarely available in sufficient quantity.

Inorganic mulch materials

These materials don't add nutrients to the soil, but are useful in some circumstances.

Plastic sheet: I prefer to avoid plastic wherever possible and wouldn't use new plastic merely to keep weeds down. I might use recycled plastic (such as that from greenhouses or cloches, if it isn't too far gone) to clear land of weeds, to warm the soil, or to mulch around newly planted trees.

Plastic is so light it may need weighing down to prevent it blowing away. You can use soil or rocks, or pin it down with pieces of wire (old coat hangers can be used).

The color of the plastic has a significant effect on its properties as mulch. Black plastic increases the soil temperature by as much as 10° F and also kills weeds. Clear plastic acts like a miniature greenhouse and can increase soil temperatures even higher (as much as 15° F), but may allow weeds to grow underneath it (if it doesn't cook them).

A big problem with plastic is that it degrades in sunlight. It is also ugly. Large areas of plastic might have an adverse effect on soil air exchange. It certainly does affect water absorption – watch that runoff.

Aluminum foil, Mylar film: These have many of the same properties as plastic, but are highly reflective which gives them some special properties. They help to keep the soil cool (they shouldn't be applied until the soil is warm) and reflect extra light back on to the surface of the leaves, increasing photosynthesis. In this way they have been known to increase yields by 100% or more. The extra light may actually disorient insect pests such as Aphids, preventing their preying upon the plants (it may also disorient the gardener as well, as it is pretty bright, as well as very ugly).

No-dig gardening

Some gardeners do no cultivation of the soil at all, instead relying on large quantities of organic mulch to provide fertility and to cover their seeds. This is the most natural way to grow plants, because it is how nature works. The soil layers remain in their natural state and are never inverted. Soil structure is improved naturally, with little work on your part, by action of earthworms and other soil organisms.

No dig systems can work very well, if you can get enough organic matter. It's been said that it takes 3 to 5 years to build up your soil using this method. If I wanted to create a no-dig garden I would probably begin with the methods outlined in this book, building up the soil by increasing its depth, adding organic matter and any necessary nutrients and then change over to permanent mulching.

The main problem with a no dig system, is that you need large quantities of organic matter. To put down a 3″ layer of mulch requires almost 1 cubic yard of material per 100 sq ft, which is a lot of material to find

No-dig garden establishment

The idea to cover the area completely with mulch, so the only plants that can grow are the ones you want.

• The day before you create your garden, water the area thoroughly to soak the soil.

• Begin by smashing all vegetation down to ground level. It doesn't have to be cut, or removed, just flattened.

• Fork the soil lightly over to allow air and moisture to penetrate. If the soil is loose and friable you can skip this step.

• Scatter a layer of nitrogen rich compost or aged manure directly on top of the cut vegetation, followed by thin layers of wood ashes, ground limestone, rock phosphate and kelp powder (or whatever nutrients you have available).

• The area is then covered with a high carbon material, such as straw, hay, dried leaves, wood chips or sawdust. The idea is to keep the ratio of carbon to nitrogen in roughly the same proportions as in a compost pile (around 30 : 1).

• Water the area to ensure everything is well saturated.

• The next layer is cardboard or newspaper. Use one continuous layer of corrugated cardboard, or 5 to 6 overlapping layers of newspaper (lapped at least 6″), to completely cover the whole garden area. This layer is intended to suppress the growth of weeds, so must be very complete. Weeds will find their way through any gaps.

• The last step is to cover the paper layer with 3″ of a weed free organic material, such as straw, shredded leaves or bark chips. This not only holds the paper in place, it also looks a lot better. This layer should be watered thoroughly as you spread it, to ensure that it is evenly moist. The bed is then ready to plant.

14   Crop planning

Planning the garden

If your garden is to realize its full potential for productivity you will need to get organized. Planning the coming seasons crops can be a lot of fun and is the kind of gardening you can do in midwinter, even if the garden is deep in snow. This paper garden may soon be altered by reality, but you will still have learned from the exercise.

The first year in the garden is probably the most difficult to plan, because you have to start everything anew. In future years you don't have to make a totally new plan, but merely refine previous ones, adding and subtracting as necessary.

Planning the garden means deciding what crops you want to grow, which varieties, how much of each, how much seed to buy, when to start seeds (indoors and outdoors), when to prick out and transplant, where to put them and more.

The easy way to start planning is to ask an experienced gardening neighbor, a local farmer or a cooperative extension office. They will be able to give you the specialized local advice you need. What crops and varieties do well in your area, when to plant, what problems to look out for and more.

You might also browse through the companion to this book The Vegetable Gardeners Handbook. It is intended to complement this book and tells you when to plant, how much of each crop, dates for succession planting, fall cropping and much more.

In future years your garden journals will be a great help in planning the coming years garden and you will be constantly referring to them. When did the Garlic mature? When did the Squash Vine borers appear? Over the years your journals will give you a bigger picture of your local climate and your gardens potential.

Step by step planning

1) Which crops?

What do you like: The first stage in planning the garden is deciding what to grow. This should be easy, just ask yourself what you like to eat and how easy is it to grow? Be sure to concentrate on crops you will actually use. There's nothing wrong with being adventurous, but don't fill up your garden with Taro, Quinoa, Oca, Skirret and Sea Kale to the exclusion of the foods you eat every day. Make a list of the crops you want to grow.

Climate: Your choice of crops will be partly determined by your climate and what grows well in your area. Each crop has its own preferred growing conditions, depending upon where it originated. Of course these change with the seasons and if you are to grow a crop with the least difficulty and the best results, you must plant it at the right time, so it gets the conditions it likes. You can try to grow Spinach in the long, hot days of midsummer, or Melons in cool weather but they won't be very tasty, productive, or easy to grow. As you get more experienced you can use various forms of crop protection to grow more exotic crops (See **Season Extension** for more on this).

Though temperature is the most obvious aspect of climate (if it's too hot or cold it won't work), day length is also very important. Some plants flower in response to certain length days (or nights) and won't flower or set fruit if the day length is too long. This is why Dahlias flower in late summer. They are short day length tropical flowers and simply wait for the days to get shorter. Day length also affects other plant functions, such as bulbing and tuber formation.

The maturation date mentioned on the seed packet is a useful indicator of how quickly a crop will mature relative to other varieties. However it is only a guide because the actual date varies according to the growing conditions. What might take 70 days to mature in a warm California summer, might take 100 days in a cool, cloudy Washington spring.

Varieties: Of course you have to choose varieties that will be able to mature in your area. Don't plant a Tomato that needs 95 warm days if you only get 80 such days, all you will get is a lot of green fruit and disappointment. This is particularly important with late plantings. See **Seeds** for more on this.

Convenience: Consider how much time you want to devote to the garden. Some crops thrive on neglect, while others wilt and die if you look at them with anything less than adoration. If you don't have a lot of time to spare you should probably concentrate on the more independent crops.

Sow or transplant?

Decide which crops you need to start inside and which you will direct sow. Generally it's more work to raise transplants inside, but you (usually) get crops earlier than by direct sowing. Direct sowing is easier, but takes longer.

Direct sow	Transplant	Either/or
Beans	Celery	Basil
Beet	Eggplant	Broccoli
Carrot	Leek	Cabbage
Radish	Melon	Cilantro
Spinach	Okra	Cucumber
Parsley	Onions	Kale
Peas	Peppers	Lettuce
Corn	Tomatoes	Squash

What to plant

Most nutritious crops
Broccoli, Kale and Collards, Parsnip, Potato, Soybean, Sweet Potato, Turnip.

Easiest crops
Bean, Beet, Chard, Corn, Cucumber, Lettuce, Onion, Squash.

Fastest growing crops (60 days or less)
Lettuce, Mizuna, Mustards, Radish, Shungiku, Spinach

Most valuable crops
Beans (Bush and Pole), Corn, Cucumber, Peppers Strawberry, Summer Squash, Tomato

Most space efficient crops
Beet, Carrot, Garlic, Leaf Lettuce, Onion, Radish, Spinach.

Most efficient crops (in all respects)
Beans (pole), Beets (root and top), Lettuce (Leaf), Onion (Bunching), Peas (Sugar Snap), Potato, Salad mix, Summer Squash, Tomato (trellis), Turnip (root and top).

Crops for moist soils
Celery, Cucumber, Endive, Lettuce, Peas, Radish, Spinach, Squash, Turnip

Hardiest crops
Brussels Sprout, Cabbage, Celeriac, Chicory, Cornsalad, Fava Bean, Garlic, Hamburg parsley, Jerusalem Artichoke, Kale, Land Cress, Leek, Parsnip, Rutabaga.

Shade tolerant crops
Beet, Brussels Sprout, Cabbage, Chard, Chinese Greens, Dill, Kale, Lettuce, Onions, Parsley, Spinach.

Drought tolerant crops
Beans, Corn, Hot Peppers, Melons, Tomatoes

My favorite crops
Basil, Pole Beans, Carrot, Garlic, Siberian Kale, Leek, Mizuna, Sugar Snap Pea, Summer Squash, Summer, Tomato

2) How much to plant

Once you've decided which crops you want, you must decide how much of each you will need (whether for your own consumption, giving away, sale or to feed to local wildlife). If you are growing for personal use you don't have to plant tons of everything, you won't need it (unless you are planning to preserve a lot for winter, or give it away). For many crops you will only need 6 or 8 plants at one time. Raising plants from seed takes some work, so don't waste time and effort on growing more plants than you can use.

I like to plant quite a few varieties, to get more diversity and interest. This means I don't usually plant many seeds of any one variety.

If you are aiming for any kind of self-sufficiency then you will need to concentrate on growing the most nutritious and productive crops. These include the high calorie or high protein crops, such as potatoes, beans and field corn. You would have a main garden of these crops and supplement them with other crops that are especially tasty or easy to grow. Your garden won't keep you alive if your main crops are tomatoes, cucumbers and lettuce.

Quantities: A family of four can consume the produce from a lot of plants and to feed a family you will need to grow crops in quantity. How about starting with 1000 Bean, 1000 Carrot, 100 Garlic, 200 Lettuce, 400 Onion, 25 Pepper, 300 Potato, 25 Squash and 50 Tomato plants. Growing this many plants requires quite a bit of organization.

3) A sowing list

Look at the planning table and write down the number of plants of each crop you will need to feed your family for a year. Subdivide this into varieties and planting dates to give you your sowing list. You will then know how many seeds to order and transplants to start.

Once you know how many plants you need, you can determine how much square footage of bed you must devote to each crop. Write down how many square feet of bed you need for each crop.

Of course all crops aren't in the ground for the same length of time. As soon as some are removed you can plant more. Early potatoes might give way to late beans, peas may make way for Zucchini. In this way you use the same space for several crops during the course of a growing season.

4) How many seeds do you need?

Once you know how many plants you require, it is easy to figure out how many seeds you will need.

When growing transplants, you will normally plant 2 to 3 seeds for each plant you need, then you can pick the very best for transplanting. You should also expect to have some losses when planting out, perhaps 10 to 20%.

With direct sown crops, where risks from pests and weather are greater, you should plan on sowing 4 seeds for every plant you need.

As you get more experienced you will learn which crops have the highest losses (when a crop has a serious pest in your area) and which are relatively problem free. In this way you may well be able to reduce the number of seeds sown even further.

5) When to plant

The first important decision was what to plant, the second one is when to plant it. When you first start gardening you should stick to the recommended planting dates fairly closely. There are enough variables involved in raising healthy crops without making it more complicated than it has to be. A complicating factor in many cases is that there are two planting dates, one for starting the seedlings and another for transplanting them out into the garden.

A number of factors determine when a crop can go into the ground.

Soil temperature: If the soil is not warm enough seeds won't germinate (in some cases they won't grow if the soil is too warm either). No appreciable crop growth occurs if the soil temperature is below 42° F and even up to 50° F it is very slow. Low soil temperature also means little activity by soil organisms, which is important because these creatures make soil nutrients available to plants. The ideal soil temperature for plant growth is said to be around 75° F. See **Seeds** for more on this.

Air temperature: Once plants have germinated growth is largely dependant on air temperature, if it is too cold they won't grow, or will only grow very slowly. The optimal air temperature for plant growth is around 70 to 80° F.

Crop hardiness: The hardy crops are much less affected by low temperatures than tender crops, because they can simply wait for warmer weather to start growing (some hardy spring crops can even be sown in autumn). Warm weather crops may be killed, or permanently retarded, by a long cold spell, so it's crucial they aren't planted too early.

Special timing: Sometimes a crop will grow over a long period, but is best planted at a specific time. This may be to avoid a pest or disease (late Peas may get viruses, late Fava Beans get infested with aphids), or to take advantage of the best growing conditions (Kale, Brussels Sprouts and Parsnips do best in autumn). Some crops may bolt if exposed to short days or long days, or may need certain day length to size up food storage organs (Onions).

After you gain some experience you will probably want to give plants protection to get them into the ground earlier, or keep them going later (see **Season Extension**).

Planting dates

There is an earliest and a latest safe planting date for each crop. For convenience these dates are usually based on the frost-free date, though this varies so much from year to year that it is only a rough guide. You simply estimate how many weeks before or after such a hypothetical date the various crops can be planted. The first and last frost dates for your location can usually be obtained from local agricultural extension offices. A rough guide to the last frost date in your location is when the Oak leaves emerge.

The earliest safe planting date depends on the crops tolerance to cold. Many people take a risk and plant the first cold weather crops slightly before this time. The plants may be harmed by a late cold snap, but they might also give you an abundant early harvest.

The latest planting date is dependent on there being enough time for the crop to mature before the onset of unfavorable conditions (summer heat, first frost, long days). To determine the appropriate time to plant fall crops, work back from the desired maturation date and then subtract the estimated number of days to harvest. You should also add a few extra days to allow for the fact that plants grow more slowly in the short fall days. They may grow as much in one long warm June day as they do in 3 or 4 cool short October days. It is a good idea to record the actual time they took to mature in your journal, so you will have a better idea next year.

Spring planting

Super hardy crops: These can be planted as soon as the ground is suitable in spring. This may be 4 to 8 weeks before the last frost date:

Leek. Onion, Parsley, Peas, Spinach, Shallots

Hardy crops: These can be sown 2 to 4 weeks before the last frost date:

Lettuce, Coriander, Mustard, Radish

Average crops: These are sown 1 to 2 weeks before last frost date:

Beet, Carrot, Parsnip, Broccoli, Cabbage, Kale, Chard, Potato.

Tender crops: These are usually sown around last frost date, or slightly later:

Beans, Corn, Squash.

Heat loving crops: These shouldn't be planted out until the soil has begun to warm up significantly. At least 2 weeks after the last frost date:

Basil, Cucumber, Eggplant, Melon, Peppers, Sweet Potatoes, Tomatoes.

Timing for transplants

Transplanted crops have two important dates; when to start the seed indoors and when to transplant the seedlings outside. If the transplants are to be ready when needed, the seed must be started the appropriate number of weeks in advance of their planting out date (see the table in **Raising Transplants**). If you miss this planting window, you will be behind before you even start (you may end up having to buy transplants).

Seedlings growing in cooler temperatures take longer to reach optimal size than those in warmer conditions, so take this into account in your planning. You can actually slow plants down by putting them in a cooler environment.

Time to grow transplants

Crop	Day Temp °F	Night Temp °F	Time/Weeks
Artichoke	60 - 65	55 - 60	10 - 12
Asparagus	70 - 80	65 - 70	10 - 12
Beans	70 - 75	60 - 65	2 - 3
Beet	60 - 65	55 - 60	3 - 4
Brassicas	60 - 70	50 - 60	5 - 7
Celery	65 - 75	60 - 65	10 - 12
Chard	60 - 65	55 - 60	3 - 4
Corn	70 - 75	60 - 65	3 - 4
Chicory	60 - 65	50 - 55	3 - 4
Cucumber	70 - 75	60 - 65	3 - 4
Eggplant	70 - 80	65 - 70	6 - 8
Lettuce	55 - 65	50 - 55	5 - 7
Leeks	60 - 65	55 - 60	10 - 12
Melon	70 - 75	60 - 65	3 - 4
Okra	65 - 75	60 - 65	5 - 7
Onion	60 - 65	55 - 60	10 - 12
Pepper	70 - 80	65 - 70	6 - 8
Squash	70 - 75	60 - 65	5 - 7
Tomato	65 - 75	60 - 65	5 - 7
Watermelon	70 - 80	65 - 70	3 - 4

Planning space

Where to plant

Once you know how many square feet of each crop you need, you have to decide what crop goes where. It may help to draw a diagram of all of the beds in the garden on graph paper so you can see how much space you have. You can then allocate the required square footage for each crop.

You won't actually need as much bed space as your list of crops suggests, because you won't be planting everything at once. Some crops will be sown in succession. For example you may want to grow 100 lettuces through the season, but you don't need to allocate 100 spaces in a bed. You may only ever have 30 or 40 plants actually in the ground at one time. Crops such as Radish and green Onions aren't usually given any space of their own, but are slotted in to available vacant spaces as intercrops.

If you find you have more space than you need, don't just plant more of the same crops to fill in the space. If you don't need them it's a waste of time and effort. It makes more sense to grow something else you will use, or plant a fast growing soil improving crop.

Arranging the crops in the beds

There are several ways you can put crops in the ground.

Crop rotation: Planting is most often based on crop rotation. This doesn't have to be too complicated, all you have to do is work it our for the first time and in subsequent years it will be automatic. See **Crop Rotation** below for more on this.

Random: You could use a completely random distribution method. Start with the long- term crops, those that take up space for a large proportion of the season and slot the rest in around them. Fill in any remaining gaps with miscellaneous crops, flowers and green manures. Don't leave any soil bare for any length of time.

Separate perennials from the annuals as much as possible, either in their own beds, or in their own sections of beds, so they don't get in the way of bed preparation. Over-wintering crops are best kept together also (in the warmest beds), so they can be protected easily and don't interfere with fall bed preparation. Tall crops are usually planted at the north side of the garden, so they don't shade other plants. Though in summer you might want the shade they cast for less heat tolerant crops.

Water requirements: Where I live we don't get any rain from June to October, which means a lot of watering. I have found that if I divide crops according to their water requirements, I can get by with using quite a bit less water and get better crops.

Fall planting

One of the best ways to increase the productivity of the garden is to plant another round of cool weather crops in mid to late summer. This will keep it going through the autumn and into early winter. Don't let the garden fade out in late summer, get vigorous new plants into the ground and it will have a whole new lease of life. See **Season Extension** for more on this.

4 months before first frost plant: Leeks

3 months before first frost plant: Beet, Carrot, Chinese Cabbage, radicchio, Rutabaga.

2 months before first frost plant: Chinese Mustards, Lettuce, Peas, Spinach, Turnip

This advice is a little more complicated in milder regions, as you can't really go by the first frost date. The first fall frost date may be so late in the year in these places, that days are getting pretty short and there may not be enough daylight for good growth. In this case you have to start your plants earlier. You want them to get big enough before the onset of cold weather, so that they can continue to grow through the winter.

You can sow the seeds of some crops in fall, to give you an early spring crop. These hardy crop include Lettuce, Spinach and Parsley.

---

6) The planting plan

When you have everything planned out on paper mark down the planting and estimated harvest dates in your journal. This will help you to remember to do everything at the right time.

Once you have worked out all of the planning details (dates for sowing and transplanting, quantities to plant, varieties, successions and more) you put all of the information into the journal under the relevant dates. You should also include any other pertinent information, when to prick out, thin, weed, harden off, fertilize, harvest dates. You can even schedule other important garden work, soil building, manure collection, compost making, the planting and incorporation of soil improving crops, vegetative propagation and pruning. If something turns out to be impractical, then change it and make a note in the journal, so you won't make the same mistake next year.

Making the most of limited space

Space saving ideas

In the vegetable garden small is beautiful, the smaller the area, the more productive it can be per square foot. The small garden should be looked upon as a challenge, not a disadvantage. You can give it all of the love and attention it needs to live up to its full productivity. Here are a few suggestions to help you use space as efficiently as possible.

*   Use transplants to reduce the time a crop is actually taking up space in the bed. Plants grow exponentially, the more leaf area they have, the quicker they grow and mature.

*   Grow the most productive and space efficient crops, those that give you the most food per square foot. Use crops that yield for an extended time, such as Pole Peas, Pole Beans, Chard, Broccoli, Kale, Tomato, Cucumber. Use short season crops (or fast maturing varieties) that enable you to get 3 or 4 crops in a season, such as Spinach, Turnip, Radish, Scallions, Lettuce. You can also grow crops that don't take up much space, such as Scallions, Carrots and use compact varieties.

- Use intensive techniques like interplanting and catch cropping, to get more than one crop from the same area of soil.

- If space is very limited, concentrate on crops that can't be purchased easily, taste better fresh, or that are always expensive (Shallots, Snap Peas, Alpine Strawberries, Radicchio). Go for quality and flavor, so you are growing things you couldn't buy at any price.

- Grow crops out of season when they are the most expensive to buy, rather than in season when they are cheap.

- Fill your whole garden with food by growing multi-purpose plants that are both ornamental and edible.

- Grow up. Train space hungry climbing plants such as Cucumbers or Snap Peas on trellises and you can increase their yield per square foot dramatically. Not only do vertical crops save space, but the produce is cleaner and has less pest damage. Be sure to put tall trellises where they won't cast shade on other crops.

- Don't try to get more food from an area by crowding the plants closer together than the soil can support. You will only succeed in reducing the yield.

- Grow cut and come again salad greens. These are harvested as individual leaves, when still very small (only a few inches long), so the plants are sown very close together (½" to 1"). Plants grown in this way may require only half the space of conventional rows.

- Once a crop stops producing remove it and plant something else. Don't try to wring that last little bit of food out of it.

- If you find you are not using a crop, replace it with something you will use. Don't waste valuable space.

Planning for continuity of supply

If you have gardened for any length of time you are probably familiar with the feast or famine syndrome. You either have to much to use, or you have none at all. It takes some thought and planning to avoid this situation.

Many crops present no problem when it comes to planning continuity of supply. If a crop is easily stored (main crop Potatoes, dry Beans and Carrots), or preserved (Broccoli, Corn and Green Beans), it doesn't matter if many plants come to maturation at once, indeed it is often desirable. You might choose to grow your entire winters supply of these vegetables in one go, at the optimal time of the year and then store it. In such a case you will plant far more of a crop than you could eat fresh.

If a crop has an extended harvest (Tomatoes, Cucumbers, Kale, Peppers) then again continuity of supply isn't much of a problem. Two or three plantings will get you right through the growing season.

Succession sowing

If a crop only stays in usable condition for a short time (Sweet Corn, Broccoli, many salad greens), you have to plan your planting carefully. This is one of the trickier aspects of vegetable gardening and needs to be worked at.

The most obvious way to get a steady harvest is to stagger the planting dates, by planting a small number of seeds at regular intervals. However this doesn't always work, because plants grow faster as it gets warmer (the old saying is: 2 weeks in March = 2 days in May). If you plant the earliest sowings too close together, they will have done so little growth in the cool weather that later ones catch up and mature at almost the same time. To get good successions you have to shorten the times between sowings as the weather warms up, for example plantings may be 16, 12, 10 and 8 days apart. In autumn the reverse happens, the days get shorter and cooler, and the time between plantings gets longer, perhaps 8, 10, 12, and 16 days. It's easier to get good succession crops with fast maturing crops, as there is less time for variation.

Another way to ensure a continuous supply is to use different varieties of the same crop, some early maturing, some standard types and some late maturing. Varieties are fairly consistent in their maturation times relative to one another and these can differ by as much as a month or more. If you plant several different varieties at the same time, they should mature roughly in order, giving you a staggered harvest according to their maturation times. These are usually planted in separate blocks, though you could also mix the seed together.

The most effective way to ensure continuity of supply is to combine the above methods. Make a number of staggered plantings of several varieties.

If you only need a few plants at a time, you can simply make it a practice to sow a few seeds in the greenhouse at regular intervals. You might plant a set number of seeds of each crop weekly and set out the largest seedlings as space becomes available. In the warmer indoor environment the plants will grow fairly steadily, so there is less chance of one planting catching up with another. You can slow down transplants by giving them cooler conditions.

If all else fails, console yourself with the thought that it isn't really necessary to grow all of the crops all of the time. You can simply substitute one crop for another: Leeks for Onions, Kale for Cabbage, Chard for Spinach.

Crop rotation

Crop rotation means planning your crops so that similar crops (or closely related ones) don't follow one another in the same soil. It is done for a number of reasons:

Rotation can reduce incidence of disease, as closely related crops are commonly subject to the same diseases (Brassicas are a notorious example). If you grow related crops in the same soil for several years then the diseases that afflict them may have time to get established. Unfortunately rotation is only of limited help in the small garden, as a disease like Clubroot can easily be spread on the soil clinging to a spade or to feet.

Rotation may also reduce the incidence of pests, which also tend to afflict groups of crops. In most gardens it's effectiveness is limited by the close proximity of the beds, as pests with any mobility can easily move to the next suitable bed. However this does make it harder for them and perhaps gives the crop a little time to get

bigger and more able to resist predation. Rotation is most effective against soil living pests such as nematodes.

Some crops really must be rotated to prevent disease or pests, notably the *Brassica* and *Solanum* families. Many others don't really need it (Corn, Beans, Spinach, Lettuce). However even they may still benefit from following certain cultural practices, such as heavy fertilization, deep digging or nitrogen fixation.

Crop rotation can be a part of good soil management. Different crops take different nutrients out of the soil (green crops like nitrogen, root crops like potassium), so if you rotate your plants everything comes out even. This isn't too critical in intensive beds as you will be replacing all of the nutrients taken by the crop and more (but it doesn't hurt). It is helpful if compost and other fertilizers are in short supply, as you rotate the heavily fertilized crops through all the beds in turn.

Rotation allows you to take advantage of the fertilization of a previous crop. For example some plants dislike rich soils and can be planted after a very hungry feeder. Some crops like nitrogen and can be planted after a nitrogen-fixing legume, some dislike lime.

Rotation may even be helpful for weed control. Vigorous growing crops such as Potatoes discourage weeds and can help clean the soil for weed susceptible crops such as Carrots or Onions. Some crops are easy to hoe, others quite difficult.

Limits of crop rotation

The usefulness of crop rotation in the garden is limited because of the close proximity of the beds (it is much more effective in the large areas of monoculture crops involved in farming). However you have to put your crops in some kind of order, so it may as well be in rotation, so long as it doesn't interfere with anything else. It may well prevent some problems from developing and it can simplify your crop planning. Don't get too obsessive though, if most crops are rotated don't worry about the occasional unrotated one.

If you have the space you should add another step to a rotation, by letting beds lie fallow under a soil improving crop for one year out of every five. This can be very useful in terms of increasing soil fertility.

If your garden is in partial shade and sunlight is precious your ability to rotate crops may be reduced.

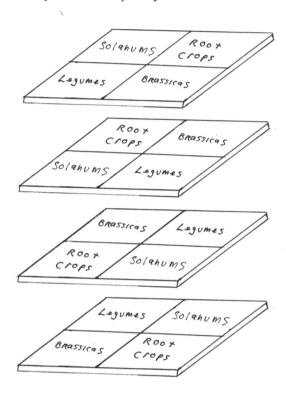

Working out a rotation

This doesn't need to be very complicated, as some crops naturally follow others, for example light feeders follow heavy feeders, nitrogen fixers follow light feeders. Ideally the following crop will not only be compatible with the previous one, but will actually benefit from its cultivation practices. For example Carrots, which are susceptible to weeds, could follow Potatoes which clean the soil of weeds and loosen the soil. Don't plant acid loving plants like Potatoes after a crop that has been heavily limed.

Some crops don't need to be rotated because they aren't susceptible to pests or disease. These can be placed anywhere which is convenient (use them to fill up the 'blocks'. Such crops include Beet, Celery, Corn, Lettuce, and Spinach.

Some possible rotations

Leaf crops (nitrogen lovers)
Fruit crops (less nitrogen)
Root crops (low nitrogen)
Legumes (nitrogen fixers)
Soil improving crop

Brassicas
Roots
Legumes and others
Soil improving crop

Brassicas
Solanums
Roots
Legumes and others
Soil improving crop

Potatoes
Brassicas
Legumes
Roots
Soil improving crop

Intercropping

Intercropping (or catch cropping) makes use of the fact that a plant doesn't need its full circle of space for its entire life, only for the final weeks when it is reaching maturity. For example a Pepper plant may eventually fill a circle 24″ in diameter, but for the first 6 to 8 weeks it's in the ground it may only need a 6″ to 9″ diameter circle. This means there is an 18″ wide space between neighboring Pepper plants that is vacant for 6 to 8 weeks, a space that could be used to grow a fast growing crop such as Lettuce. Not only will the Lettuce not interfere with the Peppers, but it may even help by shading the soil, increasing diversity and keeping down weeds (which inevitable grow on any soil left bare for 6 weeks). Sometimes you have to harvest selectively, removing the first crop to open up sufficient space for the maturing second crop

A number of fast maturing crops work well as intercrops between slow maturing ones. Lettuce with Garlic, Radish with Parsnip, Spinach with Peas.

It's very important that your intercrop doesn't interfere with the main planting. They must both get all the nutrients and water they need. If the crops end up competing with each other, neither will do well and you may end up with less than if you had grown one crop properly.

Timing is important when intercropping. You might plant the intercrop at the same time as the main crop, several weeks after, or several weeks before harvesting the main crop.

Interplanting

Interplanting is a form of intercropping whereby two crops are grown simultaneously in the same bed. It takes advantage of mutually compatible features to get the highest yield from the smallest area. It is commonly used by intensive gardeners to squeeze extra productivity out of a limited area. It can also be a method of pest control, by camouflaging the target crop from pests.

At first appearance interplanting seems to be a fairly complicated process, but if you break it down it's simple enough. Don't get too ambitious to begin with, try some of the simpler ones until you gain experience and don't overdo it. If done poorly you might not get any crop at all.

Interplanting methods

There are a number of ways to plant more than one crop in a bed, some more complex and efficient than others.

• The simplest way is to plant in blocks. This has the virtue of simplicity, but isn't particularly efficient because the plants in each block have exactly the same requirements as their neighbors and could potentially compete with one another.

• You could also plant different crops in rows along the bed. Put the biggest plants in the middle and smaller ones out to the sides. This is more efficient because you can place dissimilar, but complementary, plants alongside each other.

• You can also plant in short offset rows across the bed.

• Another ways is to alternate crop plants in the rows, when setting them out.

Spacing for interplanting

To find the correct spacing between two different crop plants add up their recommended individual spacing and divide by two. For example planting Leek (9″) and Carrot (3″) you would give you 12″ divided by 2, or a desired spacing between the plants of 6″. If the two plants are very compatible (see below) you could reduce this a little, perhaps spacing them 4″ apart.

Interplanting suggestions

Use plants with complementary growth habit. For example Corn and Beans are often grown together. The beans replace some of the nitrogen used by the Corn, while the corn provides support for the beans (this only works if the Corn is well established before the beans are planted). They should also be compatible in their requirements for fertilization and watering, so you can then treat them in blocks.

You might want to plant together crops that will be harvested at the same time, thus freeing up large areas of bed space.

Conversely you could simply plant into vacant spaces between another crop as they become available.

Complementary plants

Crops for interplanting should be mutually compatible, so take into account their complementary characteristics.

Shallow and deep rooted crops: These have different root zones and so don't compete directly with each other. Shallow rooted crops include Beans, Cucurbits, Onion, Garlic, Lettuce and Peppers. Deep-rooted ones include Beet, Carrot, Parsnips, Tomato.

Differing growth patterns: Interplanting crops with complementary growth patterns also reduces competition. Examples of this include the classic corn and beans (a tall plant and a climber) and leek and lettuce (a tall skinny plant with a short wide one).

Light loving and shade tolerant: Some plants thrive in the shade cast by larger crops, indeed in hot weather this may be the only place they do well. An example would be planting Lettuce underneath Corn or Tomatoes. Shade tolerant crops include: Celery, Chard, Cucumber, Leek, Lettuce, Mustard, Parsnip, Pea, and Spinach. Sun lovers include Corn, Melon, Peppers and Tomato,

Complementary nutrient consumers: Put plants that consume different nutrients together. For example put a heavy nitrogen user such as corn, with a nitrogen fixer such as Beans. This won't give much nitrogen to the Corn (though some research suggests that it may give some), but will replace some of that taken from the soil.

Companion planting

Companion planting has been given an almost magical significance in some circles. The basic premise is that some garden plants have a natural affinity for other plants and when planted together they will grow better and be healthier. Little of this has really been proven, in fact a lot of it seems to come from garden writers copying each other. Some people just really like the idea, so there seems to be more wishful thinking than critical thinking. Some suggestions are so silly they don't seem to have come from a real gardener at all. If you plant Horseradish with your Potatoes, you are more likely to end up with a very large Horseradish patch, rather than better potatoes.

Companion planting does work to some degree, as some plants do have special effects in the garden. In purely practical terms some combinations may work for a number of reasons. They may attract beneficial insects (especially members of the *Asteraceae* and *Apiaceae*), camouflage the smell of target plants (especially aromatic herbs), repel harmful pests, or work as trap crops (which pests will eat in preference to the crop plant).

I like the idea of companion planting and certainly think it is worthwhile, if only in that it is good to have a wide variety of plants in your garden. The best way to use companion planting is as a form of intercropping, where you are actually growing two usable crops. Otherwise the companion may actually reduce yields by taking up space that could be planted to crops (though of course it may increase their quality).

Companions that work

Bean and Corn
Broccoli and Cucumber
Cabbage or Kale and Tomato
Carrot and Onion
Celery and Leek
Potato and Tansy (what to do with the Tansy though?)
Tomato and Asparagus

Crop planning

Wblf - Weeks before last frost date   Walf - Weeks after last frost date

Crop	Germ temp °F	Germ time days	Weeks to grow transplant	Hardiness	Plants per person	When to direct sow	Start transplant	Plant out	Fall crop wks before first fall frost	Spacing inches	Weeks to harvest
Amaranth	50 - 90	5 - 14	4	Tender	10	2 walf	2 wblf	2 walf		6 - 8	6 - 8
Basil	60 - 90	5 - 10	8	Tender	5	2 walf	6 wblf	2 walf		6 - 8	8
Beans, Snap	60 - 85	6 - 18	3 - 4	Tender	40	4 walf	Last frost	4 walf		4 - 6	8
Beet	50 - 85	5 - 21	3 - 4	Half hardy	25	Last frost	3 - 4 wblf	last frost	12	3 - 5	7 - 12
Broccoli	45 - 85	4 - 20	4 - 5	Half hardy	5	2 walf	2 - 3 walf	2 walf	10 - 12	12 - 18	7 - 10
Cabbage	45 - 85	4 - 20	5 - 6	Hardy	5	2 wblf	6 wblf	2 wblf	10 - 12	12 - 18	8 - 15
Carrot	45 - 85	7 - 21		Hardy	100	Last frost			8 - 10	1 - 5	10 - 20
Celery	40 - 85	14 - 21	8 - 12	Half hardy	6	2 wblf	8 - 10 wblf	2 walf	10 - 12	9 - 12	12 - 30
Chard	50 - 85	5 - 21	3 - 4	Hardy	10	Last frost	4 wblf	Last frost	10 - 12	8 - 12	7 - 8
Corn, Sweet	50 - 95	3 - 10	3 - 4	Tender	15	2 walf	2 wblf	2 walf		12 - 18	8 - 20
Cucumber	60 - 105	3 - 10	3 - 4	Tender	2	3 - 4 walf	Last frost	3 - 4 walf		15 - 24	10 - 14
Kale	40 - 100	7 - 12	5 - 6	Very hardy	10	4 wblf	6 wblf	2 wblf	10 - 12	12 - 18	7 - 8
Leek	40 - 95	14 - 21	10 - 12	Very hardy	40	4 wblf	6 - 8 wblf	4 walf	14 - 20	3 - 6	15 - 30
Lettuce	35 - 85	2 - 15	5 - 6	Half hardy	20	2 - 4 wblf	6 wblf	2 wblf	6 - 8	6 - 15	7 - 14
Melon	65 - 100	3 - 10	3 - 4	Tender	4	4 walf	Last frost	4 walf		15 - 24	10 - 18
Okra	60 - 105	5 - 10	5 - 7	Tender	3	4 walf	2 - 3 wblf	4 walf		12 - 18	12 - 16
Onion	50 - 85	7 - 28	10 - 12	Hardy	25	4 - 6 wblf	7 - 9 wblf	3 walf	6 - 12	2 - 5	11 - 25
Parsnip	35 - 85	10 - 21		Hardy	25	2 wblf			12	3 - 5	16 - 25
Pea	40 - 85	6 - 17	4	Hardy	50	4 wblf	8 wblf	4 wblf	8 - 12	4 - 6	8 - 16
Peppers	60 - 95	7 - 28	10 - 12	Tender	4		8 wblf	4 walf		12 - 18	20 - 25
Spinach	35 - 75	5 - 22	3 - 4	Hardy	20	4 - 6 wblf	8 wblf	4 wblf	6 - 8	4 - 8	6 - 8
Squash	65 - 100	3 - 10	3 - 4	Tender	1	2 walf	2 walf	2 walf		24 - 36	7 - 12
Tomato	60 - 90	5 - 14	8 - 10	Tender	10		6 - 8 wblf	2 walf		18 - 38	11 - 16
Turnip	40 - 105	6 - 10		Hardy	5	4 wblf			8 - 10	3 - 6	6 - 12

15   Seeds

Requirements for germination

Germination is the most vulnerable stage of a plant's life and in nature most seeds don't germinate successfully (which is good because there wouldn't be room for them all anyway). A viable seed contains everything necessary to produce a healthy mature plant. For it to germinate successfully it must have sufficient warmth, moisture and oxygen (a few seeds also need light), as well as a place to put down roots.

Warmth

The optimal temperature for germination varies according to species, but most crops germinate best at temperatures of 75 to 85° F in the daytime and 5 to 10° F lower at night. Some cool weather crops will germinate at temperatures as low as 40° F, though they take much longer (and may not germinate satisfactorily above 75° F). Some warm weather crops may not germinate below 50° F.

If a seed is planted in soil that is too cold it will germinate so slowly that nothing seems to happen. This is because temperatures are too low for the chemical reactions needed for germination to occur at a reasonable speed (the time needed for germination doubles for every 18° F drop in temperature from 90° F). If the seed sits for too long carbohydrates will begin to leach out of the seed. These will be consumed by bacteria and fungi, which may eventually move on to those in the seed itself, causing it to rot.

The optimal temperature for plant growth is usually about 10° F lower than that for germination (65 to 75° F). This difference is significant because it makes it possible to germinate seeds in the warm greenhouse, (when the soil is too cold for direct sowing) and then plant them outside into cooler conditions, where they will still grow satisfactorily

Moisture

A dry seed may contain as little as 10% water. When it gets wet it soaks up water like a sponge and its water content may increase to as much as 70% . This process is known as imbibition and is a purely mechanical process that occurs even in dead seeds. If there is enough oxygen available and the temperature is right, then germination will begin (see below). Once a seed has imbibed water and started to germinate, there is no turning back. It must have everything it needs for germination and growth, or it will die.

Oxygen

As soon as a seed imbibes water its respiration and other chemical processes speed up and its need for oxygen increases (ungerminated seeds need only a small amount of oxygen). If the seed is laying on the soil surface this oxygen comes directly from the air, if it is buried it comes from the air in the soil pore spaces. If the seed is buried too deeply, if the soil surface is sealed (by crusting or algae), or if the soil is waterlogged, then the seed might not get enough oxygen and may die.

Light or dark

A few kinds of seed won't germinate unless they have been exposed to light, but most aren't particular. Of course as soon as they are able to photosynthesize they must have light.

Germination

The water absorbed by the seed during imbibition activates the seed embryo and stimulates food storage tissue in the seed to make food available. The embryo uses this food to grow, slowly breaking out of the seed coat and growing down to form the radicle (or root) and upward to form the epicotyle (or shoot).

Some seeds have species characteristics that affect germination. In some members of the *Apiaceae* (Carrot, Parsnip, Parsley) the seed embryo isn't fully developed and only matures after the seed has imbibed moisture (this is why those seeds take 3 weeks to germinate, even in the best circumstances). Beet seed capsules contain a germination inhibitor that must be leached out before they can germinate (germination may be hastened by soaking the seed overnight before planting).

Sources of seed

Local shops: The most obvious sources of seed are local retail outlets, mostly garden centers and hardware stores. These are convenient, but their selection is limited. I just went in garden center looking for a variety of Mustard. They carried four or five different brands of seed, but four of those five only had the same one variety.

In rural areas farm supply stores are usually the cheapest places to buy pea, corn and bean seed, as they sell in bulk. You may get a pound of seed for the price of a 2-ounce packet in a garden center. Their prices on seed potatoes are usually much better too. The only drawback is a limited selection of varieties.

Some gardeners frown upon using older seed, but I often buy last years seeds, at reduced prices. The best bargains are those packed in foil (they are as good as new), but even seed in paper packets may be good for a couple of years (just use promptly). Of course it helps to know which seeds are long lived and which aren't (see the table below).

Mail Order: Seed catalogs are probably the best all around source of seed. Prices are similar to retail outlets, but they have a greater selection and the seed tends to be fresher, as it is usually stored under better conditions. For many gardeners the garden year starts just after Christmas when the seed catalogs arrive and choosing the seasons crops is a treasured yearly ritual,. It helps to alleviate the midwinter urge to get out into the garden. My favorite ritual is receiving and opening the parcels of seed, it's the closest I get to the childhood feeling of opening Christmas presents! Always try to order your seeds early in the season when buying mail order, as they can sell out of favored varieties.

Seed catalogs are useful even if you don't buy from them, as they give you a good idea of which varieties are commonly available for each crop. They also tell you the differences between varieties, germination times, yields, plant spacings and more. Some catalogs are a better source of practical information than most gardening books (I like Johnnys Selected Seeds). Catalogs are advertised in the back of gardening magazines and are usually free. Once you are on their mailing list it's for life.

A word of caution, catalogs are advertising literature and you shouldn't believe everything you read. Some are pretty straightforward and honest, but others have a journalistic style reminiscent of tabloid newspapers or real estate catalogs. What they don't say can often be as informative as what they do, so you should read between the lines. They always mention the strong points of a variety, so if they don't mention something (such as flavor) it probably isn't worth mentioning.

Internet: A relatively new place to buy seeds is the internet and most mail order catalogs now have a web presence. Nothing could be easier and quicker than ordering from them, you can often have the seeds in a few days.

There are also many other smaller internet seed sellers, often individuals with an excess of seeds, looking to make a little extra money. You can find a source for any seed you have heard of on the internet. My only caution is that the quality of seed can be very variable and ranges from excellent to probably already dead.

Seed Exchanges: Seed exchanges and swaps are a fantastic resource for adventurous gardeners. You can exchange seed locally, nationally or even internationally and the variety obtainable is greater than anywhere else. Seed exchanges don't merely swap seed, but also advice and ideas and are potentially a very rich resource for the serious gardener. You can also meet new friends, in nearby gardeners, or those with exactly the same interests.

You really have to know how to save your own seed if you are going to be exchanging seed with other people. See **Seed Saving** for more on this. The seed you get through the seed exchanges may not be quite as uniform, or as high quality, as commercial seed (then again it could be even better).

Local markets: I have bought seeds of heirloom varieties of Tomatoes from farmers markets or natural food stores. You just eat the Tomato and save the seeds just as you would from your own fruit. If you are on a super low budget you can actually find all kinds of viable seeds for beans, peas, grains, herbs and spices here. You can also get vegetative material such as Shallots, Garlic, Jerusalem Artichokes, Horseradish, Sweet Potatoes, Chayote, Watercress and more. If it is locally grown it will probably do well in your garden. You do have to be aware of the potential for introducing disease however.

Choosing seed varieties

The seed business has undergone a lot of changes in the past 30 years. At one time seed companies were mostly regional, catering to local farmers and gardeners. As agribusiness developed these companies either got bigger, were taken over, or disappeared. This trend still continues and most of the larger seed companies are now owned by multi-national corporations. At the same time there has been something of a rebellion against the uniformity they represent and small specialist seed companies are springing up all over the place.

Gardeners frequently complain they are ignored by plant breeders, who concentrate all of their efforts on breeding for farmers. There is a good reason for this, 90% of seed is sold to commercial growers and a single large grower may buy more seed than a medium sized mail order seed company. For a long time plant breeders concentrated on commercially valuable traits, such as uniformity of maturation (for mechanical harvesting), shape, color, high yield and disease resistance. This was at the expense of traits the home gardener requires, such as flavor or nutrition. Fortunately this has started to change and some plant breeders now consider these traits to be high priorities. A cynic might say this is because in some cases flavor has deteriorated to the point where no amount of advertising can convince people to buy.

A lot of the new small seed companies are introducing their own varieties, or those bred by amateurs. They are also re-introducing many heirloom varieties. These were bred by generations of gardeners for their own uses.

The number of varieties available varies considerably according to crop, some have only 1 or 2 readily available varieties, while others may have 50 or 100. Some varieties are almost indistinguishable to the inexperienced, others may be so different they almost seem like different crops (e.g. Beefsteak and Currant Tomatoes). You have to evaluate what's available carefully to find the appropriate varieties for you. There are a number of criteria for selecting varieties, the relative importance of each is of course up to you.

Local adaptability: This is important because it doesn't matter how tasty or productive the variety if it won't grow well in your climate. There can be big differences in the performance of varieties in different areas. What yields well in one place may not produce at all in another (in some crops day length sensitivity is very pronounced).

The easiest way to find out which varieties grow well locally is to talk to nearby gardeners and see what they grow, most will be only too happy to give advice. You might think it a bit dull to merely grow the same as everyone else, but there is often a good reason for such popularity (such as resistance to a major local pest or disease, or simply suitability for the local climate). Of course just because a crop or variety isn't grown in your area doesn't necessarily mean it isn't suitable, maybe no one has ever tried it.

A good local nursery may be able to give you advice about varieties. Regional seed companies can also help, as their seeds are generally suitable for local conditions. You might think that local stores would only sell varieties that do well locally, but this isn't always the case. Some chain stores sell the same seeds from California to Maine.

It is good to use locally grown seed if available, as this may be adapted to your particular conditions and can do significantly better. This is another of the advantages of saving your own seed.

Flavor: Taste is a very important consideration for the home gardener, as there can be tremendous differences in flavor between varieties. This is sometimes quite subtle and often you won't notice differences between varieties unless you taste several at one sitting. If taste is particularly important to you, look for very specific descriptions of flavor such as "outstanding", "superb", "delicious" and "the best". Be wary of varieties whose descriptions neglect to mention flavor altogether, but emphasize how disease resistant or productive it is.

Season: You may require a variety for planting at a specific time of the year. Some crops have spring, summer, autumn and winter varieties, which do significantly better in their season than less specialized varieties. They may need a certain day length, be more cold tolerant, long standing, or resistant to heat, drought or certain diseases. There are also varieties bred specifically for greenhouse and cloche growing, or for over-wintering.

Other considerations: Productivity, hardiness, disease resistance, high yield, compact size, uniform maturation (for canning or freezing), vigor, beauty. Any of these characteristics might be particularly desirable in some circumstances. Don't forget that you usually don't get anything for nothing though, an outstanding feature is usually at the expense of something else. For example earliness means the plant has less time to photosynthesize and grow food, so such plants usually yield less (though in a shorter time).

There are now a few varieties out there that are considerably more nutritious than the norm. These may be exceptionally rich in vitamin A, Vitamin C, antioxidants, or other nutrients.

Evaluation
After you have grown a new variety you should record any relevant observations in your garden journal. How did it perform in the categories just mentioned? How did it compare to your old standbys? Is it worth growing again?

After a few years you will develop your own family of varieties you like and depend upon. If you save your own seed from these plants, they will slowly become adapted to your growing conditions.

Heirloom varieties
Every year new varieties are introduced to a fanfare of "NEWER, BIGGER, EARLIER, BETTER, MORE NUTRITIOUS, HIGHER YIELDING". Some of these are genuine advances and are worth investigating, however its educational to look at the 'New introductions' sections of old garden magazines, to see how these newcomers have stood the test of time. Heirlooms are the varieties that have stood this test and have been cherished by gardeners and small farmers for generations. They are plants with a history and may have come to America with Laotian refugees, Russian Mennonites or Italian peasants. They may have been grown by Native Americans, African slaves, Mormon pioneers, or Amish farmers. Heirloom vegetables have become trendy in recent years and some of the more interesting and attractive varieties have been reappearing in seed catalogs. However many can still only be obtained from seed exchanges and this in itself is a big

incentive to join such organizations. Some people even collect heirlooms as a hobby.

F1 Hybrids
To produce an F1 hybrid two distinct parent lines with the desired traits are self-pollinated for a number of generations to create two highly inbred, but very uniform, strains. These are then cross-pollinated and the resulting offspring, known as F1 hybrids, are unusually vigorous and uniform (they are almost identical genetically). This uniformity in size and maturation time (important factors for machine harvesting), along with high yields have made hybrids very popular with market gardeners and farmers. F1 hybrids are much less valuable for the home gardener, where a trait like uniformity can actually be a disadvantage (we often don't want an entire bed of Broccoli to mature simultaneously).

With a few crops (notably Corn and Brussels Sprouts) hybrid varieties are markedly superior to open pollinated varieties, but in many cases there is little advantage, except to the seed producer.

The main disadvantage of hybrids is that they don't breed true, their offspring (known as segregants) may be quite different from their parents. This means you can't reliably save seed from F1 hybrids, you have to buy new seed every time you run out (which of course is not a disadvantage for the seed company). When we sow seeds we can't grow ourselves we lose some of our independence (which is one of the reasons we garden). It's often thought that this makes seed from F1 hybrids completely useless, but this isn't always the case (see **Seed Saving** for more on this).

There are other objections to hybrids. They are often less tolerant of adverse growing conditions and seed germination can be temperamental. They may be more vulnerable to nutrient deficiency and some diseases. They may even be less nutritious, their much vaunted higher yields sometimes being merely extra water.

Perhaps the greatest objection to F1 hybrids really has nothing to do with their performance at all. The problem is the loss of genetic diversity that occurs when we simply use what is provided to us by the big seed companies (which are geared to supplying agribusiness). Home vegetable gardens all around the world could be (and should be) living repositories of genetic diversity. Each growing the crops and varieties most suited to their locations. If this happened worldwide we need not fear loss of genetic resources, we would always have the diversity we need.

I used to be very opposed to F1 hybrids, but my opposition has mellowed in recent years. I still tend to avoid them in principle (I don't even read any listing in a seed catalog marked hybrid), but I do occasionally use them. Usually if they offer a distinct advantage over open pollinated varieties and it is a crop where I probably wouldn't bother saving the seed anyway (such as Brussels Sprouts).

Organically grown seed

Some organic gardeners prefer to use organically grown seed, reasoning that this will produce better plants. There is some validity to this, but your main concern should be to obtain healthy, viable seed with a high germination rate. All other things being equal I would choose organically grown seed, but it's more important that it be fresh and of high quality. This is another good reason to save your own seed.

Treated seed

Some crops (Spinach, Peas, Beans, Corn) have a tendency to rot if planted in cold wet soils (especially poor quality seeds and certain varieties). However they must often be planted early if they are to have enough time to mature. The chemical solution to this problem is to treat the seed with a fungicide and consequently a lot of seed is sold pre-treated (some particularly susceptible varieties often aren't available without such treatment). Some seed companies will sell you untreated seed if you specify, otherwise it is treated routinely. Fungicides can be very toxic (Captan is known to be carcinogenic) and I don't want them in my garden (soil fungi are my friends). I avoid treated seed and rely on cultural practices (pre-germination, warming the soil with cloches and using transplants) to prevent seeds rotting.

Pelleted seed

Pelleted seeds are coated in clay (and maybe fungicide and fertilizer) to make little balls. They were invented to make small irregular seed more suitable for machine planting and there isn't really much to recommend them to the home gardener. They are more expensive than unpelleted seed and often don't germinate as well because the clay dries out readily (they must be kept moist).

Germination times

Crop	Germination time/ days
Artichoke, Globe	20 - 30
Bean, Bush and Pole	6 - 18
Bean, Fava	8 - 12
Bean, Runner	10 - 12
Beet	7 - 21
Broccoli	5 - 12
Cabbage	5 - 10
Carrot	14 - 28
Cauliflower	5 - 12
Celery	18 - 24
Chard	7 - 21
Chinese Cabbage	5 - 12
Collards	5 - 10
Corn	3 - 10
Cucumber	3 - 10
Eggplant	5 - 15
Endive	7 - 14
Kale	5 - 10
Kohlrabi	5 - 12
Leek	7 - 28
Lettuce	3 - 15
Melon	3 - 10
Onion	7 - 28
Parsley	14 - 28
Parsnip	21 - 28
Peas	6 - 12
Peppers	7 - 21
Radish	3 - 10
Spinach	10 - 15
Squash	6 - 10
Tomato	7 - 14
Turnip	7 - 12

Seed inoculation

If you are growing a nitrogen-fixing crop the right bacteria must be present in the soil, or there won't be much nitrogen fixation. The first time you grow such a crop you should inoculate the seed with the appropriate nitrogen-fixing bacteria. This is most important in new gardens, where the soil is very poor, or where chemicals have been used extensively. In good soil it isn't necessary to inoculate every year thereafter, as the bacteria can live in the soil for 3 to 5 years. However you should inoculate again if you don't grow the crop for a long time, or at least check plant roots to make sure nodulation is good.

Inoculant will last for at least 9 months if stored in the fridge. It should be used before its expiration date (or soon after).

Inoculation procedure

This is pretty simple, just moisten the seeds and roll them in the inoculant powder. Some gardeners add a little syrup or molasses to the water to make the inoculant stick better. They may also roll the inoculated seeds in rock phosphate powder to form pellets that supply phosphorus and protect the inoculant.

Seed that has been treated with fungicide (a lot of pea and bean seed) can't be inoculated as described above because the pesticide could kill the inoculant. In such a case you have to put the inoculant in the furrow or planting hole (some gardeners use this technique with untreated seed too). A better idea is to avoid fungicide treated seed entirely. If you forget to inoculate when planting you can try mixing it with water and water the seeds with it.

Seed storage

Seed packets often contain more seeds than you need for one season, so it's usual to have quite a collection of seed left over at the end of the growing season. If this seed is to remain in good condition for future use, it must be stored properly. It is not good to leave seed packets in warm humid places such as the greenhouse and don't let them get wet.

The factors responsible for seed losing its vigor are the same ones necessary for seed germination: moisture and warmth. They speed up seed metabolism (in preparation for germination) causing it to respire at a faster rate and use up its reserves of food. After a time the seed no longer has sufficient reserves left to grow into a healthy self sustaining seedling and is no longer viable (see **Vigor** below).

Seeds absorb moisture from the air very readily and their moisture content fluctuates with humidity. In very dry air it may be as low as 5%, while in very humid air it could be as high as 14%. Moisture content is the most critical factor in seed longevity and for every 1% rise in the moisture content of a seed (above 5%) its storage life is halved. This means that for longest life you should keep your seeds as dry as possible. If they get wet they lose their viability rapidly.

High temperature shortens seed life in the same way as moisture, by increasing the rate of respiration. For every 18° rise in temperature above 32° F the storage life of a seed is halved. This isn't quite as critical as moisture (seeds last very well when stored in foil packets), but the two have a synergistic effect.

Storage techniques

If you want to store seeds for any length of time you must keep them dry and cool. There are a number of ways to do this, depending on how long you want to keep them. Obviously if you are only going to keep the seed until the next spring planting season, then good storage conditions aren't as important as if you are starting a seed bank and hope to store them for 50 years.

Seed longevity isn't very predictable and it often lasts longer than you might expect. I recently read of some 26-year-old Cabbage seed that germinated very well, even though stored at room temperature and humidity.

Commercial paper packaging doesn't do anything to protect the seed. This doesn't matter if the seed is fresh and is to be used promptly, but means that the seed will lose viability at the normal rate when stored at room temperature and humidity (see the table below).

The best commercial seed packaging is the aluminum foil pack that keeps out all moisture until opened (I planted some nine years old foil packed Burpee lettuce that had excellent germination and growth). Once the foil packet is opened the seeds start to deteriorate at the normal rate, unless you quickly re-seal the packet with tape.

Seeds last longer if stored in the refrigerator at 35 to 50° F, however they must be kept in an airtight container, as refrigerators tend to be very humid.

The best way to store seeds for long periods is to dry them with a desiccant (see below) and then freeze them. Remember the colder you store the seeds the longer they will live. The seed must be thoroughly dry before it is frozen though, undried seed may be damaged or killed by ice crystals forming inside it.

Drying seed

Seeds must be very dry if they are to remain in good condition for any length of time. The safest way to do this is to put them in a sealed jar with a desiccant. You can use dry powdered milk (from a freshly opened packet), but silica gel is much better. This is usually treated with cobalt chloride, to make blue crystals that turn white as they absorb moisture.

Drying the seeds is simple enough. Measure out an amount of silica gel equal in volume to the amount of seed. This is roughly an ounce of seed to one tablespoon of silica gel (or 3 tablespoons of fresh powdered milk). Seal it into the airtight jar with the packets of seed. When the silica gel turns white from absorbing moisture, it should be replaced with fresh gel (do this quickly so as not to admit too much moisture). The white gel can then be re-dried for later use. Repeat this operation as necessary until the gel in the jar no longer turns white. You should then change the gel routinely every six months or so, to ensure the seeds are kept dry. When the seeds are thoroughly dry they will shatter when crushed, rather than simply being flattened.

Storage containers

Any container can be used for seed storage, so long as it is moisture proof and airtight (some plastics are actually permeable). The most popular container is a screw top glass jar with a rubber gasket (cut from an old inner tube) in the lid. Sealable plastic freezer bags (suck out the surplus air before sealing) can also be used. Ideally you will put an open container of silica gel in the container so you can see its color. Always remove the seeds and re-seal the container as quickly as possible).

Seed Longevity

How long seed will remain viable at room temperature and humidity depends on the species. The numbers in the table below are only approximations, mostly useful for comparison.

Minimum germination percentage

New seed legally has to have a minimum germination percentage and most reputable companies are reliable. I have had my doubts about a few packets of seed, but usually sowing technique is the problem rather than the seed. Seed packets usually have the date when they were packed written on them, so be suspicious of those that don't.

The minimum germination percentage tells you that you won't get a plant for every seed you sow. If seed viability is low you will have to compensate by sowing proportionately more seed. If it is very low you should start the seed indoors in optimal conditions and select only the most vigorous seedlings for planting out. If germination is very poor it's best to get new seed.

Seed vigor

Even if the germination percentage is high this doesn't necessarily correlate to good emergence in the field. You might think a 70% germination rate would mean 70 out of 100 seeds will produce plants, but it doesn't always work like this. Age doesn't only affect a seeds ability to germinate, it also affects the vigor of the seedling. Old seeds may take significantly longer to germinate and may have less vigor. This occurs because the seed has enough food to germinate, but runs out of food reserves before the seedling can begin to photosynthesize fully.

Some seed is so weak it has a hard time getting out of its own seed coat. I once acquired a large collection of unusual old seeds, averaging 6 or 7 years old which had been stored in a garden shed (some packets had even been wet at some point). A surprising number of these seeds germinated satisfactorily, but quite a few had little vigor (some Oregano seedlings sat around in their cotyledons for two months before I lost patience with them!)

Seed size

The size of a seed also affects its vigor. Large seeds have greater reserves of food than small ones, so live longer, are more vigorous and produce larger seedlings (which commonly mature faster).

Germination testing

Seed that has been stored for any length of time should be tested for germination capacity before you plant it. In this way you don't waste time and effort on non-viable seed. You can do this yourself quite easily. Select a small quantity of seeds, a minimum of 10, preferably 20, and lay them on one side of a sheet of absorbent paper (blotting paper, a coffee filter, or a strong paper towel - the kind that don't fall apart when wet). Moisten the paper (don't saturate) and then fold one side over the other to cover it. Roll up this little package, put it in a plastic bag or sandwich bag and put it in a warm place (75 to 95° F). Check the seeds every day or two, to keep them moist and look for germination. Note when the first seeds germinate (fast germination indicates high vigor) and how long it takes for the rest. Then count up how many germinate altogether to find the germination percentage. You will then have an idea of how many seeds to sow to obtain the number of plants you need.

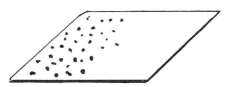

Put seeds on paper towel

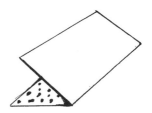

Fold in half

Completely

Roll up, moisten with water

Put in a plastic bag to keep moist

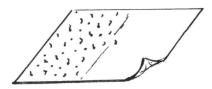

Count the germinated seeds

Seed Longevity in years

Crop	Mini-mum	Aver-age	Maxi-mum
Artichoke	4	4	4
Asparagus	2	3	3
Basil	2	4	6
Bean, Green	2	4	5
Bean, Fava	2	4	6
Bean Runner	3	4	6
Bean, Soy	2	4	6
Beet	3	5	8
Broccoli	3	5	6
Brussels Sprout	2	4	5
Cabbage	3	5	10
Carrot	2	3	5
Cauliflower	3	4	5
Celery Celeriac	2	4	5
Chard	3	4	6
Chicory	4	6	8
Chinese Cabbage	3	5	7
Chives	1	2	
Cilantro	2	4	6
Corn	1	2	
Cornsalad	3	5	7
Cow Pea	2	3	4
Cress Garden	3	5	9
Cucumber	3	5	7
Dandelion	1	2	5
Eggplant	3	4	5
Endive	5	7	10
Fennel	3	4	6
Kale	3	5	7
Kohlrabi	3	5	7
Leek	1	2	4
Lettuce	3	5	6
Melon	1	2	4
Mustard	3	4	6
N Z Spinach	3	5	6

Crop	Mini-mum	Aver-age	Maxi-mum
Okra	2	3	5
Onion	2	3	5
Pea	3	4	6
Peanut	3	4	5
Parsnip	1	2	3
Parsley, Hamburg	2	3	4
Pepper	2	4	6
Radish	3	4	5
Rhubarb	2	3	4
Rocket	2	4	5
Rutabaga	2	3	4
Sage	3	4	5
Salsify	1	2	3
Seakale	1	2	3
Sorrel	2	4	6
Spinach	2	4	6
Squash	3	6	8
Strawberry	1	2	3
Tomato	3	5	7
Tomatillo	3	5	7
Turnip	2	3	5
Watercress	2	5	9
Watermelon	3	6	8

16   Direct seed sowing

The most straightforward way to raise many crops is by sowing seed directly into the ground. Known as direct sowing, it has a number of advantages over raising transplants.

The advantages of direct sowing

•   Direct sowing is less work than raising transplants. It's quite feasible to direct sow an acre of wheat by hand, but just raising enough transplants for this would be a formidable task, let alone planting them out. Direct sown plants commonly have a higher mortality rate, but as you have so many more potential plants this isn't significant (You usually have to thin them anyway).

•   Some crops (Carrot, Parsnip, Beet, Beans, Peas, Spinach, Cucurbits) simply don't transplant very well. They can be transplanted if grown in soil blocks or plug trays, but it's rarely worth the extra effort involved. The easiest plants to direct sow are the large seeded ones, Beans, Peas, Corn and the Cucurbits.

•   Plants that are sown directly where they will grow don't experience any transplant shock.

•   It's less complicated and less expensive to direct sow. You don't need containers, soil mixes, lights or a greenhouse.

•   Sometimes you don't have sufficient transplants for your needs (whether by poor planning, negligence or act of nature). In such cases it is usually possible to simply fill in with direct sown crops.

•   Some intensive techniques use direct sowing, for example when growing closely spaced (½" apart) cut and come again salad greens. You can sometimes sow seeds directly into an occupied bed, so long as you remove the occupant before the new seedlings need the space. You can also grow transplants in this way, simply sow seed in any vacant spot and when the seedlings are large enough you can transplant them

•   If you need a lot of plants, then direct sowing makes the most sense. This is much less trouble than raising all those transplants.

Factors to consider in direct sowing

Seed viability
Seed for direct sowing should be of good viability because it may have to germinate and grow in a less than optimal environment. If your seed is less than fresh it may be worthwhile to do a germination test to give you an idea of what percentage of seeds are likely to germinate. If necessary you can then compensate by planting more thickly. Of course you could just plant more thickly anyway, but that might entail more thinning.

Soil temperature
Soil temperature is often the deciding factor in whether you get good germination or not. Cool weather crops won't germinate if the soil temperature (in the top 2″) is below 40° F, while warm weather crops need at least 60° F. These are minimum temperatures and germination will be faster and better if it is warmer than this. Very high soil temperatures can also cause poor germination, especially with cool weather crops. See **Seeds** for more on how temperature affects planting.

Before you plant

Seed bed preparation
Preparing the seed bed is physically the hardest part of direct sowing. See **Bed Preparation** for instructions on digging, shaping and preparing a bed.

A seedbed must have good drainage, good aeration and nice loose subsoil. The surface soil should be fine and crumbly, with no weeds, stones, clumps of soil, twigs or any other debris. The average size of the soil crumbs should range from that of a pea to that of a wheat grain. The texture shouldn't be too fine, as this can encourage surface crusting, or capping.

It's fairly easy to prepare a good seed bed in light soils, but heavy soils are more problematic (add lots of organic matter to improve it. If the soil is very heavy it may be necessary to make deep furrows and fill them with a mix of soil and compost

The bed should ideally be planted as soon as it is prepared, as cultivation will cause it to dry out. If this is not possible then keep it watered as you would a seedbed.

Seed treatments

Seed soaking: In warm, dry weather large seeds such as peas or beans are often soaked for a few hours (or overnight) before planting to get them off to a fast start. Some seeds can be damaged if simply soaked in a jar of water (they absorb too much water too rapidly), so it is better to put the seeds on a moist paper towel overnight. Make sure they don't dry out again before planting and don't soak them in cool wet weather (this only increases their tendency to rot). Beet and Pepper seeds are often soaked to remove a germination inhibitor and so speed germination.

Some people add a little liquid Kelp to the soak water (1 part Kelp to 400 parts water) in the belief this improves germination and reduces Damping Off disease.

Pre-germination: This is a way to make direct sowing more reliable by pre-germinating the seed indoors in warm conditions. This technique can greatly speed up growth in cool weather and may give the plants as much as two weeks head start. A seed that might take 2 to 3 weeks to germinate in cold spring soil might germinate in 4 days inside.

Pre-germination can also be used in summer, to germinate high temperature sensitive seeds such as lettuce, which don't germinate well if sown into very warm soil.

Seeds are pre-germinated in exactly the same way as you perform a germination test. Put the seeds on one side of blotting paper, a coffee filter or a strong paper towel (the kind that doesn't fall apart when wet). The paper is moistened (don't saturate), folded to cover the seed and placed in a plastic bag (or plastic sandwich bag) in a warm place (75 to 95° F). Check the seeds every couple of days and as soon as shoots begin to emerge they should go out. If you aren't ready to plant them, you can put them in the fridge for a few days.

Germinating the seed is the easy part. The hard part is getting the sprouted seeds into the ground without damaging their delicate roots. This isn't too difficult with large seeded crops such as Cucurbits, Peas, and Corn and if you are very gentle they will suffer minimal damage. Smaller seeded crops are much harder to handle without harm, in fact **Fluid Sowing** was devised as a way to plant small pre-germinated seeds safely - see below.

Inoculation: The first time you grow a nitrogen-fixing leguminous crop it must be inoculated with the appropriate bacteria. See **Seeds** for more on this.

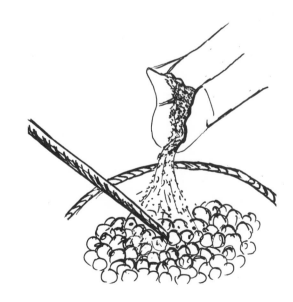

Fluid sowing

This technique enables you to plant pre-germinated seeds without damaging them, by suspending them in a thick glutinous gel of starch or alginate. Fluid sowing is most useful for planting small delicate seedlings that are easily damaged, such as Carrots, Parsnips Parsley, Onion, Spinach, Lettuce and Mustard. It is more work however.

How: Prepare the gel by mixing a tablespoon of cornstarch into a cup of water. Bring this to a boil, stir thoroughly to dissolve the powder and then allow it to cool. Put half the gel in a bowl, add the pre-germinated seeds and cover with the rest of the gel. Finally stir the mix very gently to spread the seed evenly throughout the gel. If you can't plant the seeds immediately they can be stored in the fridge in the gel for several days.

Planting the seeds: Pour the gel into a plastic bag, cut off one of the bottom corners to make a tiny hole and squeeze globs of gel and seeds out at the desired spacing. You can sow the seed in furrows, or directly on the surface, for later covering with cover soil.

It is important that gel sown seed beds be watered regularly. If the soil dries out, it can cause the gel to dry up and trap the seed. This is the commonest cause of failure when fluid sowing.

Seed planting

Depth

The depth seeds are planted affects how well they grow. If they are planted too deeply they won't germinate well for lack of oxygen, or they will waste energy getting to the surface. If they are planted too shallowly there is a danger they may dry out if not watered conscientiously. The general rule is to plant at a depth of 2 to 4 times the least diameter of the seed. The shallower measure is used in cold spring soil and the deeper one in warm summer soil.

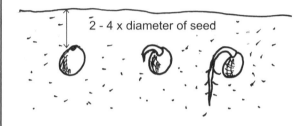

It is important that the depth of planting be consistent. If it varies a lot then germination may be uneven, some seeds appear before others, some get buried so deeply they don't appear at all and those near the surface may die from dehydration.

Density

The density of sowing is determined by several factors.

- The desired spacing at maturity (see **Spacing** for more on this).

- The vigor of the seed (especially the germination percentage), which affects how many of the seeds you plant will actually grow into viable plants.

- Whether you will thin the plants at a later date and how much thinning you are prepared to do.

- The accuracy of the person doing the seeding. Often you end up scattering more seeds than you really intend.

- An old rule of thumb for direct sowing says you should direct sow four times as many seeds as you want plants

Planting methods

Broadcast sowing

This is most often used for planting large numbers of small seeded, closely spaced, plants such as Carrot, Spinach or Mustard and for growing leaf salad crops. The theory is simple enough, seed is simply scattered onto the soil. The hard part is getting the seed evenly distributed and at the right density. It takes a little practice to get this right and you will have to experiment to find the technique that works best for you.

I broadcast the seed by moving my arm steadily back and forth, while shaking the seeds slowly off the side of my hand. You can also take pinches of seed from your palm and sprinkle them with your other hand. Usually you won't be sowing large areas, so you can afford to take your time. Very fine seed can be mixed with sand to make it easier to spread, or it can be placed in a saltshaker (or both).

When broadcasting you should pay particular attention to the edges of the bed, as these tend to get less seeds than the middle. Start by sowing these areas very deliberately and then fill in the center.

Don't scatter too many seeds on the first pass, you don't want to sow too thickly. It's easy to make a second pass to add more seed, but difficult to thin out seed already on the ground. Most people tend to sow too thickly initially and have to do a lot of thinning, so be somewhat conservative. Over-sowing wastes seed, crowds the seedlings and necessitates a lot of extra work thinning.

If you have difficulty getting an evenly distributed bed try dividing your seed into four parts and sow the same area four times. I find light colored seeds show up better if I water the bed first, as it darkens the soil and gives more contrast.

Covering: The broadcast seeds are buried at the right depth by covering them with a thin layer of sifted soil mix. It is important that this covering be of an even depth, otherwise seed germination may be uneven as well.

You can use almost anything for cover soil, old flat mix from growing transplants is good, or you can make it from a mixture of equal part of compost and soil. It is good to use cover soil on poorly structured soils as it reduces the potential for crusting.

The cover soil is scattered over the bed in a thin layer, by gently shaking a spadeful of mix over the bed (or by tapping your spade) so it falls off of the side in a fine shower. Keep the spade in constant motion to distribute the soil evenly.

If you don't want to use cover soil you can use a rake to create a series of small furrows, each the width of a rake tine. Broadcast your seed onto to this and then use the back of the rake to pull the soil from the ridges to the furrows.

A rougher and quicker method is to broadcast the seeds first and then use a rake to systematically churn up the top layer of soil. This technique is most often used for covering soil improving crops.

There is a saying... "**over-sow and under-cover**".

When the seeds have all germinated and are growing well you will have to go back and thin them to the required spacing.

Row sowing

There are advantages to sowing in rows (or drills), rather than broadcasting. It is easier to tell the crop from the weeds when they are in a line. Also it is easier to get between the plants with a hoe, so there is less need for hand weeding (you may even be able to use a wheel hoe).

Rows work best for large crops (beans, peas, corn), that are grown in closely spaced rows down the length of the bed. However they can also be used for smaller plants, you simply make more rows. You can even use them for tiny seeds (such as carrots) by simply sowing lines of seed on the bed and covering them with cover soil.

Begin by making a furrow of the appropriate width, depth and length with the edge of a rake or hoe. If the rows follow the bed you may want to use two stakes and a line to keep the row straight (dig the furrow as you walk backward down the row). If the rows run across the bed (useful when succession sowing) lay a stick or board across the bed and run a trowel or hoe along the edge to make a straight line.

The next step is to drop the seed into the furrow at the appropriate distance apart. Large seeds are the easiest to plant, as it's easy to estimate the distance between them. Small seeds can be sown by tearing a corner off the envelope and tapping out seed at the required density into the furrow. They can also be sown by taking pinches between the thumb and forefinger

After sowing you re-fill the furrow by simply dragging the back of a rake along the ground at an angle. If the soil is poor and crusts easily you might re-fill with a compost / soil mix (see **Broadcasting**). In dry areas where water is scarce it's common practice to irrigate the furrow before planting, then sow the seed and fill the furrow with dry soil (this has a dust mulch effect).

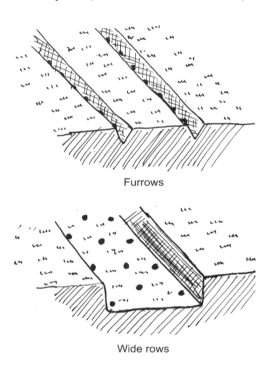

Furrows

Wide rows

If you make the furrow slightly deeper and don't re-fill it completely, you can cover the furrow with plastic to create a mini- greenhouse to hasten germination (raise one side of the furrow slightly higher than the other so rain is shed, rather than collecting in the furrow.

When planting slow germinating crops such as Carrots some people sow a few Radish seeds along with the Carrots to mark the row, so you can see where not to hoe.

Row sowing lends itself to mechanization and there are some good seed planting machines available. However I rarely find it worthwhile to use my machine because I usually only plant small areas at one time.

It is a good idea to sow a few extra seeds at the end of a row, so you have extra plants to fill in any gaps resulting from poor germination or predation.

When the seeds have all germinated and are growing well you will have to go back and thin them to the required spacing.

Equidistant sowing
This spaces the plants equidistantly all across the bed. The simplest way to do this is to make short rows across the bed.

Sow large seeds in alternate rows, so they are all an equal distance apart. Smaller seeds have been planted through a chicken wire frame to get the right spacing, or various jigs may be used (see **Spacing** for more on this).

Hill sowing
This is most often used for large trailing crops that require lots of room, such as Melons and Cucumbers. It's also good for growing crops such as Corn or Tomatoes without irrigation in dry climates (where plants must be spaced far apart to ensure they get enough moisture).

Dig a large 12″ deep hole, fill it half full of compost or other suitable fertilizer mix and replace the soil to leave a slight mound. Then make a dimple in the top of this (to hold water) and sow the seed (6 or so in the case of Cucurbits). When these are growing vigorously you thin out the weaker plants to leave only the best 3. The mound improves drainage and allows the soil to heat up faster. In hot dry areas this isn't always desirable, in which case you can flatten out the topsoil to have a flat "hill".

After you plant

Firming the soil
Traditionally gardeners used to firm down the soil with the back of a rake (or by walking on it) after planting. The idea was to ensure good contact between the soil and seeds so they get sufficient moisture. This isn't a good idea because it compacts the soil, so don't do it. It's much better to simply water the beds to get good contact.

Labelling
I've mentioned before about how important it is to label your crops clearly in the beds. The first thing you should do after planting is to write out a label with the name and variety of the crop and the date planted. Put this in the bed so it marks out the section you just planted. It's also a good idea to record this information in your garden journal in case the label gets lost or moved (if you have young children or inquisitive dogs they often do).

Support
If your plants are going to need the support of stakes, cages or trellises, it's best to set them up before planting. It's easy to damage young plants if you do it after they have emerged. See **Bed Preparation** for more on this.

Protection
Young seedlings often require protection from predators of various kinds, though the need for this varies enormously with place and time. Sometimes an unprotected bed of seedlings will be completely untouched, while at other times it may be completely wiped out. It all depends on the abundance of predators and the availability of alternative foods.

Birds are commonly a problem in early spring, when they eat newly germinated seedlings and seeds. Slugs and snails can also be a major nuisance any time, often mowing down everything as it emerges. Mice will dig and eat newly planted peas and beans (I once found a cache of Fava beans in my greenhouse, taken from a flat by a mouse). Cutworms specialize in eating young seedlings and are a common pest. Row covers are a simple way to deal with many of these pests. See **Pests** for other ways to solve these problems.

In urban areas cats can be a big problem, as they see your carefully prepared and planted bed as a lovely big litter box. One way to deter them is to lay some thorny twigs (the more vicious the spines the better) over the planted area (Black Locust twigs work great).

If birds are a problem you must have a workable system to keep them out. Netting is very effective, but is a real pain to erect and deal with. Don't neglect this protection, as birds can quickly destroy a whole planting.

Watering seed beds

Until the seeds are up and growing you must monitor the seedbed carefully and water regularly. Seeds can't start to germinate until they get all the water they need and once they have started to grow any disruption in their water supply will set them back, or even kill them.

Careful watering is another aspect of getting an evenly spaced stand. Water too heavily and you can wash seeds away, resulting in bare patches. Irregular watering can have the same result, as areas of seeds (or seedlings) die from lack of water.

A general rule for watering seedbeds is that when 50% of the surface of the bed has dried out it should be watered (this may be every few hours in hot sunny weather). Obviously the frequency of watering varies greatly according to soil type, the weather and planting depth.

It would be easy if you could just keep the bed wet all the time, but you then run the risk of waterlogging the soil and killing the seeds by depriving them of oxygen. This is particularly important in cold soil when excess water takes longer to evaporate, and seeds are slower to germinate and more prone to rot. A sign of over-watering is when the surface of the soil grows a coat of green algae. This isn't usually a serious problem, but could (at least in theory) seal the surface of the soil and prevent good air exchange.

The way to give your seed beds the even supply of moisture they require is by frequent shallow hand watering. You can use a watering can, a wand, or a hose, just make sure it has a fine rose which puts out a very light shower of water. This won't compact the soil surface, cause crusting, or wash away the seeds (causing bare spots).

In hot weather you may want to reduce the frequency of watering (and save water) by temporarily covering the soil with row covers (such as reemay), cloth, or cardboard. This keeps the soil cool and slows evaporation. Of course it must be removed as soon as the seedlings begin to emerge.

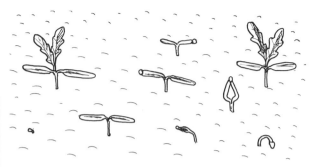

Pre-emergence weeding

It's possible to start your weed control program before your crop has even appeared, by pre-emergence weeding. There are several ways to do this.

A few days before you expect your seedlings to emerge (3 to 21 days after sowing, depending on the crop) lightly scrape a spring rake across the bed to kill any weeds that have already emerged. This will give your about-to-emerge seedlings a slight head start on the weeds. With some crops (notably Corn) you can even do this after the shoots have emerged, they won't be harmed if they are still small.

An even better pre-emergence weeding technique is flame weeding. This is most often used for slow growing, less competitive, crops such as Carrot (it's widely used for commercial organic Carrot growing), Parsley and Parsnip. A couple of days before you expect the seedlings to emerge, a flame is moved quickly across the bed to kill all newly emerged seedlings. A significant benefit of this method is that the soil isn't disturbed, so no new weed seeds are brought to the surface where they can germinate (as often happens with other forms of weeding). The big disadvantage is that you need specialized equipment and fuel (see **Weeds** for more on Flame weeding.

Yet another method of pre-emergence weeding is by sowing seeds under tape. The seed is sown in drills in the usual way, then the drill is covered with a strip of opaque paper (such as cash register or drywall tape) which is weighed down with a little soil. A day or so before you expect the seedlings to emerge you remove the paper, exposing the weed seeds that have already germinated. These will be elongated and chlorotic from the darkness and will die when exposed to strong sunlight, leaving a weed free strip of soil for your seedlings to emerge into. The weeds between these strips are hoed in the usual way.

Emergence

Most crop seedlings take from 3 to 28 days to emerge. There are so many variables in direct sowing that germination can be unpredictable. It's not uncommon to end up with some areas of a bed sown too thinly and other areas sown too thickly. Don't be too hasty to judge a planting, seeds will continue to germinate for a week or more and some seeds may be killed by pests.

Too Thin: If emergence is very sparse you have several options.

*   You can re-sow the thin areas. This is fine with fast germinating seeds, but wastes a lot of time with slower ones.

*   If the crop tolerates transplanting you can move plants from the denser spots to the thinner ones.

*   You could fill in the bare spots with transplants of another crop

*   Another alternative is to live with it. Many beds look terrible, but still produce a lot of food.

Too thick: If emergence is good and the stand is too dense you will have to thin vigorously. Excess plants are essentially weeds that will compete with your crop and must be removed promptly. See **Thinning** below.

Too irregular: If emergence is very irregular (this often happens with slow germinating seed), then the first seedlings to emerge have such a head start they will grow much more rapidly than the rest and take up more than their fair share of space. They also mature earlier than the rest, which may be okay if a staggered harvest is desirable, but it can be a problem if you need uniform maturation.

Thinning

When it's time to thin you start to appreciate the importance of good sowing technique, as a well sown bed only needs minimal thinning. However it's easy to accidentally over-sow and end up with a dense turf of seedlings.

When: Thinning (and weeding) is best done on cloudy days, or in the evening, when the soil is moist. Generally the earlier you thin the better, especially if the plants are very crowded, as they soon start to compete with each other. It's also easier to thin when the plants are small. If you get them early enough you can actually thin with a rake, ripping out large numbers of plants very quickly. If they are too big for this you will have to do it by hand, which can be quite time consuming. If plants are very close together it is usually better to pinch off the tops, rather than uprooting them and disturbing their neighbors.

Some gardeners thin out in two stages, as sometimes not all the plants you leave behind will make it (if slugs or snails are very bad you may want to thin in three stages). The first thinning concentrates on overly dense clumps and stunted, damaged, diseased or otherwise inferior plants, but leaves about twice as many plants as are needed (plants are gregarious and like to grow up with companions nearby). The second thinning occurs when the plants are really getting going and the leaves are starting to touch. This leaves only the best plants at the desired final spacing. At this stage you may be able to use the larger thinnings in the kitchen.

How: When thinning you normally leave the best plants behind and remove the inferior ones. Sometimes you have to compromise though, choosing a slightly inferior plant because it is better placed and removing whole clusters of good but crowded plants. If plants are very crowded you have to be ruthless, tearing out plants by the handful (this is no job for the timid). This may seem drastic, but I can't emphasize enough how important it is to thin adequately.

Weeding

Weeds are usually the biggest problem of direct sown beds and must be kept under control. Weed seeds germinate faster than most crop seeds and their seedlings grow faster (a 3 week old Amaranth may have a root network 5 times as large as a Lettuce of the same age.) Weeds start to compete with crop plants for moisture and nutrients about 3 weeks after the crop emerges and if unchecked may smother them completely. The initial weeding and thinning are usually dealt with in the same operation. Ideally you then weed every 10 days or so.

If you are really organized you can get a jump on weeds by actually weeding before the crop germinates. See **Pre- emergence weeding**.

After thinning and weeding

After you have finished weeding and thinning you should remove all of the dead plants to the compost pile. Don't leave them laying on the ground. In some cases the scent of a decaying plant may attract pests (notably the Carrot and its notorious Rust Fly). The remaining plants should be watered to help them recover. No matter how careful you are, some plant roots are inevitably damaged when you uproot their neighbors.

Watering seedlings

After the seedlings have emerged, you can reduce the frequency of watering. Allow the top inch or so of soil to dry out before watering again. This encourages their roots to go deeply into the soil in search of water. As the plants get larger you slowly reduce the frequency of watering, but water more deeply, until you are watering as for transplants (see **Watering** for more on this).

Feeding

Newly emerged seedlings don't have a very high demand for nutrients and can satisfy their relatively modest requirements from the soil without any additional feeding. However if the soil isn't very good (or still cold - which makes many nutrients unavailable) you may want to give them a boost once they have started to grow quickly. The best way to do this is with a foliar fertilizer. See **Foliar and Liquid Fertilizing**.

Remember:

"Not too early, not too deeply, not too thickly".

"Over sow and under cover".

Problems

If you follow all of the steps outlined above and still don't produce a healthy crop of seedlings, here are a few possible explanations.

No seeds: This sounds really stupid, but sometimes the seeds don't get planted. This most often happens when more than one person tends the garden, each person thinking someone else did it. You can usually tell when seed wasn't planted because the surface isn't raked, or there is no cover soil on it (cover soil is quite distinctive).

The seeds may have been planted, but eaten by birds and rodents before they have a chance to germinate. This is most common in early spring when food is scarce

No germination: Poor quality seed with a low germination percentage is sometimes responsible for this. Make sure you use good seed (do a germination test if necessary).

Seedlings eaten: Slugs and other small creatures may eat the seedlings as they emerge. This can look a lot like no germination. This is one of the biggest problems with direct sowing (See **Pests** for more on this).

Too dry: The germinating seeds didn't get enough water at some point and died. Perhaps watering was irregular. This may sometimes seem like poor quality seed that just didn't germinate.

Too wet: If the soil is wet all of the time the seeds may rot (especially if it's also cold).

Too cold: In cold soil germination may be so slow that seed rots before it can germinate (especially if it's also wet). This is a common problem when planting warm weather crops such as beans. It is important to wait for the soil to warm up sufficiently before planting. You can hasten this by covering the soil with plastic sheeting. or cloches, for a couple of weeks before planting.

Too warm: The seed of some cool weather crops (especially Lettuce) won't germinate if the soil is too warm. You can try cooling the soil with water or shade cloth, or pre-germinate the seed in a cooler place.

17 Crop spacing

The importance of correct spacing

It is important that plants are spaced the right distance apart. Too far apart and space is wasted, too close together and they compete with each other. Every garden book and seed catalog tells you how far apart to plant the various vegetable crops. These recommended spacings are useful relative to one another, but they may be altered in reality by a number of factors.

- The most important factor is soil fertility. The better the soil, the more nutrients are readily available and the closer you can space your plants.

- In poor soil you must compensate for the fact that there are less nutrients in the soil, by spacing the plants further apart. This ensures that each plant has enough volume of soil in which to forage for nutrients.

- After all needs for nutrients are met, competition for light becomes the main factor affecting plant growth. If plants are too close together they eventually start to compete for light. When this happens they grow tall and leggy and often fall over.

- If plants are too close together air circulation may be inhibited. This encourages high humidity and in wet climates can increase the potential for disease.

- Plants can be spaced more closely together in winter, as they grow more slowly and don't get as large. The closer spacing promotes the earlier formation of a microclimate and means less area to cover with cloches or row covers.

- Water isn't usually a limiting factor in intensive beds, because its fairly easy to replace that consumed. However in arid areas where water is scarce, water becomes as valuable as any other nutrient. You then have to space plants further apart, to ensure each individual has enough volume of soil in which to forage for water, without having to compete with neighbors. In the arid Southwest Native Americans sometimes planted their Corn 6 feet apart each way.

Other factors that affect spacing

There may be other criteria to take into account when deciding spacing, for example weeding. If your soil is very weedy, you might want to compromise on highest yield to save a lot of tedious hand weeding. You then space the plants far enough apart to allow you to hoe between them. The variety used also affects spacing, some are more compact than others.

Too close spacing

Intensive gardening books often emphasize how close you can space crops with these methods, but such close spacing requires exceptionally fertile soil. If you don't have such soil then you need to give your plants more room. If you have ever put plants too close together you will be familiar with the result. They look great while they are small, but eventually start to compete with each other and get tall and leggy. Water on the leaves makes them top heavy and they may be blown over by the wind.

Overcrowding can also cause nutrient deficiencies as roots compete for nutrients. In humid areas the poor air circulation around the leaves may encourages disease.

If you are lucky you might get a harvest from such plants, but usually not very much. It's much better to lose some yield by planting too far apart than to lose the lot by planting too close together.

Optimal spacing

In the rich deep soil of an intensive bed, roots can go straight down in search of nutrients. This means they don't need to compete with neighboring plants by sending out side roots. Consequently you can put the plants closer together than you could in a conventional row garden. Ideally crops should be planted so their foliage barely touches when they are mature. This creates a cool moist microclimate around the plants that inhibits moisture evaporation and is very conducive to good growth. If plants are closer together than this they inhibit each other, if they are further apart space is wasted and you don't get the microclimate effect.

The way to determine the optimal spacing for a crop, is to experiment with growing it at many different spacings and see what happens. Spacing plants far apart produces very large individual plants, but gives a low total yield for a given area, because there are so few plants. Closer spacing increases yield because there are more plants in the area. At a certain point the size of the individual plant starts to go down slightly, but because there are more plants in the area the yield continues to rise. Finally you get to a point where so many individual plants are packed into the area that they start to inhibit each other and yield declines.

Planting options

The spacing you use for a crop will determine how big the final harvest will be. There are several options:

- You might choose to grow a maximum number of full size plants, and sacrifice some yield, by spacing them quite far apart. This was how traditional row spacing worked, giving large individual plants, but wasting a lot of space. As a consequence the yield per square foot was relatively low. Plants that need lots of space include the Cucurbits (sprawling or bushy), Tomatoes (prone to disease if they don't get good air circulation) and Brussels Sprouts (need a lot of light to mature properly).

- To get the maximum harvest of full size plants, put them in offset rows, close enough together that they actually touch when they reach full size. This will give you the maximum number of full size plants for the area.

- The way to get the biggest harvest of all is to make do with slightly smaller mature plants, but have a lot more of them. You do this by planting them closer together, as I have just described. Some plants lend themselves to very close spacings by their shape and growth habits, such as Onion, Leek, Garlic, Celery and Carrot.

- The ultimate in close spacing is growing salad greens for individual leaves.

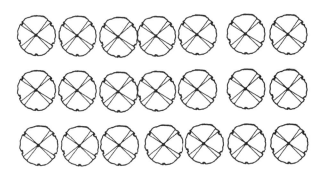

Wasted space on all sides

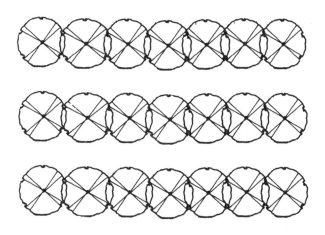

Wasted space on two sides and competition on the others

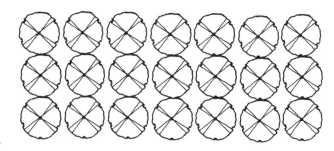

A much more efficient arrangement

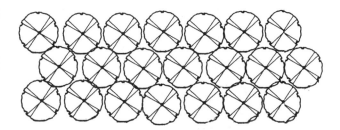

Offset rows are the most efficient way to space plants

Spacing patterns

Spacing doesn't merely involve the distance between plants in rows. One of the keys to maximizing productivity is to space the plants equidistantly over the soil, so they can take advantage of all of the available sunlight, water and nutrients and to minimize competition between individuals. This is in contrast with row crops, where plants are often crowded on two sides and have more space than they need on the other two.

The important measurement for spacing isn't the distance between plants, but rather the space the plant fills, which is a circle. By offsetting the circles (plants) you can make the most of limited space. Rows only need to be 5″ apart to get the desired 6″ spacing between individuals.

Planting in offset rows has an additional benefit of making hoeing easier. You simply run the hoe diagonally across the bed, between the rows of young plants, in both directions.

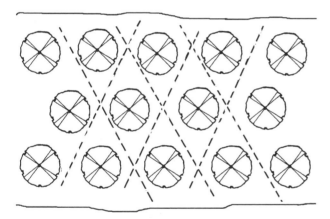

Space plants carefully for easier hoeing

Not all crops lend themselves to equidistant spacing, some do better, or are more conveniently grown, in rows or hills. Climbing vines are most easily supported if grown in rows down the bed. Very large crops may take up almost the whole width of the bed.

Keeping consistent spacing

Once you have decided upon the ideal spacing you must use it. This means spacing the plants consistently in the bed. It's no good deciding that a 9″ spacing is optimal and then setting out your plants at varying distances from 6″ to 12″ (it's happens frequently).

There are several ways to ensure you get the right spacing and stay with it. You could measure the length of your trowel or hand (measure the lengths to different points), or make a pre-measured stick (break it off to the right length). You might also make a ruler from an eight foot length of 1″ x 3″, marking off the required lengths. You then simply lay the ruler alongside the bed and put in plants at the right measurement. Some people make triangles or other jigs to ensure they get the right spacing. Once you get good at planting you will probably space the plants by eye, as it's faster and you don't need any special tools.

Crop spacing chart

Spacing recommendations may be altered by many factors, but it helps to have some guideline, so here is my chart. If you want to grow something not listed here try using the in-row spacing on the seed packet.

Crop	Poor soil	Avg soil	Rich soil	Rows
Amaranth, Leaf	8″	6″	4″	
Artichoke	72″			
Asparagus	24″	18″	12″	
Basil	8″	6″	4″	
Bean, Bush	6″	4″	3″	4″ x 18″
Bean, Fava	12″	8″	6″	4″ x 18″
Bean, Pole	8″	6″	4″	
Bean, Lima	10″	8″	6″	
Bean, Runner	15″	12″	9″	
Beet	6″	4″	3″	
Broccoli	18″	15″	12″	
Brussels sprout	30″	25″	20″	
Cabbage, Head	18″	15″	12″	
Cabbage, Leaf	8″	6″	4″	3″ x 15″
Carrot	5″	3″	1.5″	
Cauliflower	24″	21″	18″	
Celery	12″	9″	6″	
Chard	12″	8″	6″	
Chicory	12″	10″	8″	
Corn	18″	15″	12″	
Cucumber	24″	18″	12″	12″x 36″
Eggplant	24″	18″	15″	
Florence Fennel	12″	8″	6″	8″ x 12″
Garlic	10″	8″	6″	3″ x 12″

Crop	Poor soil	Avg soil	Rich soil	Rows
Kale	18″	15″	12″	
Kohlrabi	12″	6″	4″	
Leek	12″	9″	6″	5″ x 12″
Lettuce, Head	15″	12″	9″	
Lettuce, Leaf	12″	8″	6″	
Melon	24″	18″	15″	
Mustard	8″	6″	4″	
Onion, Bulb	6″	4″	2.5″	2″ x 8″
Onion,	4″	2.5″	1″	1″ x 6″
Parsley	6″	4″	3″	2″ x 10″
Parsnip	5″	4″	3″	2″ x 12″
Pea, Bush	5″	4″	3″	
Pea, Pole	5″	4″	3″	
Pepper	24″	18″	12″	
Pumpkin	36″	24″	18″	
Potato	16″	12″	9″	
Radish	4″	2″	1″	1″ x 4″
Shallot	8″	6″	4″	
Spinach	8″	6″	4″	
Squash, Summer	30″	24″	18″	
Squash, Winter	36″	30″	24″	
Tomato	30″	24″	18″	
Turnip	8″	5″	3″	3″ x 10″

18 Growing Transplants

Using transplants

Many crops do better when grown as transplants, rather than being sown directly into the ground. This involves a considerable amount of extra work, but offers a number of significant advantages that usually make it worthwhile.

Advantages

The use of transplants (rather than direct sowing) is an integral part of intensive vegetable growing. Learning how to grow the plants from seed is one of the most useful and rewarding gardening skills you can acquire. Using transplants has a number of advantages.

*   Raising transplants allows you to get a jump on the season. In cold climates you can start plants inside a lot earlier than you could sow them outside. They will also grow a lot faster in the warm conditions of the greenhouse than they would outside. When the weather warms up sufficiently for good growth, you can then set out vigorously growing plants rather then merely seeds (which would take several weeks just to reach transplant size).

*   Some crops (Eggplant, Peppers, Celery) are very slow to get started. If your growing season is short often the only way to grow them is to start them inside (where they may spend 2 or 3 months of their lives).

*   Tender little seedlings are more easily protected in the greenhouse than outdoors. By the time they go out as transplants they are much better able to withstand cold, wind, weeds and the depredations of garden creatures. This is particularly important for slow germinating and growing crops.

*   Raising transplants makes for more efficient use of space and time. It is a way to increase food production in small gardens by decreasing the time a crop occupies bed space (which gives you time for more crops). For the time the seedlings are growing to transplant size (3 months in some cases) you are in essence growing two crops at the same time, the end of one overlapping with the start of the other.

*   Some plants actually benefit from transplanting. Apparently the damage caused to their long feeder roots during transplanting, is a kind of pruning and encourages them to form bushier and stronger new roots.

*   Starting seedlings indoors conserves water. It takes a lot of water to keep a seed bed uniformly moist, but only a little to keep a flat of seeds moist.

*   Because it's easier to control indoor growing conditions you tend to lose less plants. This means you get more plants from a packet of seed, which can be important with difficult, rare, or expensive seed.

*   You can mulch transplants immediately, making them ideal for no-dig gardens.

*   Transplants can give you a better stand of plants, because you only set out the best, most advanced and uniform seedlings. The inferior plants are discarded

*   Using transplants can give your winter cover crops a little extra time in the ground. This can be significant because such crops can put on quite a lot of growth in two or three weeks of mild spring weather.

*   Raising your own transplants is more economical than buying them. It's possible to grow hundreds (or thousands) of dollars worth of plants for very little money. This may be the only way to make the garden you want economically feasible (you could easily raise 500 Delphiniums, 300 Carnations, 400 Hollyhocks if you wanted). Of course if you are growing vegetables to save money then raising your own transplants becomes almost essential.

*   Raising transplants is one of the most interesting, challenging and fun aspects of gardening. I find myself visiting my greenhouse far more often than

I really need to, looking to see what has emerged, what finally looks like it will make it, what has died (yes I do lose a seedling every few years). I also go in just to admire their beauty. There is something very satisfying about a healthy young plant that was a tiny seed just a short while ago.

- When you raise your own transplants you always have plants ready to go out into the garden. If you purchase your transplants you are dependent upon their availability. This is particularly significant for autumn crops, as many transplants are only available in spring and early summer.

Disadvantages

- When you transplant a seedling from a flat, some root damage inevitably occurs, especially to the minute feeder roots. When this happens the plant can't take up all the water it needs, so it closes its stomata to conserve water. This means the plant can't transpire, so it must stop growing until it has replaced the lost roots. This interruption is known as transplant shock and inevitably sets the plant back for a while. If a plant loses more than half of its roots it isn't merely shocked, it may die, or be so damaged that it is more susceptible to pests and disease.

- The plants that transplant most easily are those that have the capacity to replace damaged roots quickly. Such crops may actually benefit from transplanting, as mentioned above. Those that can't do this very well are traditionally direct sown. Obviously when transplanting you must do everything possible to minimize root damage and hence transplant shock. Fortunately there are now ways to raise even the most sensitive transplants with no root disturbance, so this isn't a serious problem.

- Raising transplants involves quite a bit more work than direct sowing, so it must give you a significant advantage to be worthwhile. Usually crops that need to be started early, grow slowly, are vulnerable to predation or germinate poorly are started inside, where you can give them optimal conditions for growth. There is less advantage with fast germinating and growing crops such as the Cucurbits, Beans, Peas and Corn.

- Raising transplants is more expensive and involved than direct sowing, because you need pots, sowing mix, labels, as well as somewhere to start them. However it doesn't have to cost that much if you use your imagination and recycled materials. A seed starting setup will last for many years and soon pays for itself in healthy plants.

- Young seedlings require daily attention and if you neglect them they will suffer. If you forget to (or can't) water them on a hot day they may die and a lot of time and effort can be lost. This means someone has to keep an eye on them continuously. They also need looking after for quite a while, several months in some cases.

Buying transplants

Growing your own transplants involves a significant commitment. If you really don't have the time or facilities to grow your own, or it just doesn't work out for some other reason, then you always have the option of buying them.

Buying plants can work out well so long as you are discriminating as to what crops to buy. Concentrate on plants that are hard to start or take a long time to get going, such as Tomatoes, Peppers, Onions and Eggplant. There is little point in buying easily raised, or fast growing, crops such as Corn, Beans, Peas, Cucumbers or Squash.

There are a few potential drawbacks to buying plants.

Pests: There is a danger of importing pests and diseases into your garden on purchased transplants.

Organic: Most commercial seedlings are grown with synthetic chemicals, so aren't organic.

Cost: In the long run it's a lot more expensive to buy plants, than it is to grow your own.

Varieties: There is a much more limited selection of varieties when you are buying seedlings.

What to look for when buying transplants

The quality of commercial transplants and the care they receive varies a great deal. Generally the best plants (and the most expensive) come from nurseries, where the staff know what they are doing and look after them with care. The worst plants (and the cheapest) come from the big chain stores. These have often been transported long distances and aren't always looked after adequately.

- Good transplants are short and stocky and deep green in color. Some crops should be nearly as wide as they are tall. Avoid tall leggy seedlings.

- Avoid plants with tops that are too large for the size of the pot, the roots are probably pot bound (pop one out of its cell and check it).

- Avoid plants that are already bearing flowers or fruit, they are too old. Not only they have they been around too long, but once a plant starts to flower it puts all of its energy into producing seed and so root growth slows down. It is then less able to replace damaged roots quickly and suffers more severely from transplant shock. Don't be tempted by those 18″ high Tomato plants that already have fruit on them, they won't perform as well as smaller transplants (and are a lot more expensive).

- It is important to check for visible signs of disease, damage, or insects (such as Whitefly), especially at growing points and under the leaves. Do they look deficient, are the leaves yellowish or reddish, or are they deep green in color?

- You can often get extra plants by choosing cells that haven't been thinned properly.

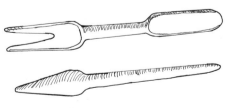

Dibber and widger

Equipment for seedling production

If you are creative it is possible to raise fine healthy seedlings with very little money or equipment, but spending a little money on quality equipment can make things easier. Here is a list of the stuff you will need and a few things you might want:

Labels: Good labels are essential. It is very easy to forget the name of a variety if you don't write it down so. Don't buy labels, you can easily make them from scrap wood or some garbage. At present I'm using strips cut from plastic yogurt cartons (any other similar plastic container would also be good). Permanent labels for perennials can be made from strips of disposable aluminum pie tins (or soda cans) and some wire. Write on them with a pencil, or an old ballpoint pen that has run out of ink.

Marking pens: You can use any kind of pen or pencil so long as it is waterproof. Wax pencils, laundry markers or special nursery pens are all good. Regular pens and lead pencils seem to write fine initially, but slowly wash off plastic labels until they are illegible. I found this out the hard way, when the writing on all of my labels became invisible.

Seed dispensing tool: Probably most gardeners get along fine with the folded envelope and tapping finger technique, but I find a seed dispenser useful for sowing fine seeds. I first bought a plastic click seeder because it was on sale and I love gadgets, but initially it irritated me with its click and hurt my thumb so I didn't use it much. However I now find myself using it for almost all small seeds, from Brassica size on down. There are a number of other patented dispensing tools available.

You may find it helpful to have a pair of tweezers on hand, so you can move seeds around if you drop too many in one place.

Pricking out tools: I use a tiny commercially made plastic dibber and a pronged pricking out tool called a widger. Since I got them all the silverware (the old standby) has gone back to the kitchen. It doesn't take long to get used to using a certain tool for a job and then you don't feel right without it.

Essentials for seed germination

Light

Light is probably the most crucial factor in producing healthy plants, if you can't give your seedlings adequate light, you are wasting your time. Light isn't usually needed for germination (except for a few plants), but it's vital from the moment the plants first seed leaves (cotyledons) appear. If emerging seedlings don't have enough light they will stretch and stretch to seek more light and the result will be spindly leggy plants. Light deprived plants are also more vulnerable to pests, diseases and other stresses, because low light means less food production.

Uneven light can also be a problem because it causes plants to lean towards the brightest direction. Serious leaning and stretching indicates insufficient light and must be corrected or your plants will be worthless. Plants sometimes lean slightly in winter greenhouses due to low light levels. If this happens simply flip the plant container around 180° and they will lean back toward vertical. If light is less than ideal, slightly cooler temperatures can help offset the adverse effect.

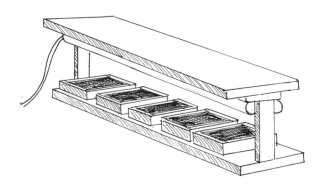

Light sources

There are a number of ways to make sure your seedlings get enough light.

Sunny windows can work quite well as mini greenhouses, though the plants commonly lean out toward the source of strongest light. You can increase light reflection on the inside of the window with mirrors or aluminum foil. Another drawback is that windowsills can get quite cold at night.

In very cold climates your only option may be to start your seeds indoors (where it's warm) under artificial light. Of all the types of artificial light commonly available the white (or warm white) fluorescent bulbs are most often used, as they come closest to natural light. Ordinary incandescent lights aren't suitable because they produce too much heat and their light is too much in the red wavelengths. There are now natural light incandescents that may be better. There are also special fluorescent grow lights available that come even closer to natural light, but they are more expensive and seedlings aren't under them long enough for this to be much of an advantage.

The commonest light setup is a pair of twin bulb four foot 40 watt fluorescent lighting fixtures (the type used in workshops) mounted on a rack. These are usually put on a timer to give the required light (day) and dark (night) periods without the inconvenience of you having to be around to turn them on and off. An 18-hour day length is usually used, as this gives you the maximum growing day length.

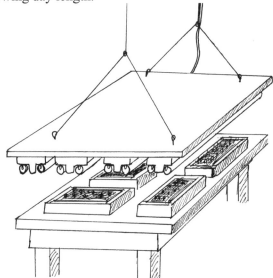

You should keep your seedlings as close to the light as possible without them actually touching it (3" is about the maximum distance). Don't mess around with movable lights, it's much easier to adjust the height of each container individually as it grows, by putting blocks underneath it.

When I moved to the milder west coast I began experimenting with inexpensive home built greenhouses. I have had such success with these that I no longer have much enthusiasm for the alternatives. For more on these structures see **Greenhouses**.

The cold frame is a poor substitute for a greenhouse, but better than nothing. It is much smaller, so heats up and cools down rapidly, so needs more careful monitoring. Also you can't go inside it in rainy weather, or to admire things. I consider the cold frame as an adjunct to a greenhouse rather than an alternative. See **Season Extension** for more on cold frames and similar devices.

Temperature
Warmth is another essential for seed germination, the warmer it is, the faster the plants will grow. If you are starting them indoors or in a heated greenhouse this is no problem, but if you are using a cool greenhouse or cold frame you may have to do some juggling to keep them warm enough. You can use soil heating cables to warm the soil and hasten germination (remember soil temperature is more critical than air temperature). You can also cover flats (or whole benches) with plastic sheeting to conserve heat (this is most useful for warm season crops, at night, or during unusually cold snaps).

You might also start the seeds in the warm indoors under lights and put the seedlings out in cooler conditions of the greenhouse or frame as soon as they are big enough. If you don't have lights you can pre-germinate indoors and then set them out in the greenhouse.

Though plants grow faster when it's warmer, this doesn't necessarily mean they are better. It is better for the plants to be slightly too cold rather than too warm (65° to 75° F is good). They may grow a little more slowly, but will be better for it (see **Seeds** for more on this). If it is too warm they may get leggy.

Sowing tips
It's important to be aware if the seeds have any special requirements for germination, such as light, extra warm or cool temperatures or stratification. This isn't the case with most vegetable crops, but is important for many shrubs, trees and wildflowers. You can easily waste time and seed by giving them the wrong conditions.

If you know the germination percentage of your seeds, you can adapt the sowing density accordingly and are less likely to end up with overpopulated or underpopulated flats. See **Seeds** for germination testing procedures.

Attention to detail
Probably no aspect of gardening is more critical than raising healthy transplants. If your transplants are of poor quality, nothing you can do for them in the garden will make up for this and your crops won't be as good as they could have been. Fortunately raising your own seedlings isn't hard and if you go about it in the right way you will be amazed at the constant stream of beautiful plants you can bring into existence.

If you are to have success with raising your own transplants you need the right equipment and materials, and must do everything at the right time. Follow the directions outlined below as closely as possible and don't take short cuts.

Sowing Quantities

Do not plant too many more seeds of a variety than you will need. I have made the mistake of over-sowing many times. The result is a cluster of plants in each cell (or flat or block) that soon start to compete with each other and show signs of nutrient deficiency. Growing crowded, stunted, deficient seedlings is a waste of seeds, time and effort, all you need is one healthy plant per cell.

You must vary the number of seeds according to the germination rate and vigor of the seeds. Generally 2 or 3 seeds per cell is plenty. When they have all emerged you then remove the excess plants, to leave only the biggest, healthiest one. An exception to this rule is when you are sowing multiple blocks (see below) and then you must be very careful to feed them as necessary.

Another mistake is sowing too much of each crop. If you only need 6 or 8 plants, there is no point in wasting container space, sowing mix and greenhouse space growing 20 or 30 plants.

A reminder: Don't plant too many seeds of each variety. Three seeds for each plant you need is enough.

Containers

Many types of containers have been used for starting seeds over the years. A competent gardener will get satisfactory results with any of the containers mentioned here. I have used them all at one time or another and use different containers for different crops. My preference is for flats and recycled cell packs.

Flats

These shallow wooden boxes are the traditional seed sowing containers and despite the introduction of some excellent alternatives they continue to be popular. This is because they are versatile, easy to make and hold a lot of plants. They can be of different depths for different crops and can also be used for pricking out.

The main drawback of flats is the considerable root disturbance during transplanting, so they are only used with plants that transplant easily. Plants that dislike transplanting should be grown in soil blocks or plug trays.

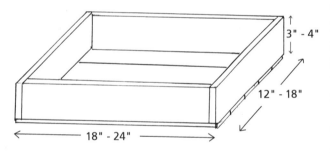

Construction: Flats are usually made with 1″ x 3″ (or 4″) sides, ½″ x 3″ bottom boards and galvanized nails. Generally a rot resistant wood such as Cedar or Redwood is best, as it lasts much longer, but I use any salvaged scrap lumber I can find. I don't really care if the flat only lasts a couple of years. If it starts to rot I simply remove the nails (for re-use in a new flat) and compost the wood.

Leave a ⅛″ gap between the bottom boards of the flat for good drainage. Flats can measure anywhere from 18″ to 24″ long and 12″ to 14″ wide, according to your preferences. Flats for sowing seeds are usually 3″ deep, those for pricking out are usually 4″ deep. A few types of seedlings also prefer the deeper flats and may bolt in shallower ones, if their roots touch the bottom. You might think it a good idea to just make them all 4″ deep, but it isn't. The flats should be filled up to the rim (for

good air circulation). This means that deeper flats are heavier and take more sowing mix.

You can buy plastic flats, but I prefer not to consume plastic. You can also use any recycled plastic, wood, or metal containers of suitable dimensions, just make sure they have enough drainage holes in the bottom. I've used the wood and cardboard boxes used to ship fruit such as grapes. They are a little deep unless you cut them down a bit, but work fine for a single planting.

Filling: Prepare flats for planting by laying a thin ½″ layer of fibrous material such as dried leaves or shredded bark in the bottom to provide drainage. Alternatively you can just put a couple of sheets of newspaper in the bottom to prevent the soil mix from falling through the cracks.

Fill the container by heaping on the appropriate mix (see **Sowing mixes** for recipes), then lightly press it down into the corners and edges with the side of your hand. Remove the excess mix by scraping a flat stick along the top edge, to leave a nice flat surface. Finally lift the flat a few inches above the ground and drop to consolidate the mix (watering the seedlings will further consolidate the mix). The surface of the soil should be almost to the top of the flat, if it's much below this air circulation is impeded and you have less depth of soil for the plants.

Sowing: Seed can either be broadcast or sown in rows. The actual spacing between the seeds depends on the crop, but ½″ to 1″ is usual. Closer than this and air circulation is inhibited which invites damping off. Further apart and you waste space, which means you need more flats, soil mix and greenhouse space.

Some people use a jig to mark furrows or dimples on the soil surface at a pre-determined spacing, I usually simply scatter it and use my judgement. The most important thing is to sow uniformly.

The seed is then covered with a thin layer (⅛″ to ¼″ depending on seed size) of sowing mix, sifted peat, or vermiculite. Experiments have shown that most seeds germinate best if not covered at all (they get more oxygen), but I find they tend to dry out quickly. I have generally had better luck when they were covered.

Fill flat. scrape off excess

Sow seeds at correct spacing

Cover with sifted cover soil

Water gently

Flats are so big it's common practice to plant more than one variety or species in a flat (it's a good way to save space and to avoid planting too much of each variety). This is fine so long as they are compatible with each other and grow at roughly the same rate (you don't want to have to prick out part of a flat, while the rest is just germinating). It is important to mark the areas of different plants clearly (I use old plastic labels or twigs to separate them). I always sow dissimilar crops side by side to make identification easier. If you have 2 varieties of the same crop side by side it won't be obvious if any seeds get mixed up (by over zealous watering or more mysterious causes).

Flat sowing mixes

These are formulated to provide the seeds with good drainage, while at the same time holding as much water as possible. They don't need to contain many nutrients. If you object to Peat Moss you could substitute leaf mold or turf loam in any of these recipes.

1 part vermiculite
1 part milled Sphagnum moss
1 part compost / leaf mold

1 part garden soil
1 part sharp sand
1 part peat moss

2 parts soil
1 part leaf mold
1 part compost

2 parts soil
1 part sand
1 part compost / peat moss

5 parts compost
4 parts soil
1 part sand
1 part leaf mold

2 parts turf loam (or loam soil)
1 part peat
1 part coarse sand

Plug Trays

Plug trays were designed as a modular growing system for commercial vegetable growers. They make it possible to transplant crops that resent disturbance (such as Cucurbits), as there is minimal root disturbance. They also lend themselves to mechanization and can be filled, sown and transplanted mechanically with minimal labor and transplant shock. They consist of plastic or Styrofoam trays, measuring about 30″ long x 10″ wide x 3″ deep and have varying numbers of cavities, depending on their size.

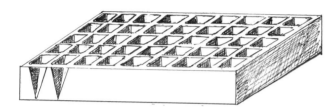

The most sophisticated plug trays have inverted pyramid shaped cavities. The idea behind this shape is that the taproot grows down though the plug of soil until it reaches the hole in the bottom and is then air pruned. The death of the tip stimulates side roots to grow, giving a bushy root mass that transplants easily.

Plug trays work very well in a mechanized and strictly monitored commercial setting, but I haven't had a lot of luck with them in my less controlled garden setting. My main objection is that the plants can dry out quickly. This is partly because there is so little soil in each cell and partly because water can't pass from one cell to another). The small volume of soil also means they need regular feeding to avoid nutrient deficiencies. They can also be hard to remove from the cells when transplanting. My final objection is that you have to buy the trays (and they are more plastic or styrofoam that you eventually have to throw away).

Filling: To prepare plug trays for planting over-fill the cavities with the specifically formulated plug tray mix, then lightly press into each segment with a finger to consolidate the soil and fill in air pockets (when you get good at this you can use all eight fingers at once). Scrape the excess mix from the top with a stick and its ready to plant.

Cell pack and plug trays mixes

These mixes need to be more moisture retentive than flat mixes because of the small volume of each cell. They also contain more nutrients than flat mixes

4 parts peat moss (+ lime)
4 parts vermiculite
2 parts compost or worm castings

2 parts compost.
1 part peat (+ lime)
1 part vermiculite

1 part compost
2 parts peat moss (+ lime)

Planting: Plant the trays by dropping 1 to 2 seeds into each compartment. If seed viability is very good then plant only one, so you don't have to thin unnecessarily. Finally cover with a light layer of mix, peat or vermiculite.

Soil Blocks

Soil blocks are fairly new in this country, but have been used for quite a while in Europe (I read a description of a gardener using them in England 50 years ago). They are a nice example of appropriate technology because they don't use any materials at all, no plastic, wood, metal or Styrofoam, just a specially formulated sowing mix. Actually you do need something to sit them on for transportation, but any board will do.

You can start anything in soil blocks, as there is no root disturbance. They are superior to plug trays in that the plants have a larger area of soil to grow in, so are less prone to drying out. Also the greater quantity of nutrients in the block means you can leave them longer before transplanting . The amount of soil in each block is so large that often more than one plant is started in each block (see **Multiple Sowing** below).

Block makers: To make soil blocks you need a special block mold to compress the specially formulated mix. These molds are available in several sizes, though you can get by with just the 2″ one. All common crops can be started in this size block, though if space is at a premium you could start them in the smaller ¾″ blocks and then transplant them (with a little adapter) to the larger ones. There is also a large 4″ block mold, but it's pretty expensive, and its just as easy to use 4″ pots. Commercial vegetable growers in Europe use automated block making machines that do everything, right down to adding the seed.

If you don't have a block maker you could make your own, using a Tomato paste can. Cut off both ends and attach them both to a dowel handle. This isn't quite as efficient as the real thing, but will work well enough.

Soil block mixes

These have to be cohesive enough to hold together when ejected from the mold. They often contain quite a lot of nutrients.

2 parts peat (+ lime)
1 part soil
1 part vermiculite

1 part compost (or leaf mold)
1 part soil

4 parts peat (+ lime)
2 parts sand
1 part soil
1 part compost

Making blocks: Measure out the pre-moistened ingredients according to one of the recipes in **Sowing**

Mixes and mix them together in a plastic tub. You want a very wet mix with the consistency of freshly mixed cement or mud, so add about 4 parts mix to 1 part water and stir thoroughly.

The key to making soil blocks lies in the moisture level of the mix. If you don't add enough water the mix will be so dry it won't fill up the mold properly, or won't eject. If you add too much water the mix may drop out of the mold prematurely, or the block may collapse when ejected. It's not a bad idea to save a little dry mix for the not unlikely event that you make it too wet initially. Some gardeners leave the prepared mix for an hour or so before making blocks to make sure the mix has absorbed all the water it can hold.

Fill the mold by pressing it into the mix 2 or 3 times. You know when it's full because surplus liquid oozes out of the top. If the mixture is deep enough you can fill the mold with one press. Scrape the mold across the top of the container to remove excess mix, put the mold on the chosen base and eject the block carefully. Rinse the mold in a bucket of water as necessary to stop the blocks sticking to them (some people do it every time).

Place the blocks close together to minimize hiding places for slugs and earwigs, but not so close that they are touching. Once the blocks are out of the mold you should handle them as little as possible, as they aren't very strong. The block becomes more cohesive as the growing roots of the plant bind it together and eventually you can handle it quite roughly without it falling apart.

The best container for holding the blocks is a flat with one long side missing (this makes it easier to slide the blocks in and out). Put the open ends of two trays together to reduce evaporation on the exposed edge. I have also used boards, plastic serving trays and odd scraps of plywood.

Planting: Sow the block by dropping the appropriate number of seeds (usually 2 to 3) into the indentation on top. Cover the seed by pinching the indentation closed, or by covering with a little peat moss (or just leave them open and be careful to keep the block moist). For seeds with very poor germination you might use the small ¾″ blocks (to save materials) and only pot on the best ones.

The blocks don't really need watering for several days, but I like to mist the surface to wet the seeds thoroughly.

Commercial cell packs

These are the thin plastic (4 to 9) segmented containers that flower and vegetable transplants are usually sold in. They are a form of plug tray, but the volume of mix they contain makes them more like soil blocks (though they don't dry out as readily and are easier to use). You can start almost anything in these containers, as they essentially eliminate the problems of root disturbance while transplanting.

I now use these for most of my seedlings because of their convenience and large volume of soil (I mostly use the larger sizes). I know I have just said that I prefer not to consume plastic and these are plastic, but I have never bought any of them. I get them for free from recycling centers, garden centers or from the side of the road (you often see them out waiting for garbage pickup).

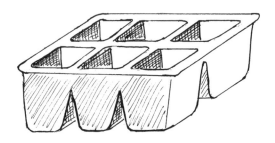

These containers are quite flimsy, but with care they can last several years (if you keep them out of the sun when you are not using them).

Filling: This is pretty straightforward, simply overfill with a plug tray type mix and scrape off the excess.

Planting: I make a light depression in the middle of each cell with a finger, put the seed (usually 1 to 2) in each depression and cover with loose mix. The larger cell packs are ideal for multi-sowing and can take up to 5 to 6 seeds in each (see **Multiple Sowing** below).

Biodegradable Peat pellets and pots

Peat pellets work on the same principle as soil blocks and are used in much the same way. They work okay, but cost more than soil blocks, often contain chemical fertilizers and have plastic netting around them (I notice that commercial growers rarely use them).

Peat pots are biodegradable containers made from compressed peat. The theory is that if you plant the pot along with the seedling there will be no shock at all. They often don't work very well in practice as seedling roots can have difficulty penetrating the walls of the pot, so they may get root bound. Also if the top of the pot is above ground it can wick water away from the plant. You can prevent the latter problem by tearing the top edge off of the pot, so that it is completely buried.

You can buy biodegradable paper pots that work much like peat pots, or you can make your own from newspaper. Simply roll a sheet of newspaper around a cylinder of the right diameter and cut it into sections of the appropriate length. Then fold over their ends and tape them down, or simply twist the end closed (or leave it open).

You can also buy a little wooden device for making paper pots. I have never tried one, but apparently they work pretty well.

Upside down turf

At one time seeds (mostly large seeded crops such as the Cucurbits) were commonly planted in sections of inverted turf. This very old technique is a forerunner of the soil block and has many of the same advantages. It is the ultimate in environmentally friendly containers because it doesn't even require a metal mould to make it. If you are ever shipwrecked on a desert island, this is the way to go.

Miscellaneous containers

Shallow plant pots are often used instead of flats for sowing small quantities of seed, especially slow germinating seeds such as trees and shrubs. Use a flat sowing mix and treat it as if you were planting small flats.

Many discarded containers can be used for growing seedlings, old paper cups, yogurt pots and milk cartons and more. The main criteria are that it hold enough sowing mix and moisture, and have good drainage Egg cartons or eggshells have been recommended by over-imaginative writers, though they are really a perfect example of what not to plant in (they are too small). Most of these containers can produce good plants and use an otherwise wasted resource. I would use these containers for pricking out if I didn't already have a good supply of old plastic 4″ plant pots. I get larger plastic plant pots from the town dump (I have to steal them though, you are not allowed to actually take anything).

Multiple sowing

Though I have emphasized the importance of having only one plant per cell or block, some plants may be grown for their whole lives in clusters of 3 to 4 (or even more). This is a useful technique to increase your output of transplants without using any extra resources or effort. You simply plants several seeds together and allow them all to mature. This can be done in multi-cell packs, soil blocks, large plug trays, individual pots, or even clusters in flats. Plants in multiple blocks are actually planted at the same density (plants per square foot) as single plants. It is just that the multi-plants are given more space between each cluster. For example if a plant is normally planted 4″ apart in rows 24″ apart, that means 2 plants would grow in a square foot. Consequently a cluster of four plants should be planted to give them two square feet of growing room.

Plants for multiple sowing

Crop	Plants per cluster	Spacing in bed in inches
Basil	3	6
Beans, pole	3	8
Beet	3	6
Broccoli	3	24
Cilantro	4	6
Corn	3	24
Cucumber	3	30
Leek	4	8
Lettuce	2	8
Onion (Bulb)	4 - 5	12
Onion (Green)	4 - 8	12
Parsley	4	6
Pea	3	6
Spinach	3 - 4	6

Seed container care

The newly planted seed containers should be kept in a warm place (ideally 65 to 80° F in the day and 10 lower at night) until the seeds have germinated. Some people cover the containers with glass or plastic to keep the seeds moist, but this isn't a good idea when using unsterilized soil mixes. The combination of moist air, warmth and lack of air circulation just invites damping off. Most seeds don't care whether it is dark or light, so if you are using lights, don't waste electricity on them until they start to germinate. Once the cotyledons appear they must be given full light.

Watering seed containers

The newly planted container should be watered thoroughly to ensure the seeds get all the moisture they need for germination. The best tool for this is a watering can or wand with an upward pointing rose that puts out a fine mist. A household spray bottle works well also. Take care that you don't apply water too quickly, as there is a danger of washing seeds around in the flat, leaving bare patches and overcrowded areas. This can be a big problem if you have more than one variety of the same crop in one container. Until the seeds have germinated you should never allow more than half of the soil surface to dry out. This is absolutely vital, if the seeds dry out they will die.

Flats: Begin watering just to the side of the container and don't make a pass over the flat until you have a good spray pattern established. Once you start moving don't stop until you have moved past the flat. If you stop, or start, over the container water will dribble down and disturb the soil. Make as many passes as you need to thoroughly moisten the container. Don't apply water any faster than it can be absorbed, otherwise it may wash seeds around, and you can wind up with bare spots and very dense spots.

Some people like to water flats from underneath, by letting them sit in a shallow pan of water until they have absorbed as much water as they can. You can also sit the containers on capillary matting (old felt carpet backing works).

Plug trays: These have to be watered very conscientiously because there is only a small quantity of soil in each cavity and water can't move sideways from one cell to another. Watch the cells at the edge of the trays in particular, because they tend to dry out faster than the rest (because they have better air circulation). Water the trays until water drips out from all of the holes underneath (they are designed to be placed on elevated racks, rather than solid tables, so you can see this).

Soil blocks: Soil blocks must be watered conscientiously because the soil isn't continuous and water can't move from one area to another. The blocks have a lot of surface area for evaporation and if you don't give them enough water they will gradually dry out over time. As with plug trays the blocks at the edge of the trays tend to dry out faster than the rest, especially if they aren't in an enclosed container. If the blocks start to dry out they gradually get harder and harder, eventually to the point where seedling roots can't penetrate their surfaces.

Blocks can be bottom watered by immersing them in a shallow pan of water and allowing them to soak up as much as they need. You can reduce the frequency of watering by setting them on capillary matting (this can be improvised from burlap or carpet padding).

Care of Seedlings

Getting seeds to germinate successfully is only the first stage in raising transplants. The next stage is looking after them, so they grow into healthy individual plants, that aren't stunted, leggy, nutrient deficient, bolted or dead.

Growing conditions

When the tiny plant first emerges from its seed case it must be looked after carefully, as it is very vulnerable. Most plants grow best at a fairly cool 55 to 70° F, so the temperature can be reduced slightly. This encourages stocky growth and discourages damping off.

The young plants most vital need is for light, without it they won't grow properly. Humidity is also important for healthy growth. Most plants like quite humid conditions, but unfortunately so do the fungi that cause Damping Off (see below for more on this). This disease can be so devastating we often have to ventilate to reduce humidity in the greenhouse.

Watering seedlings

This is one of the most critical aspects of raising seedlings and isn't simply a matter of applying lots of water. One of the commonest ways to kill seedlings is by improper watering. Under-watering is no doubt the fastest way to do this, but over-watering can be just as lethal, because of the danger of rot and damping off. Irregular watering, alternately over-watering and under-watering, isn't necessarily fatal but it can reduce growth and vigor and increase vulnerability to disease.

- One of the keys to good watering is observation. You must watch the plants carefully and learn the signs of water stress. The first of these occurs just before they start to wilt, when the leaves lose their healthy shine. By the time the leaves actually wilt the plant has stopped growing, which should be avoided whenever possible. Ideally you will always water them again before they start to lose their shine, so growth is never interrupted.

- You also have to watch the soil and note how much moisture it contains. You can allow the top ½″ of soil in the container to dry out before re-watering, to encourage roots to go deep and to prevent damping off and algal growth. When you do water be sure to thoroughly re-wet all of the soil in the container, not just the upper visible part. If you aren't conscientious the soil can slowly dry out over time. If the soil in a container starts to shrink away from the sides it is very dry and may be difficult to re-wet (bottom watering is best).

- You need to learn how much water to apply and how often. Watch how much water you need to thoroughly wet the soil, and how quickly it dries out to the point where it needs watering again. Also note how the weather affects water consumption. On very hot days you may have to water seedlings twice a day.

- You must also learn restraint to prevent over-watering. It's tempting to give them that extra dose of water "just to be sure", but continuously moist soil invites damping off. You need to be particularly careful about this on cool cloudy winter days, when water may stand around for days without evaporating (normally you don't water under such circumstances). Algae growing on the soil surface is a sign of over watering.

154

- Don't water late in the day in cool weather. Excess moisture won't have time to evaporate and will stay around all night, inviting damping off.

- Cold water shocks plants, so warm the irrigation water slightly if possible, by storing it in tanks in the greenhouse. These also serve as thermal mass and allows the chlorine to evaporate from city water. It is especially important to avoid cooling the soil in winter.

- Plants in containers outside must be watched carefully as they dry out rapidly in warm or windy conditions.

- Watering seedlings in the greenhouse in hot weather can become a chore because you need to pay attention to the plants regularly. One way around this is some kind of automatic watering system, but even that must be closely monitored to prevent under or over watering.

Thinning

When all of the seedlings have emerged and are growing vigorously, you should thin to the desired spacing. Remove the extra plants fairly promptly, along with any weed seedlings that may have appeared. Obviously you should remove the inferior seedlings where possible. Ideally you should pinch them off at soil level with your fingers or tweezers, to minimize damage to those remaining. Water after thinning to aid recovery. Proper thinning is particularly important when using plug trays.

Feeding

The mixes formulated for starting seeds are fairly low in nutrients, so older seedlings may need a feed of liquid fertilizer to keep them at optimal health. Don't wait until the plants exhibit deficiency symptoms such as yellowing or purpling of the leaves. It's best to feed lightly and frequently, rather than a single heavy feed. It's also important not to over-feed the young plants, you don't want tall, overly succulent plants.

Feeding is most important for plug tray mixes, because there is such a limited volume of soil. In commercial operations they are routinely fertilized every time they are watered (or every other time), by adding a dilute liquid fertilizer to their irrigation water.

Plants in soil blocks are less susceptible to nutrient deficiency, because of the greater volume of soil mix. However they should be fed if they are in the block for longer than 6 weeks, or if you are multiple sowing the blocks.

Seedlings in flats are less vulnerable to deficiency, because they are eventually pricked out into a more nutritious mix.

The best way to feed seedlings is with a very dilute (1 tbsp to 4 gal water) liquid fertilizer such as liquid Kelp or compost tea. See **Foliar Fertilizers** for more on this.

Pricking Out

Seedlings growing in flats will eventually run out of space and nutrients. If they are not to go directly outside, they must be pricked out into a richer soil mix and a deeper container. This should be done when the seedlings have their first true leaves (or the second set at the latest). Don't wait any longer, as young plants transplant better than older ones. If germination in the flat was very good, the roots will soon intertwine and fill the container. When this happens it becomes impossible to separate them without damage, so prick out early.

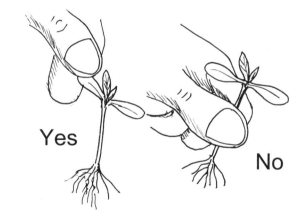

Yes   No

Preparation: Pricking out is a critical step in growing healthy transplants and must be done carefully to minimize root disturbance. This means having everything at hand and working as fast and carefully as possible. Use 4″ deep flats and a fairly nutritious pricking out mix, with the right moisture level. The seedlings should have been watered the previous day, so the soil is moist and clings to the roots, but all excess water has drained away.

How: Pricking out takes longer to describe than to do and with a little practice only takes a few seconds per plant. Begin by loosening a small clump of seedlings, so you can then remove them individually as needed. Always pick up the seedlings by their leaves or cotyledons (these will die soon anyway so minor damage won't hurt). Never pull a plant by the stem. A plant can put out new roots or new leaves, but bruising the stem could cause irreversible damage. You should have more plants than you need, so you can afford to be choosy. Select out only he biggest healthiest plants and discard the rest.

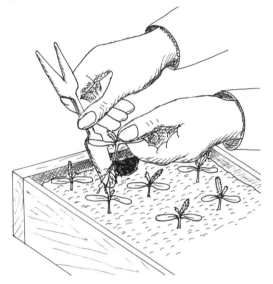

The next step is to make a hole slightly deeper than the plant roots with a dibber (or finger, knife or any tool that works for you). Then hold the seedling in the hole at the right depth and fill up the hole by pushing the dibber back into the soil an inch or so away from the seedling and pushing the soil sideways around the roots. You can also close up the hole by firming the soil around the plant with the fingers of both hands. The plant should then be firmly anchored with a little dimple in the soil. The seedling should be planted slightly deeper than it was originally, almost up to its first true leaves (bury the cotyledons). After you have transplanted a few seedlings, water them in by simply pouring a little water around their roots. Don't wait until you have planted an entire flat before watering them, as they may get stressed.

Set out the plants on a matrix (just like in a bed) to maximize efficient use of space in the flat. Some people mark out the holes beforehand to keep everything evenly spaced (they may even make jigs for precise spacing), though I usually just estimate.

Pricking out and potting mixes

These have many of the same qualities of sowing mixes, but contain more nutrients (especially trace elements).

Pricking out mix
6 parts compost parts soil
2 parts sharp sand
2 parts aged manure
2 parts leaf mold (or Peat moss)

Potting mix
7 parts turf loam
3 parts peat moss
2 parts sand
Fertilizer mix

The plants are spaced a lot farther apart than they were in the sowing tray, 1 ½″ to 3″ is usual, depending on the size of the plant and speed of growth. If they need any more space than this they are best pricked out directly into 4″ pots, or other containers. Some plants are usually pricked out twice, in which case the second container is usually an individual pot.

Put the newly pricked out flats in indirect light (under the greenhouse staging is good) for a day or so until the plants recover. You will soon learn how well you did this operation, just watch the plants and see how they react. If you did it well they won't wilt at all, if you did it poorly they will wilt severely and some may even die.

Pricking out soil blocks

Most plants stay in the 2″ blocks until their roots start to protrude from the sides of the block and then they go directly into the soil. The only times you prick out soil blocks is when using the tiny ¾″ blocks, or when growing larger plants such as Tomatoes or Cucurbits. If the weather outside remains too cool for warm weather crops, they can be potted up into 4″ pots.

Pricking out soil blocks is much easier than pricking out from flats, as there is no root disturbance. The ¾″ blocks are simply transferred into specially made 2″ blocks that have a suitably sized ¾″ indentation in the top (to make them you need a cube shaped adapter for your block maker). The 2″ blocks are just planted whole into 4″ pots or any similar container.

Potting up container plants

A potted plant must be transferred into a larger container when its roots fill the pot. Turn the plant upside down and slide it out of the pot, the root ball should show the beginning of many rootlets. If it has been left too long these roots will have wrapped around the root ball and it said to be root-bound. The common nursery practice is to pot up plants into progressively larger pots without missing a size, beginning with a 3″ pot, then 5″, then 7″ and then into a 10″ one. Apparently the regular progression stimulates the plant to grow quickly.

Water the plant an hour or two before you move it. Put some coarse woody material in the bottom of the pot for drainage. You then put a clump of potting mix into the pot, so that when you set the plant in the pot it will be at the right height. Remove the plant from the old pot, if it won't come out easily give the pot a gentle squeeze (if it's plastic), or hold upside down and tap the bottom. If it is root-bound you should cut off the encircling roots, to encourage new outward growth. Drop the plant into the new pot and fill the gap around the edge with mix, firming gently as you go. Finally make sure the plant is in a slight depression in the pot, water thoroughly and put in the shade for a few days.

Size for planting out

Almost any crop can be transplanted if the seedlings are small enough. As a general rule the younger the plant the less transplant shock it suffers. Older plants have a harder time regenerating new root hairs and roots to replace those lost when they were uprooted, so take longer to recover.

Transplants should be set out as soon as they reach optimal size. They should have at least 5 sets of true leaves and shouldn't be much taller than the depth of their container. You can put transplants out before they reach optimal size, but in cool spring weather they grow faster in the warm greenhouse and the small plants are more vulnerable to predators when outside. If you keep the plants inside for too long they start to get leggy, their roots become entangled and they can develop deficiency symptoms.

If the plants are ready to go, but it's too cold to put them outside, you can move them to a cooler place (such as a cold frame) to slow their growth. Keep feeding them though.

Hardening off

The controlled environment of the greenhouse is optimal for the growth of your seedlings (or as near as you can get it) and the young plants are a little spoiled. You are now going to send them out into the much tougher world of the garden, with its extreme temperatures, drying winds and harsh sun. Traditionally you get them ready for this by the process of hardening off, which exposes them to lower temperatures, while giving them less water and no fertilization.

Hardening off is most important when putting plants out into a much different environment, such as at the start of the growing season when the weather is cold, or when preparing warm weather crops for cool conditions (Tomatoes benefit from it). It isn't really necessary if the growing conditions outside are very good, except that it helps the plants get used to direct sunlight. Apparently plants grown indoors (without full spectrum light) produce extra cells for photosynthesis and if these are put straight outdoors they can burn (just like people).

Traditionally you begin the process of hardening off plants by putting them in the coolest area of the greenhouse. You then move them outside in the daytime, to expose them to slightly lower temperatures (not too cold - you don't want to vernalize them) They are put back into the greenhouse at night. You put them out for longer and longer periods each day for about a week, after which they remain outside until they are transplanted. You should also reduce watering, so wait until they are almost stressed before watering again. Don't fertilize again until they are transplanted out. Don't torture the plants by stressing them too hard, or for too long though. This could stunt them permanently, or cause premature bolting.

A simpler way to harden plants off is to put them in a cold frame for a few days Keep this open when it's above 50° F and close when it drops below 50° F. If frost threatens at night then cover the frame to protect the plants from freezing (or bring them back inside). Finally you leave the frame wide open for a few days before planting.

In warm weather, you just need to put plants outside in the shade for a day or two and then give them longer periods of direct sun.

Damping Off

This is such a common problem when raising transplants indoors that it gets it's own special category. Damping off may be caused by a number of species of fungi (including *Rhizoctonia solani, Pythium ultimum, Botrytis cinerea* and *Phytopthora* species) and can be the bane of the inexperienced seed starter.

The best known type of Damping Off first manifest itself as a fuzzy whitish mold on the soil surface and goes on to girdle the succulent stems of newly germinated plants. This causes the plants to keel over and die, though the stem may remain upright for a while afterward. This type is less of a problem as seedlings get older, because their stems get tougher.

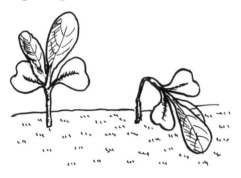

Other kinds of Damping Off kill the seed before it germinates, or rot the roots, causing their tops to turn yellow and die.

Some commercial growers avoid soil in their mixes, or sterilize it with heat or chemicals to eliminate fungal spores. Fortunately such techniques aren't really necessary. The best defense against Damping Off is to avoid giving it the growing conditions it needs. It shouldn't be a big problem if you take the precautions outlined below. You may lose a few plants occasionally, but so what.

In my experience damping off is mostly a disease of indoor seed raising. Since I started growing all of my seedlings in a well ventilated cool greenhouse I have had no problems with damping off. I actually can't remember the last time I lost a plant to damping off (lots of other reasons, but not this). However if your climate dictates that you start your seedlings inside then you have a potential problem.

Damping Off fungi need high humidity, so thin your seedlings promptly to prevent overcrowding, avoid over-watering (especially on cool sunless days when water doesn't evaporate quickly) and make sure there is good ventilation and air circulation. This may be difficult in winter when greenhouse vents are closed most of the time to maintain growing temperatures, but you have to compromise.

Sulfur powder, or a tea of Seaweed, Garlic or Chamomile has been used to treat small areas of infection and prevent it spreading. Covering the seeds with compost or Sphagnum moss (instead of sowing mix) may also help.

Sanitation

In commercial greenhouses an outbreak of disease could be economically disastrous, so they take extreme precautions (sterilization, fumigation) to keep everything clean. You don't have to resort to their measures, but you should be clean in your work habits. Good sanitation can help you prevent the buildup of disease organisms in the hospitably humid warm greenhouse environment. Don't leave thinnings and weeds laying in the greenhouse to rot. Remove any containers that are infected with Damping Off immediately. Brush the soil off of flats and plug trays before re-use and leave in the sun for the ultraviolet rays to kill microorganisms. If they get very dirty (or you have a lot of disease) wash them in a 5% bleach solution.

Problems with indoor transplants

Plants leggy
* Inadequate light.

* Too warm.

* Too much competition - inadequate thinning.

Growth slow
* Inadequate nutrient supply (they may also show deficiency symptoms).

* Too cold.

* Too dry.

Plants fall over
* If plants still look healthy they may simply have been sown too shallowly, or watered too heavily. Next time plant them deeper.

Plants fall over and die
* Damping off disease (see below).

Plants pale
* Inadequate light (usually also leggy also).

* Inadequate nitrogen.

Plants have reddish color
* See **Nutrient Deficiencies.**

No germination
* Seed not viable. This isn't likely if the seed is fairly new, as it has to legally meet minimum germination standards. However I have had some doubts about seed from some small internet companies.

* Seeds not watered, or watered too irregularly. I once sowed some seeds and had very poor germination (I muttered about the poor quality seed), but when started a second lot from the same packet I had good germination. I now believe I killed the first lot by allowing them to dry out.

* Seed not planted. Not as unlikely as you might think!

* Damping off (see below).

* A problem with the soil mix. Perhaps it contained some toxin.

Soil surface turns green
* Algae growth. This isn't usually serious but it isn't good because algae can seal the soil surface and slow air exchange. It is usually caused by excessive watering and not allowing the soil surface to ever dry off. This creates ideal conditions for damping off. Allow the soil surface to partly dry before watering again and try to improve ventilation and air circulation.

Plants eaten
* Birds, earwigs, mice, slugs, snails, sowbugs.

Outdoor nursery beds

In warm weather you can raise transplants in outdoor nursery beds. These combine aspects of both direct seeding and raising transplants and can work very well. Instead of raising transplants in containers indoors, they are started outside in a specially protected nursery bed. This has some of the advantages of direct sowing in that it's less labor intensive and you need less equipment. It also has some of the advantages of indoor starting, as young plants aren't taking up space in the main beds. They are also more easily protected in a small area and you have greater flexibility in that you always have transplants ready to go out.

These beds are most suitable for raising large numbers of hardy, tough and easily transplanted crops such as Alliums, Brassicas, Leeks, Lettuce and Onions.

A nursery bed doesn't need to be very big, any small, sunny, sheltered area will do. Ideally it should be located wherever you spend a lot of time, such as near your house or greenhouse, so you can keep a watchful eye on the seedlings. The soil should be well drained, but moisture retentive and should warm up quickly in spring. Early seedlings may even be raised in cold frames, cloches or poly-tunnels (watch out for slugs though).

Sowing the bed: The bed is prepared and planted in much the same way as other direct sown seedbeds, though you need a smaller area and can sow closer together. The soil tilth should be quite fine, though you shouldn't give the bed any special fertilization. You don't want it to be more fertile than other beds (plants should go into better soil as they get bigger).

Maintenance: The seedling bed must be weeded and thinned meticulously and protected from predators (row covers are good for this).

Holding bed

This is the second stage of outdoor seedling production and corresponds to the pricking out stage of indoor growing. The holding bed should be more fertile than the seedbed, but not as rich as the final bed.

The seedlings are transplanted here when they have one set of true leaves, in much the same way as you would prick out indoor seedlings. They should be spaced so they have plenty of room to grow until they can be transplanted. Don't put them so close together that their roots intertwine, or they could be damaged during transplanting.

Cold frame nursery bed

If you need transplants somewhat earlier than you could grow them outside, you could use a cold frame as a nursery bed. You could move the frame over the nursery bed, or you could cover the soil in the frame with several inches of a flat mix. Sow your seeds just as if you were planting in a flat. When these are sufficiently large, prick them out to give them more room.

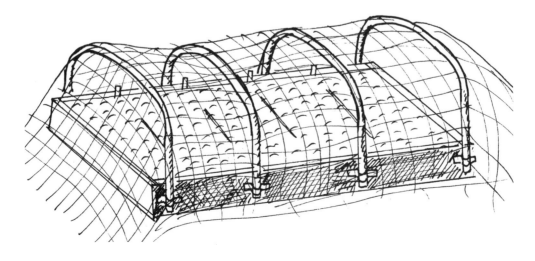

19 Sowing mixes

What are sowing mixes?

Beginning gardeners sometimes make the mistake of using garden soil for starting seeds indoors. This isn't very suitable though, as indoor growing conditions are quite different from those found outside. When used indoors in the confined environment of a container, garden soil drains poorly, has a tendency to crust and can get compacted from repeated wetting and drying. Also it doesn't hold much water (so dries out quickly), shrinks as it dries out and often contains weed seeds, pests and disease.

The formulation and preparation of sowing mixes is an important part of raising transplants. A good sowing mix has a number of specific attributes:

- It has a low density.

- It is well drained and aerated.

- It holds a lot of water.

- It has a fairly neutral pH.

- It doesn't crust easily.

- It is firm enough to provide a strong anchorage for roots.

- It has enough structural stability to resist compaction, even though it has a lot of pore space.

Buy or make?
If you are only going to start small quantities of seedlings you might want to simply buy a bag of commercial sowing mix. Just make sure it is formulated for seed starting and is 100% organic.

Making your own sowing mixes

Sowing mixes are composed of several different ingredients, each of which fulfils a certain function in the mix:

- Most mixes contain a large proportion of organic matter (compost, peat moss, leaf mold) to provide good water retention and aeration.

- The mix should contain a coarse material (sand, vermiculite, perlite) to provide good drainage, as organic material alone tends to waterlog easily.

- The mix must also contain a source of nutrients (compost, garden soil, or a fertilizer mix). It doesn't need to have a very high nutrient content, because we want the seedlings to send out vigorous roots to search for nutrients. If the mix is too rich the plants get lazy and don't do this. Pricking out and potting mixes must contain more nutrients, as the plants are bigger and have greater needs.

- The pH of the ingredients should be a fairly neutral 6.0 to 7.0, similar to that of a good garden soil.

- The mix should be free of weed seeds. It's much better if it doesn't grow more weed seedlings than crop seedlings.

- The ingredients should be free of disease and insect pests.

- The mix should also be low in salts which could burn delicate seedling roots.

161

Preparing the mixes

Sterilization and pasteurization

Chemical gardeners, farmers and nursery people commonly sterilize their soils to combat damping off fungus, either by heating it to 160 to 180° F, or with chemicals such as methyl bromide (now in the process of being banned). The problem with this approach is that it kills the soil completely, including many beneficial creatures and upsets the soil equilibrium.

Soil may also be pasteurized at 140 to 160° F, to kill many pathogens, but without affecting beneficial organisms (well made compost is actually pasteurized).

I don't worry very much about soil borne diseases (or anything else for that matter). I prefer to control damping off by giving the seedlings adequate air circulation, cool temperatures and an appropriate watering regimen.

Screening

All of the ingredients for sowing mixes are screened to take out sticks, stones and other debris, and to reduce them to a uniform texture. The ingredients for soil block or plug tray mixes should be sifted through a ¼″ mesh. Those for flat, cell pack, pricking out and potting mixes can be coarser, so sift them through a ½″ mesh.

Moisture level

Make sure the materials for the mix are at their proper moisture level (not too wet or dry). The moisture level of flat and plug tray mixes can be tested by squeezing a handful into a ball. It should hold together well, but crumble when lightly squeezed. Soil block mix needs to be much wetter (see the specific instructions for them in **Raising Transplants**).

Mixing

Small quantities of mix are usually made up in a wheelbarrow or large plastic tub. Larger quantities are most easily mixed on a concrete floor. Just spread the materials out, one on top of the other, in a big pile. Then turn the pile three times to thoroughly mix all the ingredients together. Do this by simply moving the pile a couple of feet, move it back again and then move it a third time to where you will actually store it.

Storage

Sowing mixes should be made as needed, as they dry out and deteriorate if stored for more than a few weeks. Fertilizers in the mix may start to break down and release ammonium, which can damage seeds and seedlings. It may also get infected by pests and various pathogens. Ideally you will store all of your ingredients in enclosed bins with the appropriate moisture content (and labels).

Common ingredients

Compost

Compost is the natural medium for seed germination (it covers the forest floor), so well rotted compost is the basic ingredient in many mixes. It's already pasteurized (if made properly), easily available, rich in nutrients, free of weed seeds, has a neutral pH, aids in water retention and drainage and can help suppress damping off. It isn't widely used in commercial sowing mixes because it is too variable and unpredictable and not sterile enough.

Finely sifted compost can be used as a substitute for peat in sowing mixes, though it contains a lot more nutrients. It's a good idea to sift and bag some compost in fall (write the date on your calendar), so it is ready for use in late winter, without having to mess around in the cold. If you aren't that organized, then at least keep the pile covered (it should be anyway) to prevent leaching and make sure it stays dry enough to use.

Many gardeners make a special compost pile for sowing mixes, turning it several times, to make sure it is thoroughly heated and broken down. Ideally this pile should be left under cover to age for 1 to 2 years before use.

Soil

Though seedlings shouldn't be started in soil, it is an important component of many mixes, supplying nutrients and providing support. Use the best soil in your garden, a good medium loam (not too much clay or sand) with lots of organic matter is best. Don't worry about the potential for infecting the seedlings with soil borne diseases. Some gardeners sterilize or pasteurize their soil to eliminate these, but it isn't really necessary if you use good growing techniques.

Sharp sand

Sand makes a mix more porous and improves drainage. There is quite a lot of variation in sand, some types being much more suitable than others. The best types are quite coarse, with some large ⅛″ diameter grains (such as number 2 builders sand). Beach sand is too salty, river sand is often too smooth and fine.

Composted manure

This is a good source of organic matter and nutrients and can be used as a substitute for compost if that is unavailable. Make sure it has been composted properly, otherwise it may be full of weed seeds and other problems.

Worm castings

If you have worm bins (you should), these are a good source of nutrients for the various mixes. See **Composting** for more on this.

Peat

I have already discussed the ecological implications of using peat moss (see **Fertilizers**) and you may want to avoid it altogether.

Peat has several properties that make it useful for sowing mixes. Most importantly it holds a lot of water, so increases the water retentive qualities of a mix. It has a coarse structure that helps to give good aeration. It is also light, fairly sterile, holds on to nutrients and is free of weed seeds, insect pests and toxic contaminants.

Peat is rather acid (pH 3.5 to 5.0), so lime is often added to raise the pH up to 5.0 or 6.0. Use approximately 2 tablespoons of lime per shovel of peat (4 ounces of lime will raise 8 gallons of peat 1 pH point).

Coir

This is made from the fibers that surround Coconuts and was once widely used in horticulture. It is becoming popular again in Europe because it is a good peat substitute. It works well, but it must be transported from the tropics, which seems like a waste of energy to me. If you don't want to use peat there are other suitable alternatives (such as leaf mold).

Leaf mold

Leaf mold is a very useful ingredient for soil mixes. It is similar to peat moss in that provides a mix with good aeration and helps it to hold water. Unlike peat it contains some nutrients (especially Ca, Mg and P), is a renewable resource, easily available and usually free.

You may be able to obtain already decomposed leaf mold from deciduous woods. Be cautious when using it though, as it's often very acid and can sometimes actually inhibit seedling growth. Before using it in quantity you might want to experiment to see if it has any detrimental effect. You will probably have to add lime to it to raise its pH.

It is much better to make your own leaf mold, using the leaves of deciduous trees, especially Oaks. Don't make it from evergreens (either broadleaves or conifers) as they contain toxins that can inhibit plant growth. See **Composting** for more on making leaf mold.

Turf loam

Turf loam is made from decomposed turf and rich garden soil and was commonly used for starting seeds before the widespread use of peat. It is a good source of organic matter and is also high in plant nutrients. It is made by leaving grass sod to decompose for 6 to 12 months. It is then shredded and sifted before use (see **Composting** for more on this).

Vermiculite

Vermiculite is made by heating mica to almost 2000° F, whereupon it puffs up like popcorn to 20 times its original volume. It holds up to 20 times its own weight in water and is added to sowing mixes to improve water retention and aeration. It contains some magnesium and potassium and its C.E.C. is sufficiently high to hold some nutrients. The coarser granular vermiculite is preferred for sowing mixes, because it doesn't compact as much as the finer types.

There are drawbacks to vermiculite; it is quite expensive, it must be mined, is energy intensive to produce (hence not very sustainable) and sometimes contains asbestos. In keeping with my vow to not buy things I don't need, I don't use vermiculite (or perlite).

Perlite

Perlite is made by heating volcanic silica up to 1400° F, until internal moisture causes it to puff up like popcorn. It is often added to mixes because it is light, sterile and improves the drainage and aeration of a mix.

Perlite doesn't contain any nutrients (but may contain toxic boron, aluminum and sodium), its dust is harmful to the lungs, its production is quite energy intensive and doesn't really do anything that sand doesn't.

Old flat sowing mix

The stuff left in the flat after pricking out or transplanting still contains useful nutrients and organic matter. It shouldn't be re-used for seed starting (there is some danger of disease), but it is a good addition to potting mixes and is a great cover soil for newly sown seeds.

Lime

This is used to neutralize acid ingredients such as peat moss. Dolomitic lime is preferred as it contains magnesium as well as calcium. See **pH adjustment** for more on this.

Fertilizer

A small quantity of powdered fertilizer is often added to mixes to increase their nutrient content (mix with a little sand and incorporate thoroughly). Use equal parts of blood meal, greensand and rock phosphate and about half as much Kelp powder.

Sowing mix recipes

Making up mixes is a little like cooking, some people prefer to stick rigidly to the recipe, other people prefer to improvise with what's available. See the individual types of containers for recipes (see **Raising Transplants**).

20   Transplanting

If you have been raising your plants according to the directions in this book you will have been using Alan Chadwicks' "breakfast, lunch, dinner" method. Seedlings germinate in a mix that is fairly low in nutrients (breakfast), are transplanted into a somewhat richer pricking out mix (lunch) and then finally set out in the rich soil of the intensive bed (dinner). With each step the soil gets richer and more nutritious, which encourages the plants to rapidly overcome any transplant shock. If the soil in the beds is relatively poor, you may have to give the plants a regular foliar or liquid feed).

Timing

The timing of transplanting is important. The crop must be at the right stage for planting out and the weather must be right for the crop. See **Crop Planning** for information on when to plant.

Soil condition

The soil should be fairly moist for transplanting (close to field capacity), so examine it a couple of days before you wish to plant out. If it's dry you should water it thoroughly and in two days it will be ideal. If it's wet it must be allowed to dry out (you might try to hasten drying with cloches). If the soil is ideal you could cover it with plastic sheeting if rain threatens.

Weather for planting

Seedlings grown in flats lose part of their root network when they are transplanted and so are quite vulnerable to drying out. The best time to plant them is in cool, cloudy weather, when transpiration is at a minimum. In warm sunny weather you should transplant in late afternoon or early evening. This gives the plants overnight to get adjusted before they are exposed to full sun and heat.

Plants grown in soil blocks and plug trays aren't as vulnerable to drying out as those from flats, but I still prefer to plant them out in late afternoon.

Spacing

See **Spacing** for information on this.

Pre planting treatment

Flats should be watered liberally the day before they are to be planted out (the same morning in very hot climates). This ensures they have all the water they need, but excess water has drained away. Soil blocks, pots and plug trays should be watered a couple of hours before planting out.

Plants in flats will benefit from having a knife run between the plants a few days before planting, to give each plant it's own block of soil. This severs roots that would later be broken anyway and starts the recovery process even before they are planted out.

A traditional practice to reduce transplant shock was to trim off part of each leaf. The assumption was that as root mass is lost when transplanting it was good to balance this by reducing leaf area (and hence transpiration). This is now considered a bad idea, because removing leaf area reduces a plants ability to photosynthesize and produce the food it needs for rapid recovery.

Another traditional practice was to dip the transplants roots in muddy water, supposedly to prevent them from drying out. This is also inadvisable as it may mat the roots together, which can actually increase transplant shock.

How to transplant

The type of transplant affects the method of planting, some kinds being much easier to handle than others. As I mentioned previously some vegetables resent transplanting and can only be successfully transplanted with soil around their roots (in plug trays, cell packs or soil blocks). Others can be completely bare rooted. No plant really likes being physically handled however, so you should always transplant as quickly and carefully as possible.

Hole preparation

Make the planting hole deep enough so there is plenty of space for all of the roots to spread out, without any of them folding over on themselves.

The seedling should be planted a couple of inches deeper than it was in the container, right up to its first true leaves. If a plant is only planted as deep as the cotyledons, the stem often kinks and turns woody, which slows down nutrient intake. After planting you will close up the hole, leaving a slight depression for watering. If you don't make the hole deep enough, you will be tempted to make this depression by compacting the soil. On the other hand don't make the hole so deep that the crown is buried, as this could encourage rot. In hot weather you may want to put water in the hole before planting.

I normally to use a bulb planter to make medium sized holes, as it is makes a nice even hole with one quick movement. For smaller holes you can use a narrow transplanting trowel. Some people like to use a dibber for small holes, but this may compact the sides of the hole. A dibber works best for very small holes in light soils.

In Gopher country large individual plants must be planted in wire baskets (if you don't have lined beds). Now is the time to make these.

For closely spaced plants such as Leeks you can pre-dig shallow trenches or furrows, to speed up planting. Actually I much prefer to plant Leeks in narrow holes made with a dibber.

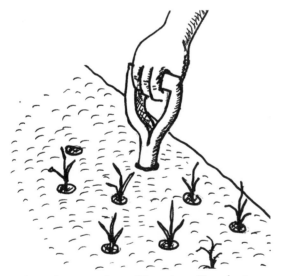

For large hungry plants (Tomatoes, Eggplants, Cucurbits) each hole is usually fertilized individually. In this case you can speed up planting by pre-digging and amending the holes.

Planting out

Flats
Even though the plants that are grown in flats usually don't mind transplanting (Cabbage, Cauliflower, Onions and Leeks can even be bare rooted) you should try to minimize soil loss and root disturbance as much as possible.

In hot weather you should keep the flat in the shade to minimize stress and perhaps cover with wet burlap to keep it moist. Remove a few plants from the flat with a hand fork as you go (in clumps if small, individually if large). Pick up each individual by the root ball or leaves (they are replaceable), never by the stem (it isn't).

Choose the best plants in the flat to plant out and discard the inferior ones. Don't just start planting at one end and plant everything.

Hold the plant in one hand and make the hole with the trowel in the other. Drop the plant in the hole, making sure the roots don't get turned up (this damages roots and so encourages disease and nutrient deficiency). The soil is then pressed around the plant quite firmly, to ensure good root contact with the soil and that no air pockets remain. The plant should now sit in the hole in a slight depression (for watering in), with its first true leaves at ground level.

Save any sowing mix remaining in the flat for other uses (see **Sowing mixes** for more on this).

Soil blocks
The usual tool for planting soil blocks is a trowel, though a number of special tools have been devised. Hold the trowel in one hand like a dagger, stabbing it into the soil and pulling backwards to open up a hole. Drop the plant into the hole with the other hand and firm the soil around it with both hands to eliminate air. The plant should be in the ground so firmly that its top would break off if you tried to uproot it.

Individual pots
If the plant doesn't come out of the pot easily give it a gentle squeeze (if plastic), or hold upside down and tap the bottom (if clay). Gently turn the plant right side up, plop it into the prepared hole and spread out any roots that are pot bound.

When planting peat pots rip the bottom off to make sure the roots can get out easily and tear the rim off so it doesn't protrude above ground and wick moisture away.

Plug trays

Planting from plug trays is very straightforward once you get them out of the trays. Ideally you can simply pull very gently on the seed leaves and the plug and entire root mass slips out, but sometimes (most often with old trays) they get stuck and you pull the leaf off. In such cases it's tempting to pull on the stem, don't though, it can cause serious bruising. You can usually push the plugs out from below by pushing a little stick up through the drainage hole.

A narrow trowel (or dibber) is the best tool for planting plug trays. The procedure is to make an appropriately sized hole with the trowel in one hand and pop the plant into the hole with the other. You then put the trowel back into the ground a couple of inches from the plant and push the soil toward the plant to firm it. Alternatively you can simply push with the backs of both hands (which leaves a nice dimple for watering).

After planting

Watering-in

Watering-in is a crucial step in transplanting. Not only does it supply the plant with necessary water, but it also fills in air spaces around the roots and bring them into closer contact with the soil. You don't have to water each individual plant as it goes into the ground, but you shouldn't wait until you have finished the whole bed either. Water everything you have just planted every 5 to 10 minutes (depending on the weather). If there is only a few plants you can use a watering can. For large numbers of plants use a hose pipe that has been turned down until water just trickles out.

Water directly into the depression at the base of the plant, to put it right where it's needed, there is no need to water the entire bed. The amount of water given to each plant varies according to weather, soil type and the size of the plant. You want to thoroughly wet the area of soil around the roots. Try a half-cup of water for a small plant and up to a quart for a very large one,

It is absolutely essential that the plants have all the water they need during the time they are recovering. If they are allowed to dry out they can be permanently retarded, or may even die. Once they have recovered they should be watered deeply, but infrequently, to encourage them to send down deep roots. See **Watering** for more on this.

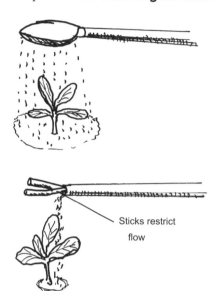

Sticks restrict flow

Label

This may seem like a minor detail, but get into the habit of labeling the plants as soon as you have finished planting them. Also make a note in your garden journal, in case the labels get moved or lost. Write the variety, dates of sowing and planting and anything else of relevance. In a large garden it's easy to forget such information and it can be useful later, especially if you save seed, or if several people work in the garden.

Protection

After your transplants are in the ground you have to be attentive to their needs until they are growing vigorously. The commonest problems are cutworms, slugs and snails. Birds can be a big problem in spring when they seem to crave the tender young seedlings (where I live Quail are a problem year round). See **Pests** for ways to deal with these problems.

In very hot weather you may want to protect your transplants from hot sun and drying winds for several days, until they have recovered completely. You can do this by shading the plants with shade cloth. Rest this on old window screens sitting on bricks. Before these materials existed gardeners had to be creative. To protect individual plants they would use wooden shingles, pushed into the soil at an angle. To protect entire beds they might use straw mats or brushwood, supported on poles. The poles were fastened to stakes to raise them several inches above the surface of the soil. The density of the mat or brushwood would determine the amount of shade provided.

Gapping up

It's not uncommon for some plants to die after transplanting, because of pests, shock, or general trauma, so don't immediately discard surplus plants after transplanting. Replace the fatalities as soon as it's obvious they won't make it (this is called gapping up) and try to remedy the cause of their loss. French market gardeners would replace all of the plants that died within 10 days of planting. After that it wasn't considered worthwhile.

Feeding

Many gardeners give the young plants a shot of liquid fertilizer as soon as they have fully recovered from transplanting. This can help them get off to a good start. Don't fertilize until they have recovered however. See **Foliar and Liquid Fertilization** for more on this.

Watering

21 Watering

Soils and water

Water isn't static in the soil, it moves upwards and
sideways by capillary action and downward by gravity.
It enters the soil as rainfall and leaves via plant roots
or by gravity (it just drains away). About 25% of the
volume of the average soil is composed of water, but the
proportions of water and air constantly fluctuate.

Infiltration

The rate at which water enters the soil is known as its
infiltration capacity and is largely dependent on the soil
structure and texture (especially of the surface layer). If
the infiltration capacity is low, water tends to puddle on
the surface, rather than soaking in. This may then run
off downhill (potentially causing erosion) and disappear.
This wastes water that could have helped us to grow
plants, so we must do everything we can to ensure that
the soil absorbs all the rainfall that lands upon it.

How water enters the soil

When a drop of water enters the soil it connects with the
nearest soil particles and is incorporated into the film of
water that surrounds them. This water is held on to the
particles by the force of adhesion, which allows the film
to build up around the particle (to a thickness of around
0.06 mm, to get specific). When each particle has as
much water as it can hold, the excess water fills up the
spaces between the particles (the micropores). All of this
water is known as capillary water, because it can move
around the soil by capillary action.

Any water entering the soil after the micropores are
full, goes in to the spaces between the aggregates (the
macropores). This water is known as gravitational water,
for the obvious reason that it moves by the force of
gravity and isn't physically held by the soil at all.

If more water enters the soil it penetrates deeper, by
force of gravity, connecting with all available soil
particles and filling up all available pore spaces, until
it hits the water table (where the soil is permanently
saturated).

If so much water enters the soil that all available pore
spaces are filled right down to the water table, the soil is
said to be at saturation point. Any more water falling on
the soil after this point can't soak into the saturated soil
and so either stands on the surface or runs off.

When water stops entering the soil, the gravitational
water in the macropores slowly drains away and is
replaced by air. When all of this water has drained off
(which may take days), the soil particles and micropores
are left holding as much capillary water as they are
physically able (the 0.06 mm thick film) and the soil is
said to be at field capacity. This is the ideal water level
for most plants, with the water forming a continuous
film from surface to water table, but with the larger
macropores still filled with air. The amount of water
the soil can hold in this state is known as its moisture
holding capacity.

How water moves in soil

The soil near the surface dries out most rapidly, as its
moisture is removed by evaporation and by plant roots.
This is replaced by capillary water, which moves through
the soil pores from wetter areas. This happens because
the film around a soil particle gets thinner as it dries out,
causing its surface tension to increase, which pulls water
from wetter particles. In this way water may move in
any direction, from wetter areas to drier ones, until all
are equally moist. In practice they never become equally
moist, because water continues to be lost (by evaporation,
or to plant roots) as fast as it can be replaced.

If water is continually removed from the soil without
replenishment, it is eventually depleted to the point
where more water can't move through the soil quickly
enough to replace that consumed. Capillary movement
is related to tension and decreases as the soil film dries
out, until it essentially ceases as the soil gets close to
wilting point. Once the continuous film of soil moisture
is broken, the plant can no longer get enough water to
replace that transpired, so it shuts down its stomata, wilts
and stops growing. If there is still moisture deep in the
soil this reduction in demand may enable more water to
move up into the soil around the root zone. If this doesn't
happen the plant may eventually die from lack of water.

169

The capillary movement of water is too slow and limited to provide plants with sufficient water for good growth, so in dry soil their roots must search out water continuously. This is actually the main incentive for roots to grow into new soil (they can only grow into moist soil). This root growth, combined with capillary movement, enables plants to get most of the available water in the soil.

Available water

All of the water in the soil isn't of equal value for growing crops. As plants suck up water, the film of moisture around each soil particle gets thinner and it takes more energy to get it. By the time the wilting point is reached, this film is so thin that plants can't extract any more water from it.

The remaining water is held tightly to the soil particles by electrical forces (at 15 times atmospheric pressure) and is known as "hygroscopic water". By determining the amount of soil suction with a tensiometer, we can determine how much water is available for plants.

The soil water that plants can use is called "available water", or the soil reservoir. That which can't be used is called (appropriately enough) "unavailable water" and includes gravitational water and hygroscopic water.

It is not good to let the soil lose more than half of its available water, as the plants then have to work harder to meet their needs. When a plant has to expend energy just to obtain water, it has less left over for growth, which then slows down. It is your job as a gardener to give your crops all the water they need, so they can grow as efficiently as possible.

Factors affecting soil water loss

Evaporation: On a hot day a bare soil can lose a lot of water through evaporation. Cultivation increases this loss by increasing the surface area of the soil and exposing soil moisture to the air. Sandy soils tend to lose less water from evaporation than clay soils, because they tend to dry out on the surface creating a dust mulch effect (and there is less capillary action to bring more moisture to the surface). Wind increases evaporation and is another reason why the garden should be sheltered from strong winds.

A layer of mulch stops water loss by evaporation almost completely. Not only does it prevent sunlight hitting the soil, it also creates a humid layer under the mulch (see **Mulch**).

Transpiration: The amount of water a plant loses through transpiration is determined by temperature, humidity and sun intensity. On a hot sunny summer day a plant may use eight times as much water as it does on a cool cloudy spring day. Wind increases transpiration losses even further.

Soils and water handling

The ability of the soil to handle water is largely determined by its texture, structure and organic matter content.

Soil texture

Sand: These soils may hold about 10% water at field capacity. The large pore spaces enable water to enter and leave easily, so it fills up or dries out fairly quickly. Such soils don't have a large reservoir of water, so must be watered frequently to keep crops supplied in dry weather. Offsetting this to some extent is the fact that roots can penetrate more easily and deeply into sandy soils in search of water. Some sandy soils are hard to re-wet if they dry out, water simply rolls off them.

Clay: These soils can hold as much as 40% water at field capacity, but a much greater proportion of this is unavailable when compared to a sandy soil. When a clay soil dries out it shrinks and cracks and these cracks can damage roots and make it hard to re-wet the soil (water drains down the cracks before it can soak into the soil). The infiltration rate in a poor clay soil is low, because water enters the small pores so slowly, it often puddles on the surface and runs off. Water also drains slowly, which can be a problem in wet climates. Clay soils have a large soil reservoir, so don't need watering as frequently as sandy ones.

Silt: These soils have characteristics somewhere between those of sand and clay.

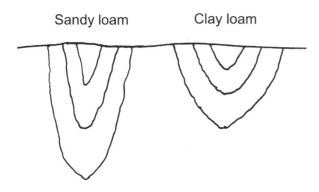

Sandy loam   Clay loam

Soil structure

A well-structured soil has a large volume of pore space, with lots of macropores that allow water to percolate freely and micropores that hold water.

Soil organic matter

Organic matter actually acts like a sponge, absorbing and holding excess water and only releasing it when the film of moisture around the soil particles is depleted. This greatly increases the water holding capacity of light sandy soils.

Organic matter also improves the crumb structure of a soil, which increases the amount of pore space. This increases aeration and improves drainage, making it easier for roots to penetrate deeply in search of water. This is particularly valuable for heavy clay soil.

Slopes

A slope drains better than flat land and so dries out faster (especially in light soils). South and west facing slopes dry out most rapidly because of their increased solar gain. Land at the bottom of a slope gets extra water as it drains down from above.

Climate

Climate affects how much water plants use and determines whether you can get away with occasional hand watering, or whether you must irrigate your plants from seedling to harvest. In hot arid areas you would expect to have to irrigate plants regularly, but even where summer rainfall is regular, loss by evaporation and transpiration often exceeds rainfall. In such cases some irrigation will be necessary to achieve maximum yields. This is especially true in intensive beds, as the fast growing, closely spaced, plants need a lot of water.

Climate and soil water

There is a considerable seasonal variation in the amount of water in the soil.

The most obvious reason for such fluctuation is rainfall. In many areas this is seasonal, some seasons being much wetter than others. Where I live on the West coast, rain is abundant in winter, but pretty much non-existent in summer.

Another reason is temperature. In the cool weather of spring and autumn there may be very little evaporation from the soil and less transpiration from plants. This means that the soil dries out much more slowly than in summer. Often there is no need to water at all at these times, especially in spring when the soil is full of water from winter rains.

Always consider the weather before watering, never water routinely. If possible don't waste water by irrigating before rain (somehow a particularly conscientious watering always seems to bring rain.) A rain gauge can help you to determine the quantity of both natural rainfall and overhead irrigation.

Water holding capacity of soils

The amount of water a soil can hold is determined by its texture and organic matter content. Soil depth is also significant, in that a deep soil has a much greater storage volume than a shallow one.

Water in top 12″ of soil

Soil	Field capacity	Permanent wilting point	Available water
Sand	1 ¾″	⅛″	1 ⅝″
Loam	2 ¼″	¼″	2″
Silt loam	2 ½″	¼″	2 ¼″
Clay	2 ½″	½″	2″
Peat	4 ¾″	1 ¼″	3 ½″

Plants and water

Why plants need water

Very little of the water taken up by a plant is actually incorporated into that plant. Most of the water is 'eventually transpired, after being used to keep the plant turgid, for cooling, or to move nutrients, wastes and manufactured foods around the plant. From 200 to 500 units of water are needed to produce one unit of dry plant material.

Plants also need the water that remains in the soil and makes up the soil solution. This is the route by which nutrient ions are transported around the soil and how they end up in plant roots. Water is also essential for the soil organisms that feed plants and is a factor in both mechanical and chemical weathering of soil, which liberates plant nutrients (see **Soil**).

Effects of too little water

In many areas water is the most common factor limiting plant growth (even in relatively humid climates). If a plant can't get enough water it closes its stomata to prevent loss through transpiration. This prevents the plant taking in carbon dioxide and without this photosynthesis can't take place. When this happens the plant must live off of its stored food reserves, so actually consumes food, rather than producing it. Consequently growth slows down, or stops completely. Of course this then affects food storage, flowering and subsequent fruiting (flowers and fruits often drop).

Water stress doesn't only slow growth and reduce yield. It may also cause plants to bolt, or affect the quality of the edible part, making them fibrous (their cells get thicker and their stems tougher), pungent or bitter. One of the reasons the French market gardeners grew such large quantities of high quality vegetables was that they ensured their crops got all the water they needed at all times.

Effects of too much water

Too much water can delay flowering and fruiting and causes plants to make succulent growth that is attractive to disease and insect pests. This succulent growth contains a lot of water, so is less nutritious and less flavorful (the latter may not be a bad thing with strongly flavored crops). If the soil becomes waterlogged there isn't enough air in the soil and roots may die.

Plant spacing and water

The spacing of plants in the bed has an effect on irrigation practices. Obviously the more plants in a given area, the more water they will extract from the soil. If you fill a bed with Tomato plants 18″ apart you may have to water every few days, if you plant them 6 feet apart you may never have to water them at all (there may already be enough water stored in the soil).

Individual plant requirements

Crop plants vary greatly in their need for water. Celery originally grew in marshes and like lots of water, while Watermelon comes from a semi- desert and can make do with very little. Deep-rooted crops generally need irrigating less frequently than shallow rooted crops. Some plants need water constantly, others have a critical stage of growth when extra water can greatly increase the final harvest (in some cases this can double the final yield).

The stage of growth affects how often you need to water. Root growth is rapid in young vigorously growing plants (as much as an inch a day), but it slows considerably as a plant matures and starts to flower and set fruit.

Young plants: These use less water than larger plants, but need it more frequently because their roots are small and their sparse foliage doesn't shade the soil very well (so evaporation is greater).

Older plants: Use more water, but have deeper roots. They also have larger leaves that form their own moist shady microclimate which reduces evaporation.

Leaf crops: These need a steady supply of moisture if they are to produce heavy yields of tasty succulent leaves. Water stress can have a dramatic effect on quality, plants may get fibrous, develop unpleasant flavors, or bolt prematurely. Keep the soil constantly moist for these crops.

Root crops: These have their greatest need for water when the roots are sizing up, but should always receive a steady supply. Water stress may cause them to bolt or develop unpleasant flavors. Irregular watering, alternately too much and too little, can stimulate them to put on little spurts of growth, which can cause them to grow unevenly and split.

Fruit and seed bearing crops: Fruit crops also respond to regular watering with heavy production of lush foliage, but this isn't necessarily a good thing, as it often delays flowering. Conversely the "stress" of infrequent watering can actually encourage flowering.

When the fruit is setting and sizing up, they need extra water, so make sure you give them enough when the flowers and fruits appear (or they may drop off). They are vulnerable to water stress at this time, not only because water is needed to size up the fruit, but also because root growth slows down at this stage. Water stress at this time can reduce the final yield considerably (though it may make the fruit sweeter).

Bulb crops: These need the most water when young, less when they are maturing and none at all when they are curing.

Watering Techniques

Observation of soil and plants
The essence of good watering is making sure the plants get all the water they need, exactly when they need it and no more. If you irrigate a plant that already has an adequate supply, it won't have any beneficial effect and you won't be using your water supply or time efficiently. Conversely if you don't water until plants wilt, their growth will be slowed (or they may even bolt), so again you won't be using your water supply efficiently.

The ideal time to water is just as the easily available water starts to run low, but before the plant has to start working harder to meet its needs (plants start to wilt much more readily at this time). Generally when half of the available water is gone from the soil you should irrigate. You have to watch the soil and plants carefully to know exactly when this stage is reached.

Signs of water stress

You will soon learn how to tell when plants are stressed merely by their appearance. Serious water stress is pretty obvious because the plants wilt, but plants begin to show subtle signs of stress long before lack of water forces them to shut down completely. As water gets harder to obtain, plants begin to lose the sheen on their leaves. As their stress increases they may sag slightly instead of standing rigidly upright and their leaf edges may start to curl. In extreme cases the growing tips and leaves go completely limp and if this continues for long they die and go dry and crisp.

Wilting isn't always a sign that the soil is dry however, in extremely hot and sunny weather plants sometimes wilt intentionally to reduce water loss. However they recover as soon as the temperature drops. Some plants are much more prone to wilting than others, especially those with thin, or big leaves, such as Rhubarb and the Cucurbits. Check your plants for water stress in the cool of early morning or evening. If they are wilting at this time, they are seriously stressed and aren't getting enough water (either the soil is dry, they are diseased, or they have root damage).

Checking soil moisture
Check the moisture level of the soil by digging down to the depth of your index finger (about 4″) and picking up a small amount of soil. If the soil is so dry it won't squeeze into a ball, it probably needs water (remember that clay forms a ball more easily than sand). Don't forget to fill up the hole again afterward.

Time of day to water
There is some controversy as to the best time of day to irrigate a garden. Some gardeners believe early morning is best, because the water has a chance to soak into the soil before the sun gets warm and is immediately available to the plants when they need it most (which might have some relevance in sandy soils). They say evening watering encourages pests and disease by leaving the soil moist all night. If you have serious disease problems you may be best sticking to morning watering. Morning watering is also best in cool climates, as the soil can warm up quickly in the morning sun.

Other gardeners prefer to water in the early evening, after the hottest part of the day, but early enough to allow the plants and soil surface to dry out before dark. At this time the soil is warm, so the water warms up quicker. Also the water has all night to soak into the soil, so there is less loss from evaporation than with morning watering. For this reason evening watering particularly lends itself to arid areas. Advocates of evening watering remind us that plants don't shut down completely at night, they still use water.

Most gardeners avoid watering in the middle of the day in hot weather, because any water on leaves, or the soil surface, will evaporate before it can do any good. This is particularly true when using overhead watering. It is often said that in strong sunlight water droplets can burn the leaves by magnifying the suns rays, but I have never seen this actually happen.

Unless there is some overriding reason for using only evening or morning watering most people water when it is convenient, rather than to some schedule. Drip irrigation can be used at any time of day or night, but I would always avoid the hottest part of the day.

Steps prior to watering

Increasing infiltration
Any soil crust should be broken up before watering, as it can impede infiltration (see **Soil Capping** below). If your soil doesn't absorb water easily, you can increase absorption by putting shallow holes in the bed with a fork, or dibbing larger holes between plants (these tricks are particularly useful when hand watering). In some cases shallow furrows made along the contour with a rake will also work. You could also put a lip around the edge of the bed to increase absorption (or simply have a flat bed).

How much water to apply
How much water to apply depends on many factors, climate, plants, soil type, plant spacing. One rule of thumb says you should give your plants 1″ of water per week in summer and about ½″ in spring and fall (but of course it all really depends on temperature and humidity). This works out to roughly ⅔ gallon per square foot, 66 gallons per 100 square feet, or 28,000 gallons per acre and should penetrate 6″ to 12″ into the ground. By observing the soil and plants you will soon know if it is too much or too little.

Intensively planted beds use a lot of water because they are producing a lot of biomass in a short time; there is a lot of growth going on. Fortunately these beds can store a lot of water because of their high organic matter content.

In rainy climates a rain gauge (or other container) is useful to monitor how much rain has fallen, so you can decide when your crops need additional irrigation.

Soil has only a limited storage capacity, so you should only apply as much water as is needed to get it back up to field capacity. If the soil is very dry this can be quite a lot. I have watered a clay soil for eight hours and only got about four or five inches of penetration. If you add more than this, not only will it be wasted, but the excess may actually damage the soil.

Over-watering: This encourages shallow rooting, making plants more vulnerable to drought and nutrient deficiencies. It may also leach away soluble nutrients and damage soil structure (especially on poor soils).

Of course over-watering wastes water and in dry areas you simply can't afford this. Even in humid areas water shortages are getting more frequent and water is getting more expensive. Over-watering also involves unnecessary work, as it takes time and effort to put water into the soil.

Irregular watering: Too much water following too little water may cause fruit such as Tomatoes to split. It can also caused splitting in Iceberg Lettuce, Cabbage and Chinese Cabbage.

How to apply water

Water should be applied to the soil only as fast as it can soak in. This means it should fall on the bed gently, approximating a light rain shower, but not so fine that water is lost in clouds of mist. If you apply water faster than it can be absorbed it will puddle and the surface structure may break down. When this dries out a crust will form, which further impedes water (and air) infiltration (this is known as capping). Of course if water runs off of the beds it will be wasted (it may also take soil with it).

When the soil surface reaches saturation point it starts to glisten and as soon as this happens (or just before) you should move the water source momentarily to allow it to soak in. Overhead irrigation does this automatically of course.

One of the commonest mistakes of novices (particularly when hand watering) is to water until the soil surface is looks nice and dark and wet and then move on. Appearances are deceptive though, the surface may be thoroughly moist, but only an inch or so down it may still be bone dry. If the soil is regularly watered in this way, plant roots will stay near the surface where the water is and the plants will be very vulnerable to fluctuations in moisture content. If you are unable to water such shallow rooted plants for a few days they will suffer.

When watering you must pay particular attention to the edges and ends, of the beds, as they dry out faster than the middle. Also watch any slopes facing away from the water source, it will get less water than slopes facing towards the water source.

Some crops like to have water applied to their leaves, but you should do it when they will dry out quickly (morning or early evening). Others (especially fuzzy ones) are very prone to disease if their leaves get wet, so you must avoid this if possible.

If you are using sprinklers or oscillators you might want to put out a jar or rain gauge, to determine exactly how much water they are putting out.

Always be careful of hoses when watering. It's easy to inadvertently drag the hose over the corner of the bed and wipe out plants.

Methods of watering

There are two schools of thought on watering, the deep infrequent waterers and the frequent shallow waterers. Deep watering works best on deep, moisture retentive soils, while shallow watering is best suited to soils that don't hold a lot of water. Initially your soil may determine which technique you should use, but as you improve the soil you can choose which you prefer. Climate and crop may also affect your choice.

Deep watering

Deep watering is less time consuming than shallow watering, but you have to be more careful. The amount of water that constitutes deep watering depends upon the soil, you must put enough water on the beds to fully replace all of the moisture lost since the last irrigation. After the soil has been thoroughly saturated you don't water again until the top few inches of soil have dried out. This forces crops to send down deep roots to search for water and such plants are less susceptible to drought.

Shallow watering

The shallow method is easier for the beginner, as there is more margin for error. It may be the best strategy for watering light soils that can't hold much water, though it will work on any soil. This method seemingly contradicts the advice I gave above about watering deeply, but it doesn't because you never allow any of the soil to dry out.

The plants are watered daily so the soil is always fully charged. Shallow watering is often done by hand, which can reduces the amount of water used. This is quite time consuming, but has an advantage in that you get to spend a lot of time with your plants and will notice the first signs of problems such as disease or pest damage. The daily washing of the leaves is said to be good for many plants

Hand watering tends to be shallow watering simply because of the time it takes to water deeply.

A variation on shallow watering in hot dry climates is to allow the subsoil to dry out. So long as you water regularly and don't allow the topsoil to dry out your plants will do okay.

After watering

Whether you water shallowly or deeply the soil should be very close to field capacity when you finish. Examine the soil carefully after irrigation (dig down again) to make sure it is thoroughly moist with no dry areas. Take note of how the soil and plants look after watering and compare the bed to one which still needs irrigating.

Soil capping

If water is applied in large droplets, or faster than it can be absorbed into the soil, the surface aggregates break down and the smaller particles wash down between the larger ones. When the surface dries out this forms a dense crust known as a cap. This most often happens on poorly structured soils, especially silt or fine sands, but heavy watering can cause it to happen even on fairly good ones. This crust not only reduces water penetration, but also hinders seedling emergence and may inhibit the exchange of air in the soil (which can cause toxic gases to build up and inhibit root growth).

Small areas of crust can be broken up with the fingers. Use a hoe for larger areas. A thin layer of mulch will help to prevent most surface crusting.

Disease and watering

In some climates careless watering can lead to fungus disease problems in vulnerable crops. If you must use overhead watering do it in the morning or early evening so the leaves and soil surface can dry out quickly. Handling wet foliage can also spread some diseases, so don't work near newly watered plants until their leaves have dried off. Wet foliage is also heavy, so wet plants may be easily damaged or knocked over.

Algae

If your soil gets covered in a coat of green algae it is usually because it is staying wet all of the time. This means you are watering too much for the prevailing conditions. While not really serious, this can be detrimental in that it tends to seal the surface of the soil, preventing good exchange of air (as with **Capping**). If this happens allow the soil surface to dry out and cultivate lightly to get air into the soil. In future allow the soil surface to dry out between irrigations.

Water sources and quality

It's worth thinking about the purity of your water source. In arid areas dissolved salts can build up in the soil and become quite toxic. Hard water contains calcium and magnesium and may raise the pH. In some areas surface water is quite acid (from acid rain) and will lower the soil pH. If you have any suspicions you can have your water tested (it may be worth having an agricultural water test done when having your soil tested).

The best water for plants is rainwater, as it contains small quantities of nitrogen, sulfur and other nutrients. On average half of all rainfall falling on the ground runs off and is lost. You should do everything you can to ensure that the soil retains as much rainfall as possible.

If you have rain barrels underneath all of your downspouts, you can collect a surprising amount of water from your roof. See below for more on **Rainwater collection**.

Probably the commonest source of water for gardeners is the utility company. City water doesn't contain many nutrients and often contains a lot of chlorine (and sometimes fluoride) which plants and soil organisms don't like (I once tried to sprout Alfalfa seed in heavily chlorinated water and it kept rotting). If you are watering seedlings you could leave chlorinated water in open barrels for a day or so, to allow the chlorine to dissipate. Don't use water that has been through a chemical water softener, as it contains a lot of salt.

City water is becoming expensive in many areas and increasingly unreliable due to droughts and hose pipe bans. One advantage is that it has good pressure for overhead irrigation.

Many suburban and rural gardeners get their water from wells. This is often superior to city water, but sometimes contains large amounts of dissolved salts. An increasing number of wells are contaminated from various industrial and farm sources, or from lawn chemicals.

In some situations you may be able to get water from clean rivers, lakes, or streams. This is usually of good quality, though you should be sure of your legal position before using it. Unless you have friends in Congress, diverting it is probably illegal.

Gray water

Gray water is any water that has been used in the house, but doesn't contain sewage (which is known as black water). Actually it may contain very dilute sewage, as well as bacteria, viruses and a variety of chemicals so it isn't completely harmless. The average house uses 100 to 200 gallons of water a day, which could be all of the water you need for your garden. This water is already piped, and just requires a little modification of your plumbing (and some of your more wasteful habits) Logic says that if you can re-use some of this water you should, though it may be illegal to do so in many places, due to health code restrictions.

In wet climates using untreated gray water isn't really worthwhile (except in times of drought). In dry climates it doesn't make sense not to use it. In an ideal world you would use the gray water for flushing toilets and would use the fresh water thus saved for irrigation. This isn't always practical though

Gray water should be used carefully as it does contain some things plants don't like. Use on perennials and shrubs rather than annuals, keep it off foliage and rotate its use around the garden (don't put it all in one place). Use fresh water in between the gray water irrigations.

The cleanest gray water is that wasted while waiting for the hot water tap to get hot. The next cleanest comes from the shower and bathtub, then the washing machine and finally from the dishwasher and kitchen sink (the dirtiest). The latter is rich in plant nutrients, but also contains grease and oils and lots of food particles, so potentially causes a lot more problems. If you are adverse to disgusting things you should forget about using kitchen sink water. Instead try washing your vegetables outdoors in the garden sink. This water can go directly onto the garden and is very clean.

If you intend to use gray water for irrigation you should alter your washing habits to reduce its toxicity. Be careful which soaps, shampoos and detergents you use, no boron, high sodium, bleach (especially), water softeners, perfumes or lanolin.

It is very important that gray water is used immediately and isn't stored for any length of time. Bacteria will start to grow after a few hours and it will soon start to stink.

A good way to use gray water is to irrigate compost crops, such as Reeds or Comfrey, grown in their own special bed. It can also be used for Willows or Bamboo. If you get really ambitious you could create your own grey water treatment marsh to purify the gray water before use.

Rainwater

Where I live we get 3 to 8 feet of rain in winter and none at all in summer. In an ideal world we could store some of that winter rain for use in summer.

Infiltration: In-soil storage is the cheapest and simplest way to store significant amounts of water. Your first priority should be to ensure that any rain that falls on your soil soaks in, rather than running off into drains. The simplest way to do this is by ensuring that the ground is covered with vegetation, so water slowly soaks

into the ground. On steeper slopes you may have to create ditches, or swales, to intercept fast flowing runoff and hold it up long enough so that it can soak in. You could also terrace the land so water doesn't run away.

Of course water that is stored in the soil isn't as convenient or versatile as water stored in a tank or pond (from which it can be directed to where you need it).

Probably the cheapest way to store water is in a pond, Runoff from roads, paths and roofs could be channeled into ponds (lined with a rubber pond liner), for later use for irrigation.

Most house already come with a ready made rainwater collection system, the roof. If you have gutters (and you should) all you have to do is direct the water from the downspouts to some kind of storage container. The water can even go uphill somewhat, so long as the tank is lower than the gutters themselves.

To estimate how much rain you are likely to collect from your roof, you must first determine the square footage of the footprint of your roof (looking down directly from above, not its actual surface area). This is usually a little more than the square footage of the upper floor of your house. Multiply this number by the average yearly rainfall in inches. Divide this number by 12 to get the number of cubic feet of water. Then multiply this by 7.5 to get the number of gallons.

For example, my roof is approximately 800 square feet and we normally get about 60 inches of rain per year. This works out to 4800, which divided by 12 equals 4000. Multiply this by 7.5 and you get 30,000 gallons of water. If only storing it were as easy as calculating it!

Rainwater storage

In areas with year round rainfall, storage doesn't present much of a problem. All you need to do is store enough water from recent rains to see you through the rainless stretches. A couple of 50 gallon barrels might be enough, or you might use an above-ground pool if you have lots of plants, or long dry spells.

In areas with no rain for long periods you need large capacity storage. The cheapest would be an above-ground pool or a hole in the ground lined with plastic (or pond liner). A much more expensive (but durable) option would be a plastic water tank (or several).

Watering Equipment

Hoses: High quality rubber hoses are expensive, but last a long time if cared for properly. Avoid cheap vinyl hoses, they kink when twisted and once kinked will repeatedly bend in the same place. They will be a source of irritation for as long as you have them.

Look after your hoses. Don't run over them with a car (especially not the threaded metal ends, they will be ruined), don't let them freeze when full of water and store them indoors in winter. In hot climates the sun is hard on hoses, not only does the ultraviolet light degrade them, but if water is left in them it can become scalding hot. This can cause the hose to swell and the layers to separate (avoid this by not leaving them full of water). Hoses will last much longer if you keep them out of the sun in their own covered spot. You can also keep plastic buckets there.

You need to have a shutoff on all hoses, so you can turn the water off without running back to the faucet.

Hand watering equipment

Watering by hand doesn't have to be a chore. It can actually be quite therapeutic and gives you a good way to wind down in the evening. It is by far the most responsive watering method, as you can water each individual plant as conditions require. It also gets you out into the garden and in contact with each plant in turn. This works best in small gardens in humid climates that have lots of rain throughout the growing season. It is totally impractical for large gardens in dry areas, don't even think about it.

There are a few tools that make hand watering easier and more efficient

Watering can: The watering can is useful for watering small numbers of plants. Nearly everyones favorite watering can is the English Haws can. It is expensive, but nicely balanced and the long spout makes it convenient for watering wide beds. It has an upturned brass rose that puts out a gentle spray and there is an even finer rose available for watering seedlings. The Haws cans are available in metal and plastic, they both use the same rose. The plastic ones are cheaper,

but aren't as durable and can't really be retired for use as garden ornaments when their useful life is over (the metal ones are really cute). Their capacity is from 1 to 2 gallons.

One advantage of plastic watering cans is that you can leave water in them for long period. If you do this in a metal cans you will shorten its life considerably, it should always be left empty.

Fan: This connects to a hose and gives a fan shaped spray for hand watering beds. It's most often used for watering seedbeds and seedlings (make sure you have a shutoff on the fan).

Tin can: Individual plants in hills can be watered by burying a perforated can next to the plants (this is done when planting to minimize root disturbance). It is filled with water, which slowly drains into the soil and waters the plant. Cans work best in slow draining clay soils, as sandy ones often drain away too quickly. If the can is partly filled with compost it will feed the plant too.

Water wand: These tools put out a similar spray to a watering can, but connect to a hose so they never run out. The best wand uses the same rose as the Haws watering can.

Alternatives to hand watering

Hand watering may be therapeutic, but it takes too much time to be practical in dry climates or in large gardens. Fortunately there are plenty of alternatives.

Overhead watering
Oscillators and sprinklers are the easiest way to water large areas of soil quickly. Sprinklers generally have a circular pattern, while oscillators have a rectangular one, otherwise they are used in the same ways. They are ersatile, fast to use and deliver water slowly to a wide area. There is minimal puddling and runoff if you use them properly. Add a timer and you can greatly increase the efficiency of your watering time.

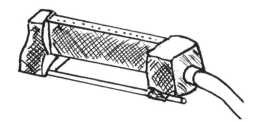

The biggest problem with overhead watering is that it wastes a lot of water. This falls on paths (where it can grow a fine crop of weeds), blows away with the wind, or evaporates from plants and the soil surface (on hot days up to 30% of the water may be lost). It also needs good water pressure.

Another objection is that overhead watering removes you from the garden somewhat, by replacing you with technology.

In general overhead watering equipment works best if it is raised off the ground a couple of feet, otherwise the jets of water are frequently deflected by tall foliage.

Spike: This inexpensive and versatile tool attaches to a hose and has a spike to hold it in the ground. It puts out a fan shaped spray of water that can be adjusted for size (and to some extent shape) by altering the water pressure. It is good for soaking small, irregularly shaped areas. This is a good example of a foolproof low-tech technology, with no moving parts to go wrong, or plastic to deteriorate in the sun.

Rose: The rose also attaches to a hose and puts out a circular spray of water. You vary the size of this spray by increasing the pressure. This is another great tool, foolproof and (if made of metal) almost indestructible.

Drip watering

Automatic watering systems use less water than other types, so are very popular in arid areas (drip irrigation was first developed in Israel). They tend to be expensive and complex to set up (some more than others), but are economical and labor saving to use.

Advantages

- They can reduce water consumption by 50%.

- They can increase yields because plants always have water easily available.

- Can work with low water pressure.

- There is less disease because foliage doesn't get wet.

- Weed growth is less because most of the soil surface remains dry, only the part around the plants gets wet.

- They reduce the amount of work needed, all you do is turn them on and off. You can even put the system on a timer to do this automatically, reducing the work of irrigation to almost nothing.

- They are the most practical way to water container plants.

Disadvantages

- These systems tend to be quite expensive, as you need a lot of parts and pipes to cover a large garden. They are also quite complex and time consuming to lay out.

- They tend to be inflexible in that they aren't easily moved once set up and are hard to work around. They are most useful for perennial plantings such as trees.

- The emitters can get clogged and tubing can be damaged by careless gardeners, rodents and sunlight (it's commonly covered with mulch to protect it from sunlight).

- They encourage you to rely on technology. You just set the timer, or turn on a tap and go indoors, rather than getting out in the garden where you will notice problems as they occur.

- They are made from plastic and eventually become garbage.

These systems are undoubtedly the way of the future in areas where water is scarce and/or expensive. If you are interested in automatic watering systems I suggest you examine the books and commercial literature. Also look at the various systems in hardware stores, garden centers and more specialist stores.

Most drip fittings are designed for watering single plants and aren't well suited to a vegetable garden, where you often need to soak the entire bed. Also most drip systems are designed for permanent installation, whereas with vegetables you need a greater degree of flexibility. You change crops frequently and need to be able to cultivate the soil without having plastic pipe in the way. There are a few products that are specifically designed for this however.

Soaker hose

This is made from recycled tires and oozes water, down its entire length. It is good for growing vegetable crops because it is fairly easy to move around. It can be buried under the soil surface so the surface doesn't get wet and grow weeds. This also reduces exposure to U.V. light.

One drawback with soaker hose is that it loses porosity over time, due to clogging from hard water, algae or small particles. This means different hoses often have different degrees of porosity (which is a pain if you want to connect two together).

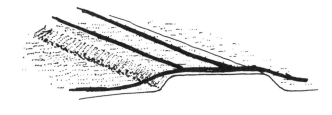

In-line drip emitters

These use the same black PVC pipe as drip irrigation, but have emitters pre-installed in them every 12″ or so. These work in much the same way as a soaker hose, but are more durable.

T tape

This is used in the same way as soaker hose, but is cheaper. I don't really like it because it is made of plastic and has a fairly short life expectancy before it ends up as garbage.

Flood irrigation

This is one of the oldest methods of irrigation. It doesn't need any special tools, but takes more specialized knowledge, as well as time to set up properly.

Sheet irrigation consists of spreading a shallow layer (or sheet) of water right across the soil. Furrow irrigation channels water through narrow furrows. It works best for warm weather crops that need a lot of water and where water in abundantly available.

Flood irrigation is very dependent on soil type and topography, and the garden must be set up carefully if it is to work effectively. The furrows must have the right gradient, so the water travels the full length of the garden and soaks in evenly, without wasting too much from runoff. This is easier on clay soils because water only penetrates slowly. On sandy soils the water often sinks into the ground before covering the entire area, or running the full length of the furrow. Beds should be narrow and fairly level and the channels must be deep and narrow so the water runs quickly. Dissolved salts can be a problem when flood irrigating, so water quality is important.

I have never worked with one of these systems, so I can't give you any advice. I just thought I should mention it.

A modern variation of flood irrigation is to use aluminum gutter or plastic pipe. Simply drill holes in it at regular intervals and lay it on the bed. This can work well as an inexpensive and simple way to irrigate.

Suggestions for water conservation

As clean fresh water becomes ever scarcer and more valuable, conservation becomes critical. In some areas this could mean the difference between having a garden and not having one. Here are some ways to reduce water consumption (taken together they can save a lot of water).

• You can cut down on water use by working a smaller number of beds very intensively.

• Mulching is one of the most important water conserving techniques you can use. It can reduce water consumption by as much as a third, by shading the soil from direct sunlight and by reducing weed competition (see **Mulching** for more on this).

- Up until there is at least 20% leaf cover, the soil loses more water by evaporation than is used by the plants. Never leave the soil bare for any longer than necessary, cover with mulch or row covers to minimize evaporation. Keeping seed beds covered not only reduces water use, but also the frequency with which you have to water.

- Put plants with similar water needs in the same bed. You can then have a bed for moisture loving plants and a separate bed for more drought tolerant crops. This enables you to more easily adjust your watering to the crop.

- The way you irrigate affects water consumption. The most water conserving methods are the drip systems, the most wasteful are overhead ones. Hand watering with a can or wand is also more efficient (but labor intensive).

- The soil is a water storage medium and one of the best ways to conserve water is to add organic matter to the soil. When a soil is high in organic matter it absorbs water like a sponge and any the water that falls on it in will be absorbed and held. It won't drain away, or be wasted in runoff.

- In row gardens, where the soil is bare for much of the time, the top couple of inches of soil was often cultivated to create a dust mulch, in the belief this would reduce evaporation. It has been found that the top couple of inches of soil tend to dry out naturally, so it really isn't necessary to cultivate. In fact cultivation may actually increase water loss.

- Though the rich soil of intensive beds holds a lot of moisture, the raised shape can increase water loss (by increasing surface area). In hot, dry climates the beds should only be slightly raised, or even flat to reduce evaporative losses. In extremely arid areas they may even be sunken.

- If water is very scarce don't use cover crops or green manures. These can take a lot of water from the soil even before you plant your crop (you should use a mulch instead). Remove old crops when they start to decline, otherwise they will continue to use water.

- Dry winds can take a lot of moisture from the soil, so make sure the garden has an efficient windbreak (a mulch will help also).

- Another useful strategy for saving water is to only water you plants at critical growth times (during germination, after transplanting and when the food part is sizing up). If you only give plants water when they need it most, you can get the highest productivity for the least consumption of water. You may get 60% of the yield, using only 10% of the water.

- Don't deprive plants of the water they need for proper growth. It's much better to grow a few plants well than a lot of plants badly.

- Starting plants inside, rather than direct sowing, can also save water.

- Some crops are more drought tolerant than others (Beans, Corn, Melons, Tomatoes), as are some varieties. If water is very scarce try to concentrate on these.

- If water is very scarce you can water plants individually, rather than wetting the entire bed (perhaps sink perforated cans by each plant).

- A few crops are so drought tolerant (Watermelons, Tomatoes) that they can be grown without irrigation, even in areas with rainless summers. They simply need to be planted further apart, to give each plant access to a larger volume of soil. In the arid southwest, Native Americans grew corn without irrigation by planting the hills 6 feet apart. Yields are lower when grown in this way, but the fruit is sweeter and better flavored. If you have plenty of space, but not much water, you may want to investigate this further.

- If your hose connections drip, then fix them.

- Don't waste rainwater. Make use of it by storing as much as you can, either in the soil or in containers. See **Rainwater** for more on this.

- Get the maximum use of your household water by using it twice. Once in the house and a second time in the garden. See **Gray Water** for more on this.

- In areas with wet winters and dry summers you might try growing your main crops in spring, while there is still plenty of water in the ground from winter rains.

181

22 Weeds

The problem with weeds

Weeds have been described as plants growing in the wrong place. This usually means growing among our cultivated plants, where they are not wanted. Weeds are pioneer plants, adapted to growing in disturbed soil and are natures first line of defense against soil erosion and degradation. When soil is disturbed by floods, foraging animals, landslides or gardeners, weeds are soon there, to quickly cover the bare soil with a mantle of vegetation. They are the first stage in a succession that, if undisturbed, could eventually lead to forest.

The garden often contains bare, disturbed soil, so the weeds come in to perform their natural role of covering and protecting it. This is a problem because these wild plants are more vigorous than most crops and better able to grow in the garden. If left unchallenged they will out-compete your crops for water, nutrients and eventually for light.

Weeds have survived despite our best efforts, because of their ability to germinate and grow quickly, forage for water and nutrients and to propagate themselves quickly. Crop plants have been selected for the traits we deem important: edibility, nutrition and yield and in the process have lost much of their ability to compete. If they are to be grow and be productive they need human protection. This is most critical when they are young and if they aren't protected from weeds at this time their yields will be reduced drastically (they may even be wiped out altogether). Neglecting to control weeds is one of the commonest reasons for failure in the garden.

Not only do weeds compete directly with our crops, they can also harbor insect and other pests, and may carry crop diseases. They may also encourage disease by crowding crops and impeding air circulation.

Beneficial aspects of weeds

There are some good aspects to weeds:

* They help to increase the biodiversity of the garden and are as beneficial in their own way as the herbs or flowers. If you removed every single weed from your garden it would be a much less interesting and healthy place.

* Many weeds are edible or have other uses around the garden. I look upon weeds as a bonus, a group of extra crops that grow themselves.

* Weeds are useful as companions and nurse plants. They quickly cover disturbed soil and protect it until the crop is big enough to take over. They also help to camouflage crop plants and hide them from pests.

* Weeds sometimes act as trap crops. For example Brassica pests are more attracted to Wild Brassicas (with their abundance of pungent oil) than to the rather insipid cultivated varieties.

* Weeds provide food for wildlife, including many important predatory insects.

* Weeds help to enrich the soil. Their deep penetrating roots can break up compacted subsoil and mine it for nutrients. They have a great ability to forage for scarce nutrients and accumulate them in their bodies (many accumulate specific nutrients). When weeds die their nutrients are released for the use of other plants. A crop of weeds can be used as a self-sown green manure crop (make sure it doesn't set seed), or can be composted. The hardier weeds can act as a cover crop to store nutrients and protect the soil over the winter.

The most beneficial weeds

Chickweed (*Stellaria*)
Clover (*Trifolium*)
Dandelion (*Taraxacum*)
Groundsel (*Senecio*)
Lambs Quarters (*Chenopodium*)
Stinging Nettle (*Urtica*)
Sweet Clover (*Melilotus*)
White Campion (*Silene*)

Annual weeds

The common annual garden weeds have selected themselves from thousands of species from all over the world. They share certain characteristics which make them supremely successful in the rich, moist, bare soil found in the garden. They have an advantage over perennial weeds in that they are more mobile and more responsive to adverse changes.

- One of the most significant characteristics of annual weeds is an ability to germinate and grow quickly. The first seedlings to appear after you direct sow a bed are usually annuals weed, which then have a head start over slower germinating crop seedlings.

- Annual weeds have an ability to produce seed quickly and abundantly (and often parthenogenically - by self-fertilization). Some weeds can set seed only a few weeks after emergence and produce several generations in a season.

- They grow and spread so rapidly they can smother competitors.

- These plants are able to effectively disperse their seeds by a wide range of ingenious methods, including hooks, explosions and parachutes. By these means they can travel very long distances and can be in the right place at the right time.

- Some species produce seeds that germinate at different times. Some germinate immediately and some have a built in dormancy period. This ensures they won't all emerge at once and face potential disaster.

- Some species have fleshy leaves that enable them to survive being uprooted long enough to set seed.

- Their seed is often very long lived and can lay buried in the ground for years. As soon as a disturbance bring them air and light and moisture they will germinate.

The commonest annual weeds include

Amaranth (*Amaranthus*)
Chickweed (*Stellaria*)
Crabgrass (*Digitaria*)
Knotweed (*Polygonum*)
Lambs Quarters (*Chenopodium*)
Mallows (*Malva*)
Purslane (*Portulaca*)
Speedwell (*Veronica*)
Storksbill (*Erodium*)
White Campion (*Silene*)
Sow Thistle (*Sonchus*)

Perennial weeds

These are quite different in character from annual weeds and most aren't a big problem in the mature annual vegetable garden, because there is too much disturbance there. They usually find their niche on soil that is disturbed relatively infrequently and eventually take over from the annual weeds. They are commonly found in perennial borders, paths, lawns and undisturbed garden beds.

Common perennial weeds
Creeping Buttercup (*Ranunculus repens*)
Creeping Thistle (*Cirsium arvensis*)
Dandelion (*Taraxacum*)
Docks (*Rumex* spp)
Ground Ivy (*Glechoma hederacea*)
Horsetail (*Equisetum*)
Japanese Knotweed (*Polygonum cuspidatum*)
Rosebay Willow Herb (*Epilobium angustifolium*)
Wood Sorrels (*Oxalis* spp)

Pernicious weeds

A few perennial weeds have adapted a similar strategy to the annuals and they can be a big problem. They spread quickly on bare soil, but instead of using seeds they take advantage of the fact that they are perennial and spread vegetatively, by means of brittle taproots, bulbs, bulbils, creeping roots, rhizomes, or stolons. These pernicious (having the power to kill or destroy) plants are the super-weeds and can be a great test of the gardeners skill and commitment to organic methods.

Pernicious perennial weeds
Bermuda Grass (*Cynodon dactylon*)
Bindweeds (*Convolvolus arvensis*)
Couch Grass (*Agropyron repens*)
Ground Elder (*Aegopodium podagraria*)

Eliminating pernicious weeds
Pernicious weeds can be very difficult to deal with. You could double dig an entire area, carefully removing every fragment of root you see and yet still have a healthy stand of weeds the following year. To eliminate such plants you have to use the right combination of techniques (see below).

If you find a pernicious weed, such as Bindweed or Bermuda Grass, growing in your garden you must get rid of it immediately, don't let it get established. If unchecked it inevitably get worse and worse. It is essential to get these weeds while they are still small, before they start to spread.

The usual way eradicate a few pernicious weeds is by digging. You have to do this very carefully to make sure you get every fragment. Gather the pieces straight into a separate bucket, don't mix them with harmless compostable weeds. Not only would you contaminate your compostable weeds, you would also create a greater volume of potentially pernicious stuff.

A large area of pernicious weeds can be eradicated by covering with a plastic mulch, either clear plastic or black. This must be left on as long as necessary to do the job. Going a step further you could solarize the soil. See **Solarization** in the section on **Diseases**.

Rototiller removal
It is possible to use a rototiller to eradicate pernicious weeds, but this should only done after very careful deliberation. If not done carefully you will merely increase the number of plants, rather than destroying them.

The weeds should be tilled (or dug) into the top 1″ of soil when they first start growing vigorously in spring, but before they start putting much food back into the roots. Two weeks later they are tilled 2″ deep, then every couple of weeks they are tilled (or dug) an inch deeper. The theory is that the shoots take energy from the roots for two weeks or more, so you allow the roots just enough time to expend energy putting out new shoots. You then incorporate them back into the soil, before they get any energy back from the shoot. The shoots also give away their location, so you can find them. You repeat this process until they are gone. This repeated cultivation damages the structure of the soil, so afterwards you must do everything you can to improve the soil.

Cultivated weeds

Some cultivated perennials can also become pests, for example Bamboo, Comfrey, Horseradish and Mints are notoriously difficult to eradicate once established. When planting them make sure you know what you are doing and put them in their own beds, or behind barriers, where they can do no harm.

Controlling weeds

Though weeds have some real benefits you can't just leave them all in the garden to do as they want. Controlling weeds is actually one of the most important garden maintenance operations of all.

Seedlings and young plants are the most vulnerable to weeds and if not protected they will soon be overwhelmed. Small weeds don't much bother larger crop plants, but you still can't afford to ignore them and allow them to complete their life cycle. If they set seed you will have even more weeds in following years. The wise old gardeners saying is "one years seeding means seven years weeding".

Though weeds must be kept under control, they shouldn't become an obsession, you don't have to remove every weed from your garden. In commercial organic farming there is a trade off between the cost of not weeding (in reduced yield) and the cost of weeding (in labor). Hand labor for weed control is one of the biggest costs for farmers, which is why conventional growers have embraced toxic herbicides and genetically modified crops so enthusiastically.

Gardeners have to make a similar compromise, choosing more crop or less work. There is always some weeding to do, even in the best kept gardens. It's like painting the Golden Gate Bridge, by the time you get to the end you have to start all over again.

Weeding tips

Weeding is a fairly simple process, but there are a few tricks that make it easier and make your weeding time more productive.

- When you establish the garden take great pains to remove all perennial weeds. This is one good argument in favor of double digging.

- You need to know which plants are weeds and which are crops, so get a good book on weed identification. If you can't identify a weed let a few seedlings grow until you can. Don't wipe out plants thoughtlessly, it may be something interesting (if it is you can pot it up and move it if necessary). Of course it's good to know whether a weed is an annual or perennial, so you know the right way to deal with it.

Volunteers

These are seedlings of garden plants that have self sown and can make gardening more interesting (many new fruit tree varieties began life in this way). They are one reason for not wiping out seedlings blindly without first identifying them. Useful volunteers can be transplanted to where you want them to grow. Seedling fruit trees can have selected scions grafted onto them.

Volunteers of some crops (e.g. Potatoes) are discouraged because they can provide a source of infectious diseases, or help pests to survive the winter.

- The earlier you weed, the easier it will be. Newly germinated seedlings are the easiest to eliminate, but its pretty straightforward up until they have their first few leaves (you can simply run over them with a Dutch or oscillating hoe). If you leave it much later than this they will be so big you can't use a hoe easily. They may also re-root, or sprout from the root (if perennial).

- Don't use a hoe until the crop seedlings have emerged and you can see the plants clearly. If you hoe too soon you may damage the emerging crop seedlings. There are ways of weeding before the crop emerges, see **Pre-emergence Weeding** in the section on **Direct Sowing**.

- Weeds begin to compete with a direct sown crop about 3 weeks after the crop emerges, so don't wait too long. Once weeds start inhibiting a crop they will reduce the final yield, or delay maturation.

- Research has shown that weeds some distance away from the crop have a greater deleterious effect than those near by. Apparently this is because the closer weeds are partly suppressed by the crop, whereas those further away are able to grow so large they inhibit the crop.

- Cut off annual weeds just below ground level (and below the crown) and most will die. Perennials often re-sprout from the root and may need cutting several times before they die. A few plants need more than this, they must be dug out very carefully, so you get every fragment of root - see **Pernicious Weeds**.

- Weed regularly to keep on top of it, ideally every 10 to 14 days and you will always be dealing with small weeds. This is an important maintenance operation and you can't afford to neglect it.

- Get into the habit of weeding for a few minutes whenever you are in the garden. Remove the biggest weeds first, as these are closest to setting seed.

- It's better to weed a small section thoroughly, than halfheartedly weed a larger area. If you try to do too much, too quickly, the garden can easily get overgrown and you can get discouraged. If you can't get through the entire garden in time then it is time to evaluate its size (or get help).

- If weeds hopelessly swamp a bed it may be better to clear it completely and start over.

- Don't disturb the soil any deeper than necessary when hoeing. Weed seeds sprout when cultivation brings them close (within 2″) to the soil surface and exposes them to air (and sometimes light). Seeds left buried deeper than this don't germinate and will eventually die ("let sleeping seeds lie").

- Though it's easier to weed in moist soil, weeds die faster if the soil is dry. Normally you don't water for a couple of days after weeding, as watering may help them to re-root and recover. If you disturb the remaining crop plants too much, you may have to water however.

- Don't simply uproot weeds and leave them on the bed, or on the path. Remove them to the compost pile. Some weeds can survive uprooting (notably the fleshy ones like Purslane) and re-root or set seed. Also decaying plant material may encourage disease. Throw the weeds straight into a bucket when hand weeding, or throw them on to the path and rake them up into a wheelbarrow after you finish.

- Don't slacken off on weeding at the end of the season, otherwise the hardier weeds, which set seed late in the year, will come back to haunt you. After the last harvest, skim the bed of weeds and apply a much, or plant a cover crop to prevent weed growth.

- Keep going after perennial weeds until they are no longer a problem, never let up.

- Make sure you return the nutrients contained in the weeds to the soil, either by burying them, using as mulch, or by composting.

Hoeing

Hoeing is the commonest way to weed large areas quickly and doesn't have to be a chore if done right.

It helps if you set out your plants to make hoeing easier. Plant on a matrix and leave enough space between the plants (the width of a hoe plus a couple of inches). Hoe diagonally from one side down each row, then cross to the other side of the bed (so you can hoe in the same direction) and hoe down the opposite rows (see illustration). Finally hoe around the edges.

As the crop grows larger it's helpful to have a narrow 3″ hoe for getting in the narrower spaces.

One of the keys to efficient hoeing is to keep the blade sharp, so it cuts cleanly rather than tearing or bulldozing. It should be sharp enough to cut you, especially at the corners (file from the inside of the blade). If you are doing a lot of hoeing sharpen it every 20 to 30 minutes.

Hoeing not only removes weeds, it also creates a loose dry surface that is less hospitable to weed seedlings.

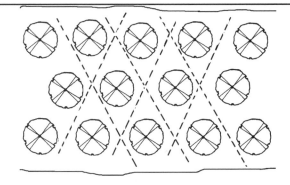

Hoes

There are many different types of hoe, each designed for a specific purpose and it pays to find the right one for the job. The problem with many hoes is that if used improperly they penetrate too deeply, damaging roots, bringing up weed seeds to the surface where they can germinate and damaging the soil (ideally they should enetrate to a maximum of 1″).

Draw hoe

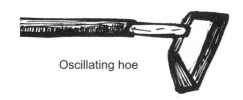

Eye hoe

Oscillating hoe

Dutch hoe

Warren hoe

Oscillating hoe: The blade of this tool tilts so it is at the right angle for cutting on both the push and pull strokes. It is one of the best hoes for removing small seedlings (the smaller the better), as it only scrapes the surface of the soil and doesn't uncover more weed seeds. It doesn't work well with a dense growth of larger weeds.

Dutch hoe: This hoe is used for much the same purpose as the oscillating hoe. It's low angled blade works parallel to the ground and is moved backwards and forwards to cut off roots just below the soil surface. Used properly is doesn't damage shallow crop roots, or stir up the soil too much. Hold the handle fairly low to keep the blade nearly parallel with the soil (but keep your back straight).

Draw hoe: The blade of a draw hoe is fixed at a sharp angle, so that the blade is parallel to the ground when the handle is held at an appropriate angle. With the blade almost parallel to the ground, you don't disturb the soil very much when cutting shallow weeds. For tougher, deeper-rooted weeds you increase the angle of attack to penetrate more deeply. You then use a heavier downward chopping motion, breaking off and pulverizing a small section at a time. It isn't as precise as other hoes.

Onion Hoe: This miniature draw hoe is used for precise close up weeding.

Warren hoe: The arrowhead shaped blade is useful for precise cultivation and furrowing, however it isn't very sharp so can't cut weeds very well.

Wheel hoe: As the name suggests, this consists of a hoe mounted on a wheel and is pushed with two hands. Though specifically designed for hoeing long rows quickly, it can be used on beds in some cases. Fitted with an oscillating blade it can be very fast and precise. Unfortunately it is also quite expensive.

Fork and Spade: These aren't hoes, but these multi-purpose tools are often used for weeding. The spade is good for skimming densely packed weeds from paths and beds and for digging up deep rooted perennial weeds. The fork is used for loosening deep rooted weeds so they can be hand pulled. The smaller border fork is particularly useful for this.

Other ways to tackle weeds

Chickens

If chickens are confined in a small area they will eat all weeds, weed seeds, soil pests and everything else. The best way to do this is with a mobile hen run (known as a "Chicken Tractor"). This is placed over the area to be weeded and when the chickens have eaten everything, it is moved to the next area.

Crop selection

Crops vary in their ability to compete with weeds. Robust fast growing crops with large leaves, like Chard and Cucumber can compete against weeds much more effectively than narrow or lacy leafed plants like Onion and Carrot. If your soil is very weedy, you might grow only the most weed tolerant crops until you get the problem under control.

Design

You can reduce weed problems by designing the garden carefully. Keep bare disturbed soil to a minimum at all times, make paths fairly narrow (so there is less area for weeds) and use deep mulches.

Flame Weeding

This ingenious method uses a flame from a specially adapted torch (old-fashioned flame guns used kerosene, modern ones use propane) to kill weeds. Used like a scythe, it works quickly and with little effort. Flame weeding is most effective with small annuals, but can also kill perennial if used regularly. It's also good for weeding paths and close to trees (it won't hurt them).

The flame actually passes a few inches over the weeds and doesn't really burn them, but merely heats them slightly. A surface temperature of 60° C is all that is necessary to burst their cell walls and kill them (almost like freezing). The flamed weeds darken slightly, but don't immediately look much different, so you have to work carefully to make sure you cover the entire area.

In very dry areas you need to be very aware of the danger of starting a fire. I rarely use mine in summer and then only after I have thoroughly watered the area (it doesn't make it any less effective). Even then I keep a hose handy.

No Digging

Any kind of soil cultivation brings weed seeds to the surface where they can germinate. If you don't disturb the soil this doesn't happen. No-dig gardeners rely on mulch to feed their soil and to suppress weeds. Such a garden can be relatively weed free in a few years (see **Mulch**).

Mulch

Bare soil is a direct invitation to annual weeds, it's as if you prepared it just for them. If you cover the soil with mulch, they can't get established. See **Mulch** for more on this.

Plant Potatoes

Potatoes are a good cleaning crop for weedy soils, because the soil is cultivated three times when growing them. Once when planting out, again when earthing up and for a third time when harvesting the tubers. You can uproot and bury weeds at each stage.

Plastic mulch

A continuous plastic mulch can be a very effective way to kill large areas of weeds. The color of the plastic you use is important. Black plastic works best, because it deprives the plants of light and increases the soil temperature by as much as 10° F. Clear plastic is less effective, as in cool weather weeds may continue to grow underneath it. In sunny weather it can increase soil temperatures by as much as 15° F, in which case it will probably cook the weeds.

Rotation

Crops that are vulnerable to weeds should follow a vigorous crop that suppresses weeds (such as Potatoes). Some crops are easy to hoe, so are easily kept weed free, while others are much more difficult.

Hand weeding

Hand weeding is the most effective way of weeding in between plants. Even when using a hoe you often have to do some hand weeding, as it's the only way to weed close to plants without damaging them. When weeding you might sit, kneel (get something to kneel on), bend, or crouch, depending on the number of weeds. After a little practice you can speed up weeding by using both hands simultaneously.

Edible weeds

Many of the most common garden weeds are actually edible and can be very good if gathered at the right time (often as good as the crops you are trying to grow). These are plants you will have to remove anyway, so all you have to do is prepare them. Using them increases the productivity of your garden with no extra work. If you want to learn more about edible weeds and other useful wild plants check out my book The Uses Of Wild Plants.

The most useful edible garden weeds include.

Amaranth (*Amaranthus*) P
Burdock (*Arctium*) R, P
Chickweed (*Stellaria*) P, S
Dandelion (*Taraxacum*) R, P, S
Docks (*Rumex* spp) P
Ground Elder (*Aegopodium podagraria*) P
Ground Ivy (*Glechoma hederacea*) S
Japanese Knotweed (*Polygonum cuspidatum*) P
Lambs Quarters (*Chenopodium*) P, S
Mallow (*Malva*) P, S
Miners Lettuce (*Montia*) P. S.
Plantain (*Plantago*) P. S.
Purslane (*Portulaca oleracea*) P, S
Rosebay Willow Herb (*Epilobium angustifolium*) P, S
Shepherds Purse (*Capsella*) P, S
Sorrel (*Rumex*) P, S
Stinging Nettle (*Urtica*) P
Sow Thistle (*Sonchus*) P. S.
Thistles (*Cirsium*) R, P
Wild Lettuce (*Lactuca*) P. S.
Wintercress (*Barbarea*) P. S.

R - root, P - potherb, S - salad

Smother crops

Smother crop are plants that grow so vigorously they cast a dense shade and smother all competing plants beneath them (even pernicious perennials). The commonest smother crops include Mustard, African Marigold, Buckwheat, Hemp and Sunflower (see **Soil improving Crops** for more on these).

Any crops that form a continuous canopy of shade over a bed also act to suppress weeds to some extent. Not only does the reduced light inhibit weed growth, but it has recently been found that the light filtering through green leaves doesn't stimulate seed germination.

Weed Barriers

Creeping pernicious perennials can be prevented from invading the garden by a 6″ deep ditch (some people go right down into the subsoil to make sure). If you don't want an open ditch then bury some kind of barrier (plastic, metal, wood).

Soil Improvement

Some weeds prefer poor (acid, wet, infertile) soils and can be discouraged by improving the soil, liming, draining and fertilizing.

Solarization

This can be used to kill weed seeds and most pernicious perennials. See **Diseases** for more on this.

Spacing

Crop plants should ideally be spaced for maximum weed suppressing effect. The smaller the plants the closer together they must be spaced. Widely spaced, slow growing, plants should be intercropped to keep the soil covered, or you should use mulch.

Use transplants

If weeds are very bad, you could start almost all of your crops as transplants. These have a head start over weeds and so are much more able to compete with them.

Weed killers.

The very idea of weed killers is anathema to organic gardeners, but there are situations where they might be useful. The most obvious is when faced with a newly introduced pernicious perennial weed such as Bindweed or Bermuda Grass. In such a case the benefits of completely eradicating such a serious pest quickly might outweigh any other consideration. There are some organic herbicides, though most of them aren't tough enough for serious perennial weeds.

Weeding in the Dark

An experiment in Germany found that weeding at night reduced the number of weed seeds germinating. This is probably because many seeds are photosensitive and need light to germinate. Of course this presents other problems, you might accidentally weed out crops if you can't see what you are doing (hopefully we will soon be able to find cheap Iraq war surplus night vision glasses)

Disposal of weeds

Most weeds should be returned to the soil, either by composting or burying them. Pernicious perennial weeds and annuals with seeds, can't be recycled in this way (unless very dead) as they may well come back to haunt you. It would be a waste to simply dump or burn them however, so I would suggest composting them in the middle of a very hot pile. Another way to get rid of them would be to anaerobically compost them in a plastic bag (see **Composting**).

Weed seed bank in the soil

If you are negligent about weeding, seeds will slowly build up in the soil (there may be as many as 7000 seeds per square foot). Unfortunately there isn't any good way to reduce these numbers quickly. You might think you could germinate them all, by cultivating the soil and watering it as for a seedbed. However only a small percentage of the seeds present will germinate at any one time, so this approach won't have much effect. The top layer of soil provides the warm moist conditions that shorten the life of seeds, and up to 50% of the seeds in this layer will normally die in the following year (far more than you could remove by germinating them). Seeds buried deeper in the soil have better storage conditions and can last much longer (up to 40 years in some cases).

Weed seeds last longer in impoverished chemically fertilized soils, than they do in rich biologically active soils. There they are attacked by soil organisms such as bacteria, fungi and weevils.

This doesn't mean that it's a waste of time to sprout seeds in the soil. They are a good source of organic matter for compost piles and provide a free green manure crop. In spring you can use plastic cloches to warm the soil and encourage weed germination (weed seeds germinate more readily in spring). You can then remove the young plants for compost or green manure, prior to sowing or transplanting.

Stripping the top inch or two of soil from the beds can reduce the numbers of seeds in the soil. This is some of

your best soil though, so you don't want to lose it. You could put it in a compost pile to kill the seeds and then return it to the garden in compost.

The most significant thing you can do to reduce the number of seeds in your soil, is to stop more being added. If you conscientiously remove weeds before they set seed, the bank of viable seeds in the soil will decline markedly in a few years.

Don't import weeds

Though some weeds transport themselves to the garden, many are inadvertently imported by gardeners.

- Imported manure is almost certain to bring in weeds, especially from the bedding or feed mixed in with it). It should be composted thoroughly before using it in the garden.

- Hay is often full of all kinds of seeds. In fact using weedy hay as a mulch is almost like planting a lawn (add it to the compost pile instead.)

- Weed seeds may also be introduced with cover crop seeds such as Alfalfa, Buckwheat or Clover.

- Quite a few annual weeds are frequent flyers and will arrive by air. If you can eliminate nearby sources of airborne seed (Thistles, Dandelions, Wild Lettuce), before they scatter seed all over your garden, you will save some work.

- Purchased transplants and potted plants may contain weed seeds, or roots of perennial weeds, so be vigilant when bringing plants into the garden.

- Weed seeds may also come into the garden on wheels, feet, pets and clothes.

---

23 Garden pests

Garden wildlife

When gardeners talk about pests they mean any insect, mammal, bird, mollusk, human and other creature that damages or destroys crops and so reduces their yields. Pests may be as large as an Elk or as small as an aphid. In this section I am mainly talking about insect pests and their kin, though I briefly mention larger pest at the end.

Chemically dependent gardeners look upon pests as malevolent forces that prey upon helpless and innocent plants, much like evil spirits. They attempt to protect their plants by killing the pests with an arsenal of weapons, cultural, biological and (mostly) chemical.

Organic gardeners look upon pests as indicators that there is an imbalance or other problem in the garden. One that places the affected plants under some kind of stress and weakens them, making them more attractive to pests. They attempt to defeat pests, not by simply killing them, but by correcting the problem that is causing the stress. From this point of view the pest is actually helping you, by pointing out a problem (you might have some difficulty convincing yourself on this).

Friend or foe?

You are never alone in your garden, many other creatures live in it too (some no doubt think of it as 'their' garden). Most of these creatures are harmless, or beneficial (they pollinate crops, break down organic matter, aerate the soil, clean up diseased material, prey on insect pests). They should be left alone to pursue their own lives, if not actively encouraged. Only a few creatures are potentially destructive (in some circumstances) and these are the ones we label pests. The organic grower should attempt to learn about all of the gardens inhabitants, so she won't worry about non-existent problems, or act rashly and indiscriminately.

I have a fairly lenient approach to pests, because I like to think that I'm cultivating a garden, rather than simply a selection of crops. I'll accept quite a lot of damage so long as it doesn't significantly reduce the final harvest. If

---

Notice

I have used the word pest many times in this book as a convenient word to describe creatures in the wrong place at the wrong time. I mean no offense to these creatures and recognize their right to their own existence, so long as they recognize mine (and the rights of my plants).

---

the pest is particularly interesting (such as a Swallowtail Butterfly) I will even tolerate a considerable reduction in yield (I guess I'm a sucker for a pretty face).

Unpredictability of pests

Many factors influence the size of insect populations, so they fluctuate enormously from year to year. Some pests tend to be around all the time (Cabbage Moths), but most are quite erratic, appearing in large numbers some years and barely at all in others. Pests may attack one plant and leave seemingly identical neighbors alone. In one garden their effect may be negligible, while a nearby garden may be devastated. Sometimes a pest may appear on your crop when there isn't another crop like it for miles around.

Insects have the capacity to reproduce very rapidly if conditions are right. If a single moth can lay 1000 eggs, it only takes 20 moths to lay 20,000. Fortunately insect mortality is also very high. It was once estimated that of 10,000 Large Cabbage White Butterflies, 6000 were killed by disease, 3400 by parasites, 420 by birds and 220 died as pupae.

How pests find plants

Insect pests locate their favored food plants by sight and smell and then taste it to verify it is the right one. They have a very highly developed sense of smell and can often smell plants that are odorless to humans. Some insects can detect their preferred plants from a considerable distance (Carrot Rust Fly is said to be able to smell bruised Carrot foliage from a mile away).

Organic growers believe that pests are most attracted to the least healthy plants. Plants with succulent sappy growth from having been fed too much soluble nitrogen, plants whose roots have been damaged during transplanting and plants growing in less than ideal soils, or an unsuitable climate. These weaknesses may not be immediately detectable to humans, but insects quickly identify and exploit them.

Though the organic ideal is to eliminate all causes of stress in the garden, this is not really possible in practice. An intensive garden is an artificial creation and you want to grow the crops you will eat, rather than those which are ideally suited to it. This means there will always be some conflict and some pests.

Killing

An intensive vegetable garden is an artificial situation that favors certain insects, just as it favors certain plants – weeds. Having created such a situation the gardener

must sometimes intervene to maintain some kind of balance (or there may not be anything to harvest).

Many newcomers to gardening are hesitant to kill pests and this is a fairly natural reaction (I still feel uncomfortable killing things). If you absolutely refuse to kill pests under any circumstances (a valid standpoint), you can try deporting them. If you do this you must take them far enough away or they may return. You could also plant extra crops, or just make do with a little less.

I almost never kill anything, not because I don't have any pests, but because I don't care if plants get damaged, so long as they still yield a reasonable crop. I must admit that here in the Santa Cruz mountains we are blessed with a relative scarcity of serious insect pests and diseases. However we do have deer, gophers and quail to stop gardeners from getting too complacent.

Pests in the garden.

Pests can be a big problem when starting a garden, because soil fertility is relatively low and growing conditions aren't ideal. This can be a difficult situation for beginners, as the initial enthusiasm can quickly turn to discouragement when everything you put into the ground gets mutilated. It is important not to get too

disheartened, the damage is often less serious than it appears. Your garden may not look like the pictures in Fine Gardening magazine (mine never has either), but you can still get good yields.

Unfortunately, even after the first couple of years, you aren't necessarily out of the woods. Pests tend to increase in variety for several years, as they discover you have created a 24 hour salad bar for them. Eventually however, the garden reaches a state of ecological equilibrium and pests gradually become less troublesome. The plants are healthier, predators become more abundant and you discover the most effective ways to deal with them. By this time you main pests may not be insects at all, but larger animals. In my first garden slugs were my biggest problem, but in later years I progressed through rabbits, groundhogs, raccoons and finally to deer (I moved before the pests got any bigger than that.)

Tolerable pests

Most plants can tolerate considerable damage with little effect on the harvest (it is not in a pests interest to kill its host, because it could destroy its food source). Logic would lead one to conclude that if an insect is feeding on a plant it must be harmful, but recent evidence suggests this isn't always the case. A plant can often lose 30% of its leaf area without appreciably affecting the yield, because it produces more leaves than it really needs (presumably as insurance against just such an eventuality). They can also repair minor damage quite easily, by putting out new growth. Older basal leaves will often get shaded out and die anyway as a plant matures.

Minor predation has even been shown to increase yields in some cases (which would make some pests beneficial and not pests at all!). For example small colonies of aphids have increased wheat yields, weevils have increased Strawberry, Pea and Bean yields, Mites have increased Cucumber yields, Asparagus Beetle has increased Asparagus yields (in following years). It isn't really clear why minor damage would increase crop yield, perhaps it's a form of pruning and so stimulates growth.

Many pests don't appreciably affect plant health and cause negligible damage to edible parts. Such pests may be both common and hard to control, but because of the nature of their activities they can often be tolerated. The Corn Earworm is such a creature, it is very common, but causes mostly cosmetic damage and it isn't worth the effort required to eliminate it. Conventional commercial growers merely chop the damaged tip off of the ear and the buyer knows nothing.

As home gardeners we have one big advantage over commercial growers. If we lose a crop it doesn't really matter, we aren't going to go hungry and we aren't going to go out of business.

Intolerable pests

At the other end of the spectrum are those pests that kill, or permanently stunt, their host plants. Some of these are very persistent and discouraging, repeatedly killing or seriously damaging a large proportion of a planting, or rendering it inedible (Carrot Rust Fly is an example).

The first such pest I encountered was the Squash Vine Borer, which caused me to pretty much give up growing Summer Squash for a while. Other such pests include Slugs, Snails, Bean Beetles, Cabbage Maggot and Carrot Rust Fly. Every gardener has (or has had) their nemesis. Some are very specific in their feeding habits (such as the Squash Borer), while others will eat a wide variety of things (slugs and snails). If you want to grow their favorite crops, you must find ways to deal with such creatures.

Dealing with a pest problem

When an organic gardener talks about pests, she usually means the most difficult and destructive creatures that are hard to ignore. Fortunately if you use the right techniques you can usually reduce their depredations to tolerable levels, even if you can't eliminate them entirely.

Observing

This is the single most critical aspect of pest control, because if you don't notice a problem you can't do anything about it. A couple of nights of neglect may be long enough for an entire seedbed to be destroyed by slugs. It's disheartening to notice a pest after it has destroyed a plant, when a little observation and action could have prevented the damage. This is another reason to have the vegetable garden close to your house.

Get in the habit of walking around the garden every day to check things out. Take some of these walks at night with a bright flashlight and you will see a different world. Time spent looking at things in the garden is always well spent. The better you get to know the garden the easier it is to control pests. Write down in your garden journal when you first notice a pest each year, and you will know when to anticipate it in the future.

Identifying

I once read a novel that explained how learning the name of something gives you power over it. It is a good practice (and interesting) to learn the names of every insect you find, regardless of whether it's a pest or not (you may even want to draw, or photograph, them). Don't forget that immature insects often look quite different from adults (the Ladybird Beetle is a good example). You could even make a net from a coat hanger, a piece of old panty-hose and a stick, to help you catch them. Collect them in a jar for identification and then release them.

What did the damage?

If your plants are getting damaged, you must find out which creature is responsible. You don't want to interfere with the many harmless or beneficial creatures out there. You need to think like a detective to find the perpetrator of the crime. It is not always the most visible insect that is the guilty party. Insects feed off of plants by chewing, boring, mining, sucking and forming galls. The type of damage they inflict will help you to deduce what kind of creature is responsible. Some pests live inside the plant and you may not be aware of their presence until the plant wilts, or shows deficiency symptoms (Carrot fly, Cabbage root maggot, Squash borers).

What to do

Once you have identified the culprit you can determine if the problem is serious enough to warrant action. As a gardener you can be selective as to how and when, you control your pests. Worry about those that kill plants, or reduce yields considerably and ignore those that cause mainly cosmetic damage. Some pest damage is tolerable and to be expected. Don't get paranoid and regard every insect you see as a potential threat and every chewed leaf as a cause for retaliation.

One important reason to take action is to reduce the reproductive potential of a pest, so it doesn't develop into a problem. The theory being that it's better to kill a few individuals now, than to have to kill a lot more after they have seriously damaged your crops. All pests should be watched closely. If they start to multiply rapidly,. the situation could get out of hand. If you act quickly and decisively you may contain an infestation and prevent serious damage.

Some mortality of plants is acceptable, but if it goes above 15 to 20% you will probably have to take action. Seedlings and small plants are more vulnerable to damage than larger ones, as there is less of them to eat and they are less resilient. You can afford to lose higher proportion of direct sown seedlings, than you can the relatively few, widely spaced, labor intensive transplants.

Integrated pest management

Integrated pest management means always using the least damaging method of pest control at your disposal. Some people see IPM as a public relations ploy to make pesticide use seem more responsible, but organic gardeners and farmers have used it for years. It is actually a major shift in philosophy for conventional growers because it doesn't seek to wipe out all pests, but rather to keep their numbers below a certain threshold.

Cultural: The safest control options are merely good horticultural practices and aren't directly connected with pests at all. They include proper site selection, appropriate fertilization, using resistant varieties, sanitation, cultivation, planting dates, crop rotations, trap crops, fertilization and more.

Physical: If the above cultural options don't work you have to take more aggressive action, such as using barriers, dogs, repellants, hand picking, spraying with water, trapping, or removing infected plants.

Biological: The next level of escalation is biological control. Using the diseases and predators of pests, either by encouraging them (which you should always be doing anyway), or by introducing them

Chemical: Finally, if none of the above controls are enough, you may have to resort to chemicals. Begin with soap and plant sprays, then possibly B.T. The last resort is the 'organic pesticides' such as rotenone and pyrethrum.

Pest control options

By the act of planting and cultivating their favorite food plants, we make the intensive garden a favorable place for pests. Therefore we must endeavor to make other conditions less favorable. Over the years an enormous array of tricks have been devised to combat pests and every gardener has her favorites. However pests are unpredictable and without doing a carefully controlled experiment it can be hard to know if a remedy actually worked, or whether they disappeared for some other reason. Sometimes a trick works only under very specific conditions.

Cultural controls

Companion planting
There has been a lot of hype about companion planting in organic literature and in truth a lot of it doesn't really work very well. However it can help reduce pest problems by increasing diversity, providing food for predatory insects and by disguising the scent and sight of food plants (so pests have a harder time finding them).

Crop selection
Some crops are rarely affected by pests, while others have a whole series of often lethal pests and diseases which can make growing them difficult. Initially you might want to emphasize the former, which include Basil, Beets, Chard, Cilantro, Endive, Leek, Parsnip, Peppers and Rocket.

The incidence and severity of pest attacks varies enormously from place to place. In California Summer Squash is remarkably trouble free, but when I lived in Connecticut I gave up growing them, because of the Squash Vine borer.

In some cases you can grow resistant varieties of crops. Though this rarely gives complete protection, it can be another way to help reduce a problem to tolerable levels. Another aspect of this is not to plant varieties that are particularly vulnerable to pests.

Extra planting

If you figure that pests are going to consume 20% of a crop you could simply try planting 20% more. This simple solution can solve many pest problems. After transplanting you should keep a few plants in reserve, ready to replace any early fatalities.

Interplanting

Interplanting means growing more than one kind of plant together. It is useful for pest control because it reduces the concentration of a crop planting. Each individual is surrounded by dissimilar plants, which makes the target crop harder to find and reduces the spread of pests. If you interplant with flowers this also provides habitat for predatory insects. See **Crop Planning** for more on this.

Rotation

In small gardens rotations are only useful for controlling soil dwelling creatures such as nematodes and then only to a limited extent. Most garden pests are sufficiently mobile to move from one area to another as the vegetation changes. See **Crop Planning** for more on this.

Sanitation

Pest control begins with good sanitation. Remove and compost all crop debris as soon as possible after harvest. Don't leave it in the garden to decay and don't leave unharvested crops in the ground over the winter). You should also remove excess weeds, though more to reduce the incidence of disease than for insects. Minimize hiding places for pests such as slugs and snails, by keeping the garden free of unnecessary debris, such as planks, rocks and brush.

Soil improvement

It may seem improbable that by improving your soil you can fight pests, but this is the key to organic pest control. If plants are well fed they can often outgrow pest attacks. By improving the soil you also improve the health of your plants, which makes them less attractive to pests. Chemically dependent gardeners are sometimes surprised on kicking their habit, to find that they don't have any more pests than before.

Timing

Some pests can be avoided by planting a crop at a specific time, either earlier or later than normal. Pests usually appear at specific times of the year, because their activity is dictated by season and temperature. Most insects don't become active until the temperature reaches at least 60° F.

Pests don't appear at exactly the same time every year, because the temperature on a given day varies considerably from year to year. The last frost date may vary by up to six weeks in some cases. This could make it difficult to anticipate exactly when a pest will appear, but fortunately plants are affected by the same temperature fluctuations as insects. All you have to do is find out which plants normally appear at the same time as the anticipated pest and then wait for the appearance of the plant. In this way you can comfortably predict when certain pests will appear and you will know when to go after them. Note in your journal when these pest and plant combinations appear.

If plants are planted early they may be large enough to tolerate otherwise serious attacks.

Trap Crops

Some plants are very attractive to pests and will be attacked in preference to certain crops. For example aphids may attack Nasturtiums in preference to Brassicas.

Transplanting

Plants are most vulnerable to pests when germinating and when very young. As they get older they are more able to survive some damage. If a direct sown crop is consistently attacked and destroyed, then try growing it from transplants.

Physical controls

Barriers

Often the best way to deal with a serious pest is to create a physical barrier between pest and crop. Cutworms, Cabbage Root Fly, Carrot Rust Fly, slugs and snails are all most effectively stopped with barriers (see their individual listings below).

Cultivation

Cultivation of the soil surface can help control some pests, by burying them or exposing them to predators (it can also damage the soil though, and expose fresh weed seeds).

Fencing

A well-designed and constructed fence is the most effective way to deal with problem animals such as deer, raccoons, groundhogs and more. In fact it may be the only effective way. In extreme cases an electric fence may be necessary (such as to keep Raccoons out of Sweet Corn). The main problem with fences is their cost. They are also pretty ugly, though you can hide them with vines (this also makes them more productive).

Hand picking

This works well for slow moving creatures such as slugs, snails and caterpillars and is often the most low impact way to deal with such pests in the small garden. If you only have a few plants this may actually be quicker and easier than mixing up some spray, spraying and then cleaning the sprayer. Look for eggs, larvae and mature insects when hand picking and make sure you examine the undersides of leaves also. This is also a good time to look for disease, weeds and other problems.

Netting

I hate plastic netting, but it is the most effective barrier against birds. I dislike it for many reasons. It is hard to deal with, it interferes with access to plants, is ugly and can entangle and kill beneficial creatures such as snakes and insectivorous birds. If you use netting then check it frequently for tangled animals, if you wait too long they will die.

An alternative to plastic netting is to make chicken wire cages. These are easier to use, but bulky and harder to store.

Row covers

Row covers made from a non-woven synthetic fabric (Reemay is the best known) are a simple solution to some otherwise intractable pest problems. If used carefully they can exclude all pests from a bed and so are a way to defeat root pests such as Carrot Rust Fly and Cabbage Root maggot. They even work against insects that lay eggs on leaves, such as leaf miners and caterpillars. They also cut down the wind and create a warm microclimate under the cover, which can speed growth in cool weather.

Row covers have their drawbacks, they are ugly, non-recyclable and inconvenient (you also have to buy them). In hot weather the ground can get too hot underneath them and can cook the plants. In this case you have to support them with hoops to improve air circulation.

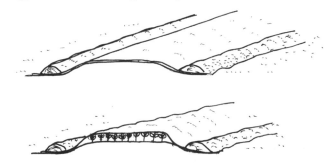

A row cover must be large enough to completely cover vulnerable plants, with enough left over to bury the edges in the soil (make a shallow furrow, put the edge in and re-fill it). There should be a good seal all the way around, so pests can't get at the plants. Don't stretch the cover too tightly, as the plants need room to grow. If there isn't enough room they may pull the edge of the cover out of the ground, or the plants will get crowded .

Water

A strong jet of water from a hose will wash Aphids and other tiny creatures from plants.

Biological controls

Releasing predators

There are specialized predatory insects that prey on a single species of mite, scale, aphid or whitefly. They are often released in large numbers by commercial growers, as a means of insect control on farms. Unfortunately they aren't as effective in the small space of a single garden, because they are very mobile and often simply fly away. Insect release projects are most effective when undertaken on a larger scale, such as an entire neighborhood.

These insects can be very effective in enclosed spaces such as greenhouses, or in the soil. Obviously soil dwelling predators such as Nematodes have to stay where they are put, they can't just move.

Encouraging predatory Insects

Though insect predators aren't usually abundant enough to have a major impact on serious pest infestations, they are an important factor in preventing such outbreaks from occurring. This fact often becomes apparent after they are wiped out by insecticides sprayed to control a pest.

The simplest and best ways to keep insect pests at low levels is by encouraging predatory insects to live in your garden. You do this by planting the kinds of herbs and flowers that provide them with food. Many predatory insects are very small and can't get nectar from large flowers. They are most attracted to small, nectar laden, flowers, such as members of the Daisy, Mint and Carrot families. Generally native plants work best, though many exotic species are also good. Highly bred cultivars are often sterile and useless.

The most important insect predators include:
Assassin Bugs
Big Eyed Bugs
Ground Beetles
Ladybird Beetles
Lacewings
Pirate Bugs
Predatory Mites
Praying Mantises
Rove Beetles
Spiders
Syrphid flies
Tachnid Flies
Wasps (Brachonid, Chalcid, Ichneumon, Trichogramma)

Don't forget to encourage (or at least not discourage) larger predators, snakes, frogs, toads (and other amphibians), lizards, bats, birds, coyotes and cougars. You can attract birds and bats by providing them with suitable roosting and nesting sites. Some people feed birds in winter to encourage them to stay around. Frogs and toads are attracted by nearby water, which is another good reason to have a pond in your garden.

The larger insect predators need places to hide and feed, so ideally perennials should form the framework of the garden. Any wild areas in the garden will act as a refuge. Outdoor patio lights attract many insects, which makes them popular feeding stations for predators.

Releasing disease organisms

Disease causing bacteria, protozoa, viruses, nematodes and fungi are commercially available for use as pest control agents and work well in the right circumstances. The best known of these is the bacteria *Bacillus thuringensis* (commonly known as B.T.) This is lethal to many varieties of leaf eating (it must be eaten to be effective) caterpillars, some types of flies and members of the hymenoptera (grasshoppers). It is now so widely used that resistant strains of some pests are now developing (a sign of indiscriminate use).

Dogs and cats

These have their drawbacks in the garden, but there is no denying that they do control some pests. An active cat can be a very effective Gopher catcher. An active dog will keep raccoons, deer and other mammals away.

Chemical controls

Soft soap sprays

Soft soap (soap made from potassium carbonate rather than sodium hydroxide) kills small soft-bodied insects such as aphids, sawfly larvae and mites (it may also kill small predators). Prepare a spray by mixing 6 tablespoons of soft soap (Ivory Snow works well) in one gallon of water. There are commercial insecticidal soaps available, but they aren't much better and are more expensive). Liquid soap is sometimes mixed with other pesticides to help them to stick better.

Plant sprays

Repellent, or poisonous, plants such as Tansy, Artemisia, Tomato, Garlic, Onion, Cayenne or Rhubarb can be made into a spray for use against many insects. Make a spray by boiling 2 lb of leaves (or 20 cloves of Garlic) in 2 quarts of water for 30 minutes, then strain and allow to cool. This is then mixed with ½ ounce of soft soap flakes (to help the spray penetrate) dissolved in 1 liter of hot water. Sprays can also be made by putting the leaves through a blender.

Bug juice

This simple spray can be used for Colorado Potato Beetles, Cabbage Loopers and Mexican Bean Beetle Larvae. We don't really know how it controls pests, it may spread disease (in which case it is actually a biological control), or it may act as a repellent. It is made by hand picking as many of the problem insects as you can find and putting them in a blender with twice their volume of water. Puree for a minute or so, then strain and dilute with 3 parts water to one part juice (don't use the blender for food again). This brew can be stored in the fridge for several days. Spray whole plants as often as necessary (don't forget the undersides).

Organic pesticides

Pesticides are considered a kind of panacea by chemically dependent gardeners (see insect damage - get the spray gun). Organic gardeners are sometimes guilty of this kind of thinking also, but they use sprays made from extracts of leaves, flowers and roots, in the belief that these 'natural' products are somehow more benign than the synthetics. Unfortunately this really isn't true, some botanicals (such as nicotine) are extremely poisonous (probably too poisonous to use in fact). The advantage of botanicals over the synthetics is that they break down quickly and don't persist in the environment. However this is actually a disadvantage in the short term, because you may have to apply them repeatedly to be effective.

The fundamental problem with pesticides really has nothing to do with how toxic they are and applies equally to organics and synthetics. The problem is that they treat a symptom as if it were the problem and upset the delicate natural balance of predator and prey. Even if a pesticide is so selective that it only kills the target insect (and not it's predators as well), in doing so it deprives the predators of food, so they die as well. With the predators gone, the pest will recover more quickly (predators take much longer to recover than prey) and can become an even more serious problem. The more persistent pesticides also get into the food chain and into your body fat.

Organic pesticides have a minor place in organic gardening, but only as a last resort, to save a crop when all else fails. However the need to use a pesticide indicates a failure of some kind and shouldn't become a habit.

The pesticides mentioned below are in order from least toxic to the most toxic. If you feel you must use a pesticide always use the least toxic one that will do the job.

Botanical pesticides

Quassia: This is the most benign of the botanical insecticides and is used on soft-bodied insects such as aphids and small caterpillars (though it may also kill some small predators). It comes in the form of chips and is prepared by boiling an ounce of chips in a quart of water for 30 minutes (often with a spoonful of soft soap flakes). Allow the mixture to cool and dilute with 3 parts water.

Pyrethrum: Actually a number of compounds, this is derived from several species of Daisy. It is relatively harmless to most mammals, but is toxic to most sucking and chewing insects (and to beneficial insects and fish). It is available either as a dust or spray, or you can make your own by soaking the dried flowers in water.

Derris: Also known as rotenone, this pesticide is very toxic to aphids, whitefly and beetles. It is also poisonous to fish, birds and some mammals (it's also more toxic to humans than was previously thought). It is most commonly used in the form of a dust, though liquids are also available

Nicotine: A highly toxic plant spray can be made by boiling a cup of Tobacco leaves (or cigarette butts) in a gallon of water (add a spoonful of soap flakes to increase its effectiveness). The fresh solution is very toxic to most creatures (including humans), but breaks down within a couple of days (don't use on plants within a month of harvest). It doesn't cost anything to make, but is unpleasant and rather dangerous. It is actually illegal in some places.

Garden insects

I don't really have the room to go into detail about the pests of individual crops. Instead I am going to discuss some of the worst pests and give examples of how to deal with them. Only a few pests (Aphids, Root Flies, Cabbage White Caterpillars, Slugs) do most of the damage in gardens nationwide, so begin by learning how to control these.

So you don't get the impression that most wild creatures are harmful to the garden, I am also going to mention the various types of beneficial insects.

The insects are the most significant garden pests. They have jointed limbs, an external skeleton and their bodies are divided into 3 parts (head, thorax and abdomen). They also have 3 pairs of legs and 2 pairs of wings. They are divided into several significant groups, the name of which refers to the type of wing the possess.

Coleoptera (Sheath Winged)
Beetles
The beetles are the largest insect group and contain some of the worst pests and the most valuable predators. They have hardened wing coverings that meet in a line down their backs.

Beneficial species: Firefly, Ground, Ladybird, Rove, Soldier, Tiger and other Beetles.

Harmful species: Asparagus, Blister, Click, Colorado Potato, Japanese and Cucumber Beetles. Also weevils.

Notable species
Wireworms: These leathery, golden brown creatures are the larvae of the Click Beetle. They are most common on grassland, but can also be a problem in gardens (especially those newly created from grassland). They will eat the underground parts of most common vegetable crops, but are most often a problem with younger plants (they often kill seedlings).

Flea Beetles: These tiny jumping beetles chew little holes in the leaves of the Brassica crops and their relatives. Generally I ignore them because their damage is generally minimal and plants will usually grow out of it. Young plants with little leaf area sometimes suffer badly and seedlings occasionally die (a foliar feed may help them to recover). One suggested remedy is to move a grease covered board along the row of plants, the idea being to catch the beetles as they jump (but what do you do with a grease covered board afterwards?) If they are really bad use a botanical insecticide.

Mexican Bean Beetles: These are the bad cousins of the Ladybird Beetles and look somewhat similar. In sufficient numbers they can completely defoliate whole plants. They can be controlled by early planting, hand picking and by encouraging predators. If all else fails use pyrethrum or rotenone.

Ground Beetles: These large black beetles (Staphylid, Carabid and other species) are probably the most important general predators in the garden. Every day these extremely active creatures eat their own body weight in cutworms, slugs, snails, Cabbage root maggots and any other insects they can catch (and also their pupae and eggs). Their larvae are also predatory. These beetles dislike bare and disturbed soil, so encourage them by providing mulch or other refuges (the foam disks used to control Cabbage Root Maggots make great hiding places).

Ladybird Beetles: These are probably the most familiar predatory insects, praying on aphids, thrips and mites. The larval form is less familiar, but equally voracious. Encourage them to stay in your garden over winter by giving them areas of undisturbed vegetation.

Lepidoptera (Scaly Winged)
Butterflies and Moths.

Harmful species:
All of the Lepidoptera are plant eaters.
European Corn Borer, Cabbage Looper, Corn Earworm, Cutworms, Hornworms, Cabbage Worms, Squash Vine Borers.

Notable species
Cabbage White Butterflies: Perhaps the most widespread and worst of the caterpillar pests, the

Cabbage White attacks all Brassica crops. The voracious caterpillars can strip small plants down to the midribs in a very short time. They are preyed upon by Ground Beetles and spiders and are parasitized by small wasps. They are unattractive as food for birds because they store mustard oil in their bodies.

If the caterpillars aren't too numerous the best control is to hand pick. They are often well camouflaged so can be hard to detect (the damaged leaves alert you to their presence, while fresh droppings give away their location). If there are too many you might try a spray of B.T.

Squash Vine Borer: The number one pest of Summer Squash, east of the Rockies, this is one of the worst pests of any plant you are likely to encounter in vegetable gardening. It will kill Summer Squash almost every time unless drastic measures are taken. If you aren't very observant, by the time the damage is apparent the plant is wilting and close to death. Once a plant starts to wilt the commonest course of action is to cut the plant open and pry out the worm-like caterpillars. They give away their location by the sawdust-like frass that comes out of little holes in the stem. You should also bury the damaged stems in soil so they can root at several places.

Another course of action is to inject B.T into the stem, where the caterpillar will eat it.

It's better if you can prevent the borers from entering the plant in the first place. One idea is to lay a sheet of aluminum foil 'mulch' under the plant - ostensibly to fool the parent moth so she doesn't find the stems. You might also wrap the stem with aluminum foil.

Cutworms: These caterpillars are the larvae of Noctuid moths. They are adapted to spending their days underground and their nights feeding on the surface. Their modus operandi is to wrap themselves around the stems of plants and feed on them until the plant falls over. They can be a big problem with small seedlings. During the day they hide in the soil near the fallen plant, so if you suspect cutworm damage (the fallen plants are

quite distinctive), dig down into the soil around the plant to find the culprit, it's almost always there. If Cutworms are very bad you can deter them by putting little collars of cardboard or aluminum foil around the stem of each seedling. Night patrols can catch cutworms in the act.

Diptera (Two Winged)
Flies
These species have only two wings rather than the usual four. They are small and fast and can be hard to identify. Several species are very serious pests of vegetable crops and a lot of time and effort is spent dealing with them.

Harmful species:
Cabbage Root Maggot, Carrot Rust Fly, Leaf Miners, Mosquitoes.

Notable species:
Cabbage Root Fly / Maggot: This fly is probably the most difficult insect pest of the Brassicas (and they have more than their fair share). It lays its eggs at the base of the plant and the newly hatched larvae burrow down to the roots and eat them. If there are enough maggots the root system of the plant may be completely destroyed and it will die. There may be three generations of this pest in a year, the first hatching in mid spring, the second in early or midsummer and the third in early or mid fall.

The first sign that something is wrong is when the plant wilts in sunny weather, even though there is plenty of water available. If this happens examine the roots for small white maggots (they look like grains of cooked rice). Once a plant has reached this point all you can do is feed it and pile soil against the stem in the hope it can put out more roots, but it may well die. Dispose of badly infected plants and next time take precautions to prevent their taking hold (see below).

Probably the best way to control root maggots is with 6″ circles (or squares) of foam carpet backing (get used stuff that is thrown away by carpet stores.) The disk is cut down its diameter and a small cross is cut in the center. This enables the disk to fit snugly around the stem and prevent the newly hatched larvae from tunneling down to the root. These foam disks work very well, as the foam can expand as the stem enlarges. Tar paper was once widely used for this purpose, but doesn't expand in the same way, so isn't as good.

These disks not only makes it harder for the fly larvae to get into the root, but also act as a mulch and provide a refuge for predatory Ground Beetles and spiders (these eat the eggs and larvae). These disks may reduce damage by as much as 70%, which is as good as most pesticides.

Root Maggots can also be controlled by using row covers, which prevent the fly getting near the plants.

Carrot Rust Fly (Psila rosae): The Rust Fly is similar to the Cabbage Root Fly, in that its larvae tunnel into the root. Though it doesn't usually kill the plant, it causes rust colored lesions that render the root pretty much inedible. Carrot Rust Fly may also attack the related Parsnip, Celery and some herbs.

The first line of defense against Carrot flies is hygiene. They are said to be able to smell damaged Carrot foliage from great distances, supposedly up to a mile. Keep thinning and weeding (which might bruise the foliage) to a minimum and never leave the foliage laying around. Also don't leave the remains of an overwintering Carrot crop in the ground, as it can mean a big increase in the incidence of Carrot rust fly. Always dig and compost old carrots.

If the fly problem is severe some kind of barrier is the best solution. You can use row covers to keep them from ever getting near to the plants. It's said that a simple plastic screen 30″ to 36″ high around the plants will also work. Apparently the flies always fly close to the ground and will go around the screen, but not over it (so long as then bed is no more than 36″ wide).

There are two generations of flies each year, the first in late spring and another in late summer. It is possible to avoid them by carefully timing the planting and harvesting.

Four rows of onions to one row of carrots is said to disguise their smell, as is a mulch of fresh grass or sawdust. Ground Beetles will eat the eggs. Winter cultivation can expose the larvae to foraging birds.

Leaf miners: As the name suggests, the larvae of these flies tunnel into the leaves and eat them from the inside. If the damage is minor, you can simply remove and destroy the affected leaves (make sure you don't eat them.) If they get really bad you will have to cover the plants with row covers.

Hemiptera (Half winged): True Bugs.
One pair of wings are hard and don't look like wings, the other pair are membranous. They can be identified by the triangle on their backs.

Beneficial species:
Assassin Bugs, Pirate Bugs, Orchard Bugs
You don't usually need to encourage these species, just don't kill them. They don't like bare soil, so a mulch will help.

Harmful species:
Squash Bug and Tarnished Plant Bug

Tarnished plant bug stages

Homoptera (Same winged)
These species have two pairs of similar membranous wings.

Harmful species:
Aphids, Cicadas, Leafhoppers and **Whitefly**. There are no beneficial members of this family.

Notable species:
Aphids: These creatures feed by sucking the sap from plants and need to consume a lot of sap to get the protein they need (the sugary sap is then excreted as honeydew). In small numbers aphids aren't a problem, but under favorable circumstances they can multiply rapidly and remove so much sap from a plant they stunt its growth. They may also transmit virus diseases.

Aphids have been called the mice of the insect world, because they provide food for so many creatures. The best way to control Aphids is by encouraging predators such as Ladybird beetles, Ground beetles, Lacewings, Hoverflies and birds. If they get too numerous they can be washed from plants by simply spraying them with a strong jet of water. If this doesn't work then try a soap spray. Rain can be a very effective control.

Thysanoptera (Fringe Winged)
Thrips
These tiny sucking insects have toxic saliva and are all harmful to plants.

Hymenoptera (Membrane Winged)
Ants, Bees, Wasps
Members of this group have two pairs of clear wings

Beneficial species: All species are beneficial. This is an extremely important family of insects. The Bees are our most important pollinators of course. The Wasps are all beneficial in that they are either predators, or parasites of pests. Ants break down organic matter.

Notable species:
Wasps: The tiny wasp species (*Brachonid, Chalcid, Encarsia, Ichneumon, Trichogramma*), parasitize caterpillars and other pests by laying their eggs on them. They can be encouraged by growing lots of plants with small, nectar rich flowers (especially those in the *Apiaceae* and *Asteraceae*). The larger wasps kill and eat many pests, so should be left alone where possible. Don't destroy their nests just because you can.

Orthoptera (Straight Winged)
These have large back wings and leathery front ones.

Beneficial species:
Praying mantis

Harmful species:
Crickets and Grasshoppers

Notable species:
Grasshoppers and **Crickets**: These voracious insects eat many types of vegetable and garden plant. They can be hard to control because they are so mobile. Row covers are probably the best option for small areas. The bacteria known as Milky Spore disease (*Nosema locusta*) is a good control, but is most effective when used on a larger scale than a single garden.

Praying Mantids: These fascinating creatures are voracious predators, preying on anything they can catch (including beneficial insects). Some people buy the eggs sacs, but this isn't a good idea if there are native species in your area, as the aliens may displace the natives. You can encourage Praying Mantids by having wild areas in the garden.

Neuroptera (Nerve Winged)
Lacewings
Members of this group have lacy transparent wings.

They are all beneficial as their larvae eat aphids, mites and scale insects. It's been estimated that the offspring of a pair of Lacewings could eat 13 million Aphids in one season. Encourage them by planting small flowered herbs and flowers (see Wasps) as a food source.

Other garden creatures

Spiders
Spiders are justly famous as voracious predators. They will eat anything they can catch, including springtails, flies, aphids and moths. Encourage them by providing refuges.

Harvestmen
These beneficial Arachnids prey on caterpillars, aphids and anything else they can catch.

Nematodes
Commonly known as Eelworms, these minute creatures are an important part of the soil microfauna (there may be 30 million per square meter). Most nematodes are

harmless or beneficial (some break down organic matter, others control insect pests), but a few suck juices from plant roots. In small numbers nematodes don't do much damage (though disease can enter through their lesions and they sometimes transport viruses). In a healthy soil nematodes are usually kept under control by fungi, insects and other predatory nematodes. However they sometimes build up in the soil to the point where it becomes 'sick'. Plants growing in such soil show signs of nutrient deficiency because of serious root damage.

The simplest way to deal with nematode infestations is to plant resistant varieties when available. Crop rotation also helps. In serious cases you might try solarizing the soil (see below). Ultimately you could just not plant susceptible crops for 3 to 5 years.

The most commonly encountered harmful nematode species include; Potato Cyst Eelworm, Bulb Eelworm and Root Knot Nematode.

Nematocidal Marigolds

One way to deal with nematodes in the soil is by planting Marigolds (*Tagetes*). The most effective species is the large African Marigold (*T. minuta*), but this isn't very practical for small gardens as it may grow to 10 feet in height. Some ornamental types can also be effective, Crackerjack, Sparky and Nemagold are all good. Generally the more scent the variety has, the more effective it will be. For maximum effectiveness the plants must be sown in a solid block, covering the entire affected area (like a cover crop). Scattered plants or small blocks won't work very well, no matter how good the variety.

Millipedes, Centipedes

Centipedes are voracious predators of mites, nematodes, small slugs and many small soil organisms. Encourage them by providing refuges.

Some clues to pest damage

Tiny random holes:
  Flea Beetles

Plants snipped off and gone:
  Mammals, Rabbit, Deer, Groundhog, Human

Plant parts still present:
  Birds, Cutworms

Plant parts pulled down into a hole:
  Gophers

Leaves randomly chewed, mostly at edges, slime present :
  Slugs, snails

Leaves randomly chewed with large holes, small green droppings present:
  Caterpillars

Plants look fine, but wilt at midday, even in cool weather (root damage):
  Cabbage Maggot

Leaves have tunnels in them:
  Leaf Miners

Leaves sticky:
  Honeydew from Aphids

Slugs and snails

In cool humid climates there may be 200 slugs on every square yard of your garden. They generally prefer to eat old decaying material and are important decomposing organisms, but if that isn't available they will eat almost any crop plants (though they have their preferences).

Slugs can be a real problem in cool wet conditions. They are extremely voracious and when abundant they can devour an entire bed of seedlings in a night, or strip almost mature plants. They also reproduce rapidly and can produce up to three generations annually. They are hermaphrodite so don't even need to mate and each one is capable of producing 400 round white eggs annually.

You can usually identify their Mollusk handiwork by the shiny trail of mucus they leave behind as they move. They tend to chew leaves from their outer edges and may devour a young plant right down to the stem and a few of the tougher leaf midribs.

Slugs originally had shells like snails, but abandoned them in favor of the ability to hide in crevices in the soil and under rocks (they burrow down into the soil when it gets too cold or hot). They also hide under boards, rocks and leaves, so keep such debris out of the garden. Boards can actually be used as slug traps, so long as you check them every morning.

Snails hide in dense vegetation, or cracks in walls, during the day and come out to eat at night. The easiest way to eliminate snails, is to remove all of the places that can act as a refuge. I've seen beds of cover crop completely defoliated on the side neighboring dense vegetation, while the other side was almost untouched (though the defoliation was slowly spreading). Clearing an old crop may force the snails to move elsewhere, so be prepared.

Hand picking: The most effective and low impact way to control slugs and snails is by hand picking. This is best done at night or early morning and must be done regularly if it is to have much effect (I once collected over 2400 slugs in 5 consecutive evenings). You will soon learn to find their hiding places. Slugs commonly hide down in the crevices in the soil and you can often dig down around a damaged plant to find the culprit.

You can squash these creatures as you pick them, or drop them in a bucket of salt water. If you don't want to kill them you can collect them in a bucket of leaves and transport them a few miles. If you have any gardening rivals you could drop them in their gardens.

Barriers: Hand picking alone won't solve all your Mollusk problems. They may move at a snails pace, but they are surprisingly mobile (some can walk a mile in a few days) and more can simply come to where there is food. Ideally you could erect some kind of barrier, such as a 2-foot wide path of cinders or crushed oyster shells. Sharp sand, wood ashes or sawdust also work apparently, but must be kept dry or replenished frequently. The razor sharp fragments of diatomaceous earth are lethal to the soft bodies of slugs and snails (they don't do human lungs any good either - wear a mask). Other barriers are copper strips (they won't cross it), wire screen, tilted boards with grease on the undersides and tiny barbed wire fences.

Trapping: Cups of beer, milk or yeast (dissolved in sugar water) will catch quite a few mollusks (and a few other creatures). Put this in a cup with the rim about a half-inch above the soil surface. There needs to be a lot of these traps to be effective, at least one for every square yard. Traps can also be made from cabbage leaves, boards, grapefruit skins and cut potatoes, though these don't kill, they merely make collecting easier (you must check them daily).

Avoid mulch: Slugs can easily hide in mulch. so it is usually avoided in areas where they are a big problem.

Ducks: These birds love slugs and snails and are one of the best controls. Chickens like them as well, but do more damage to crops. Toads, snakes, birds and Ground Beetles (probably the most important) all kill slugs and snails. There are even predatory slugs (Testacella species) which eat other slugs (cannibal slugs).

Metaldehyde: This poison is widely used for killing slugs, but probably only kill about 10% of those present. They are also poisonous to Ground Beetles (a main predator) and mammals, so must be used with caution (poisoned slugs may poison slug predators). They work best in the greenhouse, where predators are usually absent.

Larger garden creatures

The larger animal pests can do so much damage, so quickly, that they can't be tolerated if they come into the garden. You can either fence them out, catch and transport them, or kill them. The first option is most preferable and the last is the least desirable. Killing some animals because they are garden pests would wipe them out completely (I heard of one person shooting six black bears to protect his garden.) Of course many animals are beneficial, birds, bats, shrews, lizards and snakes and you should encourage these species in any way you can.

Birds

Some birds relish the tender growth of new seedlings and may also eat newly planted seeds. They can be particularly bad in early spring when other foods may be scarce. The best way to keep birds out of the garden is to be working there, or have cats working there. If this isn't possible, you may have to put nets over vulnerable transplants and seedbeds. Some people suggest putting out a little old seed in the paths for birds to eat, so they won't bother the crop (if you don't explain this to them very clearly, they will probably just eat it in addition to the seedlings).

Of course you only want to keep birds out of the garden at certain times. For most of the year they eat enormous numbers of pests and should be actively encouraged. Attract them with nesting boxes and feed them in severe winter weather.

Deer

As the suburbs creep out further into rural areas more gardeners are having problems with deer. The deer population has increased in many areas in recent years. This is because we have eliminated their predators (wolves and cougars), but don't allow hunting in residential areas. Deer can be a serious problem, because not only will they eat a lot, but they will keep coming back for more.

Probably the easiest way to keep deer out of the garden is with an aggressive dog. What is the ideal breed of dog for guarding gardens? It would have to be big and aggressive enough to scare away potential pests, agile enough to catch gophers and smart enough not to walk on the beds. If you are a dog breeder here is a worthwhile challenge for you!

The only 100% guaranteed way to keep deer out of the garden is a secure fence, but to be effective it must be strong and high. The cheapest commercial deer fencing is the eight foot tall plastic mesh. The best thing about this stuff is that its dark color is almost invisible. You can buy special 8 ft high metal wire deer fencing to keep out deer. This is much more secure, durable and permanent, but is too expensive for me.

I kept deer out of my last garden by attaching four foot sticks to the top of my existing metal fence posts and stringing 2 or 3 highly visible lines across them (I used old electrical wire because I found some, but string works just as well). The whole arrangement was very flimsy, but looked too tall to jump and so worked very well. At my new garden I·bought the cheapest 2″ mesh chicken wire and attached it to metal fence posts. This gave me a 6 foot tall fence, which has been enough to deter the lazy deer around here. I started to increase its height as just described, but have never actually got around to finishing the job because it hasn't been needed.

Opaque fencing doesn't have to be as tall as a transparent one, because deer (rather sensibly) won't jump over something if they can't see where they will land. A double fence is also effective, if wide enough so they can't clear both at once, but narrow enough that they can't jump each of them singly. A variation on this is one fence, with a parallel strand of wire at the right distance out from it.

Gophers

Gophers are the curse of many western gardeners (or should I say many western gardeners curse Gophers). They will eat almost anything, even the roots of fairly well established trees. They are most often kept under control by trapping (especially in early spring before they breed), or with hunting cats, but they are difficult to eliminate entirely.

These animals only tunnel, they won't walk on to the bed and dig down from the surface. You can keep them out of a bed by lining it with wire mesh. This is expensive and time consuming for a large garden, but you can certainly line some special beds for growing those crops most favored by them. The mesh must be put down carefully. These creatures aren't stupid, they seem to know there is something good on the other side and will work to find chinks in the barrier.

Groundhogs

These rodents have a voracious appetite and once they move into your garden they stay there. Dogs are probably the best deterrent. The Groundhog is a solitary animal, so if you can live trap and transport it, this may solve the problem. It may return if it isn't taken far enough, or the vacated hole may prove attractive to another animal. You can also fence them out, though you have to bury the base of the fence at right angles so they can't tunnel under it.

Supposedly Groundhogs can climb to some extent, though the one in my garden in Connecticut tried frantically to dig down under my two-foot high fence (it failed because I had bent it out at the bottom). It never thought to go over it though (maybe it was below average Groundhog intelligence).

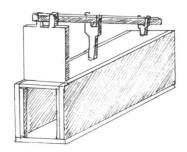

A final word

Gardening shouldn't be an aggressive activity. Don't look upon the creatures that share your garden as a problem. Learn their names and how they live. Appreciate their beauty and the things they add to the garden. It wouldn't be the same without them.

Rabbits

Everything I said about Groundhogs applies to rabbits also (though they can't climb). Dogs and wire fencing are the most effective means of control.

Raccoons

If Raccoons get into the habit of visiting your garden they can become intolerable. These intelligent and agile creatures will harvest many crops before you can (especially Sweet Corn), so you must deal with them. A really good fence might keep them out. A dog will too, if it's big and tough enough (and out in the garden at night).

Rats

Many people are blissfully unaware that they have a rat supermarket in their back garden. If you have a poorly made compost pile, full of half decomposed food in your garden, you probably have rats as well. Dogs and cats are a good control, as are anticoagulant poisons.

24 Disease

Disease has been defined as a disruption in plant functioning as a result of a continuous irritation. The effects of disease vary widely, they may kill a plant in a matter of hours, or there may be no obvious symptoms at all, merely reduced yield and increased vulnerability to stress. For a disease to infect a plant the conditions must be exactly right, in fact it can be quite hard to infect a plant intentionally. When conditions are right a disease can move with devastating speed, wiping out all susceptible plants within a day or so.

The basis of organic disease control is the belief that healthy plants, growing in the right conditions aren't susceptible to disease. We believe that disease is one of natures ways of eliminating plants that are stressed in some way (wrong climate, wet soil, damaged roots, acid soil). If a crop is heavily diseased, something is wrong.

Types of disease

Disease may be classified by the type of agent that causes it.

Bacteria: Most of these minute organisms are either harmless or beneficial and they are very important for healthy soil function. However a few rogue species can cause serious crop diseases, including; Fire Blight, Leaf Spot, Crown Gall, Bacterial Canker, Bacterial Wilt and Soft Rot.

Bacteria enter a plant through wounds or natural openings. They need moisture to survive and are usually transported to plants on soil moisture, such as when soil is splashed on to leaves, or from fingers, insects or wind). Generally they prefer warm moist conditions so are most problematic in tropical areas. In a healthy soil bacteria are controlled by viruses, protozoa, actinomycetes, earthworms and other organisms.

Fungi: Commonly called molds, these are perhaps the most important plant disease causing agents. Fungus diseases are highly infectious and include the Powdery Mildews, Downy Mildews, Rusts, Early and Late Blights, Botrytis or Grey Molds, Clubroot, Fusarium

Wilt, Verticillium Wilt, Septoria Leaf Spot, Dutch Elm Disease, Honey Fungus and Damping Off.

Some fungi prefer cool conditions for growth, others like warmth. They all need moisture, so they are most common in wet or humid conditions (they are spread by water or wind). Their spores can be found almost everywhere and enter plants through wounds or natural openings. In healthy soil actinomycetes and bacteria keep them under control. If you allow the surface of your soil to dry out regularly, then fungal diseases are much less able to get established.

Viruses: These smallest of pathogens can't survive outside of living cells, so aren't found in the soil. They must be transmitted from one living thing to another (most often these are insects such as aphids and mites). They are very infectious and can be spread by any physical contact, such as from fingers, sap or clothing. They can also be carried in seeds, or in any parts used for vegetative propagation (this can be a big problem). Some viruses are very specific as to a single host plant, others are very adaptable. Common virus diseases include Cucumber Mosaic, Tobacco Mosaic and Curly Top.

Viruses may be present in a plant without it being very apparent, but if the plant becomes stressed in some way they can become a problem. They get into the cells of the plant, causing systemic infections and are among the hardest diseases to identify. The commonest symptoms of virus disease are stunted plants, distorted leaves, spots on fruit, and mottled or streaked color changes in the leaves, but often the only symptom is low vigor and slow growth. If you are giving your plants everything they need, but growth is still poor, then virus disease could be the reason.

Once a virus gets into the plant cells there is no way to cure it, all you can do is keep the plants well supplied with nutrients and hope for the best, or burn it to prevent the disease spreading. You can help to reduce the spread of virus disease by eliminating potential sources of contamination (some weeds harbor viruses) and by controlling aphids and other sap sucking pests.

Diagnosis of disease

The first step in dealing with a plant disease is to identify the organism responsible. A disease may manifest itself in a plant in many ways, swellings, stunting, wilting, deformed growth, galls, death of tissue and color changes. There may also be visible signs of an infectious agent, such as mildew or rust. On the other hand there may not be any symptoms at all, except slow growth and poor yield. It's also possible that the visible signs are not symptoms of a disease at all, but some other problem, such as a nutrient deficiency (see **Nutrient Deficiency** for more on these). Diseases are so specific to crops that I won't discuss individual diseases here, but I do want to mention some general control measures.

Disease control measures

Most diseases are specific to a particular crop plant, or family of plants. They may be spread by insects, water, hands, spores, soil, seed, vegetative material, or they may come in with infected plants.

Once a plant is infected with disease it's usually too late to do much about it, except to remove and burn it. In some cases once a disease gets into the soil it is there for 10 years or more, so prevention truly is better than cure. There are quite a few ways to minimize the risk.

Air circulation
When the air is still and plants are spaced closely together, the transpiration can create locally humid conditions in which fungal diseases can thrive (they need 85% humidity to get established). To prevent this from happening you must ensure there is always some air movement (prune and stake if necessary).

Burning
The safest way to get rid of diseased plant material is to burn it. The problem with burning is that you lose all of the organic matter and a lot of the nutrients (notably nitrogen and sulfur). Potassium and phosphorus remain in the ashes in a very soluble form and should be returned to the garden. As soon as the fire is cool collect the ashes (sift to remove any charcoal and save this for the next fire) and store them in a dry place. If they get wet they will lose most of their nutrients.

To minimize the pollution from incomplete combustion the fire should be as hot as possible, which means all of the material must be dry. To minimize fire hazard the best time to burn is immediately after rain (in which case you need to cover the material beforehand to keep it dry). Be very careful about what you burn along with the diseased plants, avoid treated or painted wood, glossy magazines, plastics and synthetic materials of any kind.

Climate
Growing a plant in unsuitable conditions (too wet, dry, warm, cold) is one of the easiest ways to create an outbreak of disease and in some circumstances you can practically guarantee it (such as growing Tomatoes in cool wet conditions). Only very cold weather doesn't favor some kind of disease, but of course that doesn't favor plant growth either.

Fungicides
Powdery Mildew and some other fungus diseases, can sometimes be controlled by using a 5% solution of diluted urine as a fungicide. A teaspoon of baking soda to a pint of water may also work, as may a spray of Garlic, compost tea, copper sulfate, sulfur, borax, or Equisetum.

Nutrition
Good plant nutrition can reduce the incidence of disease, just as it reduces the incidence of pests. It not only prevents deficiency diseases, but also makes plants strong and vigorous enough to resist infection. At the same time don't give your plants too many soluble nutrients (especially nitrogen and potassium), as this may increase their vulnerability to disease.

Importation of disease
Diseases (as well as weeds and insect pests) may be inadvertently imported on manures, or in the soil sticking to boots, boxes and tool.

Disease can also be introduced with plant material (especially viruses), so buy certified disease free stock where available (Potatoes, Garlic) and be careful where you obtain material for propagation. Purchased transplants are a common source of disease, which is one good reason to grow your own. Some gardeners avoid buying Brassica transplants for fear of introducing Club Root disease into their soil.

Resistant varieties

Some diseases can be controlled by planting resistant varieties. This isn't 100% effective (what is?) but it is simple and can certainly help. Locally adapted varieties may be more resistant to local afflictions than those from completely different climates. They will certainly be more at home.

Rotation

Crop rotation can help reduce the incidence of disease (see **Crop Planning** for more on this).

Sanitation

The first rule of sanitation is to keep your garden clean and free from possible sources of infection. If a plant begins to show signs of disease remove and destroy it immediately. By removing potential sources of infection as soon as they become apparent, you may be able to prevent a serious outbreak. It isn't a bad idea to remove all plants once they are past their prime, as they often become more susceptible to disease and may pass it on to younger ones. In fall you should remove decaying plant material and crop debris, as this can help diseases survive over the winter. Some gardeners dig and store root crops so they can't act as hosts for disease. Some weeds may act as alternate hosts for diseases.

Seeds

Some plant diseases can be carried in seed. Most commercial seed suppliers take a lot of trouble to make sure their seed is disease free, but you can't be so sure of home saved, or swapped, seed.

Other plant ailments

Your plants symptoms may not be caused by a disease at all, but may have some other cause. Here are a few possibilities:

Nutrient deficiencies and excesses: It is sometimes hard to differentiate these from diseases, as the symptoms may be similar. See **Nutrients** for more on this.

Salt burn: An excess of salt can cause leaf tips and margins to die. This first occurs on older leaves, but may then spread to younger ones.

Sunburn: Areas between the leaf veins turn yellow and die. This often happens to houseplants when they are moved outside in spring. It can usually be prevented by giving the plants sufficient moisture. A lack of chlorophyll can also lead to sunburn.

Water deficiency: See **Watering** for the symptoms of this.

Blossom end rot: This is generally caused by inconsistent watering when the fruit was small, and/or lack of calcium.

Air pollution: This sometimes burns or bleaches both sides of the leaf.

Ethylene: An excess of ethylene from organic soils can cause leaf petioles to curl. This isn't really a problem, but indicates inadequate air circulation.

Soil

The more active and healthy your soil, the less plant disease you will have. This is because beneficial soil organisms compete with pathogens and suppress or kill them.

The pH of the soil affects the incidence of disease. Some pathogens prefer acid soils (Clubroot is rarely a problem if the pH is above 7.0), some like more alkaline ones (Scab is more of a problem at high pH). Ideally the soil should be fairly neutral.

Timing

Diseases usually need very specific conditions to get established. You can sometimes avoid these conditions by delaying planting or by using transplants.

Water

Many pathogens need water to get established, or for transportation, so avoid wetting foliage when watering. If this isn't possible then at least water early enough, so plants have time to dry out before nightfall and don't stay wet all night. You should also avoid touching the wet plants if possible, as many diseases are spread in this way. In poorly drained soils there is a much greater risk of fungus disease such as Damping off, Clubroot and Root Rot. Conversely a lack of water may increase susceptibility to some diseases.

Soil solarization

This is in essence an organic method of soil fumigation and can be used to eliminate many insect pests, diseases (including Verticillium, Fusarium, Damping Off and sometimes Clubroot), as well as most weeds (not Bindweed), weed seeds and other problems.

Solarization is a way of pasteurizing the soil up to 140° F to a depth of 12″ without moving it. Temperatures above 120° F kill most pathogens in a few hours. Even a temperature of 105° F can be effective, though this will take several weeks to achieve the same result.

Solarization must be done carefully if it is to be effective. It works best in hot sunny climates (as far north as Canada) and may not work at all in cloudy, cool ones. In cooler areas it must be done during the sunniest and warmest part of the year, when the sun is high in the sky, and even then you must make sure the area is sheltered from cool winds. Raised beds may not heat up very well on their northern edges, so you might want to flatten them out.

To start the solarization process, remove all surface vegetation and then flatten the soil, so there is good contact with the plastic and no large air pockets. Then water the area thoroughly to help it conduct heat. The next step is to cover the whole area with a continuous sheet of clear polyethylene and bury the edges in a shallow trench to seal in the heat. The best plastic sheet for this is only 1 to 2 mil thick, as this heats the soil more effectively than thicker plastic (though it is prone to tearing, which would probably stop it working). It is usually most convenient to solarize the soil one bed at a time.

If the air temperature exceeds 90° F, leave the plastic on for 3 to 4 weeks. If temperatures are in the 80's then give it 6 weeks. If they are only in the 70's you will need to give it 8 weeks. You can speed up the process by using 2 sheets of plastic, simply lay down the first as described above, then lay down a second layer separated by soda cans or small plant pots, at suitable intervals.

An interesting side effect of solarization is improved growth of plants. This probably occurs because the heat kills many of the microorganisms in the soil and their subsequent decay releases the nutrients in their bodies.

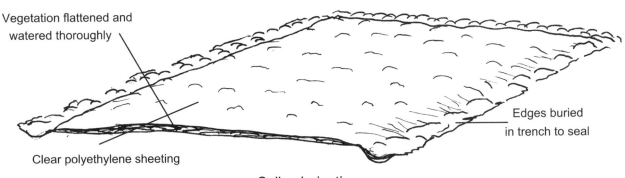

Vegetation flattened and watered thoroughly

Edges buried in trench to seal

Clear polyethylene sheeting

Soil solarization

25 Harvesting

Harvesting is one of the most rewarding aspects of gardening. You finally reap what you have sown and fill your basket with the bounty of the garden. Harvesting begins a few weeks after the first spring sowing (when you pick the first salad greens) and continues right through summer, autumn and well into winter. In milder climates you can actually harvest year round.

Record keeping

It's helpful to keep records in your garden journal of when you start harvesting a crop and whether the yield was good, bad, or indifferent. If you are so inclined you might also record roughly how much you harvest, its quality and any other relevant details. This information, along with the planting dates, will be helpful in planning the next year's garden, It also gives you a basis for evaluating your techniques, varieties and other actions.

When to Harvest

It's important to pick a crop at the right stage of growth. If you pick too early the flavor may be inferior, the harvest will be smaller and it may not store well (vegetables for storage must be fully mature). If you harvest too late, the flavor is usually inferior and you may lose the crop altogether. It may bolt, turn bitter or woody, or may simply become inedible.

Some crops stay productive, or in peak condition, for a while and can be harvested for quite a long period (Carrots, Chard, Tomatoes). Other crops come to their peak of ripeness and are then over-mature, so need to be harvested at exactly the right moment (Corn, Snap Beans, Peas).

Some crops must be harvested promptly and frequently to keep them producing well (Beans, Peas, Summer Squash, Spinach, Broccoli). As soon as these crops start yielding, you must start picking. Don't wait for them to give you enough "to be worthwhile", harvesting stimulates production. Regular picking of leaf crops encourages them to put out new fresh growth and delays the tendency to bolt.

You can start harvesting many crops (Scallions, Cabbage, Beets, Lettuce) before they are fully mature. By doing so you can extend the harvest and avoid having a sudden glut when it all matures at once. This is especially important for spring crops, as they don't last long before summer heat (and long days) causes them to bolt. You need to make the most of them.

Though you will usually harvest a crop when you want to eat it, there are other reasons to harvest also. It is actually an important maintenance operation and you should always harvest anything that is ready, whether you intend to use it or not (even if you merely compost it). If you leave it on the plant it will get over-mature and may slow or stop production. It may also make the plant susceptible to diseases and pests. Impending frost may force you to harvest tender crops such as Tomatoes and Peppers, before they get damaged. Sometimes a crop is better harvested and stored, than left in the field where it will quickly become over-mature.

How to harvest

Use a sharp knife for harvesting. It will cut cleanly, which is faster and leaves a clean cut which heals rapidly. Bruised and torn tissue is an invitation to rot.

Vegetables begin to deteriorate once picked, so try to harvest just before you plan to use them. Some crops are actually best if cooked within minutes of harvest, most notably the old-fashioned Sweet Corns. If you are harvesting food for your own consumption, you usually don't have to worry about keeping it in good condition, it won't be around that long.

If you are harvesting for storage, or sale (in which case it may have to stay in good condition for several days), you have to be careful how you treat the crop. A vegetable isn't killed when it is harvested, it continues to live until it has used up its stored food reserves. To keep it alive and in optimal condition for as long as possible, you have to help it make those reserves last.

Heat hastens decay, so commercial growers usually harvest their crops in the cool of early morning, when

211

the plants are as cold as possible. In large operations they may then be cooled even further (with water, ice or in a refrigerator), to remove as much latent heat from them as possible. Leave air spaces around the vegetables for fastest cooling. The crop is then put into a cool, humid environment, to keep it cold and retard water loss.

When harvesting vegetables intended for storage, you need to be especially careful not to damage them. Never throw them into containers, or on to the ground, as the slightest cut or bruise exudes nutritious sap that can give decay causing organisms a foothold. If something does get damaged it must not be stored for any length of time, as it may infect the healthy stuff around it. After you finish harvesting sort out the badly damaged stuff for immediate consumption, slightly damaged stuff to be eaten soon and only the most perfect stuff for storage.

Try to avoid harvesting when the plants are wet, as this can encourage the spread of some diseases. Avoid harvesting leaf crops when it's too hot, as they contain less water at this time and so don't keep so well. In dry weather you should water the day before harvesting, to make sure the crops are fully charged with water.

Repeat harvesting

Many leafy crops can be harvested one leaf at a time. By taking a leaf or two from many plants you can actually harvest a complete dinner salad with no noticeable impact on the garden. It may be best to avoid the large outermost leaves (which tend to be the toughest) and take some of the tender inner ones instead. Leave the large outer leaves in place to produce more food.

If you leave an inch or two of stem (maybe even a few leaves) when harvesting Lettuce, Chard, Spinach and Cabbage, the plant may then send up tasty new growth which can be harvested at a later date. This is often better than harvesting single outer leaves because you get succulent new growth.

Though these techniques are very useful for extending the harvest, at some point you have to say enough. When a plant starts to fade it may be more productive to replace it with a fast growing young transplant and get another full crop.

Harvest thinning

A good way to increase the harvest of leaf vegetables is by initially planting at a closer than optimal spacing. You then slowly harvest thin the plants, as they grow larger, until they reach the final spacing.

Extra harvests

We need to get over the idea of one harvest from a crop. We can make out gardens much more productive by harvesting plants at different stages. Many crops will produce more than one type of food if you let them. These are the little bonus crops that can turn a meal into a gourmet delight. Obviously you have to know what's edible before you do this, some parts of some garden crops are poisonous. Don't scatter Tomato flowers on your salad, or cook up a pot of Rhubarb leaves. Here are just a few suggestions on possible extra uses for crops.

Peas: The shoots are edible as well as the peas and/or pods and flowers. Dry peas can be sprouted.

Garlic: The young leaves, flower stalk, rounds and bulbs are all good.

Kale: Use the flower buds, edible flowers and leaves, young leaves in salads, sprouted seeds.

Chinese Cabbage: Use the compact heads, individual leaves, flower stalks, flowers, seed sprouts.

Brassica: You can eat the flower buds of pretty much any Brassica that bolts, if you get it early enough and it isn't infested with aphids. Also edible green seedpods and flowers.

Squash: Use the flowers and fruit.

After harvest treatment

Don't forget about the plants after harvest. If they are to be harvested frequently, you may want to give them a liquid feed occasionally to keep them growing vigorously. If they are finished then remove all crop debris and prepare the soil for the next crop.

Storage

Garden crops have the most flavor and the highest nutritional value when freshly picked, so are best eaten at this time. However in temperate climates winter makes this impossible. Consequently gardeners in those areas have had to devise ways to store the summers produce for winter use.

Not surprisingly the vegetables that store the best are those that are intended as food storage organs: taproots, tubers, bulbs and thick fleshy leaves. Onions are a good example, their food storage tissue is well protected by a thick waterproof skin, so they can be stored for months. Cabbages are another.

Some vegetables can't be stored for any length of time, because they lose moisture rapidly when harvested and so deteriorate quickly. The thin leafed vegetables such as Amaranth, Basil, Spinach and Watercress are most prone to this and soon become inedible (they are best cooked and frozen to preserve them).

Harvested vegetables are still alive and so must respire, consuming stored foods and losing moisture in the process. As these food reserves are the part we want to eat, the plant gradually becomes less useful as food. To keep vegetables in the best condition, for the longest time, we must minimize the rate of respiration and water loss. We do this by increasing the humidity and lowering the storage temperature.

Humidity
Vegetables continue to lose water after harvest and by the time they have lost 5% of their stored water they become limp and unusable. This loss of moisture can be minimized by keeping the vegetables in a humid environment. Most vegetables need at least 80% humidity or they will deteriorate quickly. This is why they keep so much better in the fridge when stored in a plastic bag.

Temperature
Temperature affects humidity and they should always be considered together. Cold air holds less moisture than warm air, so less moisture is needed to saturate it .

Crops last longer when stored in cool conditions because for every 18° F (10° C) drop in temperature, the time needed for a chemical reaction (such as decay) doubles. Most crops last longest when stored just above freezing point (between 32° to 40° F). The temperature should not drop below freezing, because this would damage plant cells and cause them to rot (unless of course you are intentionally freezing them and keeping them frozen).

Low temperatures have an adverse effects on the frost tender vegetables, especially Tomatoes, Potatoes and the Cucurbits. They may lose all of their flavor, or develop an off flavor (this is why we don't keep them in the fridge of course). They should be stored at a slightly higher temperature.

Air circulation
This doesn't actually extend the physiological life of the crops, but it is important because it reduces the incidence of rot causing fungi. It is the reason why most crops are stored in slatted wooden boxes on slatted shelves and why there is ideally a space between each individual vegetable. It is also why the Alliums are suspended in braids or mesh bags.

Air circulation is also important to vent ethylene out of the storage area, as this gas encourages sprouting, ripening and eventually rotting.

Curing
A few crops will rot if not cured properly before storage. Winter Squash, Pumpkins and the Alliums should be left in a warm sunny place for 1 to 2 weeks, so their skins can dry and harden.

Rotting
Only the very best produce must be stored for any length of time. The slightest injury to a vegetable can cause it to decay and this can cause adjacent vegetables to rot as well (in this way the entire store can be ruined). Even the most durable vegetables rot occasionally, so make it a habit of checking stored crops regularly and remove spoiled individuals promptly.

Storage Methods

If they are to last for any length of time, vegetables must be stored in cool humid conditions. There are a number of ways in which we can achieve this.

Store in the fridge

The commonest short-term storage method is to keep vegetables in the refrigerator. Most fridges run at 35 to 40° F, which is ideal for most temperate crops. Refrigerators are humid enough for most crops, but not for leaf vegetables. These should be kept in plastic bags to increase the humidity even further.

Warm season fruits should never be stored in the fridge, as it spoils their flavor. They should be eaten fresh, within a day or two of picking.

In ground storage

In areas with cool or cold winters the easiest way to store crops is to leave them where they are, in the ground. This is less work, there's less room for error and they usually stay in better condition. The crops that can be stored like this were the staple winter foods in northern Europe for centuries.

The hardier leaf crops, Cabbage, Leeks, Kale, Brussels Sprouts, can all stand very cold weather and may actually improve in flavor from exposure to frost. They may lose some outer leaves to frost damage, but the interior will be fine.

The hardy root crops, Carrots, Parsnips, Turnips, Jerusalem Artichokes, can all be stored in the ground and generally improve in flavor with frost. In very cold areas they must be covered with a thick mulch to prevent freezing and rot (and so you can physically dig them). The depth of mulch depends on how cold it gets, but should be at least 6″. Mulching also protects the plants from frost heaving.

A problem with in-ground storage is that pests such as mice can cause severe damage, especially under mulch. If this is a problem, you might try laying down a layer of wire screen mesh over the crop before applying the mulch. In-ground storage can also help insect pests and diseases survive from one year to another, because there are almost always a crop in the ground.

Clamp storage

A traditional way to store large amounts of root crops, such as potatoes and carrots (also Apples, Cabbages and more) is in a clamp. You can store different vegetables in the same pile. One of the advantages of a clamp is that you use what is already available in your garden and don't have to buy anything. One of the disadvantages is that there are a lot of variables involved, it may work great, or you may lose everything. Clamps don't work very well if the winter is very cold, if rodents get inside, or if individual roots rot (they can infect the entire clamp).

The clamp works best in light, well drained soil and should be in a sheltered site. Start by digging out the soil to a depth of 10″, then lay down a 3″ to 6″ layer of straw or dry leaves. A piece of perforated pipe is arranged in the center and the roots are placed around it to form a cone or prism shaped pile (if you don't have any pipe a vent can be constructed from straw). The pile is then covered with a 6″ thick layer of straw or leaves (more in very cold climates). Finally the straw is covered with a 6″ thick layer of soil, which is packed down with a spade. Some of this soil comes from the original excavation, the rest is obtained by digging a drainage trench around the clamp. Keep the vent open on top of the clamp, unless it gets very cold, when it should be temporarily closed with straw..

In mild areas you can remove the crop as needed and re-cover the clamp with soil, but in very cold weather the roots in a disturbed clamp may rot. In such a case you have to gather them all and store indoors.

Other storage ideas

A simpler alternative to a clamp is to bury a rodent proof box 2 to 3 ft deep in well-drained soil. The vegetables are packed in dry leaves or straw and covered with a thick layer of the same. You can use almost any kind of box; old garbage cans, 50 gallon drum or crates, but perhaps the best (if somewhat cumbersome to handle) containers are 36″ sections of 18″ to 24″ concrete pipe. Dig a hole, install the pipe, put a wire screen (to keep out rodents) in the bottom, and some gravel (for drainage). Cover the top with a wire screen and a foot of mulch.

In mild winter areas an old broken fridge or freezer can be used as a storage container. Lay it on its back, remove the shelves and lock, and fill with vegetables packed with straw or dry leaves. This would work in colder climates as well, but you would have to bury it in the ground to prevent the contents freezing.

A cold frame can also be used to store winter crops and is often otherwise empty in early winter. Pack the vegetables in straw or dry leaves and cover with more of the same to prevent them freezing. If rodents are a problem, seal the base of the frame with fine wire mesh.

Root cellar options

The best and most convenient way to store a large volume of crops over the winter is in a root cellar. Traditionally this was dug into the earth (usually the side of a steep bank) to benefit from the humidity and cool stable temperature found there (a root cellar should always stay above freezing). This kind of root cellar takes a lot of work to build, but if you have the time and energy it will be worthwhile.

A perfectly functional root cellar can be constructed in any basement. This is actually better than an outside root cellar in one respect, as it is more convenient for the cook. It should be built on the cooler northeast side of the house (away from heat pipes), on an earth or concrete floor and should have a window to vent to the outside. The house provides two walls, so you only have to build and insulate two walls and a ceiling. Cover the inside with a vapor barrier to keep the humidity up and cover the window to keep the room dark. Put in plenty of slatted shelves and store the vegetables in open slatted wooden fruit containers.

You can store your crops in any outbuilding, garage or unheated part of the house, so long as it doesn't freeze in winter.

Using the root cellar

It helps to have a maximum minimum thermometer in the root cellar, so you know how cold and warm it gets. You can have quite a lot of control over the storage conditions in the root cellar. Ideally the average temperature will be around 35° F, though this will vary from floor to ceiling. This difference can help you give the various vegetables the differing conditions they require. If humidity gets too low you can sprinkle water on the floor. You will need to vent occasionally to keep the air inside from getting stagnant. If it gets too warm (above 40° F), open the vents on cold nights. If it gets too cold (much below freezing), then open them on

warm days. If temperatures fluctuate wildly you could pack the vegetables in boxes filled with straw or dry leaves.

It is important to check on your stored crops regularly and remove spoiled vegetables before they affect their neighbors. Keep fruit and vegetables separate, as fruit may exude ethylene and cause the vegetables to age more rapidly.

Processing methods

Of course you can also store vegetables by freezing, canning, drying or other methods. These are beyond the scope of this book however.

26 Seed saving

Saving seed was once an integral part of growing your own food. If you wanted to plant seed, then you had to save seed. Only relatively recently has it become the norm for gardeners and farmers to purchase seed annually. We now have a situation where many gardeners don't even think about the possibility of saving their own seeds.

Some garden writers seem to have a curious prejudice against saving seed from the garden. Why this should be I can't imagine, as it doesn't even take much time or effort. I have heard some fairly feeble explanations as to why you shouldn't bother saving seed. For example hybrid seed doesn't come true, so you shouldn't bother saving any seed. How did they reach that conclusion? Maybe such writers think seed saving is an anachronism, when there are all those new and improved varieties coming out every year.

If someone tries to tell you it's too difficult for the layperson to save seed, remember that uneducated pre-industrial subsistence farmers bred all of our major crops. By faithfully and lovingly saving the best seed from their crops to replant the following years they transformed a few wild plants into the crops that made civilization possible. Besides their achievements, the work of todays scientific breeders pales into insignificance.

Reasons for saving your own seed

- Saving seed is a basic part of the craft of gardening, as natural as raising your own seedlings, making compost, or harvesting. If you can grow high quality crops, you can save seed that is as good as, or better than, any you can buy.

- Saving seed is an important component of ecologically sound agriculture. By selecting seed from the best plants in your garden you can develop strains that are ideally suited to your growing conditions. If a lot of people start doing this we could eventually have locally adapted strains of crops for every region, just as we used to.

- In many cases saving your own seed is so easy, there is no reason not to. All you have to do is gather it before it gets dispersed. I often collect seed automatically and then decide what to do with it later.

- There is also a serious reason to save your own seeds. In recent years many seed companies have been bought up by multi-national corporations and many of the old varieties of vegetables have disappeared from their catalogs. Except for a few small companies, the varieties of seed available over the counter already has an alarming uniformity. In Europe the disappearance of old varieties has been hastened by seed patenting laws, that have in effect made it illegal to sell many rare seed varieties.

- Though it is no longer possible to buy the seeds of many excellent varieties, you can still get hold of them. There are networks of home gardeners, dedicated to growing and exchanging the seed of old varieties and these have saved many old varieties from extinction. The Seed Savers Exchange is the best known of these in this country. Saving seed enables you to trade seed in organizations such as this, and gives you access to an enormous number of seed varieties.

- Seed saving makes you more self-sufficient by reducing inputs, lowering costs and making your seed source more secure. Of course you can still buy as many seeds as you want (experimenting with them is fun), but if they are open pollinated you will only have to buy them once.

- Seed saving is one of the more satisfying aspects of gardening, You get to see your crops complete their life cycle, rather than always stopping them half way. Putting fresh seed back into the packets you emptied in spring completes the cycle and is a good way to end the gardening year.

Problems of seed saving

There are a few reasons why you may not want to save seed.

- Growing seed crops takes longer than growing vegetable crops and so can upset rotations and successions.

- Saving seed makes the garden messier, as there are small numbers of seeding plants scattered around taking up bed space. You can sometimes solve this problem by moving the plants to a special seed bed (especially biennials).

- Seed bearing plants are often still in the ground while you are planting the next years crop. This could help pests and diseases to survive from one year to the next. Fortunately you don't have to save seed from every crop every year. Most seed can be stored for several years.

- If you aren't careful some seed varieties can cross-pollinate with others and their unique characteristics will be lost. They used to say that the seed had 'run out', but this isn't a very appropriate term. If you want to trade seed you must take care to ensure that it remains pure and true to type. This isn't usually difficult, but takes a little extra work (See below)

- Some virus diseases may be transmitted through infected seeds. These include Lettuce or Tobacco mosaic viruses and Celery Leaf Spot. If you don't know what to look for, you can perpetuate these problems and perhaps spread them to other gardens. If plants show any hint of virus disease don't save seed from them.

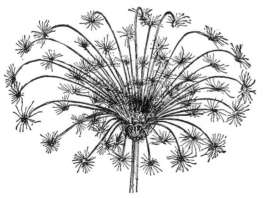

Getting started in seed saving

Basically saving seed consists of allowing plants to do what nature intended, which is to produce seed. Sometimes you have to assist them, and sometimes they do it whether you like it or not. You gather the seed when it is ripe, dry it thoroughly and store it. I don't have room to go into detail about saving seed of individual crops, so I will merely give you some general ideas about what this entails.

- The easiest plants for the beginning seed saver are those that are self-pollinating and are grown for their ripe fruit (Tomato, Eggplant, Melon, Pepper). It's merely a matter of collecting the fruit and separating out the seed (the actual cleaning is the hardest part). Other easily saved, self-pollinating, crops include Bean, Lettuce, Pea and Spinach (these are known as inbreeders). Tomato and Pea can both cross-pollinate to some degree (not with each other), so are best isolated if possible.

- Cross-pollinated crops include Corn, Beet, Brassicas, Carrot and Onion. The latter three can also self-pollinate if necessary, but seed produced in this way is usually inferior.

- Make sure the quality of a variety doesn't deteriorate over succeeding generations. Select the best and most typical plants for collecting seed and mark them prominently so no one harvests them accidentally. Avoid poor looking plants and off types (seed growers remove these to prevent their becoming pollinators). Good cultivation practices increase the size of the crop and of individual seeds (which makes for better seed), but doesn't affect the size of following generations.

- Don't collect seed from the first plants to flower (or the first year in the case of biennials), as you don't want to develop an early bolting variety.

- Keep good records. This is especially important if you will be trading seed with other gardeners.

- If you need the space in a bed, you can transplant long term seed plants (Beet, Carrot, Cabbage,

Leek, Onion) to a special seed plant area. Do this while they are dormant.

- Wait until seed is fully ripe before gathering, don't get impatient and gather early. The only exception to this is if wet weather threatens to ruin the seeds (on of the commonest causes of seed crop loss). In this case harvest the whole plants and finish drying them under cover

- You can also save seed of soil improving crops, to provide another level of self-sufficiency. Most species are fairly easy to save from (especially Buckwheat, Brassicas, Legumes and Sunflowers).

- If you only have a small quantity of a particularly precious seed variety, don't plant it all at once. If an unforeseen disaster strikes you could lose it all.

- Seed has only a limited lifespan. If you are trying to preserve unique old varieties, you will have to grow out the seeds every few years, to get fresh seed.

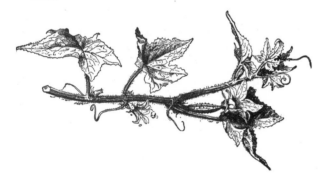

Maintaining genetic purity

If you are just saving seed for your own use next year, then it isn't absolutely necessary that your variety be 100% pure. However if you are attempting to preserve a variety for posterity, or want to trade seed with others, then you need to be sure it is what you say it is. Depending upon the crop this may mean isolating it from all other potential pollinators.

The easiest way to isolate is with time. If only one variety is flowering at any one time, it can't cross-pollinate with anything else. This isn't always as clear cut as you might think, because some crops can cross with closely related wild plants. Also you don't necessarily know what is growing in neighboring gardens.

Another way to isolate the plants is with distance, though this varies considerably according to crop. It may be as little as 20 yards, or as much as a mile.

The other way to isolate plants is to cage them, so no pollinating insects can get in to pollinate them. You then have to hand pollinate, or introduce insects to do it for you.

The alternative to isolation is hand pollination. This isn't as difficult as you might imagine and can be quite simple with some of the bigger flowers.

Maintaining genetic variability

When we save seed we tend to take it from the best plants in the garden, those with the biggest fruits, highest yield, best flavor and more, but this isn't always the best policy. In selecting for highest yield you may be losing important traits such as disease resistance, or drought tolerance. Traditionally gardeners selected seed from a wide variety of plants and mixed them together to maintain genetic diversity. Native Americans bred their Corn for diversity rather than purity, because they wanted plants that would be adaptable to any possible adverse conditions. They tried to ensure that their seed corn was pollinated by as many different plants as possible. In its native land they even left a closely related wild Corn in the fields to help pollinate the crop.

Many common vegetable seeds are very inbred, and to maintain a reasonable degree of genetic variability you will need to gather seed from more than one plant. The actual number of plants varies considerably with the crop, it may be as little as 5 plants or as much as 100. You don't need to worry about this with self-pollinating crops.

Gathering and cleaning seed

I gather most of my seed into paper grocery bags, by bending the heads over the bags and gently loosening the seed. I clean it of husks and debris with a series of different mesh sieves, along with some careful winnowing. I then put it in a paper grocery bag to dry. It is important that the seed is completely dry if you intend to store it for any length of time.

To get seed from a soft fruit like a Tomato or a Cucumber, simply squeeze it from the ripe fruit (eat the rest), stir in a little water and let it ferment in a warm place for a few days. Then pour off the clear liquid and seeds, and rinse several times to remove bits of flesh. Strain the cleaned seed and dry it in a warm dry place.

Saving vegetative material

Saving tubers and bulbs is quite simple in most cases. The hardier types can even be left in the ground for the winter. If you have to dig them and store them inside, make sure you cure and store them properly (see **Harvesting**). You also have to be aware of the possibility of transmitting viral disease from one generation to another.

Saving F1 hybrid seed

It is often said that you shouldn't save seed from F1 hybrid plants because it doesn't come true to type. The offspring (the F2 generation) won't resemble the parents, but will show the segregation of it's grandparents. It is sometimes said that such seed isn't viable, though this isn't usually true.

Though F1 seed doesn't generally breed true, in some varieties you can still get a fairly good (if very variable) crop straight away, so it may be worth experimenting with it. Hybrids can be converted into open pollinated varieties, by planting the F2 seed and in subsequent years selecting seed from the plants with the most desirable characteristics. In some cases common varieties labeled as hybrids may actually come close to breeding true.

Breeding your own varieties

Seed savers are most often concerned with maintaining the purity of established varieties and maintaining them for posterity, but this isn't all there is to seed saving. If you are adventurous, the next step (and a logical one) is to start breeding your own new varieties and altering old ones to make them more suitable for your needs and local growing conditions. Plant breeding opens up a whole new vista for the ambitious gardener and isn't very difficult. It is how out ancestors produced all of our common crops and their many varieties. You could even create entirely new kinds of crops, as very little breeding work has been done on most potential food plants. Professional plant breeders mostly work for large companies, breeding varieties useful to large scale farmers. Breeding garden seeds has pretty much been left to the small seed companies and amateur breeders.

27   Season extension

Extending the growing season means pushing the start of the season back into early spring (or even late winter) and pushing the end of the season into late autumn or early winter. Some gardeners get really into this and grow crops right through the winter, even in cold snowy climates. I am not going to go into great detail here, I just want to make you aware of some of the possibilities.

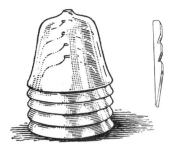

Obstacles to plant growth

Cold
The most obvious factor limiting outdoor plant growth in winter is temperature. The rate of plant growth is halved for every 18° F drop in temperature (down from 90° F). So even if it's not actually freezing, plant growth will pretty much stop when the temperature gets down near 40° F (it gets very slow below 50° F). We can get around this problem by growing crops under glass (or more often plastic) as described below.

Short days / weak sun
Unfortunately merely warming up the environment around the plants to above 50° F won't necessarily give us good crops. The days are much shorter in winter and the sun is a lot lower in the sky (and hence weaker). There may be only an eighth as much solar energy around as in summer. For 4 to 6 weeks on either side of the winter solstice there may be too little sunlight for any appreciable plant growth (of course this depends upon where you live).

Frost
Frost is most likely to occur on calm clear nights, following cold clear winter days. It is most severe in the early hours, after the heat in the ground has been

radiating out into space all night. Cold air (and hence frost) gathers in valleys and the lowest hollows to form frost pockets (see **Site Planning**). Frost kills plants by freezing and bursting their cells, but it doesn't affect all plants equally. Tender plants such as Eggplant, Basil and Peppers can be killed as soon as the temperature drops to freezing (32° F). The hardiest plants (Brussels Sprouts, Kale, Leeks) can come back from being frozen solid and may take temperatures as low as 0° F.

Spring gardening

When the calendar says it's time to start planting the garden in early spring, the weather can be very variable. It may be sunny and mild, or there may be deep snow. The last frost date commonly varies by as much as 4 to 6 weeks from one year to the next. There is no need to be intimidated by the fickle weather however. The day length and sun intensity is increasing and you can start gardening. By using crop protecting devices you can largely eliminate this variability in weather. Early spring planting is one of the best ways to increase the productivity of the garden. The earlier the plants start growing, the more food you can get out of the garden.

Planting: When you start planting in spring the soil and the weather are still quite cold. Your main objective is to get the plants established and growing. From then on time is on your side, as growing conditions can only improve, as the days get longer and the sun gets stronger.

Early bed preparation: Many gardeners prepare their spring beds in autumn, so they don't have to wait for suitable spring weather to get started. The prepared bed can be covered with a thick mulch, to protect them over the winter. Earthworms love this mulch and thrive under it (as unfortunately do slugs).

Warm the soil: In early spring the days are lengthening rapidly and the air is warming up nicely. Unfortunately the soil is still cold (it warms up much slower than the air), so your main priority must be to warm the soil. If you had a mulch on the bed to protect it over the winter, this should be removed, as it insulates

the soil and keeps it cold. You can hasten soil warming by covering it with a hoop house, cloche or plastic sheeting for 2 to 3 weeks.

Early sowing: Many crops can be direct sown in the fall, to overwinter as seeds or seedlings and do most of their growing in early spring. Some very hardy crops can be direct sown under cloches in mid to late winter to mature in early spring. You may be able to give these crops a fast start by pre-germinating as described in **Direct Sowing.**

Use transplants: Plants will often grow quite happily at temperatures that would be too low for the satisfactory germination of their seeds. Hence transplanted crops can give you a considerable head start over direct sown ones. Larger plants are better able to cope with cold conditions and so grow faster, and mature earlier, than smaller ones.

Fall gardening

Planting a fall garden is one of the easiest ways to increase and extend the garden harvest. Many gardeners run out of enthusiasm for anything but harvesting by midsummer and pretty much abandon the garden for the year. This is a big mistake, if you don't plant a fall garden you are not really trying.

Fall gardening begins in mid summer, when you start the autumn crops. The soil and weather is warm at this time, so the plants grow fast. As fall comes on the days get shorter, the sun gets weaker and temperatures gradually drop. The autumn crops should be almost mature by the time the hard frosts arrive and growth slows dramatically. They can then sit in the cold garden in an edible state for weeks, waiting to be harvested. In very cold climates they stay in much better shape if protected with cold frames or cloches. They may even continue to grow.

The hardy autumn/winter crops become important when nighttime temperatures regularly drop below 50° F and continue bearing until temperatures drop down into the 20's.

Early frost protection: The simplest season extending technique is to protect the tender crops from the first occasional autumn frosts. Even the lightest frost will kill such plants if they are not protected. The first frost may be followed by several weeks of good

growing weather before the next one, so the simple act of covering your plants for a night or two may reward you with several more weeks of harvests. Almost anything will give protection from light frost; cloches, cold frames, old blankets, row covers, plastic sheeting, hay or straw mulch. Tall plants such as Tomatoes can be unstaked and laid down on the ground for easier protection. For protection from more severe frosts you can cover crops with cold frames or cloches.

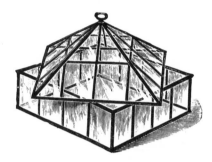

Protect the tender crops for as long as there is good growth in the daytime. It isn't worth protecting them once the days get cold, as they won't thrive. It is better to replace them with hardy crops.

A quick freeze does a lot more damage to plants than a gradual decline in temperature (which gradually hardens them off). If unprotected plants are hit by an unexpected frost you may be able to revive them by washing the frost off with a spray of water. This must be done before the sun hits them and thaws them out too quickly.

Commercial citrus and strawberry farmers protect large areas of crops by running water sprinklers all night. As the water turns to ice it gives off heat and so prevents the plants from freezing. This has been effective at protecting Citrus groves down to 15° F. In an emergency you could emulate them and leave a sprinkler on for the coldest part of the night (don't turn it off until all ice has melted).

Crop timing: Fall crops commonly take longer to mature than spring or summer crops, because the sun is weaker and the days are shorter. To determine the right time to plant fall crops, you must decide when you want them to mature (normally just before the weather turns too cold for good growth). You must the find out the number of days the crop needs to reach maturation (add extra days to allow for the shorter autumn days). Subtract this number of days from the maturation date and you have the sowing date. It's a good idea to plant a few successions at this time, to make sure you have crops at the right stage. It helps to keep notes on actual maturation times in your journal, as it makes next years planning much easier.

Crop selection: Some cool weather crops are much better suited to growing in autumn than in spring. Often by the time it's warm enough for plants to mature in spring, the days are getting too long and so they bolt (short day crops such as Spinach and Oriental Cabbage are notorious for this). The warm temperatures adversely affect their flavor as well. Such crops do far better in autumn, growing quickly in the warm days of late summer and slowly maturing in the shorter colder days that follow.

For cold weather growing it is best to stick to the tried and true hardy crops; Cabbage, Kale, Leek, Brussels Sprouts, Cornsalad, Carrot, Parsnip and Chard. It is important to use the right crop variety at this time of year, as hardiness varies considerably within a crop. You want the varieties that have been bred to withstand adverse cold growing conditions. Often spring or summer varieties just won't make it.

Site for winter crops: The beds for winter crops should receive all of the sunlight available, so make sure they won't be shaded. Remember the sun will be much lower in the sky at this time, so there will be a lot more shade. A south facing slope is the best choice as it gets extra heat from the sun. Some gardeners shape winter beds so they tilt slightly to the south, to give them a little extra solar gain. The beds should be well protected from cold winds, which chill plants and soil, and drain heat from cloches and frames. Don't plant the winter garden in low lying areas, as these are frost pockets and much colder than more elevated slopes.

The soil should also be well drained, as dampness is often as great as enemy of winter plants as is cold (much of the value of cloches and cold frames is due to their protecting plants from moisture).

Crop protection devices

If the growing season is short and cool the variety of vegetables that can be grown without protection is quite limited. To get the most out of your garden in such circumstances you have to modify the climate with crop protection devices. Even the simplest of these can be very effective and they greatly expand the gardens productive potential. They can be used in several different ways.

- These devices keep the soil warm and provide the plants with a much better growing environment than can be found outside (the interior of the cloche can be 10 or 15° F warmer). They also block out cold winds and keep plants drier and cleaner.

- They can be used to warm the soil for spring planting and so enable you to start crops earlier in the spring than you could otherwise.

- They provide young seedlings with frost protection and a warmer growing environment.

- They can be used instead of a greenhouse for raising transplants, hardening off transplants and overwintering hardy plants.

- They can be used to protect tender crops from low temperatures and for protecting late maturing fall crops from frost. The more sophisticated devices can be used to grow fresh vegetables right through the winter (even in the snow).

- They can be used to give extra warmth to hot season crops.

Problems with these devices

- They can give you a false sense of security and encourage you to grow plants at the wrong time.

- If not well ventilated they can heat up rapidly in sunny weather. This makes the plants vulnerable to heat damage.

- Weeds, slugs, snails and other pests find the protected environment as hospitable as do the crops. To control these problems the devices must be easily movable, so you have access to the plants and soil.

Choosing the right protection

The type of crop protection you use depends upon your needs and your finances. Generally the portable devices are the most useful, because you can move them around. Using them to get a crop established and then moving them on to another crop. However the permanent devices are more effective at protecting plants from severe cold.

Poly tunnels

The larger poly tunnels are known as hoop houses, smaller ones are called tunnel cloches. They are cheapest way to protect large areas of plants.

The hoop house is basically a giant cloche and can cover several beds at once. It can be used for growing crops for their entire lives (including tall ones). The gardener can work inside it, which is very convenient for watering, harvesting and weeding and very pleasant in cold weather. It's great to run out to your tunnel in cold wintry weather and do some spring gardening. Hoop houses can be used to grow a crop to maturity, hardy crops in winter and heat loving ones in cool summer areas. Some gardeners in cooler climates have rigged up moveable poly tunnels and use them to start crops. When these are up and growing they move them to another site to start another crop. The ability to move the greenhouse around neatly avoids the problem of pests building up in the soil.

In very cold weather you can actually grow plants in cold frames inside the poly tunnel, for double protection

Tunnel cloches usually cover the width of one bed and may be of any length. They are usually made of flexible plastic or metal pipe, but could easily be made of Bamboo canes or Willow wands.

The cover is usually 200 gauge plastic sheeting (thicker plastic cuts out too much light, while thinner stuff is too flimsy) or vinyl (see **Greenhouses**). One edge of the cover is buried in the soil to weigh it down, while the other is simply weighted down with stones (or anything heavy), to facilitate opening and closing. Make sure the cover is firmly anchored, as if any part comes loose the wind will rip it apart. Cover rough parts of the frame with tape to prevent it abrading the cover and if tears do appear, repair them as soon as possible with transparent plastic tape. The cloche is ventilated by raising one side.

Modular Cloches

The word cloche means bell in French, because the first cloches were bell shaped glass jars. Then the British started making them from flat panes of glass held together with special wire clips to give various configurations. These glass cloches last indefinitely (if they aren't broken) and can be made from recycled materials. In recent years plastic has been used instead of glass and one piece molded cloches are now available.

Modular glass, or plastic, cloches aren't very popular in North America, but have been widely used in Britain and other parts of Europe. They are easily moved, let in a lot of light and are modular so can cover as large or small an area as you need. They are most often used as temporary protection until a crop is established and are moved once growth is well under way. They aren't usually tall enough to protect mature crops, don't hold much heat in cold weather and heat up quickly when it's sunny. A small space is left between each module to vent them (this can be increased by uncovering both ends).

You don't normally have to remove modular cloches to water the plants. Simply water the cloche, water running off the top will move sideways into the soil under the cloche. Direct sown crops should be watered thoroughly after planting, before covering with the cloches.

You can make a simple rigid plastic tunnel from a sheet of transparent corrugated plastic. This is simply bent to the required shape over a bed and held in place with pegs or baling wire. Several of these may be needed to cover the length of a bed.

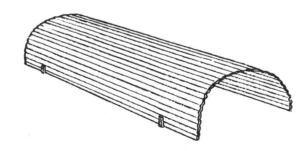

Large cloches can be made from 2″ x 1″ (or 2″ x 2″) lumber and plastic sheeting, braced with wire to keep them rigid. These can be quite large, 10 x 5 feet or even 20 x 5 feet. They are used like the poly tunnels described above, but are easier to move.

Cold Frames

A cold frame is essentially a small greenhouse and can be used like one for raising seedlings and protecting plants. They are also ideal for hardening off seedlings before they go into the garden. Frames stay warmer than cloches in winter because they are better insulated. Like cloches they can quickly overheat in sunny weather if not vented carefully. They are vented by propping the frames open slightly in cool weather, or removing them entirely if it gets very warm.

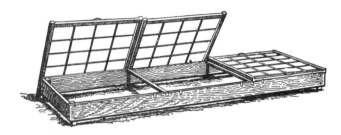

I consider the cold frame as an accessory to the greenhouse, rather than a substitute for it. It is a good place to put almost mature transplants, to free up room in the greenhouse

In Britain many tender crops were traditionally planted in cold frames. When they grew large enough (and it was warmer) the glass lights were taken off. The larger kitchen gardens often had row upon row of brick cold frames for early lettuce, carrots, potatoes, strawberries, melons and peppers. They were sometimes used in conjunction with hot beds (see below), or soil heating cables for growing out of season crops.

Types: Dutch light frames are simple glazed frames that resemble window sashes (in some cases they actually are old single pane window sashes). They are simply rested on wooden boards (the back board is slightly wider than the front to give the frame a slight pitch). If you use aluminum sashes it is even possible to rest the frames on a mound of earth (wood ones will rot quickly). More complex frames might have a gable roof, which is higher in the middle and slopes to each side.

Cold frames used to be made of rot resistant wood, but most commercial frames are now made of aluminum. Most gardeners make their own frames out of scrap wood, old window sashes and plastic sheeting. Don't use commercial wood preservatives on cold frames, because it may leach into the soil. Since the bottom edge of the

cold frame is the part most prone to rot (it sits directly on the soil), it's a good idea to nail a wooden strip to the bottom of the frame. When it eventually rots you only have to replace the strip, rather than the entire frame.

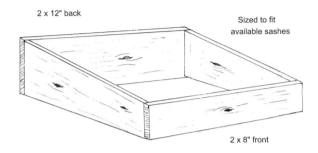

Row covers

Row covers, consisting of non-woven polyester fabric or perforated plastic sheeting, are a recent innovation. They are so light they can simply be laid over a seedbed or bed of transplants. As the new plants grow they lift up the fabric, creating a protected microclimate (or you can support them with wire or plastic hoops - I use short lengths of flexible ½″ polyethylene irrigation pipe). Seeds are sometimes sown directly into unusually deep furrows (and not re-filled fully) to give them some time to grow before they have to push up the cover.

These covers protect young plants from pests and wind and raise temperatures slightly, thus providing a more hospitable growing climate. They can be removed when the weather is warm enough and the plants are old enough to look after themselves. If the weather is very sunny, it can get hot enough under the cover to cook the plants. Avoid this by supporting the cover on hoops, to improve air circulation and prevent overheating

Miscellaneous devices

To protect individual plants you can use commercial hot caps, newspaper hats, bottomless gallon plastic water or milk jugs or large soda bottles (take the cap off to vent it).

Wire Tomato cages can be wrapped with plastic sheeting to protect the plants inside.

If plants are grown in furrows (or soil is mounded up on either side) you can cover them with a sheet of glass, rigid plastic or polyethylene. Make sure this is vented well, or the first warm sunny day will cook the plants.

Water filled containers such as inner tubes (or commercial tubes such as the wall O' Water) can be placed around individual plants to protect them from freezing.

Hot beds

The French market gardeners were masters of extending the growing season by the use of hot beds. This seemingly primitive way of heating is not only a very efficient use of resources, but also surprisingly effective. An experienced gardener can carefully control the amount of heat produced. Hot beds work best in spring, as the soil temperature would be slowly rising anyway. In fall there is the chance that the bed will suddenly cool rapidly when the pile finishes heating.

Hot beds can be built in brick cold frames, or the glass frames can be supported by wooden stakes at each corner. It's even possible to build up the manure to form a raised lip and just lay the framed directly on this. However it shortens the life of the frame, unless you use metal sashes (old double glazed aluminum windows would be perfect for this)

The first step in building a hot bed is to water and turn the manure, to encourage it to heat up. It is turned every few days for two weeks to prevent it heating too rapidly. You can also reduce its temperature by mixing it with an equal volume of leaves or aged manure.

Prepare the bed by laying down a deep (24″) layer of manure, compact it slightly to slow the heating, by packing it with a spade. Leave the manure for five days, then cover with a 4″ to 6″ layer of soil for the plants to grow in (the depth of soil depends upon the crop). The glass is then placed on the bed and more manure is piled up around the sides. Don't plant the bed until the temperature of the pile drops to 60 to 70° F. At night and in very cold weather, the frames were covered with straw mats to hold in the heat.

An alternative method of making a hotbed is to dig a 12″ deep pit and fill it with 12″ of manure. This is then covered with 4″ to 6″ of a mix of half soil and half manure and the cold frame is put over it.

If you don't have (or don't want to use) manure, you could make a hot bed over a newly built compost pile, but it doesn't work as well. You could also use moist chopped leaves (you need a lot). The modern way to make a hotbed is with electric soil warming cables (once again substituting fossil fuel energy for knowledge).

Forcing

Forcing is another approach to season extension and allows you to harvest fresh salad vegetables in winter and early spring, even in extremely cold areas. It is most commonly practiced with Chicory, but a number of other crops can also be forced (Seakale, Dandelion, Rutabaga, Rhubarb).

Forcing is a simple process, the roots are dug after the plants go dormant in late autumn and planted in a box of sand. This is stored in a cool dark place until required. To start the shoots growing they are watered and moved to a warmer (but still dark) place. The pale shoots are harvested as needed and the roots will go on to produce a second crop (and sometimes a third).

The Victorians forced Rhubarb and Seakale in the garden. After it has died down in autumn it was covered with a pot (they used special forcing pots, but a plant pot, or an old bucket, will do) and a foot or so of fresh manure was piled up around it. The heat from the manure stimulated the plant to produce new shoots in about 4 to 5 weeks.

225

28 Greenhouses

A greenhouse makes gardening so much easier, pleasanter and more productive that I consider it to be pretty much an essential. You might imagine that a greenhouse must inevitably be expensive, but it is possible to get a functioning greenhouse without spending very much money. I have built a variety of low cost greenhouses over the years and all have worked really well. So well in fact that I no longer raise any seedlings under lights.

I also bought a second hand greenhouse for $300, which would have worked great also, except that I never got around to anchoring it down properly. One stormy night, not long after I bought it, the wind moved the concrete blocks holding it down, picked it up and demolished it. Fortunately I was able to salvage most of the polycarbonate glazing and built a larger greenhouse. The moral of this story – anchor your greenhouse firmly to the ground straight away.

The most important use of the greenhouse is as a nursery for raising transplants from seed, but it is only really packed with seedlings in spring. In winter it can be used to grow hardy cold season crops, in spring and autumn you can grow cool weather crops and in summer you can grow hot weather crops.

There are already plenty of good books on greenhouse design, construction, siting and related stuff, so I won't get into as those topics here. If you have lots of money and want to create a state of the art greenhouse, there are a lot of commercial greenhouses, kits and designs to choose from. If you don't have much money I suggest you consider one of the low cost options mentioned below. Whatever you do don't deprive yourself of the pleasure of a greenhouse because you don't think you can afford it.

Types of Greenhouse

Solar greenhouse
The name is somewhat misleading name because all greenhouses are solar heated to some degree. These have several innovative features that make them more energy efficient and economical than their predecessors. Solar greenhouses are most often used in very cold climates, where their special features come into their own.

Generally a solar greenhouse will have a solid insulated north wall to reduce heat loss. There is not much reduction in light from this wall being opaque, because the sun is always well to the south in winter. The bottom sections of the side and front walls may also be solid and insulated, to further reduce heat loss (again without reducing light levels significantly). These opaque walls are often painted white to increase the reflection of light on to the plants.

This drawing is perhaps 100 years old, which shows that solar greenhouses are not really new.

The south facing glass front is angled to ensure maximum light penetration in winter when the sun is low. This actually reduces light penetration in summer, when the sun is high and very hot .

There is usually some form of heat storage, set against the solid north wall (this may double as a shelf). This absorbs some of the heat entering the greenhouse during the day, making it slightly cooler. It makes it significantly warmer at night, when the heat radiates back into the greenhouse. In very cold climates there may even be thick insulated opaque curtains or shutters, that can be closed at night, or in very cold weather, to reduce heat loss.

Attached solar greenhouse

One of the most cost-effective way to utilize solar energy in the home, is to add a solar greenhouse on to the south facing side. Attached greenhouses are not only useful, but also provide a wonderful living space, that is not quite inside and not quite outside. There is a symbiotic effect that enhances both the greenhouse and house. The greenhouse come alive (quite literally when it fills with plants) and becomes more than just the workshop of the garden. It even gives surplus heat to the house during the day and receives heat from the house on cold nights (this can sometimes cause humidity problems in the house however). As the many virtues of attached greenhouses become more widely known, I believe they will eventually become an essential part of every well designed temperate climate house.

Gable roof greenhouse

The traditional gable roof greenhouse is very efficient in terms of light and space and you can fit a lot of plants into it. They are ideally suited for mild cloudy climates, as there is very good light penetration, even in summer. However they don't conserve heat very well. Mine works well enough in our mild winters, but it doesn't stay very warm. Some of these greenhouses have slightly sloping sidewalls to admit more light in winter. Those with glass to the ground are more versatile, but those with a solid base stay warmer. These greenhouses are sometimes attached to buildings, in which case they have many of the advantages described above.

Hoop greenhouse

I already mentioned poly tunnels in the section on Season Extension. The largest poly tunnel, the hoop greenhouse, is one of the cheapest greenhouses you can build. It consists of a series of metal or plastic hoops covered with plastic sheeting. It can be of almost any size and covers the greatest area for the least expense. Commercial growers commonly use hoop houses for raising seedlings, because of their low cost. They are also fairly moveable, which is an advantage if you don't own your own garden land. Hoop houses are usually free standing, but could easily be adapted to make a low cost lean-to (a half hoop house!)

There are drawbacks to hoop houses. They aren't very efficient at retaining heat (though better than the smaller tunnel cloches. They heat up quickly in sunny weather and can be hard to ventilate properly unless you use an electric fan. They aren't very attractive either.

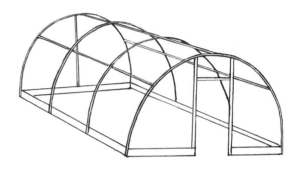

The hoop house usually consists of a rectangular wooden foundation frame, to which a series of metal or plastic hoops are bolted. These hoops are adjustable so that once the cover is attached you can push them up to tighten the cover (this makes it very taut and resistant to wind damage). The cover is usually U.V. resistant polyethylene, or PVC and should be installed on a warm day to minimize sagging. The outer edges of the hoops are often covered with foam covered tape to prevent chafing and potential damage. The ends of the hoop house are enclosed with plastic covered, semi-circular wooden frames, with doors and vents.

A-frames

An A-frame greenhouse can be made quite cheaply from wood or pipe (plastic or metal), covered with polyethylene sheeting, corrugated plastic, or salvaged glass. They tend not to have much room inside them, unless they are very tall. One way around this is to create a pit greenhouse, whereby you dig a trench to walk in down the center of the greenhouse, and have the plants at ground level. This design was once quite popular, as it is inexpensive to make and quite energy efficient. However it must be drained carefully, or it may get waterlogged. The best way to accomplish this is to build the greenhouse into the side of a hill.

Greenhouse Glazing

When the sun hits the greenhouse, the light rays pass straight through the glazing unhindered (because of their wavelengths) and heat up the interior of the greenhouse and any objects within. When these objects heat up they emit heat radiation of a wavelength which doesn't pass through the glazing so easily (it is essentially opaque to them), thus heat is trapped inside. This heat builds up quickly on sunny days, even if it is very cold outside and makes the greenhouse interior nice and warm. You have no doubt heard of the greenhouse effect recently, well this is it.

To maximize heat gain the greenhouse must admit as much light as possible. This is especially critical in the short, often gloomy, days of winter and early spring. This means using clear, rather than translucent, glazing where possible and keeping glazing bars to a minimum. It also means keeping the glazing clean, and even removing condensation if it gets too thick.

If it is to stay warm the greenhouse needs to be airtight. Any small gap will allow a lot of heat to escape (and allow pests to enter). In very cold climates greenhouses sometimes have a second layer of glazing, as this can reduce heat loss by as much as 40%. This could be a plastic sheet, separated from the main glazing by 1″. This second layer also reduces the amount of light inside (each layer cuts out as much as 10% of light), so should only be used if really necessary.

Rigid glazing is best in snowy areas, as plastic sheeting tends to sag under the weight of a heavy snow and may even break.

Polyethylene sheeting: This stuff isn't very environmentally friendly, it doesn't break down very well, has a short life span, can't be recycled easily, fossil fuels are used in it's manufacture and toxins are produced as by-products. It is also quite ugly and so translucent you can't see outside. However it also has some unique and very useful properties for inexpensive greenhouses. It is versatile, cheap, available in large continuous sheets and so light it needs little structural support.

Ordinary polyethylene sheeting has a short lifespan (as short as 6 months) when used outside because it degrades when exposed to the ultraviolet rays in bright sunlight. Ultraviolet resistant polyethylene is available specifically for agricultural use, but even this only lasts for about 3 years. Some organic purists object to the use of plastics in the garden altogether and its true they soon end up as garbage. We really do need better, more durable, yet recyclable (or at least biodegradable) plastic sheeting. It works so well for this purpose, that it's hard to imagine building a really inexpensive greenhouse without it.

Plastic sheeting isn't very resistant to abrasion and if any part flaps in the wind it will eventually wear away and rip. To prevent this from happening it must be kept taut at all times. It is usually attached to the wooden frame of the greenhouse with narrow wooden battens. If these are screwed in place they are easily removable when it's time to replace the plastic.

Vinyl sheeting: This is more durable than polyethylene and may last 6 years or more. It is also more expensive.

Glass: In many respects glass is still the best material for glazing. It lasts indefinitely, is made from abundant natural materials, can be recycled and is so clear it lets in more light than other types of glazing. There is even a special greenhouse glass that lets in a more complete spectrum of light (it is more expensive though).

The main drawback with glass is that it is heavy and needs a strong support structure (which tends to be more expensive). It also breaks fairly easily and is quite expensive (though cheap used glass is often readily available).

Other materials: There are several types of proprietary rigid plastic glazing for greenhouses, some even have double walls.

Polycarbonate is the glazing I have had the most experience with. It is superior to glass in that it is easy to work with and doesn't break (I have accidentally folded a sheet, it just popped back flat). It is also very light and doesn't need a big heavy supporting structure (which is a big advantage).

Greenhouse design Factors

Heating

If the greenhouse isn't warm enough, you won't get good plant growth. Plants like the same conditions as humans, so we automatically know when they are right, it feels good. This means temperatures of around 70 to 80° F in the day and 10° lower at night. A maximum minimum thermometer is very useful to monitor the greenhouse temperature.

Traditionally greenhouses were classified according to how warm they stayed in winter. A cold greenhouse merely keeps its contents from freezing, a cool greenhouse doesn't go any lower than 40 to 50° F, whereas a warm one is always kept above 55° F (usually with supplemental heat).

Heat storage: Heating the greenhouse in cold weather is expensive and not very energy efficient, so modern greenhouses mostly rely on storing solar heat. They do this with thermal mass, which is any dense material that holds a lot of heat. Thermal mass helps to lessen the extreme temperature swings that often take place in the greenhouse, between sunny days and frosty nights.

The most commonly used thermal mass is water, which can be stored in any container that doesn't rust (50 gallon plastic drums work well). To maximize heat absorption these containers are usually painted black. Large water tanks have been used to grow fish in solar greenhouses. The thermal mass of the tank helps to keep the greenhouse warm at night (and cooler in the day), while the greenhouse warms the water in the tank for the fish.

Masonry walls, stone or concrete foundations and floors also store heat, especially if dark in color. You can also use concrete blocks to rest the staging (shelves) on and for paths. The outside of the foundation is sometimes insulated to help it retain heat.

Siting

To make the best use of available sunlight a solar greenhouse should face as close to south as possible and there should be no obstructions to block the sun. This is especially critical in winter, when the sun is low in the sky. There should be no trees nearby, as these not only cast shade, but also drip sap (which makes the glass dirty) and drop leaves (which can collect on the glass).

The greenhouse should also be sheltered from cold winter winds, as they can increase heat loss enormously. Wind can also cause structural damage, so in windy areas the greenhouse must be anchored firmly (remember my experience). Modern greenhouses tend to be light and fairly flimsy at the best of times.

Flooring

The floor of the greenhouse can be bare soil, concrete blocks (which add thermal mass), gravel or wooden boards.

Size

I suggest that you make the greenhouse fairly large. If you are serious about growing plants and producing food you won't have any difficulty filling it up. My second greenhouse was twice the size of the first, but still filled up completely. However even a small greenhouse can produce a lot of plants (put the biggest transplants in a cold frame for their last few weeks before planting out).

Ventilation

The rule of thumb for ventilation is that the area of vents should equal one fifth of the floor area. There should be vents at both bottom and top for good airflow. You keep the vents open when it's hot and close them when it's cold. You can buy automatic vents that work by compressed gas and counter-weights and open at a pre-determined temperature. A thermostat and electric fan can also work well, though I prefer to keep things simple where possible. I found I had to put netting over the vents to keep out birds and other pests.

Very Low Cost Greenhouses

If you are creative and handy with tools, you can construct a perfectly functional (if not particularly attractive) greenhouse very cheaply. In fact finding a suitable site is usually more of a problem than cost, especially in suburban areas where the rather rudimentary appearance of a temporary structure might not be appreciated by some neighbors. These inexpensive structures can pay for themselves in one season in extra crops and transplants.

For a long time I raised seeds on windowsills and under lights, because I thought couldn't afford a greenhouse. After working in a greenhouse at the University of California Santa Cruz and learning their advantages, I wasn't prepared to go back to my old ways, so when I moved up to Washington state I was forced to build my own. With almost no money I went to work with salvaged materials and discovered that a perfectly functional greenhouse could be constructed for next to nothing.

My first structure, a 10 x 6 foot lean-to, took about 6 hours to build and actually cost around two dollars. I spent a dollar for a sheet of plastic (actually a painters drop cloth on sale) and used about a dollars-worth of galvanized nails. The salvaged Cedar 2 x 4's I used for framing had been laying on the ground for a couple of years and many were half rotten, but I cut off the worst parts and used the worst of the remaining ones for non structural purposes. The performance of this crude greenhouse far exceeded my expectations and must have produced more than a thousand healthy transplants over the course of the summer (enough to fill the garden to overflowing).

When the flimsy plastic on this greenhouse began to look a little tattered at the end of the summer, I tore the whole thing down and replaced it with one twice the size (10 x 12 feet). I actually didn't spend any more money on this second structure, as in the meantime I had found a large sheet of U.V. resistant greenhouse plastic. I also had more salvaged Cedar 2 x 4's lying around. This house lasted for several years. It was a wonderful feeling going into that warm, moist greenhouse full of growing things, while outside it was cold and wet. All the more so as it didn't really cost me anything, apart from my time.

The key to constructing an inexpensive greenhouse is to be creative with what is available for free, or at low cost. I used salvaged 2 x 4's because they were laying there for free. In a later garden I made a hoop house out of discarded plastic well pipe, some rebar and more plastic sheet. I have seen a design for a ultra low cost greenhouse made from hay bales, flexible Bamboo and plastic sheeting. I have also seen a greenhouse made from long flexible shoots of Vine Maples, tied together in the manner of a Native American wigwam or sweat lodge. You could use an old discarded tent or dining canopy frame, just cover it in plastic.

Greenhouse management

Here are a few suggestions to keep your plants happy in their new home.

- Maintaining the desired temperature in the greenhouse often involves adjusting the vents during the day. Opening them to cool it down, or closing them to warm it up.

- If the greenhouse temperature gets much above 90° F, spray water on the walls and paths (a process known as damping down), to cool the place by evaporation. Damping down is sometimes done to increase humidity for some crops, or to reduce the frequency of watering. Remember that fungus diseases like humidity however and keep the place well vented when damping down, or you may also get damping off!

- If the greenhouse gets too hot every day and venting doesn't help, you can use shade cloth to keep it cooler. Traditionally the glass was coated with whitewash to keep it cooler, but this is a hassle to remove in autumn.

- Temperature varies considerably from one part of the greenhouse to another. Heat rises so the higher parts get the hottest, while lower ones stay much cooler. You can move plants around as necessary to take advantage of these differences.

- If you need to heat the greenhouse in an emergency, kerosene heaters are probably the simplest and most economical.

- My greenhouses have all been unheated and get quite cool on cloudy winter days. Because of this I sometimes start early seedlings indoors in warmer conditions (they don't need light to germinate). I move them outside as soon as the first seedlings appear. They may be a little disappointed that they don't get the 80 degree weather they germinated in, but grow into stocky and vigorous plants anyway. If you can't start things indoors, you could use soil-heating cables to provide the necessary warmth for germinating seeds. Or you could make a propagator using light bulbs as a heat source. Many cool season plants are perfectly happy when sown straight into the cool greenhouse.

- The greenhouse is a warm hospitable enclosed space, far more comfortable than the outside. You find it is a nice comfortable place to be and so do many other organisms. Consequently it is important to have good sanitation to prevent the buildup of disease and other pests. Don't leave thinnings or weeds in the greenhouse to rot. Don't use it as a storeroom for flats, plug trays, pea poles and other items. Examine the interior of the greenhouse regularly for signs of pest infestation, look under leaves, flats and staging, for damage from mice, whitefly, slugs, earwigs and damping off. If pests get established they can be a big problem, so try and keep them out. Put netting over vents, nail copper strips where slugs could enter.

- When the greenhouse is empty (or nearly empty) in early winter clean it out thoroughly. Remove old plants and weeds, and if disease is a problem wash the interior thoroughly with detergent. If possible move any tender plants indoors and open all the vents so it can cool down to the outside temperature for a while (if it's cold enough this may kill some pests). This is also a good time to wash the glass, both inside and out. Put this chore on your calendar so you don't forget it.

- In cold weather you could enclose part of the greenhouse with plastic, to create a warmer area for germinating seedlings and rooting cuttings.

- In winter slatted staging is important for air circulation and disease control. In summer this may be covered with plastic and capillary matting to reduce watering.

- Have a daily morning and evening routine, where you check the greenhouse and its inhabitants.

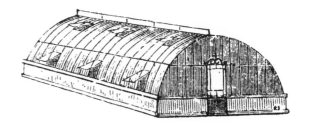

Watering

Watering is one of the most critical jobs in the greenhouse. In hot weather it must be done every day, so someone always needs to be around to check on things. I usually do it before I go to work and then again when I get home. If you like to go away for days at a time in summer you might want to set up some kind of automatic watering system. The simplest of these is capillary matting (old felt or foam carpet padding will work) or sand. You simply place the containers on this and they soak up moisture as needed by capillary action. A more complex alternative is to use a drip or mist system attached to a timer. See **Watering** for more on these.

In winter it is good to warm up the irrigation water by storing it in tanks in the greenhouse (these also serve as thermal mass). Very cold water could cool the soil and shock plants.

See **Raising Transplants** for more on watering seeds and seedlings.

Venting

Venting is another important operation, and if you neglect it the plants may get cooked or chilled. In winter you have to watch the weather carefully. If it is cold and cloudy you keep the vents closed to conserve heat. If it is sunny you must open them up fully to avoid too much heat buildup. In very cold weather you close the greenhouse windows early in the evening, to allow heat to build up for the night. In hot weather you leave all of the vents open all of the time, to cool down the house as much as possible. Generally it's better to keep the greenhouse too cool rather than too hot.

If you don't have the time to monitor your greenhouse carefully you can use an automated venting system.

Ventilation not only affects the greenhouse temperature, it also affects humidity by regulating the airflow inside.

29 Tools

Buying tools

You don't need many tools in the intensive garden (especially once you have the garden beds established), so you may as well get good quality ones. It's something of a cliche to say cheap tools are expensive, but often they don't stand up to hard use and don't last very long. A good tool lasts a lifetime (or longer) and actually gets more attractive over the years, as the wood and metal are polished to a smooth patina by hours of hard work (are they dirty words?)

Examine tools carefully before buying them. Cheap tools are often made of crimped sheet metal, rivets, molded plastic and thin spot welded steel and feel light and generally flimsy. Good tools are forged from solid pieces of steel and have a balance and a strong feel that is quite different from a cheap tool. American manufacturers appear to have stopped making durable high quality tools, especially forks and spades. This is probably because in affluent America we have developed a throwaway mentality, when it breaks you buy a new one.

The best gardening tools you are likely to find are English, because in that less affluent country you don't throw away a spade, in fact your kids often inherit it after you die. However even in Britain cheap throwaway tools are taking over and its getting harder to find good ones. We are now getting cheap Chinese copies of expensive English tools. Despite my better judgement (I really should know better by now) I bought a Chinese stainless steel spade, it looked beautiful, but it snapped before I really got to use it. I had a similar experience with Chinese secateurs, they snapped when I tried to cut a woody branch, rather than a flower stem.

Good tools are pretty expensive if you buy them new. If you don't have the money you have to be more creative and look for old tools at flea markets, thrift shops and garage sales. The nice thing about old tools is they had to be well made to become old tools.

As you learn to use your tools properly you will come to respect and prize them. They enable you to quickly and accurately perform a task which would be almost impossibly difficult without them. They have acquired their present forms over centuries of use and experimentation and do the jobs they were designed for very well.

Essential tools

These are the basic tools it's very hard to do without.

Spade and fork

The workhorses of the garden, they are commonly used together and it's nice to buy a matching pair from the same manufacturer. These should be of high quality as they get more hard use and abuse, than any other tools. Cheap ones simply don't last; you could go through several cheap forks for the price of a good one and they are not as nice to use.

There is a choice of handles with the spade and fork. Most American gardeners like the long straight handle, as the long length gives good leverage and can be easier on your back. English gardeners mostly use the shorter D type handle, as it gives more control. However they can take some getting used to if you are used to longer handles. The handle may be made of split ash, plastic, fiberglass, wood reinforced with metal, or steel. You can get beautiful stainless steel tools that look like sculpture or jewelry. The rationale for using them is that soil

233

doesn't stick to them as easily as to forged steel, but they are much more brittle and fork tines tend to snap if over-stressed (forged steel merely bends). They are also more expensive.

Fork

Fork: The fork is probably more useful than the spade. It can be used for digging, spreading and incorporating amendments, breaking up clods, tilthing the soil, harvesting root crops and for digging up deeply rooted weeds. Strength is even more critical in a fork than it is in a spade, as there is less metal to do the job. It should be forged from one piece of metal and the tines should ring like a tuning fork when rapped. If you are very strong, you will soon break a pressed or welded fork.

The most commonly used type is the garden fork, which has square tines and a head about 12″ x 8″. The spading Fork (or potato fork) is about the same size, but has flattened tines, designed for digging potatoes and other root crops. It is the best tool for opening up heavy soil (this is why it's called a spading fork) and for incorporating amendments. The border fork is a smaller version of the garden fork, with a head about 8″ x 5″. It is intended for use in confined spaces such as borders, though it's often favored as a digging fork by people with less strength.

Though a good fork is very strong, it can be damaged if used carelessly. You need to develop some sensitivity when digging, especially in heavy or compacted soil. If you feel resistance when a tine hangs up, stop levering immediately. Any fork will bend if you put all of your weight on to a single tine. For that matter never use a fork (or spade) for levering heavy things out of the ground.

Spade: The spade is used for digging, skimming, weeding, planting and chopping. The normal size for a spade is 12″ X 8″, though larger ones are sometimes available (you need to be pretty strong to use them effectively). The border spade is smaller (about 8″ x 5″) and is intended for working in confined spaces. The top edge of the spade blade should have a flat flange attached, to give your foot more area to press against.

Shovel: Many people confuse spades and shovels. A spade has a flat square blade and is intended for digging. A shovel has a pointed blade (or a square blade with rounded sides) set at an angle to the handle and is designed more for scooping than digging.

The pointed shovel is often used for digging, in fact many American gardeners use them for their whole lives. However it isn't as effective, because the head is angled too much and the pointed edge doesn't dig to an even depth.

You will want a shovel as well as a spade (and perhaps a square shovel too), as it's much better for scooping and moving sand and gravel.

Rake: The rake is used for combing debris from the soil, leveling soil, collecting stones, breaking up crusted soil and burying seeds. The quality of a rake isn't nearly so important as with the fork and spade, as it doesn't get such rugged use. The strongest rake consists of steel pins on a rigid back, but I prefer those made from one piece of metal with the handle attached to the head from either end. The back of these rakes is ideally suited for shaping beds.

It's useful to have a narrow rake for working in confined areas, such as in the paths between beds, and a wider one for shaping beds and general cleanup. Make sure the handle is long enough to use comfortably.

Trowel, hand fork: As with their larger cousins, the most important aspect of these tools is strength. It is very easy for a strong person to break a weak hand fork or trowel. Unlike the spade and fork these tools are relatively cheap and easily available, so there's no excuse for not buying good ones. I would never buy a trowel, or hand fork, that was stamped from a piece of sheet metal. Almost without exception they will eventually bend or break where the metal is creased to form the neck. The solid cast aluminum ones are good (in this case the cheap Chinese copies are a really good deal), as are the ones with a solid neck and welded blade.

The trowel is the most useful of the two tools and is used for potting up, transplanting and weeding. Narrow trowels intended for transplanting, are known as transplanters.

The fork is good for hand weeding, cultivating and separating seedlings in flats. It can be used like a trowel in heavy soils.

These tools are small and it's easy to accidentally cover them with soil or debris and lose them. A brightly colored handle helps to prevent this from happening.

Buckets: I don't know how gardeners used to get along without plastic 5 gallon buckets. They have so many uses in the garden, making compost tea, carrying water and amendments, collecting seeds, harvesting, weeding, carrying tools and more. You can't have too many buckets (keep a few of the tight fitting lids as well). You can often get food, paint or joint compound buckets for free, from restaurants or building contractors.

Hoes: These are most often used for weeding of course, but some can also be used for making furrows, earthing up and more. See **Weeding** for more on hoes.

Knife: This is used for pruning, harvesting, sharpening, propagation and general cutting. You could get someone to buy you a nice one for Christmas, but any good pocket knife will do if you keep it sharp.

Pruning shears: Also known as secateurs, they are used for pruning small branches (up to a half inch or so), deadheading and harvesting. There are two types of pruners. The bypass type work like scissors, with two blade sliding past each other (the Swiss Felco shears are considered the standard). The anvil types work like a guillotine, with one blade coming down onto the other (Rolcut are good). Each have their advocates. Some people say the bypass types are the most precise and claim anvil pruners tend to crush the wood.

Good secateurs are much nicer to use than cheap ones. They feel better, hold their edge longer and cut more cleanly. It's important to keep your pruners sharp and not to try and cut branches that are too thick (use loppers or a pruning saw for thicker branches). Carry your secateurs in a holster so they are available at all times.

Seed starting equipment: See Seed Starting.

Sieve: Also known as a riddle, this is used for sifting materials for sowing mixes and cover soils. They generally come in two sizes, one with ½″ mesh and one with ¼″ mesh. It's easy to make your own sieve from scrap wood and you can get away with making only one frame (simply insert the ¼″ screen on top of the ½″ one).

String: You will need string for laying out beds, marking rows, tying and many other things. I prefer light colored biodegradable sisal in most cases, though some people prefer rot resistant nylon. You will also want some stakes to set out lines for beds and planting.

You will also need to tie plants to their supports. You can buy wide plastic horticultural tape for this, or you could tear up some strips of cloth. Don't use string, as it cuts into the plants stem.

Watering Equipment: See Watering for more on this.

Wheelbarrow: The wheelbarrow is a fairly expensive item, but it's essential in all but the smallest gardens. It will get a lot of hard use so you should get a good "professional" or contractors wheelbarrow. A "homeowner" barrow is fine for small loads, but I've always overloaded and broken them.

The best wheelbarrows have a pneumatic tire for easier wheeling. I always used to wonder why no one produced a puncture proof solid rubber tire, and now you can actually get one. The weight in the wheelbarrow should be forward over the wheel, rather than over the handles and it should tip easily for emptying.

I avoid plastic wheelbarrows. They may not rust but they often crack and definitely aren't as durable as steel. They also aren't as rigid and tend to flex under heavy loads, making them harder to steer.

Keep the wheelbarrow under cover and it will last much longer than if left outside. If you must leave it outside turn it upside down to prevent water collecting in it and causing rust. The wood will still deteriorate of course.

Other useful tools

Though these tools aren't essential, they make many jobs easier and faster. It's nice to always have right tool for the job. I have a tendency to accumulate tools of all kinds, from yard sales and the like. Some of them you can make yourself.

Aerated compost tea maker
If you want to make this kind of compost tea, you need a special setup. You can buy one of these, but it is very simple (and much cheaper) to make your own. See **Foliar Fertilizers** for information on this.

Axe: A small axe has many garden uses, cutting and splitting wood, sharpening and pounding posts, making stakes.

Broadfork: This tool is designed for quickly preparing established intensive beds. It works great and I highly recommend it if you have a lot of garden beds.

Cart: A large two wheeled garden cart is very useful for the bigger garden, as it's large capacity enables it to carry bulky things more easily than a wheelbarrow. You can carry up to 300 pounds quite comfortably, as all of the weight goes over the wheels.

I got a very large garden cart with the idea that bigger is better. A big one could carry more, which is obviously good, right? Wrong, it is too big to go in many places and so doesn't get used. One day I will build a series of wide freeways around my garden and I will be able to use it.

Many of these carts aren't very rugged and don't stand up to hard use very well, so you have to be careful with them. The best carts are expensive, but if you have the right skills you could build your own.

Dibber: This cone shaped piece of wood or metal is used for planting out bare root seedlings (especially Leeks). You can buy some fantastic dibbers (the classic hardwood with the brass tip, or the high tech aluminum and rubber), or you can make one from a broken spade or fork handle. You could even whittle one out of a hardwood branch (or a whole set: 1″, 1 ½″ and 2″ and more). The tip should be fairly blunt, so it doesn't leave an air pocket under the plant. You can mark out various depths on the side of the dibber, to facilitate making holes of uniform depth and for spacing plants accurately.

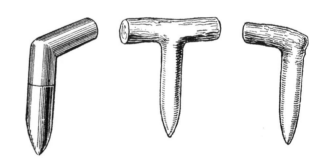

If you get into making dibbers, you might also make an extra long one, to use standing up. Make it out of an old broom handle.

Digging bar
This is a 5 foot long steel bar with a chisel point on one end. It is very strong and is the tool for levering stubborn roots out of the ground. If you get one it will probably save you from breaking several other tools.

Flame weeding gun: This is used to torch annual weeds, especially when preparing seedbeds (see **Weeds**).

File: This is used to sharpen spades, hoes, axes and other tools.

Hand cultivator: Useful for weeding and breaking surface crust. It doesn't need to be very strong, so can be quite inexpensive.

Machete: This is useful for chopping compost materials and clearing brush. Don't use it for pruning fruit trees.

Manure fork: A manure fork is quite different from a garden fork. It has long narrow tines that penetrate the manure easily, hold the loose material in a clump (it doesn't just fall through the tines) and then let go of it equally easily. It is used for moving bulky fibrous materials such as manures, compost, hay, prunings and green manures. It is THE tool for making compost piles. It isn't used for digging in the ground as the tines are too flimsy.

There are actually two kinds of manure forks. The commonest type has four to six tines and a head about 9 inches wide. It's useful for moving manure, hay and leaves. The other type has a shorter D shaped handle and 10 to 12 tines in a head that is up to 18″ wide. It is specifically designed for moving large volumes of loose manure quickly and works better for this than anything else.

Most manure forks have long straight handles for extra leverage, but I now have a T handled one that is just great. The first time I used it I was amazed at how much more control it gave me.

Marker pen or pencil: Any pen or pencil that is waterproof and permanent will do. There's nothing more frustrating than having your carefully written labels fade into illegibility. Laundry pens work as well as anything.

Mattock: This tough, all purpose tool has one blade that looks like a pick or blunt axe and another like a blunt adze. It is invaluable for the grunt work involved in digging out trees, rocks and small shrubs, cutting roots and dealing with compacted soil.

Measuring cup: This is used for measuring out powdered amendments. Make one by cutting the top off a gallon jug and marking out pre-measured amounts.

Measuring stick: This is a six foot length of 1″ x 2″, with 3″ intervals marked upon it. It is used for laying out plants in rows.

Netting: This is often necessary to protect plants from birds. Discarded fishing net works great if you can get it.

Rain gauge: Used for determining rainfall and irrigation needs.

Scythe: Used for cutting weeds, green manure, mulch and compost material. The best scythes are made in Austria and have a very thin and light blade that can be honed to razor sharpnesss. Scything looks easy and can be, but the scythe must be used with the right motion, must be the right size, must be adjusted to fit your body and must be kept sharp, otherwise it is hard work. When you get used to scything is fast and efficient, but if you don't do it very often, it will make your muscles ache the next day.

Sharpening stone: A good stone is essential for sharpening knives, pruners and more. I like the diamond impregnated sharpening tools, as they are more convenient than an oil or whetstone. Mine has its own little belt pouch so is always conveniently available alongside my secateurs.

Sledgehammer: Used for breaking concrete, pounding stakes (don't use your spade, it can break) and more.

Soil block maker: Used for making soil blocks of course. See **Raising Transplants** for more on this.

Sprayer: You may want a sprayer for foliar feeding and spraying pests. The commonest garden sprayers consist of a hand pressurized plastic tank (with a carrying strap) and have an adjustable nozzle.

Spring tine rake: This rake is designed for raking up leaves, weeds and other loose materials. It can also be used for thinning direct sown seedlings quickly.

Supports: Climbing crops need a strong support structure. This could be made from Bamboo canes, poles from the woods, or 1" x 1" dimension lumber. You can buy wire Tomato cages, but it's better to make them yourself from concrete reinforcing wire. This is cheaper and you can make different sizes. They can be used to support many kinds of plants, not just tomatoes. See **Bed Preparation** for more on this.

Thermometer: A maximum minimum thermometer is useful for recording temperatures in the garden and greenhouse.

Power tools

Power tools tend to fall into 2 categories of quality. Commercial grade stuff is designed for small farmers and market gardeners, it is good, but also expensive. There is also the 'homeowner' grade equipment for people who like to own stuff, but don't want to pay a lot for it. The latter doesn't stand up to sustained use very well. If you don't fall into either category, you may have problems finding suitable equipment. I try to find gently used commercial equipment.

Lawn mower: I don't own a lawn mower, but when I had access to one I found it useful for shredding dry tree leaves for mulch.

Rototiller: For reasons I already mentioned (see p 73), Rototillers don't really have a place in the intensive organic garden. They might be helpful in the initial establishment of very large gardens on poor soil, but don't let them encourage you to start a garden that is too big to look after properly.

If you need a tiller for any reason, it makes the most sense to rent . Make sure it has the muscle for real work (at least 4 or 5 h.p), as smaller tillers merely scratch the surface.

Shredder: Much of what I have said about tillers also applies to shredders. These can be useful for chipping woody material as an alternative to burning, but you need a fairly hefty machine. If you want to do this you should rent a big industrial shredder/chipper (ideally with neighbors, to share the cost). Time will also break down woody material, you just need to be patient.

Other necessities

Tool Shed
You will need a place to store all of these tools. A tool shed is the best place (hence the name) and can also be used to store boots (have a boot scraper), work clothes, seeds, amendments and other equipment. Ideally it will have a work bench for various tasks and will be adjacent to the greenhouse, propagation and nursery areas. It may even have a covered area, where you can work in the rain and harsh sun.

The tool shed can easily descend into chaos if it isn't carefully organized. Hang the tools from racks so the handles stay straight and they don't fall into a big pile on the floor. You might even draw an outline of each tool, in its proper place, so you know which tool goes where, and can see if anything is missing.

Calendar: Hang a calendar in the tool shed (with a pen on a piece of string) and mark it with things to do, when they were done and other observations. This can be a convenient substitute journal, or a place to record things to be entered into the journal later.

Chalkboard: I have a chalkboard in the tool shed, where I write tasks to be accomplished and cross them off as they are completed. It's an easy way to prioritize your activities.

Care of tools

Good tools can easily last a lifetime, but only if they are looked after properly. Never leave garden tools outside overnight, put them away after work. If left out in rain (or even damp night air) the metal will start to rust and the wood will repeatedly swell and shrink until the grain starts to separate and splinter. This not only weakens the handle and greatly shortens its life, but also makes it rough and unpleasant to hold.

Tools should be cleaned after each use, though this doesn't always happen when you are tired at the end of a long day. The commonest way to do this is to scrape off the mud and soil with a piece of sharp wood, called a 'man' (or wash them with a hose) and then plunge the metal part into a bucket containing sand and old vegetable oil (not the toxic used motor oil that used to be recommended). You could also wipe them with an oily rag. If you leave mud caked on to the metal for long periods it encourages rust.

Hang all tools in the shed after use. This protects the tools from damage and also protects you from potential injury. You will appreciate this if you have ever stood on the head of a rake and been hit in the face by the handle. Tools should be kept away from young children for the same reasons.

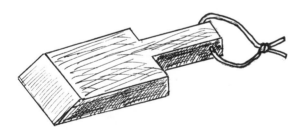

Rejuvenate old handles by smoothing them with fine sandpaper and giving them a coat of linseed oil. If you do this every couple of years, the handles won't dry out and split and will last much longer.

Secateurs and loppers must be kept sharp if they are to cut easily and cleanly. Put a little grease (oil dissipates too quickly) between the moving parts to lubricate them. If they get wet, dry them off and wipe with oil. Don't just forget about them, or they may rust. Bypass pruners are only sharpened on the beveled side. If you sharpen the flat side they won't cut properly.

Care of the spade

Spades should be sharpened with a 45° angle to the back, with a coarse file. It shouldn't be razor sharp, as this wastes metal and the edge will simply be blunted as soon as it is plunged into the soil. However it should be sharp enough to slice cleanly through vegetation and roots. People in a hurry sometimes use an electric grinder, but this requires a very light touch, or you will just grind away useful spade. There is also a danger of burning the metal and drawing the temper. Don't become fanatical and sharpen your spade every day, you will simply shorten its life by filing it away. Spades are actually self-sharpening to some degree, often the only maintenance necessary is to file out nicks

To replace a broken spade or fork handle

Remove the fastening pin (or pins), by filing off the head (or use a hacksaw) and then hammer it out with a punch.

Clamp the handle firmly in a vise and hammer on the head to loosen it from the handle (protect the head with a piece of wood).

Plane or whittle the end of the handle to the right shape to fit into the head. It should be very tight. If there is any play at all, the handle will move ever so slightly in the socket.

Hammer the handle into place (make sure the handle is in line with the head) and re-drill the holes.

Hammer in the new pins (use large nails if you don't have new pins, just cut them off with about a quarter inch to spare) and hammer the ends of the pins to spread and flatten them. Put the opposite end of the pin on the jaw of the vise to back it up while hammering.

File off any sharp edges so everything is smooth.

Index

About the author

Frank Tozer was born and raised in England, but moved to the United States when in his 20's. He has been a compulsive gardener for over 30 years, with a particular obsession with food plants. His 2 ½ acre garden in the Santa Cruz Mountains of California is an evolving mix of English cottage garden, edible landscape, French intensive vegetable garden, wild (mostly edible) plant garden, forest garden and more. He is pretty much a self taught gardener, except for a happy year and a half he spent at the U.C.S.C. Farm and Garden (the garden started by Alan Chadwick at the University of California Santa Cruz). He is also the author of The Vegetable Growers Handbook and The Uses Of Wild Plants

Green Man Publishing

P.O. Box 1546

Felton

CA 95018

The Uses Of Wild Plants
Frank Tozer

This unique guide to the wild plants of North America describes the uses and cultivation of more than 1200 species in over 500 genera. A treasury of information on every aspect of plant use, it describes

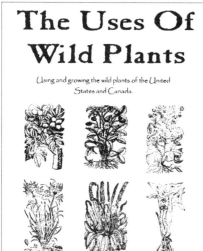

how wild plants were used for food in the past, how they can be used today and how they might one day become new crops. It is one of the most comprehensive guides to North American edible wild plants available.

It describes how plants have been used to treat sickness, and how they can help to enhance health by providing superior nutrition. How they can be used for dyes, cosmetics, soap, paper, fuel, clothing, perfumes, glues, craft materials, and many other home, commercial and industrial uses.

Looking to the future, it shows how wild plants could help us to create an ecologically sustainable society, by providing new crops for food, medicine, fuels, renewable energy, chemicals and building materials. How they could help to clean our rivers and lakes, desalinate soil, remove toxic chemicals from polluted groundwater, recover valuable nutrients from waste, and maybe even reduce global warming.

A unique feature of this book for gardeners is that it also discusses the cultivation of these plants. It also describes their uses around the garden, homestead and farm, as new crops, fertilizers, fence-posts, fencing, hedges, mulch, screens, green manures, insecticides, groundcover, and more.

$24.95

ISBN 0-9773489-0-3

Green Man Publishing

P.O. Box 1546

Felton

CA 95018

The Vegetable Growers Handbook
Frank Tozer

The companion to The Organic Gardeners Handbook, this is a very practical guide to growing over 70 common vegetables. There are specific step by step, instructions for each crop; soil requirements, variety selection, raising transplants, direct sowing, protection, watering, harvesting, seed saving, storage, extending the growing season and more. It forewarns you of potential problems with each crop, and explains how to deal with them. This is a book with imagination, so it doesn't stop there, but also discusses unusual crops, culinary herbs, edible flowers, enhanced nutrition foods, unusual growing ideas, additional uses for common crops, and even how to use common edible garden weeds. There is also a small selection of outstanding vegetarian recipes.

$22.95

ISBN 978-0-9773489-3-0